the WISDOM *of the* RENAISSANCE

ALSO BY MICHAEL K. KELLOGG

The Greek Search for Wisdom
The Roman Search for Wisdom
The Wisdom of the Middle Ages

Three Questions We Never Stop Asking

the WISDOM
of the
RENAISSANCE

Michael K. Kellogg

 Prometheus Books

59 John Glenn Drive
Amherst, New York 14228

Published 2019 by Prometheus Books

Cover image of *Allegory of Grammar*, by Laurent de La Hyre (1650),
acquired by Henry Walters with the Massarenti Collection (1902)

Cover design by Nicole Sommer-Lecht | Cover design © Prometheus Books

Inquiries should be addressed to
Prometheus Books
59 John Glenn Drive
Amherst, New York 14228
VOICE: 716–691–0133 • FAX: 716–691–0137
WWW.PROMETHEUSBOOKS.COM

23 22 21 20 19   5 4 3 2 1

Library of Congress Cataloging-in-Publication Data

LCCN 2019002884 (print) |
ISBN 978-1-63388-519-6 (ebook) | ISBN 978-1-63388-518-9 (hardcover)

Printed in the United States of America

For Camille,

Heavenly Rosalind! . . .
With all graces wide-enlarged.

—*As You Like It*, 1.2.178, 3.2.140

CONTENTS

INTRODUCTION

W hen we hear the word *Renaissance*, most of us rightly turn our thoughts to quattrocento (fifteenth century) and early cinquecento (sixteenth century) Italian art: Fra Angelico's *Deposition from the Cross* (ca. 1432), Filippo Lippi's *Madonna and Child* (ca. 1440), Botticelli's *Birth of Venus* (ca. 1485), Leonardo's *Last Supper* (1495–1498), Raphael's *School of Athens* (1509–1511), or Michelangelo's Sistine Chapel ceiling (1508–1512). The vibrant colors, classical forms, and increasingly rich details in these and so many other paintings literally changed the way we see the world and conceive of ourselves. In Rome, Naples, and the city-states of Milan, Venice, and, above all, Florence, a profound transformation was taking place that was dazzlingly reflected in the art, architecture, and even the music of the time, a transformation that quickly spread beyond the Alps to northern Europe, down through France to Spain, and eventually across the channel to England.

There are numerous excellent studies of these aesthetic trends by experts in the field, complete with full-color plates and elaborate descriptions.[1] Our focus here will be different if nonetheless inextricably related. It will be on the conception of man to be found, not in paintings and sculptures, but in the poems, plays, letters, novels, essays, and treatises of the time. As we will use the term, the Renaissance refers both to a period—roughly from the death of Chaucer in 1400 to the death of Shakespeare in 1616—and to a progression in human consciousness that brought us from the Middle Ages to the early modern era.

Our word *Renaissance* derives, via the French, from Petrarch's *rinascita*, which literally means "rebirth." Petrarch claimed that, in his work, the humanist tradition of ancient Greece and Rome was being redis-covered and reconceived following the benighted Dark Ages. He even arranged to have himself crowned poet laureate in Rome, reinstating a classical tradition. But Petrarch was a self-promoter and prone to exaggeration. As I was at pains to show in my last book, the classical tradition was never fully lost during the Middle Ages, and powerful stirrings of the Renaissance can be traced at least to the twelfth century, two hundred years before Petrarch.[2] There was never a sharp break. But, after Petrarch, the pace and magnitude of change was sufficiently marked that calling this period the Renaissance is still illuminating as well as inevitable.

Fernand Braudel, the great historian of the Mediterranean world in the sixteenth century, downplayed the importance of specific events and specific individuals. He focused on the *longue durée*, the glacial perspective of geography, climate, food sources, shifting trade routes, and the gradual development of cities and technology as drivers of economic and social change.[3] He is undoubtedly right, and his work is a useful corrective to the more traditional focus on individual achievements and dramatic events. Civilizations developed around the Mediterranean—like frogs around a pond, as Plato once noted—as a source both of food and mobility. Geographic features—such as mountains, plains, and rivers—determined livelihoods and defenses. Technological developments—in navigation, architecture, tools for farming, and drift nets for fishing—only gradually compensated for or took increased advantage of natural features.

But correctives can be one-sided too. Indeed, they are so by definition. As Aristotle suggested in discussing character traits, the only way to straighten a bent stick is to bend it in the opposite direction. I have bent my stick in the direction of extraordinary individuals: specific writers and thinkers who both embodied and drove the dramatic expansion of individual consciousness during the Renaissance. As Ben Jonson said of Shakespeare, he was the "soul of the age," and yet "he was not of an age but for all time!"[4] Perhaps the great writers of the Western tradition are just flotsam on the tides of history. But they did not conceive of themselves in those terms, and we can celebrate and learn from their achievements without ignoring the *longue durée* that envelops and sustains them, even as they transcend it.

In each of the chapters that follow, I try to provide sufficient historical background to place each author in context. At the risk of some repetition, however, I want briefly to note four broad, closely intertwined trends that accelerated the pace of change in western Europe during the fifteenth century and beyond.

THE RISE OF SOVEREIGN NATIONS

In 1453, the Hundred Years' War between England and France came to a decisive end. English pretensions to the French throne were finally abandoned, as were English continental possessions other than a last redoubt in and around Calais. A period of relative peace descended on Europe that lasted close to fifty years, until the religious wars triggered by the Protestant Reformation and Catholic Counter-Reformation. "Relative" is still the operative word, however. Rebellious Burgundy was not brought under the full control of France until 1477. The Wars of the Roses over dynastic succession were waged between 1455 and 1487 by English nobles who were disgusted with the monarchy's expensive failure in France and jealous of their own prerogatives. And the Reconquista (expulsion of the Moors) in Spain was finally completed only with the conquest of Granada in 1492. But those were largely internal struggles of consolidation. Strife between nations was significantly reduced, allowing the material conditions of everyday life to improve.

Europe was finally recovering from the ravages of the plague in the fourteenth century, which had killed as many as half its inhabitants. The absence of global warfare, a milder climate, and a longer growing season (as well as severe labor shortages) improved the lot of the post-feudal peasant class. Increased trade within Europe led to a new middle class of merchants and artisans. Cities expanded as cultural, artistic, and administrative centers. Bureaucrats and diplomats flourished. Great merchant banking families, such as the Medicis in Florence and the Fuggers in Germany, financed both the armies and the artistic patronage of popes, kings, and princes. During the fifteenth century, western Europe completed its transition from a localized, feudal society to one dominated by nation-states ruled by more or less absolute monarchs. The map of modern Europe was taking shape.

Yet it was in fractured and fractious Italy that the Renaissance had its start. Italy would remain divided until the nineteenth century, when Giuseppe Garibaldi and his thousand Redshirts began to realize Machiavelli's dream of a united Italy. In the fifteenth century, there were five principal centers of influence: the Kingdom of Naples, the Papal States surrounding Rome, and the great city-states of Florence, Venice, and Milan, with numerous smaller cities acting as satellites and often pawns of the larger powers.

Naples was contested and alternately controlled by Spain and France. Rome was a shell of its former self until a trio of powerful popes—Sixtus IV (r. 1471–1484), Alexander VI (r. 1492–1503), and Julius II (r. 1503–1513)—restored its grandeur and enhanced its influence throughout Italy and beyond. Florence was an off-again, on-again republic controlled largely by the Medici family. Milan was dominated by the Viscontis for almost two centuries, until the line of succession ran out and the *condottiere* Francesco Sforza used his military expertise to establish his own dynasty in 1450. The Republic of Venice was the most stable of the five regions, with elected doges acting as CEOs and overseeing the phenomenal growth of the city's trade. One cannot but think that this constant tension and sense of competition between the various regions of Italy contributed to the artistic and intellectual ferment that made Italy the breeding ground of the Renaissance.

But the lack of unity also made the Italian states an inviting target for the growing power of the European monarchies and their professional armies. In 1494, Charles VIII of France invaded Naples, at that time a dependency of Aragon. His passage down the peninsula led to the overthrow of the Medicis in Florence. A brief period of theocracy (1494–1498) under the fanatic monk Girolamo Savonarola was followed by a fragile democracy. Little more than a decade later, however, the Florentine Republic—which now foolishly backed the French—was forced to capitulate to the Holy Roman emperor, Charles V, of Habsburg Spain. The republic collapsed, and the Medicis returned to power. Pope Clement VII also backed French claims in Naples. In 1527, unruly troops of Charles V sacked Rome and held the pope a virtual prisoner in the Castel Sant'Angelo. The independence of Milan was also a casualty of war, becoming a duchy of Habsburg Spain in 1525.

If the Renaissance of the fourteenth and fifteenth centuries belonged to Italy, the sixteenth century was the golden age of Spain. When Ferdinand of Aragon and Isabella of Castile married in 1469, they united a Spain that was almost as divided as Italy. They completed the Reconquista, recapturing the last Muslim stronghold of Granada in the same year they sent Columbus on his voyage to find a western passage to India. Through astute marital alliances, their grandson became heir to three dynasties: Spain, the Burgundian possessions in the Netherlands, otherwise known as the Low Countries, and Habsburg Austria, as well as vast territories in the New World of America. As Holy Roman emperor, Charles V attracted the fear and envy of other European nations and strained his resources fighting on three fronts at once: the Italian wars with France; wars to prevent Muslim encroachments into Europe; and wars with Dutch and German princes who supported the Reformation. His son, Philip II, continued to fight incursions by Islam generally and the Turks in particular, culminating in the great naval battle of Lepanto, at which Miguel de Cervantes fought, in 1571. But Philip's efforts to protect trade in the Mediterranean were less successful. A series of battles in North Africa proved inconclusive. And, despite Spain's new dominance at sea, Islamic piracy continued largely unchecked.

The title of emperor went to Philip's brother Ferdinand, who now controlled the Austrian lands of the Habsburgs. But Philip was also king of Naples, Sicily, and Portugal, as well as the Duke of Milan. He even had a brief stint as nominal king of England during his four-year, childless marriage to Queen Mary I, the Catholic daughter of Henry VIII and his first wife, Catherine of Aragon. Spain under Philip had vast resources from American gold and silver, eastern spices, Castilian wool, and Dutch textiles. But Philip dissipated those riches in a vain attempt to suppress Protestantism in the Netherlands and the various principalities of central Europe. He imposed ruinous taxes on his many subjects and mortgaged Spain's future to foreign bankers. The Netherlands began a revolt in 1568 that, aided by England, lasted eighty years. Philip's efforts to invade England, depose Queen Elizabeth, reinstate Catholicism, and put an end to English interference in the Netherlands culminated in the collapse of the supposedly invincible Spanish Armada in 1588. Spain went bankrupt five times during the reign of Philip II. By the time he died in 1598, Spanish hegemony was waning.

France's turn to wax would be next, beginning in the latter half of the seventeenth century and continuing well into the eighteenth. The Italian Wars between France and Spain lasted intermittently until 1559. In the end, France was forced to renounce all claims on Italy, but it at least managed to consolidate its own borders, securing Provence, preserving the Alsace, and regaining Calais from the English.

France solidified those borders just in time to see itself torn apart internally by the wars of religion between Catholics and Huguenots. The Huguenots, who followed the teachings of John Calvin, were decidedly in the minority, but they had strongholds in urban areas, particularly in Paris. The civil war is discussed at some length in the chapter on Montaigne, who played an important role in trying to negotiate a peaceful resolution. But that resolution came only after his death, when Henri IV, the first Bourbon king of France (r. 1589–1610), issued the Edict of Nantes in 1598, which guaranteed freedom of religion and full civil rights to the Huguenots. Henri himself had been a Huguenot but reconverted to

Catholicism—or, more accurately, renounced his Calvinism, reputedly with the words "*Paris vaut bien une messe*" (Paris is well worth a mass).

The wars of religion were not at an end, however. They soon inflamed the rest of Europe. The Habsburg Empire at that time spanned much of central Europe and extended into the Low Countries not controlled by Spain. It was a highly decentralized empire with hundreds of separate principalities, each jealous of its independence. In 1618, the newly elected Holy Roman emperor, Ferdinand II, tried forcibly to impose Catholicism throughout the Habsburg territories. The reaction was immediate. Bohemia, Saxony, parts of the Netherlands, and other principalities rebelled. Spain joined the side of the Habsburgs in an effort to control its own Dutch rebels. Sweden entered on the side of the Protestants in 1630, turning the war into a full-scale European conflagration. James I's attempt to send military aid to his son-in-law Frederick V in the Rhine was stifled by Parliament, and his punitive reaction became a causal factor in the English Civil War that ultimately would lead to the deposition and execution of his son Charles I. France, though Catholic, ended up joining the anti-Spain and anti-Habsburg forces in 1635. Eight million Europeans died in what became known as the Thirty Years' War, either directly from the violence or from the plagues and famines that ensued. Various treaties known as the Peace of Westphalia were signed in 1648. They were a formal acknowledgment of the territorial boundaries of the sovereign states, including the newly recognized Dutch Republic, and an informal acknowledgment of the changing balance of power within Europe.

THE EXPANSION OF LEARNING

From the fourteenth century on, there was a steadily increasing interest in the works of ancient Rome. Humanists, inspired by the example of Petrarch, hunted for forgotten classics in monasteries throughout Europe, where they had been dutifully copied and preserved throughout the Middle Ages. Scholars labored to collate manuscripts and to provide accurate texts. Detailed commentaries were prepared that depended on close textual analysis. These humanists were not isolated scholars, however. There was a widespread belief that the study of the classics made for better, more productive citizens. Those reading Virgil, Cicero, Livy, and Seneca imbibed practical and rhetorical skills appropriate to law, administration, and foreign relations. They served the modern state as secretaries, speechwriters, and diplomats. As the premier Renaissance historian, Jacob Burckhardt, would later explain, the classical learning of the humanist "had to serve the practical needs of daily life."[5]

Yet there was still only limited knowledge of the Greek classics. The works of Aristotle, preserved and carefully annotated by Arab scholars in Alexandria, had already been translated into Latin. Homer and some of the tragedians were available in poor Latin translations. But other Greek classics were largely unknown, and the ability to read ancient Greek was rare. That changed in 1453, when Constantinople fell to the Turks. The Eastern Roman Empire, which had survived the fall of Rome by almost a millennium, was at an end. Greek scholars fled to Italy and other parts of western Europe, bringing their knowledge of ancient Greek and their libraries with them. Classics of Greek literature, as well as scientific and medical texts of Galen, Euclid, Ptolemy, and others, became available, and western scholars scrambled to learn to read them in the original. Others eagerly awaited accurate translations by an increasing cadre of philologists. Most important, the *Dialogues* of Plato were translated into Latin in the 1460s by the Italian scholar Marsilio Ficino. Neoplatonism, given a Renaissance cast by Ficino's most brilliant student, Giovanni Pico della Mirandola, began to rival, if not displace, the Scholasticism derived from Aristotle among progressive theologians.

The revival of classical learning was at first thought to serve the needs of religion as well as those of the state. These were not *secular* humanists, as we use that term today. Ficino was a Catholic priest. Pico was a devout Christian, as were Desiderius Erasmus and other proselytizers of ancient learning. They believed strongly that humanism and religion were not only fully compatible, but reinforced one another. That was equally true among those who studied science. They viewed nature itself as a book consistent with, and every bit as important as, the Bible. Both came from God.

The church, however, took a dim view of the application of philology and close textual analysis to the Bible itself. Catholic humanists thought there was nothing more important than ensuring that the Word of God was stated accurately and that people could read or at least listen to scripture in the vernacular. But the church fiercely resisted any attempt to undermine the Latin Vulgate Bible then in standard use or to allow congregations to form their own views as to the meaning of scripture without the mediation of the church.

In 1450, Johannes Gutenberg was already at work on a printed version of the Bible. It was a proper Latin Vulgate Bible. But the new technology could not easily be kept within the bounds approved by the church. Gutenberg's printing press was quickly duplicated throughout Europe. Engravings from woodcuts and copper plates allowed readers to study illustrations, maps, diagrams, and tables, all of which were important for many new works on astronomy, botany, geography, medicine, and other disciplines. By the end of the fifteenth century, as many as fifteen *million* volumes of forty thousand different titles and editions had been printed. Ten times that number had appeared by 1600, including vernacular works in Italian, German, French, Spanish, and English.[6] The hunger for learning seemed inexhaustible. Knowledge was no longer the exclusive preserve of Latinists. The impact of any one writer could be magnified a thousandfold, much to the horror of the Catholic Church. Publishing's first blockbuster best sellers were produced by Erasmus, who, even fifty years earlier, would likely have remained an obscure former monk known to just a few scholars. Instead, he was celebrated throughout Europe until he was alternately blamed for, and excoriated by, the Protestant Reformation.

The publication of vernacular versions of the Bible, and the Catholic Church's efforts to ban them, became a core issue of the Reformation.

Of longer-term significance, however, was the plethora of literary, philosophical, and scientific works that the Catholic Church also concluded were inconsistent with or inimical to the Catholic faith. When Nicolaus Copernicus (1473–1543), Johannes Kepler (1571–1630), and Galileo Galilei (1564–1642) demonstrated that the earth revolves around the sun, rather than vice versa, a crusade against learning was launched that the church could not win but was unwilling to abandon. Its *Index of Forbidden Books*, published in 1559, became an ever-lengthening honor roll for great authors until its abolition in 1966. The Catholic Church turned its face resolutely away from the new learning and back toward the Middle Ages. The church bade time stand still, just as it insisted that the earth stood still. "*E pur si muove*" (And yet it moves), Galileo would reputedly murmur, after his forced public recantation.

THE AGE OF DISCOVERY

The Crusades—a papal-driven attempt to reclaim Jerusalem and the Holy Land for Christianity—lasted from 1095 to 1291. Despite some early successes, the Crusades were, in the end, a military and moral disaster. But they did expand the horizons of western Europe by introducing to it the spices, silks, and superior learning of the Arab world. Where once European states sought to conquer in the name of God, they now sought to conquer in the name of trade. Navigation and overland routes improved, and trade expanded to India, China, and elsewhere in the Far East. A rising middle class of merchants, bankers, and artisans grew wealthy. Commercial arrangements were streamlined, and Arabic numbers, double-entry bookkeeping, bills of exchange, and maritime insurance became commonplace. Textiles, spices, coffee, tobacco, sugar, and brightly colored dyes poured into western Europe, along with the pigments critical to the palettes of Renaissance painters. Eyeglasses were produced for the nearsighted as were lead pencils for the literate. The seven major guilds in

Florence—cloth finishers, wool merchants, silk weavers, bankers, notaries, druggists/spice merchants, and furriers—give a fair indication of the growing importance of trade in developing a new, urban middle class.

Trade, in turn, drove exploration. The so-called Silk Road connecting the Middle East and the Far East with the Mediterranean was, in reality, a variety of routes: up the Persian Gulf and overland across the Arabian Peninsula; up the Red Sea and through Egypt. Heavy tolls were exacted along the way, where the routes were not closed altogether by the growing Ottoman Empire. A purely maritime route to the Far East became a commercial imperative, and the Portuguese, already situated on the Atlantic, were in an ideal position to obtain it. Prince Henry the Navigator (1394–1460) funded explorations of West Africa and the Canary Islands. Aided by magnetic compasses and rapidly improving navigation charts, the Portuguese gradually worked their way down the west coast of Africa, establishing valuable ports in Madeira, the Azores, and the Cape Verde islands. In 1488, Bartolomeu Dias first rounded the southern tip of Africa, which he called the Cape of Good Hope. And in 1497, Vasco da Gama left Lisbon with four ships and 170 men bound all the way to India and back, a voyage celebrated in the sixteenth-century epic poem *The Lusiads*, by Luís Vaz de Camões. Portugal established the first global trading empire, to which it added Brazil in 1500. But, by the time *The Lusiads* was written in the 1570s, that empire had already declined, and Spain was now the dominant force in world trade.

It is ironic, though, that two of the most important Spanish-sponsored explorations were led by non-Spaniards. In 1492, the Italian Christopher Columbus convinced Ferdinand and Isabella to fund his attempt to find a western route to the Far East. By this date, educated people had long known that the world was round. The first extant terrestrial globe was coincidentally produced by the German mariner Martin Behaim in the same year Columbus set sail in his three small vessels. But cartographers had underestimated the circumference of the world by as much as a third.[7] They also were ignorant of the fact that North and South America were situated between Europe and the Far East. Accordingly, when Columbus finally made landfall in the Bahamas, he mistook it for India.

Juan Ponce de León, who accompanied Columbus on his second expedition, explored Puerto Rico, landed in Florida in 1513, and later attempted unsuccessfully to establish a Spanish colony there. The Spanish had greater success in South America. Vasco Núñez de Balboa reached the Isthmus of Panama and set eyes upon the Pacific Ocean in 1513.[8] And in 1519, the Portuguese sailor Ferdinand Magellan sought to prove that a western route to the Moluccas, the so-called Spice Islands, was still possible. He was backed, however, not by Portugal—which rejected his proposal as implausible—but by Spain. It took Magellan three years, and ultimately cost him his life in a native skirmish into which he senselessly interjected himself. But he had quelled a mutiny, reached the southern-most tip of South America, passed through what became known as the Straits of Magellan, and crossed the vast, uncharted waters of the Pacific Ocean. The tiny remnants of his crew finally rounded the Cape of Good Hope and returned, without Magellan, to Spain and glory in 1522.

Unlike the Portuguese in the Far East, the Spanish had little interest in peaceful trade with the indigenous peoples of South America. The primary objective of their conquistadors was exploitation. Hernán Cortés all but wiped out the ancient Aztec civilization in Mexico between 1519 and 1521. Francisco Pizarro did the same with the Incas in Peru between 1531 and 1533. Priests bearing crosses and intent on conversion accompanied the troops, but in the end there were few left to convert. The indigenous population quickly fell by more than 80 percent. Many succumbed to smallpox and measles, diseases against which they had no natural defenses. Indiscriminate slaughter and forced labor in the silver mines accounted for the rest. Slaves were imported from Africa to fill the void. Gold, silver, and other goods made the return journey to Spain. But the golden era of Spain would also soon fade, if not as quickly as Portugal's had.

England laid its own hypothetical claims to the east coast of North America based on the 1497 voyages of John Cabot, an Italian mariner employed by Henry VII. Sir Francis Drake—pirate or patriot, depending on your perspective—performed a second circumnavigation from 1577 to 1580, seizing Spanish treasure ships and laying claim to California along the way. Drake would play a significant role in defeating the once-invincible Spanish Armada in 1588. His many voyages made him a rich man and established a tradition of English maritime dominance that lasted through the nineteenth century.

English settlements were founded in Jamestown, Virginia, in 1607 and in Plymouth, on Massachusetts Bay, in 1620—the first purely commercial, the second driven by Puritan separatists. Meanwhile, French traders and trappers spread across Canada and down into the unchartered territories below. Conflict among the great powers was inevitable, but that is beyond the scope of this volume. The critical point is that, by the start of the seventeenth century, the map of the world, at least in its outlines, was largely complete. Western Europe was spreading its influence—sometimes benign but often baleful—throughout the world. It received two things in return: wealth—sometimes from trade but often from theft—and knowledge. The latter proved far more important in the development of Western consciousness. Just as Copernicus dislodged the earth from the center of the solar system in his 1543 book, *On the Revolutions of the Celestial Spheres*, so too the great explorers made it clear that western Europe was just a portion, and a small portion at that, of a much larger, more varied world. Travel literature poured from the new printing presses: accounts of voyages, descriptions of new lands and old tribal societies—sometimes accurate but often sensationalized. This literature fed the hunger for learning that had already been ignited by the rediscovery of classical texts and the development of the printing press.

REFORMATION AND UPHEAVAL

The One, Holy, Catholic and Apostolic Church dominated the religious life of western Europe throughout the Middle Ages. It was the main source of cohesion and social stability after the collapse of the Roman Empire. At the same time, it was also a force for rigidity and repression. By the end of the fifteenth century, most Jews and Muslims had either converted or been expelled from Spain, Portugal, and much of the rest of Europe. Even the *conversos* (converted Jews) and Moriscos (converted Muslims) faced constant suspicion and discrimination. Amsterdam and a few cities in Italy provided rare safe havens for practicing Jews.

Though it showed no tolerance for other religions, the Catholic Church was hardly a monolith. The Great Schism of 1054 had split the Western, Roman church from the Eastern Orthodox one based in Constantinople. And the Western church itself was divided between rival popes from 1378 to 1417, one residing at Avignon and the other at Rome; each had his own College of Cardinals. An effort to resolve this Western Schism in 1409 led instead to the existence of three popes before the Council of Constance finally deposed all three and settled on Martin V (r. 1417–1431). An attempt was made soon thereafter to unify the Eastern and Western churches. In the face of a growing threat from the Ottoman Empire and hoping to obtain military support from western Europe, representatives of the Eastern Orthodox Church agreed to a decree of union in 1439. But the decree was soundly rejected back in Constantinople, and in any event the city itself soon fell. The Ottomans proved more tolerant than Christians—just as the Arabs had been in the Middle Ages when they controlled much of Spain—and allowed Christians and Jews alike to practice their faiths during the ensuing centuries. But the center of the Eastern Orthodox Church shifted to Russia.

The Western church, meanwhile, was rotting from within. The Council of Constance may have guaranteed that there was only one pope at a time, but it could not ensure that only good popes were elected by the now unitary College of Cardinals. Alexander VI (r. 1492–1503), the Borgia pope, bribed, murdered, and fornicated his way to power. Julius II (r. 1503–1513), the warrior pope, drove the French from Italy and set the various Italian states against one another so that none would gain hegemony. Leo X (r. 1513–1521)—who reputedly said upon his election, "Since God has given us the papacy, let us enjoy it"—spent money like a Medici, which was to be expected since he was the second son of Lorenzo the Magnificent. These were all secular, not religious, leaders. And the church over which they presided reflected that. Ecclesiastical posts were openly bought and sold, when they were not granted *gratis* to the "nephews"—that is, the bastard sons—of popes and cardinals. As many as half the clergy lived openly with women, and illegitimate children of priests were commonplace. The sacraments were a moneymaking proposition. Parishioners were tithed at every religious milestone in their lives, including baptism, confirmation, marriage, and extreme unction. The church even found a way to continue charging after death.

Purgatory—where souls worked off their sins before being welcomed into heaven—had no basis in scripture. But it was an established and by now extremely lucrative bit of church doctrine. Through prayer and buying masses, it was believed one could shorten the stay of those in purgatory. Eventually, the prayers and masses were deemed superfluous. The faithful could buy "indulgences" directly to save themselves—and their deceased loved ones—a long, painful sojourn in the waiting room of heaven. This "purgatory industry" helped to build Saint Peter's Church and filled the Vatican Museums with priceless works of art. It also, finally, was the wedge that split the church apart. The printing press helped spread the Reformation. The rise of nation-states, eager to stop the outflow of funds to Rome and greedily eyeing rich church lands, helped to protect the Reformation. But it was the sale of indulgences that provided the initial spark of protest.

Others had tried before Martin Luther. Jan Hus, a Czech theologian, was burned at the stake in 1415 for criticizing the sale of indulgences, the corruption of the clergy, and the misguided Crusades. The Lollards, led by John Wycliffe in fourteenth-century England, argued for numerous church reforms, including the abolition of church property, and for an English-language Bible that would eliminate priests as intermediaries between the people and their God. But the Lollards, too, were actively persecuted until finally absorbed into the Church of England. Martin Luther affixed his "Ninety-Five Theses" to the church door at just the right time (1517, when printed pamphlets spread rapidly throughout Europe) and in just the right place (Wittenberg, where the powerful elector of Saxony protected the young monk).

Although he began with an attack on indulgences, Luther's core teachings were the primacy of scripture over church doctrine and of faith over works. He took a dismal view of human nature. We are all sinful. We are all condemned except insofar as God grants us the grace of salvation. We cannot save ourselves; we can only pray and hope. Indeed, much of the reason for Luther's rebellion was that, as a monk, he found himself incapable of imitating the example of Christ. Nor did he think the church could bridge that gap. To the contrary, the church interposed itself between man and God, preventing a more direct relationship. The faithful had to rely on the priesthood to present and interpret a Bible that most could never hope to read or even to have read to them directly. Luther wanted people to listen to the Word of God in their own language, and indeed, Luther's vernacular translation of the Bible became the foundation of the common German language, just as the King James Bible would determine the future of the English language.[9] His many hymns still reverberate powerfully through churches today. Luther also wanted to do away with many of the everyday religious rituals by which Catholics marked their passage through life. He argued that only two sacraments have a basis in scripture: baptism and Communion. He also rejected the isolation and hierarchy of priests. Luther himself married a former nun and fathered six children. All members of the community, he argued, are worshipers together; all are flawed human beings whose salvation depends not on good works but on faith in the grace of God.

When called upon formally to recant at the Diet of Worms in 1521, Luther declined: "Here I stand, I can do no other," he said. Thomas Carlyle called it, with pardonable exaggeration, "the greatest moment in the modern history of men."[10] By that, Carlyle—who stressed the role of "great men" in history—meant that individual conscience was finally claiming its due. But, in fact, the Reformation was not a humanist development in favor of individual conscience. Luther—like the other main figures of the Reformation, John Calvin and Huldrych Zwingli, who disagreed with Luther and with one another on doctrinal issues such as whether Christ is really present in the Eucharist—had no intention of tolerating dissent from his new orthodoxy.

The Reformation was as much a nationalist, economic shift as a religious one. The reason Luther could decline to recant and escape burning at the stake was that he was protected by Frederick the Wise, the elector of Saxony, who had an important vote in choosing the Holy Roman emperor. He and other German princes felt that the papacy was exploiting Germany and usurping its wealth. Not only was the outflow of funds to Rome slowed by the Reformation, but religion became a local affair, and rich church properties were subject to state control. When the First Act of Supremacy of 1534 made Henry VIII head of the separate Church of England, he immediately set Thomas Cromwell to work shuttering all the monasteries, dissolving their orders, and selling their lands. The sale of church lands was extremely popular with the landowning class and helped solidify the position of the Church of England.

The iconoclasm of the Reformation was quite literal. Religious images and artworks were destroyed. Religious rituals were abandoned. The worship of saints and their relics was rejected as gross superstition. Church music was simplified. Religion became an altogether grimmer but not thereby more enlightened affair. Belief in demons was still strong. Witches and heretics were still burned. And predestination—the belief that everyone's fate is determined by God and not by the will of man—was standard doctrine.

Rome did not seriously awaken to the challenge posed by the Reformation until 1540, when the Society of Jesus was established under Ignatius of Loyola. The Jesuits were the shock troops of the Counter-Reformation, establishing schools and proselytizing throughout Europe and the rest of the world. Rome set up its own Inquisition in 1542 to combat heresy. The ecumenical Council of Trent, meeting from 1545 to 1563, articulated the principles of the Counter-Reformation. It reaffirmed the authority of the pope, the critical role of priests as mediators between God and the lay congregation, and the sanctity of all seven sacraments, including the transubstantiation of the bread and wine into the body and blood of Christ at Communion. It also confirmed the existence of purgatory and the veneration of saints and their relics. It even allowed the continued sale of indulgences, though at a reduced level. Actual reforms were few and far between. But the council did condemn the sale of church offices and insisted that priests and nuns must observe their vows of chastity.

Italy, Spain, and Portugal remained solidly Catholic. Aside from the five years (1553–1558) when Mary I tried to reimpose Catholicism, England was firmly Anglican, especially after the failure of the Gunpowder Plot in 1605, when Catholic recusants tried to blow up the Houses of Parliament. The Counter-Reformation was too little and too late to preserve Catholicism in much of northern Europe. Under the Peace of Augsburg of 1555—forced on the emperor by a military alliance of Protestant princes known as the Schmalkaldic League—the rulers of states within the Holy Roman Empire were allowed to choose whether their subjects were to be Catholic or Lutheran. "*Cuius regio, eius religio*" (whose realm, his religion) was the unfortunate motto. Internal dissent was not tolerated, although members of the minority religion were granted time to migrate to other states. This winner-take-all approach had particularly harsh consequences in France, where it led to sixty years of brutal and destructive warfare between Catholics and Huguenots. It was Ferdinand II's attempt to repudiate the Peace of Augsburg that led to the Thirty Years' War. Only in 1648, with the Peace of Westphalia, was Calvinism recognized, along with Catholicism and Lutheranism, as a legitimate state religion, and the European wars of religion finally came to an end.

TEN RENAISSANCE AUTHORS

"Nothing [is] more wonderful than man," wrote the fifteenth-century Italian philosopher Pico della Mirandola.[11] Man stands between the physical world of nature and the spiritual world of God and the angels. If he cultivates his sensuality, he will become one with the beasts. But if he cultivates his intellect and recognizes "the dignity of th[e] liberal arts," "he will be an angel, and a son of God."[12]

This is a truly remarkable statement: man can become like a god. The sentiment seems to come right out of the pagan, anthropomorphic mythology of the classical world. Yet Pico never doubted that humanist studies were fully compatible with Christian revelation. Thomas Aquinas had attempted two centuries earlier to harmonize Aristotelian reason and church doctrine. Whole waves of lesser scholar-theologians toiled in his wake and brought discredit to the enterprise. Scholasticism became a term of derision and abuse, though whether it was because reason was distorted to serve religion or because religion was distorted to serve reason depended on the perspective of the critic.

Pico, however, was advocating something very different. He had little interest in doctrinal issues. He simply wanted to celebrate the capacities of man as given by God and thereby partaking of the divine. For him, the various schools and sects were but stepping-stones to enhanced consciousness of man himself, "like the sun rising from the deep."[13] Pico imagined God addressing his creation:

> I have placed thee at the center of the world, that from there thou mayest more conveniently look around and see whatsoever is in the world. Neither heavenly nor earthly, neither mortal nor immortal have We made thee. Thou ... art the molder and maker of thyself; thy mayest sculpt

thyself into whatever shape thou dost prefer. Thou canst grow downward into the lower natures which are brutes. Thou canst again grow upward from thy soul's reason into the higher natures which are divine.[14]

If we insist on a definition of the core Renaissance ideal, we could do worse than "thou art the molder and maker of thyself." Pico and many other writers insisted on the essential goodness and perfectibility of man, as well as the transformative power of art and the humanities. In the Middle Ages, man was cast into shadows by the twin institutions of feudalism and the Catholic Church. The rapid breakdown of that existing order—driven by the dynamic economic and political changes noted above—brought individual man back into the classical sunlight and irrevocably altered our consciousness and our sense of personal identity.

Jacob Burckhardt aptly captures the transformation:

Man was conscious of himself only as a member of a race, people, party, family or corporation—only through some general category. In Italy this veil first melted into air; an *objective* treatment and consideration of the state and of all the things of this world became possible. The *subjective* side at the same time asserted itself with corresponding emphasis; man became a spiritual *individual*, and recognized himself as such.[15]

We can see this recognition and celebration of the individual in the paintings of the Renaissance. We can even hear it behind the soaring, searing harmonies of the great masters of polyphonic church music: Josquin des Prez (ca. 1450–1521), Giovanni Pierluigi da Palestrina (1525/6–1594), and Thomas Tallis (ca. 1505–1585), who, along with his younger pupil and colleague William Byrd (1539/40–1623), was literally granted a monopoly on polyphonic music by Queen Elizabeth. And it is laid plainly on the surface in Claudio Monteverdi's *L'Orfeo* (1607), the earliest opera still in the modern repertoire. If ever there was an art form that focuses on the individual, in triumph and desperation, it is opera, the modern heir to Greek tragedy.[16]

The ten authors we will study in this book all played important roles in the development of the subjective side of individual consciousness. They provided us with a new vision of men and women as makers and molders of themselves. Simultaneously, they attempted a more or less objective treatment of the state and worldly affairs. In the tension between those two perspectives lies much of their most fruitful, as well as their most comic, work.

Petrarch (1304–1374) embodies this divided consciousness, though he is never deliberately comic. If ever there were a writer who took himself with unrelieved seriousness, it is Petrarch. He invented the sonnet form as an intense and condensed way to convey thoughts and emotions. His letters to fellow scholars are a rallying cry for humanism and the study of classical texts. And his private account of his own spiritual turmoil shows that he recognized the inherent tension, denied by others, between humanism and Catholicism. Although his dates would seem to situate him in the medieval world of Dante and Boccaccio, he is in fact remarkably modern and deserves his place in the vanguard of the Renaissance.

Erasmus (ca. 1466–1536) was a best-selling anthologizer and popularizer of classical adages. He was a strong advocate for the power of a humanist education in shaping Christian citizens and leaders. But he also had a taste for satire. He may be the first writer to stress the importance, or at least the inevitability, of folly in everyday life. That is a point his contemporary, **Martin Luther** (1483–1546), should have understood but did not. Despite his dark, counter-Renaissance view of human nature, Luther had complete faith in his own infallibility. He took Erasmus's measured calls for church reform and turned them into an uncompromising attack on the pope and the corruption of the church, seeking to remake religion in his own image. Erasmus was caught in the middle, between a reactionary church and a bomb-throwing Luther, and his efforts to find a middle ground were condemned by both.

Machiavelli (1469–1527) also took a dark view of human nature. His advice to the Medici prince who he hoped would unite Italy and drive out foreign invaders was thoroughly pragmatic and deliberately amoral. Although he favored a republican form of government like that of ancient Rome, Machiavelli was willing to settle for a competent strongman, and he thought that Christian values had no role to play in the political rough-and-tumble necessary to obtain and retain power. If you want to be a Christian saint, he advised, join a monastery and stay out of politics.

Thomas More (1478–1535) is more famous as a Catholic martyr than a great writer. But he was England's most important humanist and a close friend of Erasmus before he set himself against Henry VIII's divorce from Catherine of Aragon and England's consequent divorce from the Catholic Church. More's *Utopia* is a slight book, yet it has resonated through the centuries and still generates strong opinions as to both the possibility and the desirability of the society he depicts. More shared a love of satire with Erasmus, and he deliberately suffused *Utopia* with a teasing ambiguity.

Castiglione (1478–1529) turned his attention away from the prince and toward the courtiers who serve him. His imagined courtier is the perfect Renaissance man: educated, articulate, and skilled in all the arts of pleasing and impressing others. His most important quality is *sprezzatura*, a word coined by Castiglione, which refers to an almost superhuman grace and ease, a studied nonchalance that disguises the tremendous effort that goes into any form of mastery. Castiglione's courtier is truly the maker and molder of himself. Yet Castiglione does not shrink from exploring the moral and personal ambiguity of the courtier's subservient position in a world of absolute sovereigns.

Rabelais (1483–1553) is an earthy writer. At times, he borders on the obscene. Many of his characters are the embodiment of excess; that is to say, they are Rabelaisian. But the excess is not just of food, drink, and sex; it is also of knowledge, experience, and humor. This former monk turned doctor and novelist—beloved of kings and bishops if not of the theology faculty at the Sorbonne—believed that laughter is natural to man and that, along with our godlike capacity for knowledge and love, we received a generous admixture of absurdity that we cannot escape and therefore might as well embrace.

Montaigne (1533–1592) directly challenges the Renaissance belief that men can become like gods. "They want to get out of themselves and escape from the man," he writes. "That is madness: instead of changing into angels, they change into beasts; instead of raising themselves, they lower themselves." Montaigne stresses man's inherent fallibility and urges us to find wisdom, not in abstractions, but in a close attention to experience. Without the aspirational tyranny of absolutes, Montaigne is free to value experience on its own terms. He teaches us how to live without the ethical, social, and religious conventions by which most of us do live but which falsify the human condition.

Cervantes (1547–1616) wrote the first, and many would say the greatest, novel. Instead of the classical ideal of *mimesis*—art imitating life—Cervantes adopts a more modern notion: life imitating art. Alonso Quixano, a fifty-year-old bachelor of modest means, grows obsessed with books of chivalry and, in a parody of Renaissance self-fashioning, decides to remake himself in their image. As Don Quixote de la Mancha, he is inspired to genuine acts of love and feats of courage. But his literary ideal repeatedly clashes with a very different reality. In the heroic absurdity of Don Quixote, we find both comedy and pathos. We come away from reading the book with a greater sense of our common humanity and the possibilities of being human. For each of us is, to some extent, compelled to be the author of our own fictional universe. That is how we give meaning to our lives in a world abandoned by God.

Shakespeare (1564–1616) excels even Homer, Virgil, and Dante as the poet of human experience. No matter how often we read him or watch his plays, his riches cannot be exhausted. Harold Bloom credits him with the invention of the human. Shakespeare had more than a little help in that regard from Montaigne and Cervantes, not to mention the twelfth-century abbess Heloise. But there is still a profound truth in

Bloom's praise. Shakespeare is both the culmination and the termination of the Renaissance: the soul of his age and for all time. In Shakespeare we find, and remake, ourselves.

Chapter 1

THE THREE FACES OF FRANCESCO PETRARCA

I am like a man standing between two worlds; I look both forward and backward.[1]

This dual vision is the essence of Petrarch. Indeed, it is the essence of the Renaissance that Petrarch did so much to bring into being. The Renaissance looked backward, beyond the Middle Ages, to the classical tradition of ancient Rome and ancient Greece. And the Renaissance looked forward, in an explosion of creativity, to new forms of thought and expression freed from medieval constraints. But Petrarch also looked within, to explore his own soul, and he was tormented by his seeming failures and inadequacies.

Petrarch has long been called the first modern man.[2] That appellation is not necessarily a compliment. The unified medieval worldview shaped by Augustine and Abelard, perfected by Aquinas and Dante, and leavened by Saint Francis provided a broader context within which their thoughts and sensibilities found expression. It anchored them as men and thinkers. We can still discern that fading superstructure in the romances of Chrétien de Troyes, Giovanni Boccaccio's secular stories, and even Chaucer's earthy pilgrimage.[3]

But the medieval synthesis was irrevocably shattered in Petrarch. Petrarch's work was as fragmented as his *Canzoniere* (Songbook), originally titled *Rerum vulgarium fragmenta* (Fragments in the Vernacular). Petrarch himself was a mass of contradictions, large and small. He was a religious seeker who found rest for his troubled soul only in the study of ancient literature. He was a devout Christian who had no patience for the scholastic thought of Abelard and Aquinas. He was a cleric with illegitimate children. He was an amazingly productive writer who rarely finished projects. He was a dedicated Latinist whose most famous writings were in Italian. He was an indefatigable traveler who praised nothing more than a quiet life in the country. He was committed to freedom yet voluntarily lived under tyrants. He sought the patronage of the great while denouncing worldly ambition. He was a hypochondriac who disparaged doctors even as he sought their advice. He was a sentimentalist who disparaged sentiment and a lover who disparaged love. He was by turn magnanimous and petty, generous to those who admired him while grudging in praise of his two greatest contemporaries, Dante and Boccaccio. He was a relentless self-publicist and a relentless self-critic, questioning everything but his own importance.

Petrarch was a fox trying to be a hedgehog.[4] He tried to be Dante in his *Canzoniere*, and failed. He tried to be Augustine in his *Secretum*, and failed. He tried to be Virgil in his *Africa*, and failed. He tried to be a combination of Cicero and Seneca in his reflections on rhetoric and moral philosophy, and failed.

Where Petrarch succeeded was in being himself, in all his contradictions. He launched the discovery of the individual that is the essence of the Renaissance. He was the first true humanist. Petrarch loved scholarship, poetry, and philosophy, not just as ends in themselves but as means to a greater understanding of the self, as roads to wisdom. In his many volumes of letters, written throughout his life, he includes the reader in this process of self-discovery. He even wrote letters to the great literary figures of the ancient tradition: Homer, Livy, Virgil, Horace, Cicero, and Seneca, among others. He praised their virtues and in some cases, especially Cicero, chided their shortcomings. He used the study of literature as a means of self-examination. He thought he could discover the modern self through the rediscovery of ancient authors. Petrarch believed that the self was an object worthy of contemplation and study and that enhanced self-consciousness was our desideratum. In this, he was more a precursor to Montaigne and Rousseau than a successor to Augustine.

Indeed, we might well claim that Petrarch was the first postmodern man.[5] His constant themes were exile and fragmentation and inexorable change through time. He was a man driven from the garden by angels brandishing flaming swords. Even his beloved Augustine was valued more for the dark night of his soul than for the alleged illumination that followed his conversion. With the loss of the medieval synthesis, Petrarch sought to reconstruct a new self from the fragments of ancient wisdom. That self was not given; it was created. It was fashioned through the study of literature. Petrarch sought a rebirth—a *rinascita*—in the act of writing.[6] For Petrarch, writing was a moral act and a personal necessity. He may not properly be numbered among the greatest thinkers and writers of all time, but he was the indispensable man of his own time. He was the pivot on which the medieval world turned toward the Renaissance.

LIFE

Francesco Petrarca, known to us as Petrarch, was born on July 20, 1304, in the city-state of Arezzo, about forty-five miles from Florence. Dating back to Etruscan times, Arezzo is most famous today for its recently restored fresco by Piero della Francesca and for the Casa del Petrarca.

Although he was born in Arezzo, Petrarch always considered himself a Florentine. His father was exiled from Florence by the Black Guelfs in 1302, the same year Dante was condemned *in absentia* and forbidden to return.[7] Ser Petracco moved first to Arezzo in rural Tuscany and then to the papal court at Avignon, where his wife and two sons joined him in 1312. Petrarch accordingly grew up and spent much of his life in Provence.

Petrarch was homeschooled and, from an early age, showed a great love of the Roman classics. His father, however, was of a more practical bent. He sent Petrarch at the age of twelve, along with his younger brother, Gherardo, to study law, first at Montpellier and later at Bologna. "A full seven years I spent in that study," Petrarch would later write. "It would be more truthful to say I wasted them!"[8] His father sought to quench his continued interest in the classics by burning the books Petrarch had painstakingly collected. Petrarch groaned as if he himself had been tossed on the same fire. In response to his tears, his father snatched back two books—a volume of Virgil plus Cicero's *Rhetoric*—and handed them to the boy. "'Take this one,' he said, 'as an occasional recreation for your spirit, and this one as a prop for your law studies.'"[9] The story likely contains more symbolic than literal truth, for those two authors exercised the greatest influence on the young Petrarch. He considered them his true patrimony.

While the two boys were at Montpellier, their mother died. When their father also died a few years later, Petrarch quickly abandoned the study of law and returned to Avignon in 1326. Whatever money was in his father's estate apparently went to a stepmother, and Petrarch and his brother were left with limited resources. Fortunately, Petrarch had a knack for attracting patronage, and he became a favorite of the powerful Colonna family from Rome, including the father, Stefano, and his sons Giovanni and Giacomo, both of whom became high-ranking church officials. Petrarch also formed close friendships with the Belgian musician Lodewyck Heyliger, whom Petrarch called "Socrates," and with Lello di Pietro Stefano dei Tosetti, whom Petrarch rechristened "Laelius," after the loyal friend of the Roman general and conqueror of Carthage, Scipio Africanus.[10] Petrarch's collected letters are full of epistles to, and about, these cherished friends.

But his most famous and life-altering encounter was with the elusive "Laura" on April 6, 1327, when Petrarch was still twenty-two. Petrarch always claimed it was Good Friday, though in fact Good Friday did not fall on that date in 1327. He also later claimed that she died at exactly the same hour of the same day, twenty-one years later, in 1348. The symmetry may be a convenient fabrication for symbolic purposes, but the reality of the meeting and its effect on the young Petrarch are generally accepted. Petrarch saw Laura at church and was struck, like Dante for his Beatrice, with a lifelong passion that was his greatest joy and his deepest anguish. Petrarch recorded all his family and other milestones on the flyleaves of his copy of Virgil. This is where he registered his first meeting with Laura, as well as her death from the plague in 1348.

Laura was already married to someone else, and Petrarch's love was unrequited though nonetheless recognized and sometimes tolerated, if not encouraged, by its object. Petrarch first obtained fame for the Italian sonnets he began writing to Laura, love poems inspired by Dante and other masters of the *dolce stil nuovo*.[11] Dante had died in 1321, when Petrarch was seventeen. But Dante nonetheless was a decisive influence and rival, though Petrarch pretended not to have read Dante's *Commedia* until 1359, when Boccaccio sent him a copy.[12] Even then, he offered at best faint praise for the greatest of all Italian poets and only grudgingly acknowledged that, of the "three crowns of Italian literature," Dante held the first place, with himself in second and Boccaccio in third.[13]

Petrarch became a cleric in 1328, though purely, it would seem, as a matter of convenience. He never took holy orders or actually functioned as a priest. But he soon received a canonry from his friend Cardinal Giovanni Colonna, with a modest income and even more modest duties. In fact, he became something of a collector of no-show benefices over his career from various patrons. Although the incomes from each were small, collectively they gave him a solid living. Yet neither his canonries nor his devotion to Laura kept Petrarch from fathering two illegitimate children by unknown women. His son, Giovanni, was born in 1337 and his daughter, Francesca, in 1343. He arranged for both children to be legitimized by Pope Clement VI.

In 1337, with assistance from his friends, Petrarch purchased a country house in Vaucluse, a small, "closed valley" ending in a rock face, from which a fountain provided the source of the Sorgue River. Here, with the help of a rural couple, Petrarch sought solitude from the busy papal court at Avignon and the freedom to write and to appreciate nature at leisure. Morris Bishop called Vaucluse Petrarch's Sabine Farm, after Horace's own rural refuge from Rome.[14] And just as Horace's farm was near Mount Soracte, made famous in one of his finest odes,[15] Petrarch's riverside cottage was close to Mont Ventoux, made famous in one of Petrarch's most important letters, in which he describes an ascent to the summit undertaken with his brother for no other reason than to enjoy the view from the top.

Petrarch's retreat to the countryside was shocking to his contemporaries, who could not imagine voluntarily absenting oneself from the papal court and its opportunities for advancement. But Petrarch was vigorous in criticizing a city existence driven by ambition. Such a life, he wrote, is "filled with toil, lacking in repose, directed toward others, forgetful of oneself; the entire lives of men of affairs are wars without a truce. . . . They are everywhere but with themselves; they often speak with others but never with themselves."[16]

In a verse letter to Giacomo Colonna, Petrarch stressed the advantages of solitude in the midst of nature for the work he wished to do and the life he wished to live:

> I want nothing, content
> with what I have. . . .
> . . .
> If she so wills, may Fortune keep for me
> this bit of land, the small house and dear books,
> and keep all else herself. . . .
> . . .
> Just let her not touch the wealth that comes
> from poetry, or my free time, that misses
> none of the worries of extravagance.[17]

It is a lovely vision. Petrarch retreated to Vaucluse to rediscover and reinvent himself. He regarded the solitude of nature both as a soothing balm for his unrequited love and as a contemplative space for self-knowledge, a place to speak with himself and to be with himself.

Yet, however sincere Petrarch's love of Vaucluse, he often left it to travel throughout Europe, and however sincere Petrarch's disdain of worldly ambition, he pursued glory and influence with fierce intensity. In 1341, after a relentless lobbying campaign, he arranged to have himself crowned poet laureate in Rome on the Capitoline Hill, the first since the fall of Rome. He was proclaiming himself and getting others to proclaim him a modern successor to Virgil, Horace, and Ovid. Petrarch underwent a three-day "examination" by Robert of Anjou, king of Naples, before accepting the laurel crown in Rome on April 8. His coronation oration was a celebration of humanistic ideals, carefully recovered from antiquity after the dark years of medieval Europe. It was also a call to arms for cultural renewal, for politically engaged poetry, and for the obligation of writers to forge a renewed sense of community based on classical ideals.

Petrarch was only thirty-six when he was crowned at Rome. He was later deeply embarrassed by the premature accolades and his own part in calling them forth. Indeed, the people of Rome, most of whom undoubtedly had never heard of Petrarch, must have been puzzled by the whole affair, in which they nonetheless participated with enthusiasm. At that time, Petrarch had only a limited body of work on which to lay such a claim, most notably a small portion of his sonnets to Laura and the beginning of an epic poem on Scipio Africanus. This poem, *Africa*, takes its conscious starting point from Virgil's *Aeneid*, with Dido's curse hurled at the departing Aeneas and promising "endless war" between Carthage and Rome: "No love between our peoples, ever, no pacts of peace!"[18]

Africa was never finished, though Petrarch continued to work on it intermittently until his death, sometimes thinking it the equal of the *Aeneid* but mostly, and correctly, viewing it as a failure. Petrarch was a poet of the fractured self, a poet of introspection. He lacked the prerequisites for epic poetry: sustained narrative drive, structural coherence, and detailed characterization. *Africa* is, by common consensus, tedious and pedestrian. Even its most ardent advocate, the Italian scholar Aldo Bernardo, admires the poem not for its epic verse but for the humanistic vision embodied in the character of Scipio.[19]

Petrarch traveled frequently to Italy, often on diplomatic missions to and from powerful figures. Petrarch met Boccaccio in Florence in 1350. He condescended to the younger man to a certain extent, but there was genuine affection and devotion on both sides through the years, and many of Petrarch's most famous letters were written to Boccaccio. In 1353, Petrarch moved permanently from Provence to northern Italy, living under the patronage of a succession of Italian strongmen, princes, and despots in Milan, Venice, Parma, and Padua. He served them as secretary, ambassador, court poet, and literary ornament. This patronage, added to his benefices, made him reasonably wealthy. Petrarch occasionally chafed at his public obligations and turned down the post of papal secretary on several occasions, yet he clearly did not want to give up being a public figure. As he explained in a somewhat defensive letter to Boccaccio, he considered himself a combination of courtier and humanist,[20] a combination Baldassare Castiglione would turn into the ideal type of the Renaissance man.

As he aged, Petrarch shifted away from poetry to scholarship. During his extensive travels, he always sought out ancient manuscripts in monasteries and church libraries. His greatest find was Cicero's *Letters to Atticus* at the cathedral library in Verona, and he used those letters and the letters of Seneca as models for his own carefully shaped and preserved correspondence. Petrarch longed to create a sort of humanistic monastery, with a group of like-minded friends devoted to scholarship, literature, and friendship. But more and more of those closest to him died, many of plague, some of violence: Laura, Giovanni Colonna, Socrates, Laelius. His letters are full of accumulated grief and his increasing weariness with life. His son, Giovanni, died of the plague in Milan in 1361, shortly after Petrarch had ended his own eight-year residence there.

For a time, Petrarch re-created his Vaucluse retreat with a house and garden outside Parma. He loved the spot dearly but was frequently absent and perpetually restless. Around 1368, Petrarch and his daughter Francesca (with her family) moved to the small town of Arquà, near Padua. There, he lived an ascetic, scholarly, and pious life. "I wish that death would find me reading or writing, or, if it please Christ, praying or weeping."[21] He had his wish on July 18, 1374, just short of his seventieth birthday.

In his will, Petrarch granted various legacies to his brother and his remaining friends, including fifty florins to Boccaccio "to buy a warm winter dressing gown." He left the house at Vaucluse to the couple who had cared for him there for so long. His library was claimed by Padua, but the rest of the estate went to his daughter and her family. Petrarch's true legacy, though, was the divided consciousness that is the hallmark of modernity.

PETRARCH IN LOVE

Petrarch first saw Laura on April 6, 1327, at the church of Sainte-Claire d'Avignon. His instant passion for her could only be compared to (and was clearly intended to rival) Dante's love for Beatrice. Indeed, Petrarch, in his poetry, is in constant dialogue with Dante as model and foil.

Some, even among Petrarch's friends and contemporaries, suspected that Laura was nothing but a poetic creation and not a flesh-and-blood woman. But Petrarch insisted otherwise, and most scholars now agree. Laura is generally identified as Laura de Noves, a member of the Avignon nobility, who was married in 1325 at the age of eighteen and became Laura de Sade. Her inaccessibility seems to have been part of her hold on him.

Petrarch wrote poems to his Laura over a thirty-year span. His devotion to (or, more accurately, his obsession with) her sometimes wavers but never breaks. He worked on the collection throughout his life, revising, discarding, and reordering the individual poems. He put them in their final form only in the last year of his life. The original title of the collection is *Rerum vulgarium fragmenta* (Fragments in the Vernacular), which is preferable to the commonly used *Canzoniere* because the fragmentation is a deliberate part of the poet's intention constantly to undermine any straightforward narrative. Petrarch himself referred to the poems as *Rime Sparse* (Scattered Rhymes), perhaps echoing Horace's injunction to *sparga rosas* (scatter roses). The poems are indeed roses scattered throughout Petrarch's life, and yet they fail to leave a clear trail.

There are a total of 366 poems in the collection—one for every day of a leap year—which Petrarch divided into two parts, corresponding roughly to poems written before and poems written after the death of Laura on April 6, 1348. But it is not a neat division. Part one contains poems about Laura's death, while part two contains poems in which Laura is still very much alive. Petrarch deliberately plays tricks with chronology, resisting even as he invites a simple autobiographical reading.

There are 317 sonnets in the collection, as well as a variety of other poetic forms, such as canzoni, sestinas, ballads, and madrigals. Not all the poems are about Laura. Some are political or religious. There are even poems about other women that Petrarch could not resist including, just as Dante did in his *Vita Nuova*.

Over time, the *Canzoniere* became Petrarch's most famous work, a fact that undoubtedly would have shocked him and may well shock modern readers, many of whom will find the poems tedious and overwrought. But the poems were remarkably influential. Petrarch is the father of lyric love poetry in the vernacular, more so than the Provençal troubadours or even Dante. Petrarch offers us a changing portrait of human love through time, not an allegorical or a religious journey. The prime subject of that portrait is the poet himself, the lover rather than the beloved. He extols his beloved's beauty and goodness and decries her coldness and cruelty. But the focus is almost always on the poet's feelings rather than the actual object of his affections.

We are today most familiar with Shakespearean sonnets, written in iambic pentameter, with three four-line stanzas, known as quatrains, and a final rhyming couplet. The rhyme scheme is conventional: *abab cdcd efef gg*. Petrarch's sonnets, which he derived from earlier models, also contain fourteen lines but generally consist of two quatrains and two tercets, which are three-line stanzas. The two quatrains have an interlocking rhyme scheme, *abba*. The tercets are generally more flexible, but Petrarch often used *cde* followed by *cdc*.

Here is the first of the Petrarchan sonnets to Laura:

Voi ch'ascoltate in rime sparse il suono
di quei sospiri ond'io nudriva 'l core
in sul mio primo giovenile errore
quand'era in parte altr'uom da quel ch'i' sono,

del vario stile in ch'io piango et ragiono
fra le vane speranze e 'l van dolore,
ove sia chi per prova intenda amore,
spero trovar pietà, nonché perdono.

Ma ben veggio or sì come al popol tutto
favola fui gran tempo, onde sovente
di me medesmo meco mi vergogno;

et del mio vaneggiar vergogna è 'l frutto,
e 'l pentersi, e 'l conoscer chiaramente
che quanto piace al mondo è breve sogno.[22]

My (relatively) literal translation makes no attempt to capture the rhythm or rhymes of the original Italian:

You who hear in scattered rhymes the sound
of those sighs with which I nourished my heart
in my first youthful error
when I was in part another man than I am now,

for the various styles in which I wept and sang
between vain hope and vain sorrow,
from those who have traveled on the road of Love,
I hope to find pity and forgiveness.

But I see now, yes, how people
have long told tales about me, so that often
it fills me with shame;

of my vanities, shame is the fruit
and penitence and the clearest knowledge
that what pleases the world is but a fleeting dream.

Two things in particular are worth noting about this opening sonnet, obviously written later in time to serve as an introduction to the collection. First, it is an *apologia* for the poems that follow. Petrarch will present his poems—with all their sighs and hopes and sorrows—but he recognizes that these efforts through the years capture moods and feelings that are often far from admirable. Taken together, these moments paint a portrait with the infinitely variable hues of love, some beautiful, some ugly. The Lover is by turns adoring and wounded, fatuous and petulant, hopeful and miserable, chaste and lustful, pious and profane, naive and bitter, quickened and prostrate. He is, as Mark Musa remarks in the introduction to his excellent translation, the "personification of the hapless lover as antihero."[23] There is in these poems both sincere feeling and a strong element of self-mockery. Morris Bishop calls the *Canzoniere* "an autobiographical novel in verse."[24] If so, the novel has neither plot nor narrative, and the autobiography is, as Musa point out, largely "fictional."[25] The Lover of the sonnets is every bit as much a literary creation as Dante's Pilgrim, and any simplistic identification of Petrarch and the Lover will lead the reader astray.

Second, and relatedly, the poem starts with a deliberate reference to the first of Dante's *Vita Nuova* poems, which begins:

O voi che per la via d'Amor passate,
attendete e guardate
s'elli è dolore alcun, quanto 'l mio, grave.

O you who travel on the road of Love,
pause here and look about
for any man whose grief surpasses mine.[26]

Dante's direct address to and engagement of the reader (*voi che*) is copied by Petrarch, and I have accentuated the echoes by having Petrarch also refer to those who have "traveled on the road of Love," a loose if legitimate translation of "*chi per prova intenda amore*" (literally: those who have tried to test love). The reference to Dante, however, is intended by Petrarch less as a tribute than as a challenge and a contrast. Dante offered a coherent narrative for his *Vita Nuova* poems, including prose connectors to try to draw them together. His *Commedia* is an even more explicitly narrative account of how his love for Beatrice has led him to God.

Petrarch will have none of that. His scattered rhymes speak only of the moments that occasioned them. No coherent narrative will connect those moments. Indeed, there is no coherent narrative through time that would not falsify the singular experiences he attempts to capture in the poems. Each memory embodied in a poem is *è breve sogno* (a brief dream). But fellow travelers on the road of love will recognize truth in these scattered rhymes. Petrarch is writing about human love—in all its longings and frustrations. Laura is not a proxy for the divine. There are religious poems in the collection, but those, too, capture moments in time, rare moments of rapture and transcendence. They do not turn Laura into a religious allegory or provide any lasting apotheosis for the Lover. Dante's Pilgrim and Petrarch's Lover are two of the most influential fictional creations in the Western tradition. Yet, in the end, they serve very different gods and reflect very different poets. As Petrarch makes clear toward the end of the collection, "my faith is to the world and to my lady."[27]

Yet it is a particular kind of faith, one that expects no fulfillment and no settled state in which desire is fulfilled. He can neither possess his lady nor conquer the world through his poetry. He can only provide fragmentary glimpses of each and thereby glimpses of his own fragmentary self. There is no fixed self to order those experiences and no fixed reality to anchor them. Petrarch captures moments and feelings that are often at odds with one another: "Caught in contrasting winds in a frail boat / on the high seas I am without a helm."[28]

And yet, Petrarch insists, "not through a thousand turnings have I moved."[29] What has stayed fixed and true amid time and change is his attempt to transmute his love for Laura into poetry. Indeed, he makes the identification explicit when he puns on Laura and *lauro*, the laurel that crowns the successful poet:

> I'll chase the shadow of that lovely laurel [*dolce lauro*]
> throughout the hottest day and through the snow
> until the final day closes my eyes.[30]

Petrarch's pursuit of Laura is one with his pursuit of poetic glory. There is a complicated symbiosis between the two, as each feeds on the other.

Through poetry, Petrarch is able to capture and fix his memories of Laura and thereby appear to pause the inexorable march of time. He wrote fifteen anniversary poems explicitly commemorating the day he first saw her and measuring the changes in both of them through the years. But all the poems in the collection are such commemorations. Laura ages, but Petrarch's memories are fixed in poetry, brief moments captured forever. The poems give life to Laura and to Petrarch.

> Love gives me life through memory alone;
> so if I see the world in youthful guise
> as it begins to clothe itself in green,
> it is as if I see in unripe age
> that beautiful young girl who's now a lady.[31]

Writing poetry is an act of meditation upon experience and past desire. Meeting Laura created desire. Poetry is a way of rekindling that desire in the hope of transcending loss. Yet the very act of writing reconnects the poet with his past desires, their transitory nature and the losses he has experienced. There is clear irony in trying to transcend time and desire by immersing oneself in both. But poetic glory is a way of partially escaping the flux and loss of time.[32] "I hope through her to live," he writes, "long after people think that I am dead."[33] Conversely, even after her death, Laura continues to live in his memory and in his poems: "*ancor è in vita*!" (She's still alive!).[34]

Shakespeare would take this contrast between evanescent time and poetic immortality as a principal theme, echoing Petrarch in one of his most famous sonnets:

> Since brass, nor stone, nor earth, nor boundless sea
> But sad mortality o'ersways their power,
> How with this rage shall beauty hold a plea,
> Whose action is no stronger than a flower?
> O, how shall summer's honey breath hold out
> Against the wrackful siege of batt'ring days,
> When rocks impregnable are not so stout
> Nor gates of steel so strong, but Time decays?
> O, fearful meditation! Where, alack,
> Shall Time's best jewel from Time's chest lie hid?
> Or what strong hand can hold his swift foot back,
> Or who his spoil of beauty can forbid?
> O, none, unless this miracle have might,
> That in black ink my love may still shine bright.[35]

Shakespeare's sonnets have eclipsed those of Petrarch, but Shakespeare's debt to Petrarch is undeniable. Indeed, there is something even more elusive about Petrarch's protean moods, and his faith in poetry as a means of conquering time is decidedly more ambiguous.

Petrarch compares his pursuit of Laura to Apollo's pursuit of Daphne:

> So far astray is my insane desire
> to chase this lady who has turned in flight,
> and light and liberated of Love's snares,
> flies off ahead of my slow run for her.[36]

Apollo never captures Daphne. Swift of foot, she flees his advances. A human girl cannot, in the end, outrun a god, but praying for deliverance to her father, the river god Peneus, she is turned into a laurel tree as Apollo finally closes in. Daphne is never possessed; nor will Petrarch ever possess his Laura. That failure is the essence and impetus of Petrarch's poetry. What he seeks—Laura and poetic glory—always eludes his grasp: "*vivo del desir fuor di speranza*" (I live in desire beyond hope).[37] His fragments will never coalesce into a coherent narrative. He will never be finished. He will never be satisfied. He will never reach either transcendent bliss or perfect expression. As a human, he always falls short and yet never stops trying. The goal of poetry is to stop time, but time cannot be stopped. "*La vita fugge et non s'arresta un'ora*" (Life runs away and never rests a moment).[38]

Petrarch's pursuit of Laura and of poetic glory is also a pursuit of himself through time. The experiences embodied in the poems made him the person and the writer he has become. But he cannot fix himself outside of time or give his experiences a single, definitive meaning.[39] He cannot impose a clear narrative of the self and its development, while being true to the components of his experience. In this, he is very much a modern consciousness. Our sense of self through time, he believes, is inherently unstable and fragmented. Petrarch can offer us only those fragments in all their contradictions. That is the true portrait of a life, a series of such fragments. Petrarch himself captures them and pins them in his collection like butterflies. He imposes order of a sort, but it is a contingent order. The narrative of transcendence eludes him.

Or perhaps it is more accurate to say that he deliberately rejects the narrative of transcendence as a falsification. Dante overcame time through a coherent and unified narrative of redemption in the perfection of desire and poetry. Petrarch's faith in his lady (desire) and the world (poetry) is every bit as strong. But he sees them both in a very human and imperfect state. Daphne, who embodies both, is always out of reach.

PETRARCH'S SECRET

In 1333, when he was twenty-eight, Petrarch was given a pocket-sized copy of Augustine's *Confessions*. The book made a powerful impression on the young man, and he carried it with him at all times. Augustine came to rival Virgil and Cicero in his thinking. Christianity and antiquity wrestled for his fractured soul.

Nine years later, Petrarch wrote his own confession, *Secretum meum* (My Secret), the same year his brother, Gherardo, became a Carthusian monk. It recounts his failings as a person and as a Christian with remarkable frankness and clarity. In 1909, Petrarch scholar Maud Jerrold said that "it remains one of the world's great monuments of self-revelation, and ranks with the *Confessions of St. Augustine.*"[40] Pardonable exaggeration, perhaps, but nobody much reads the *Secretum* anymore. Indeed, the most accessible translation dates from 1911. The high-water mark for admiration of the *Secretum* was more than a hundred years ago, whereas the *Confessions* increasingly has become an indispensable work.

There is ample reason for that. Augustine tells the dramatic, autobiographical story of one man's struggle to find virtue and God, and he ends with a triumphant conversion and a revelation both personal and intellectual. Petrarch neither tells a story nor ends in triumph. Augustine describes his sins in vivid and concrete detail. The reader lives through them and through the anguish that leads to Augustine's final conversion. Petrarch presents his own faults abstractly, and his self-flagellation

49

(or, rather, the flaying administered to him by Augustine) is painful and embarrassing to the reader, rather than an invitation for sympathetic identification and self-improvement.

And yet the book is well worth reading, not just for what it reveals about Petrarch the man but for what it reveals about the sources of human unhappiness, the lies we constantly tell ourselves, and what truly matters in a human life, whether Christian or not. For all the talk of immortality and God's grace, which Petrarch himself embraces only tentatively in the end, the *Secretum* is not ultimately a religious book, or at least it can be read with profit without such an overlay. Petrarch is sufficiently honest that he does not even pretend to follow the Augustinian way, any more than he followed the Dantean way in his *Canzoniere*. However much he might like to, he simply cannot do it. And for that recognition and his courageous commitment to personal integrity, we must admire him.

The *Secretum* is an imagined dialogue in three parts between Augustine and Petrarch. In a preface, Petrarch claims it is a private work as an aid in his own meditations. That is not merely a literary device. He never published the book in his lifetime, and it was not circulated until some years after his death. Yet he surely knew that such circulation was likely if not inevitable.

Augustine comes to Petrarch, as Virgil came to Dante, to lead him out of his current misery and into a communion with the divine. Augustine chastises Petrarch for succumbing to a plague of false desires when he should be focused on God and his own mortality. Petrarch is unhappy, Augustine claims, because he has chosen worldly seductions over virtue and truth.

Petrarch puts up only a mild defense at first because it is clear that he does not take Augustine's attack seriously. He of all people has dedicated his life to the pursuit of virtue and truth. He has sought neither wealth nor power. He has led a modest life of independence, reserved for writing and scholarship. He has loved deeply and unselfishly. He is unhappy, yes, but that is a product not of choice nor lack of virtue but of ill fortune, and in particular his unquenchable passion for Laura. "What man exists," he asks Augustine, "so ignorant or so far removed from all contact with the world as not to know that penury, grief, disgrace, illness, death, and other evils too that are reckoned among the greatest, often befall us in spite of ourselves, and never with our own consent?"[41] We cannot will ourselves to be happy. We must instead accept unhappiness as our common lot and deal with it as best we can. No one is more cognizant than he of human frailty and human mortality.

Augustine dismisses Petrarch's easy answers as an exercise in self-deception. We deceive ourselves and esteem ourselves more than we deserve and in the process deceive others. He urges Petrarch to "be jealous for truth more than for disputation."[42] There are two key steps to overcoming the distresses of mortal life. The first is to meditate upon death and man's misery; the second is to develop the will to rise above one's current state. Petrarch has failed on both counts.

Augustine denies that Petrarch meditates on mortality. He grieves the deaths of others and acknowledges the inevitability of his own, but he does not feel it at the center of his being as the most important facet of life itself. He intellectualizes it and therefore distances himself from it: "It has not sunk down into your heart as deeply as it ought, nor is it lodged there as firmly as it should be."[43]

Augustine further denies that Petrarch has truly willed to change for the better: "I have witnessed many tears, but very little will."[44] Augustine starts with the Stoic premise that no one can be unhappy against his will because happiness depends only on virtue, not external circumstances. The will is superior even to fortune, and "the desire of virtue is itself a great part of virtue."[45] But wishing to be better is not the same as truly willing it. Petrarch's desires for liberty and for an end to his misery have been too feeble and ineffective. His mind is overcrowded, and his strength is dissipated on trifles. Every lesser wish must be set aside so that all desire is focused on the chief good. All other desires and passions must be extinguished before the fetters of the world are broken and desire is free. Otherwise, the mind will turn back upon itself in anger and loathing, and the soul will return to its crooked paths.

With this groundwork established, Augustine, in the second dialogue, launches a furious assault on Petrarch's character. He begins with the greatest sources of Petrarch's pride: his intellect, his learning, his writing, and his eloquence. What value is that vaunted intellect, Augustine asks, when it is "no match in skill for some of the meanest and smallest of God's creatures?"[46] How have you benefited from your vast reading, when you forget more than you retain? What profit is it, in any event, to know the courses of the stars or unravel the secrets of nature when you are ignorant of yourself? What good is eloquence if you convince others but stand convicted in the court of your own conscience? "What worse folly than to go on blind to one's real defects, and be infatuated with words and the pleasure of hearing one's own voice?"[47] For the things that truly matter, words are altogether inadequate. All your writing and scholarship, Augustine tells him, are so much "vanity and gaining the empty praise of men."[48]

Petrarch is looking with brutal honesty at the pillars on which he has built his life and his reputation. He places the words in the mouth of Augustine, but the scrutiny is his own. He is asking himself what is truly worthwhile in a human life and whether he has misspent his energies. "Here, unless I am mistaken," Petrarch has Augustine say to him, "are the causes that inflate your mind with pride, forbid you to recognize your low estate, and keep you from the recollection of death."[49] Petrarch as character in the dialogue resists these points. Yet Petrarch as author, in the character of Augustine, is relentless in pursing them.

Augustine extends the list of charges by noting that even Petrarch's devotion to literature and learning, misguided though it may be, is only half-hearted. He accuses Petrarch of cupidity and ambition. He left his quiet life in the country and took on the busyness of city life and travel for the sake of wealth and power: "You only concede to what is Good and Beautiful the moments you can spare from avarice."[50] Petrarch strongly disputes this charge, claiming that no one is freer of this fault than himself. He has never sought riches or power but instead has been content with enough only to secure his needs and his independence. Augustine turns that admission against him: "What greater riches can there be than to lack nothing? What greater power than to be independent of everyone else in the world?"[51] Augustine then twists the knife still further, accusing Petrarch of practicing "the art of ingratiating yourself in the palaces of the great, the trick of flattery, deceit, promising, lying, pretending, dissembling, and putting up with all kinds of slights and indignities."[52] Those who know his biography know how much truth there is in those words and how much it must have cost Petrarch to write them.

Finally, Augustine adds physical vanity and lust to the list of charges. Although Petrarch claims to have asked God to free him from the latter sin, Augustine echoes the most famous line of his own *Confessions*: "You have always asked that your prayers may be granted presently," just not yet.[53] But the most interesting addition is provided by Petrarch himself, when he confesses to a deep-seated melancholy that sounds remarkably like clinical depression. Petrarch notes that the passions attack him in short bursts, but he has longer bouts with gloom and despair. "In such times I take no pleasure in the light of day, I see nothing, I am as one plunged in the darkness of hell itself, and seem to endure death in its most cruel form."[54] Here, Petrarch's *Secretum* takes a modern turn as he provides us with additional insight into why he not merely wallows in but appears to relish the misery of his love for Laura. Cause and effect may be difficult to untangle, but there is a decidedly bipolar aspect in the *Canzoniere* that is distilled here in a self-diagnosis.

Oddly, though, Augustine's proposed cure for these many faults and troubles has nothing to do with religion. To the contrary, he urges Petrarch to study Cicero, Seneca, and Virgil, and to commit their most important maxims to memory so that they are always at hand to fortify his will and to aid him against pride, avarice, ambition, melancholy, and lust. Since Petrarch has spent his life studying those authors, Augustine's advice seems a validation rather than a reproach, and a validation of precisely the learning and scholarship Augustine has just dismissed as so much vanity. But what Augustine is really saying is that reading these authors is not the same as internalizing their teachings. They must shape the will, not just occupy the mind. If approached in the proper spirit, pagan literature can do much in reconciling one to fortune, conquering passion, curing the sorrows of the heart, and putting reason in control of one's life.

All that may be true, but it seems a rather glib prescription for the litany of ills that has gone before. And, indeed, at the start of the third dialogue, Augustine acknowledges that he has "not at all as yet touched upon the deep-seated wounds which are within."[55] Petrarch, he says, is still held in bondage by two strong claims: love and glory. Only when those are defeated will he truly be free.

Petrarch is deeply shocked. He considers love and glory to be "the finest passions" of his nature.[56] They are treasures rather than fetters. Thanks to love he has gained renown as a poet. Thanks to love he has been ennobled as a man. Petrarch insists that love is virtuous as long as the object is herself virtuous. His love is honorable, with no admixture of the flesh or desire for earthly rewards. He loves Laura's immortal soul, not its physical embodiment. She has led him to God.

"Do you mean to assert," Augustine counters, "that if the same soul had been lodged in a body ill-formed and poor to look upon, you would have taken equal delight therein?"[57] Of course not. The purified Beatrice who led Dante to God is a dangerous myth. His passion for Laura has tied his heart to worldly things—"the sight of the object, the hope of enjoying it,"[58]—and detached his mind from heaven. It has led him into misery. Augustine openly mocks Petrarch's younger self as a pale, wasted figure who "felt a morbid pleasure in feeding on tears and sighs,"[59] a sentiment with which any reader of the *Canzoniere* must concur. Augustine compels him to admit that his deep melancholy began at the same time as his love for Laura. He has expended sixteen years of effort and grief in loving and celebrating a delusion. Only renouncing his love for Laura and never turning back will provide a cure.

Petrarch accepts Augustine's counsel "heartily and with thankfulness" and resolves to shut his life to Laura.[60] The irony is rich for a modern reader. Petrarch finished the *Secretum* in 1342 or 1343. But Petrarch kept writing sonnets to Laura until her death in 1348, which occasioned a new outpouring of more than one hundred postmortem poems. Petrarch may have embraced Augustine's advice intellectually, but his heart still belonged to Laura. No wonder Petrarch kept the *Secretum* as a private work in aid of his own meditations. He never convinced even himself.

The same is true of glory. Augustine chides Petrarch for seeking too eagerly the praise of men. Worldly glory is a small and feeble thing, quickly passing. It is particularly perverse for Petrarch to seek the applause of the common herd he so despises. Yet Petrarch cannot bear the thought of leaving his *Africa* half-finished. Augustine responds with a killing dig: this work, he says, "greatly excellent as you think it, has no wide scope nor long future before it."[61] Yet Petrarch insists that there is nothing wrong with hoping for worldly glory and seeking it here, while still making it secondary to virtue and the more radiant glory of eternal life.[62] In any event, he concludes simply, "I have not strength to resist that old bent for study altogether."[63] You can hear Augustine sigh: "Want of will you call want of power. Well, so it must be, if it cannot be otherwise."[64]

This is neither a satisfying nor a definitive ending. But it is an honest one. Petrarch cannot follow Augustine in leaving all earthly desires behind and reconstructing his life's narrative as one of Christian salvation. He cannot and does not wish to abandon desire and poetry. Nor, as we have seen, can he claim to bring them to the perfection sought by Dante. For all its medieval antecedents, the *Secretum* is not a medieval book. Petrarch is unwilling to let go of this world in favor of the next. He admires virtue but not the denuded virtue of abstract religion. Petrarch will cling tenaciously to what he most values—love, poetry, learning, glory—and let the immortal chips fall where they may.

I do not think to become as God, or to inhabit eternity, or embrace heaven and earth. Such glory as belongs to man is enough for me. That is all I sigh after. Mortal myself, it is but mortal blessings I desire.[65]

PETRARCH AS HUMANIST SAGE

Petrarch was an inveterate letter writer, addressing his vast correspondence to intimate friends as well as to the important political and intellectual figures of his day. Inspired by the philosophical letters of Seneca and by the letters on contemporary events written by Cicero—particularly those to Atticus that Petrarch himself had discovered in a church library and preserved for posterity—Petrarch decided to publish his own correspondence. He approached the task as carefully as he did his *Canzoniere*, selecting, rejecting, extensively revising and polishing, and even creating new letters after the fact to fill chronological and narrative gaps. The letters were intended as a standalone work of art, not just a miscellany. He organized his first collection, which he called the *Familiares* (Letters on Familiar Matters) into twenty-four books, like Homer's *Odyssey*. Each book contains anywhere from six to twenty-two letters. He followed this with the *Seniles* (Letters of Old Age) in eighteen books. He prepared another collection of Verse Letters, as well as a set of "uncollected" letters that did not make the cut for either the *Familiares* or the *Seniles* but were nonetheless preserved.

Petrarch's topics are as varied as his correspondents. He seeks to merge the moral and philosophical concerns of Seneca with the more personal and political reporting of Cicero. In keeping with his understanding of his vocation as a man of letters—to gather knowledge and to dispense wisdom—Petrarch closely follows contemporary events. He writes to emperors, kings, princes, popes, and cardinals, offering counsel and sometimes criticism. The scholarly Petrarch even purports to give military advice on occasion. And he is a tireless proponent of ending the Babylonian Captivity and returning the papacy to Rome, as reflected in a lengthy letter to Pope Urban V.

The letters are also a running commentary on the intellectual currents of the day, currents often driven by Petrarch himself. He wrote letters to and about philosophers and poets. Some of his most important were written to his younger contemporary Boccaccio, whom he called "my most loving brother."[66] Petrarch, in a remarkable series of letters gathered at the end of the *Familiares*, wrote directly to dead poets, historians, and philosophers of ancient Greece and Rome, including Homer, Cicero, Livy, Virgil, Horace, and Seneca, among others. He treats them—as they indeed were for him—as intimate acquaintances and daily companions.

The letters are rightly treasured as historical documents, giving us a portrait of the troubled fourteenth century, a time of plague, war, random violence, religious turmoil, and growing intellectual ferment. But they are even more valuable as the self-portrait of a single, remarkable man at the center of his age—a man with a gift for friendship, a powerful intellect devoted to the life of the mind, curious about new places and people, in love with nature and solitude yet fully engaged with his time, and seeking, always, distractions from his hopeless passion for Laura. Even more than the *Secretum*, the letters are Petrarch's *Confessions*.

From the letters, we know Petrarch as intimately as we will come to know Montaigne, warts and all. Petrarch himself disclaims such knowledge: "I certainly do not know what kind of man I am," he explains, "because we all deceive ourselves in judging ourselves."[67] He notes that, in reading them over, he discovered that "the letters were so different that . . . I seemed to be in constant contradiction," and thus "to be contradictory was my only expedient."[68] In that respect, the letters are very much in keeping with the widely variable moods of the *Canzoniere*. They are additional scattered fragments from the mind of this infinitely complex man. Yet, as Morris Bishop writes, taken as a whole "they reveal to us a total man, a great poet and scholar, wise, absurd, penetrating, vain, uncomprehending, cruel, introspective, self-conscious, enlightened, ancient, modern—one may add a whole thesaurus of adjectives."[69]

Petrarch both discovered and created himself in his letters. He sought, through writing, to learn how to live. "I am not teaching you, dear friend, but myself," he wrote to one correspondent, "and in addressing you, I admonish myself and learn by listening to myself."[70] Petrarch believed that the study of history, particularly Roman history, rather than philosophy or even religion, was the foundation of a moral education. Like Plutarch, he wrote numerous biographies of Roman heroes, focused on greatness of character and the virtues of personal discipline, self-sacrifice, courage, love of liberty and country. His *Africa* is a poetic tribute to Scipio Africanus, the hero of the final Punic War. Reading about such figures, he claimed, supplements and shapes our experience: "There is nothing that moves me as much as the examples of outstanding men. They help one to rise on high and to test the mind to see whether it possesses anything solid, anything noble, anything unbending and firm against fortune, or whether it lies to itself about itself."[71] The study of such examples is critical to the formation of our human identity.

In his letters, however, Petrarch seeks to turn himself into an exemplar of a very different kind, not a warrior or political leader but a man of letters, steeped in the learning and wisdom of his day and eager to extend the bounds of both. In the process, he creates a new humanistic ideal, the cultivation of the self through reading, thinking, and writing. He considers that cultivation of the self to be our highest duty as human beings, superior to the demands of country and even religion.

The ideal life for Petrarch is a quiet literary engagement far from the madding crowd struggling for wealth and advancement. It is a life focused on developing human reason, human thought, and human language. We can neglect neither care of the mind nor the proper use of language. Each depends upon the other.[72] Petrarch considered reading and writing to be spiritual exercises, focused on the ordering of the self and its desires.[73] Reading and writing are the means of finding, forming, and realizing one's ideal self. In such a quest, he notes, "a scholar's spirit knows no restraint."[74]

Petrarch believes that quest is aided by solitude and communion with nature, an idea that would have a huge impact on the poets and writers of the romantic period. "I spend a large part of my time in the country, and even now, as ever, I am desirous of solitude and quiet; I read, I write, I think; this is my life, this my joy, which has been with me since youth."[75] This is not, however, the ascetic isolation of the desert fathers; it is the solitude of the scholar in his remote hut, walking among trees and rivers, who sits down to a simple dinner and rich conversation with a friend or two. In his *De vita solitaria* (On the Solitary Life), Petrarch outlines the duties of the man of letters:

> To devote oneself to reading and writing, finding alternately labor and solace in each, to read what the first men wrote and write what the last men may read, and since we can't thank our elders for their gift of learning, to show our gratitude by passing them on to posterity, to keep fresh their names, whether unknown to the masses or fallen into oblivion, to dig them out of time's ruins, to transmit them clothed in honor to our children's children, to guard them in our hearts and keep them sweet on our lips; and in short by loving, remembering, celebrating them in every possible way to render them the gratitude which, though not adequate to their merits, is their due.[76]

In perhaps his most famous letter, Petrarch writes of his ascent of Mont Ventoux, which he climbed one day with his brother, "led solely by a desire to view the great height of it."[77] He could see the mountain from his hut in Vaucluse and had long entertained the prospect of climbing it. He is impelled to do so one day after rereading in Livy a description of King Philip of Macedonia climbing Mount Hemo in hopes of seeing from the top both the Adriatic and the Black Seas. Life is imitating, or at least inspired by, literature.

Laura was a real woman whom he loved, but in Petrarch's poems she is also the embodiment of poetry. Mont Ventoux is a real mountain that he climbed—indeed, an ascent of Mont Ventoux is today a regular stage on the Tour de France—but in Petrarch's letter it is also the embodiment of his intellectual and spiritual quest. His climb has deliberate echoes of the opening of Dante's *Commedia*, when Dante the Pilgrim is lost in a dark wood and cannot summon the strength to take the upward path to where the light of heaven shines.

Mont Ventoux is just under 6,300 feet, but "it is a steep mountain with rocky and almost inaccessible cliffs."[78] The hikers' early enthusiasm gives way to weariness as they make their way slowly upward. Perseverance is all, in hiking as well as in life. But whereas his brother heads straight up over sharp ridges, Petrarch continually searches out a more gentle access, which just as continually eludes him. He wanders far afield, often descending and lengthening his journey without easing his passage. In the end, he must climb straight up to join his brother. This happens several times, and the exhausted Petrarch, "proceeding from the physical to the metaphysical,"[79] sits down and draws the obvious moral lesson: his experience in climbing this mountain is precisely his experience is searching after virtue. There is a narrow road to the top, "and one must proceed from virtue to virtue with very deliberate steps."[80] Yet he has been constantly beguiled by what appears to be the "less impeded road of earthly and base pleasures," which takes him back into the valleys and away from the summit.[81]

Summoning all his reserves, Petrarch reaches the top with his brother. In a mood familiar to all future climbers, he writes, "Moved by a certain unaccustomed quality of the air and by the unrestricted spectacle, I stood there as in a trance."[82] He looks at the Alps, "frozen and snow-covered, through which that wild enemy of the Roman people [Hannibal and his Carthaginians and his elephants] once crossed," and beyond them toward the sky of Italy, "which was visible to my mind rather than to my eyes."[83] He even thinks back to Athos and Olympus. In effect, Petrarch surveys from his vantage point the whole of Western history and culture, from the Greeks onward. His awe in the face of the high mountains merges with his awe of the human spirit, in all its nobility.

There is a strong religious component to Petrarch's musings, but somehow that is not what one retains from the letter. The critical moment in the *Confessions* occurs when Augustine, choosing a passage from scripture at random, abandons his worldly concerns and turns to God. Petrarch, at the top of Mont Ventoux, opens at random the small volume of the *Confessions* he carries with him everywhere. In it, he finds an apt reminder from Augustine that too many go to admire the summits of mountains, the vast expanses of the seas, and the revolutions of the stars but overlook themselves. Petrarch reproaches himself for admiring worldly things, but his thoughts turn immediately not to God but to the pagan philosophers, who taught him to "consider nothing wonderful except the human mind compared to whose greatness nothing is great."[84] The distant humanism of antiquity retains its hold upon him.

Mont Ventoux is Petrarch's mountain of purgatory, from the top of which he surveys an earthly paradise. But, unlike Dante, who ascends from there to the celestial sphere, Petrarch makes his long way back down the mountain. And, like most climbers, Petrarch has stayed too long on the summit, and he and his brother are overtaken by darkness on the descent.

Petrarch is overtaken by darkness many times in his letters as well. He constantly stresses the uncertainty of fortune, the empty futility of the struggle for wealth and power, and the fleeting nature of life: "O labors and cares of men, O brief and lost time, O vanity and pride over nothing!"[85] He confronts the deaths of Laura, his closest friends Socrates and Laelius, and various members of the Colonna family, among many others. Throughout, he strives to follow the advice he sometimes too easily dispensed to others in his youth: to "be in possession of one's self" and to not give way to despair.[86] That resolve is sorely tested on the death of his son, Giovanni, at the age of twenty-three. "I cherish him in my thoughts," he writes, "hold him in my heart, embrace him in my memory, and, alas, seek him in vain with my eyes."[87] Even more devastating is the death of his beloved grandson, Francesco.[88] "I live only for this," he laments, "to hear daily of the deaths of friends and dear ones."[89]

And yet a kind of peace and wholeness and renewed sense of purpose is to be found in the letters of his old age. Petrarch remained a devout

Christian throughout his life, but he separated out the questions "What may we hope?" and "What ought we to do?" Like Marcus Aurelius, who concluded that it ultimately does not matter whether there is a divine providence or just the chance interaction of atoms and the void, Petrarch believes that our task here on earth is the same under either scenario. He dismisses scholastic disputes as a childish waste of time: "I do not love sects," he writes, "but the truth."[90] And he found that truth in "the wealth of the liberally educated mind," a mind that "possesse[s] characteristics that result from such studies—mainly, kindness, faith, generosity, and steadfastness."[91] Petrarch was passionate in his defense of literature and the growth of knowledge. "We are all exiles and foreigners, with no permanent city here," he wrote,[92] but books "speak with us, advise us and join us together with a certain living and penetrating intimacy."[93] In his correspondence, he sought to foster a community of such humanists.

Petrarch's aging friend and fellow writer Boccaccio was accosted by a mad monk who prophesized that Boccaccio would suffer the torments of hell if he did not repent of his literary writings and devote himself solely to religion. Petrarch sent an encouraging letter to the deeply affected Boccaccio, condemning the attack: "It is an ancient custom to draw the veil of religion and sanctimony over lies and invented stories in general so that belief in divinity covers human trickery."[94] Literature, Petrarch insists, is critical to our spiritual and emotional development. "Literature does not impede, but rather helps a man of good character who masters it; it advances the journey of life, it does not delay it."[95] No one is harmed by "the delightful, precious treasures of literature gained through study,"[96] and a life devoted to such study does not preclude but may even promote the highest saintliness. Elsewhere, in an anthropomorphic account of the development of religion, Petrarch writes that "poetry is not in the least contrary to theology." Rather, theology itself arose out of poetry, and the first theologians were simply poets trying to make sense of their lives and the world.[97]

For Petrarch, the act of writing and creating is thus critical to the development of human consciousness. To be sure, writing is inevitably tainted with the thirst for glory. But it is also a noble activity and our most important tool for self-examination, self-criticism, and the search for virtue. The self is a text in need of constant revision and emendation.[98] Writing honestly is therefore a moral act, a way of caring for the soul and learning and conveying the art of living: "For me writing and living are the same thing and I hope will be so to the very end."[99] That labor will only end with his life, for "life without energy is not life but a sluggish, useless lapse of time."[100]

In an early letter, Petrarch compares his own restless travels through the cities of Europe to the wanderings of Ulysses.[101] He reinforces the analogy by adopting for his *Familiares* the twenty-four-book structure of the *Odyssey*. Yet surely he had most firmly in mind Dante's Ulysses, who refuses to temper his search for truth and virtue. In Dante's retelling,[102] the aging Ulysses, with a small group of his most loyal comrades, sets sail in a small boat over the Mediterranean Sea to the Gates of Hercules (i.e., the Straits of Gibraltar), the limit of the known world. They sail on together, to follow valor's lure and wisdom's quest, into the Southern Hemisphere until they come within sight of the mountain of purgatory. There, a whirlwind turns their tiny vessel around three times before sending it prow first down into the darkness of the sea.

Petrarch, like Ulysses, did not recognize divine constraints on human striving. The quest for knowledge cannot remain within limits imposed by faith: "Never will the road to the investigation of new ideas be blocked to keen minds."[103] Petrarch does not promise us the transcendence of an Augustine or a Dante. He offers instead a never-ending, inherently flawed but nonetheless noble undertaking, to understand our classical, pagan past and to build with it "a world made new."[104]

Chapter 2
ERASMUS: THE MAN IN THE MIDDLE

Erasmus posuit ova, Lutherus eduxit pullos.[1]

Less than a century separated the death of Petrarch in 1374 from the birth of Erasmus, probably in 1466. The two men had much in common. Each was recognized as the most important intellectual figure of his day. Each was a Latinist, humanist, and scholar. Each corresponded on terms of equality with emperors, popes, kings, and princes (both secular and ecclesiastical), as well as with writers throughout Europe. Each traveled widely and restlessly and enjoyed a wide circle of friends and acolytes. And each man was deeply religious, accepting the central tenets of the Catholic religion while dismissing the arid dialectics of medieval scholasticism as at best a distraction from, and at worst an obfuscation of, those core beliefs.

But the two men were also totally different from one another, and much had changed in Europe and in the church between the age of Petrarch and that of Erasmus. Petrarch was passionate in his vernacular poetry, tortured in his religious confessions, and giddy with excitement at the rediscovery of the classics. While always a practicing Christian, Petrarch's thinking had a stronger tinge of ancient, pagan Rome. Petrarch assumed rather than reasoned that his humanism and his religion were compatible; regardless, as we have seen, the former was in the end more important to him. Petrarch seemed to think, or wished to think, that all would be well with the church if the pope simply returned from Avignon to his rightful place in Rome.

Erasmus had no such comfortable illusion. The pope was back in Rome, but all was decidedly not well with the church. It had grown ever more powerful, ever more magnificent, and ever more sordid in the intervening years. The popes were secular and military leaders, fighting to expand their wealth and their influence. The church itself had become a vast pyramid scheme and patronage network, a sort of Renaissance Amway. The mendicant friars of the Dominican and Franciscan Orders had long since abandoned their vows of poverty in favor of enormous land holdings and rich donations. Ecclesiastical posts were openly bought and sold. Even down to the level of the parish priest, everything had its price: from baptism through confirmation, marriage, burial, and beyond, with paid masses for the repose of souls. Tithes were collected from the poor and then passed up the line with the ruthless efficiency of ancient Roman tax collectors, each intervening church official extracting his share. Purgatory—where souls worked off their sins before being welcomed into heaven—had no basis in scripture, but the desire to shorten one's stay there provided a prime opportunity for the sale of indulgences to the living and for the dead. Make a gift to the church and save your loved ones—and yourself—a long, painful sojourn in the waiting room of heaven.

Vast wealth flowed to Rome and to bishoprics throughout Europe. Splendid cathedrals were built, culminating in Saint Peter's Basilica, designed by the noted architect Donato Bramante, with later assistance from Michelangelo. It took more than a century to complete. The adjacent Vatican Museums were begun by Pope Julius II, who commissioned Michelangelo to paint the ceiling of the Sistine Chapel. Raphael, Titian, Botticelli, and many others were sustained at one time or another by papal patronage. The art supported and purchased by the church was sublime. But the morals of the churchmen were too often appalling.

As many as half the clergy lived openly with women. Illegitimate children of priests—of whom Erasmus was one—were commonplace. Popes regularly made bishops and cardinals of their "nephews" (that is, their bastard sons). It is hard to pinpoint the nadir of the church's corruption, but certainly the reign of the Borgia pope, Alexander VI, from

1492 to 1503, is a strong candidate. He poisoned rivals, kept a string of mistresses, and even fathered a child with his own daughter, Lucrezia. The popes were more *condottieri* (professional soldiers) than bringers of Christ's peace. They were no better, and in many instances worse, than the Italian strongmen with whom they formed and broke alliances: Ludovico Visconti and Francesco Sforza in Milan; the doge Francesco Foscari in Venice; the Medicis in Florence; Federico da Montefeltro in Urbino. Appalling violence and war spread through all of Italy, even as the ideals of the Italian Renaissance crossed the Alps into northern Europe.

This is the world into which Desiderius Erasmus was born. He had a northern, not a southern, temperament and was much more measured and phlegmatic than the Italian-born Petrarch. There was no Laura in his life, but he had a gift for friendship and effortlessly inspired loyalty in others. He seemed to suffer no intellectual or spiritual crises, no dark nights of the soul. He wore his faith comfortably even when the great crisis of his age arose. He viewed Christianity not so much as a set of doctrines but as a way of life, a life of humility, tolerance, and kindness. Except when his scholarly ire was up, which was often, or in his later years, when he succumbed with some justification to persecution paranoia, he did try to live by those principles.

Erasmus lived everywhere and nowhere. Born in Holland, he resided at various times in France and England, as well as Italy, Belgium, Switzerland, Germany, and elsewhere. He was a citizen of Europe, but the only true home Erasmus had was the Latin language. Latin was still the common bond of educated Europeans, though it would soon give way before the vital energy of the vernacular tongues. Erasmus was the last great thinker who wrote always and only in the Latin language, fusing the classical and medieval traditions in a prose that was lively, flexible, and elegant. He was also the first to benefit so notably from Johannes Gutenberg's printing press, circa 1440, an innovation quickly copied in cities throughout Europe. Erasmus's works became international best sellers among the cadre of scholars, theologians, and humanists dedicated to expanding classical learning and rescuing Christianity from the corruption and abuses of the church.

Erasmus's fundamental insight was that these two goals—the expansion of classical learning and the purification of Catholicism—were conjoined and that the former was the means to the latter. His Renaissance became the church's Reformation. As the Latin quotation that begins this chapter explains, "Erasmus laid the eggs, Luther hatched them."

Erasmus, like Petrarch, was devoted to *bonae litterae*—the literature and culture of classical antiquity. His favorites were the moral writings of Cicero and Plutarch, the poetry of Virgil and Horace, and the dialogues of Plato, which he cherished both for their portrait of "Saint Socrates"[2] and for their distinction between the world of transient physical phenomena and the unchanging, intelligible realm of the spirit. Erasmus brought the entire world of ancient thought vividly alive for his contemporaries through his *Adages*, an extensive collection of excerpts and proverbs from Greek and Roman authors, along with his own commentary.

Erasmus was also strongly influenced by the movement known as the *devotio moderna*, a simplified religious practice focused on piety, humility, and charity. He dismissed the medieval scholasticism of Aquinas, Duns Scotus, and others as useless logic chopping. He had little patience even for doctrinal tenets many thought essential to the faith, such as the Trinity, the Immaculate Conception, and purgatory. Erasmus thought that all Christians should establish a direct relationship with God through constant exposure to the scriptures and the writings of the church fathers. Everything else—the ceremonies and trappings of the church, the veneration of saints' relics, the purchase of indulgences, pilgrimages, fasting and abstinence, and even the sacraments—was too often a substitute for that personal relationship with God. The true church for Erasmus was not a hierarchical institution of great wealth and power but a community of men, women, and children dedicated to a closer relationship with God and to the imitation of Christ.

Erasmus's love of *bonae litterae* reinforced the *devotio moderna* in three respects. First, he used ancient writings to develop more fully the idea of man articulated in the Gospels and in the writings of Saint Paul and the church fathers. Erasmus believed that human nature had not changed in its fundamentals and that the philosophical and moral writings of the Greeks and Romans had much to tell us about how to live as Christians. Second, he took the principles of classical philology learned in dealing with ancient texts and applied them to the New Testament and the writings of the church fathers. Creating proper editions by collating and correcting extant manuscripts and engaging in close textual analyses were tools appropriate to sacred as well as profane writings. *Ad fontes* (to the sources) became a rallying cry for a reconnection with the original faith. Third, and most important for our purposes, he combined classical models and reforming zeal in his two satirical masterworks, the *Praise of Folly* and the *Colloquies*.

Erasmus's ideals of Christian humanism swept through Europe—not just among the intelligentsia but also among secular and religious leaders. His widely read works might have led peacefully to significant internal reforms in the church. But that became impossible after Martin Luther nailed his "Ninety-Five Theses" to the door of the Castle Church in Wittenberg on October 31, 1517. Erasmus was an incremental reformer. Luther was an intransigent revolutionary, and the revolution known to us as the Reformation became all but inevitable when the church chose to condemn Luther, to burn his books, and to brand him a heretic. Political resentments against Rome in northern Europe, combined with genuine grievances with the church, fueled the break. The backlash known as the Counter-Reformation, and its by-product, the Dominican inquisition, seemed to leave no room for a middle ground. Yet Erasmus, soon despised and ridiculed by both sides, sought to occupy it. "The center cannot hold," Yeats would later write,[3] yet Erasmus held to it with a courage and wry humor for which he is rarely given the credit he deserves.

EARLY LIFE

Erasmus was born in South Holland, the Netherlands, probably in 1466, though the exact year is unknown. He had a brother, Peter, who was three years older. Both boys were illegitimate. Their father, Gerard, was a Catholic priest. Little is known of their mother except that she died of the plague around 1483. Gerard died of the same cause the following year, and the two boys were left in the care of three guardians.

Until their father's death, the brothers had received excellent educations in Latin in the ancient town of Deventer. That changed when the guardians took over. They refused to send the boys to university but instead pushed them to enter monasteries. Erasmus later alleged that they did so to disguise their mishandling of the small estate the boys had received from their father. Peter entered an Augustinian monastery near Delft. Erasmus resisted for a time but eventually, weakened by his own bout with the plague, acquiesced. Sometime between 1486 and 1488, when Erasmus was between twenty and twenty-two years old, he entered a different Augustinian monastery, this one at Steyn. Erasmus later claimed that he was only sixteen, perhaps to accentuate his claim that he became a monk due to pressure from his guardians rather than as a considered choice.

Erasmus was ordained a priest in 1492. But he detested monastic life. He found the early hours, the ascetic conditions, and the scanty, barely edible food detrimental to his health. More important, he thought that his fellow monks had lost the connection between their faith and their observances and rituals so that the latter had become spiritually empty and mind-numbing. Erasmus seized what time he could to study the classics and began a correspondence with other like-minded monks. Gradually, he made a name for himself as a Latinist, and in that role he found his freedom.

Erasmus received a temporary dispensation to leave the monastery in 1493 to serve as a secretary to the bishop of Cambrai, who wanted to give a humanist polish to his correspondence. The bishop was planning a trip to Rome and enlisted Erasmus as part of his entourage. In the end, the bishop never left for Rome, but Erasmus did not return to Steyn. Instead, with the bishop's permission and a small, inadequate stipend, he went to study at the University of Paris. Long a bastion of rigid scholastic philosophy based on Aristotle, Paris gradually was warming to Renaissance humanism. Erasmus found a sympathetic Italian scholar with whom to study and steeped himself in Cicero, Plutarch, Virgil, and Horace. Free of the restraints of monastic life, moreover, his literary interests turned increasingly toward religious reform.

Erasmus supported himself in Paris by tutoring the sons of wealthy aristocrats. One of these, William Blount, the fourth Baron Mountjoy, invited Erasmus to accompany him to England in 1499. There Erasmus became lifelong friends with John Colet, a humanist theologian and dean of Saint Paul's Cathedral, and with Thomas More. Erasmus even met the future King Henry VIII, then only eight years old, who would later have More executed for refusing to accept Henry as the head of a separate Church of England.

Erasmus made three trips to England. He even taught at Cambridge for a time and considered staying on as a professor. But he found the climate damp, the food poor, and the wine unpalatable. His health, always delicate, suffered. Yet he developed many of his more important ideas in conversations and correspondence with Colet, More, and their friends and colleagues. By the time he left England the first time, Erasmus had found his life's mission: to unite learning and culture with piety and theology, to reconcile humanism and religious reform.[4]

When he was not in England, Erasmus lived mostly in Paris, Louvain (then part of the separate duchy of Brabant), Basel, and the imperial German city of Freiburg im Breisgau. He also traveled to Italy and other parts of Germany. He paid only brief and sporadic visits to his native Holland. After 1501, he never returned there, and for good reason. His "temporary dispensation" from monastic life had long since lapsed, and his increasing fame made him an ornament his former monastery was eager to reclaim. It was not until 1514, however, that he was officially summoned back to Steyn. He flatly refused to go, claiming that his health would not stand it and that he could better serve the church as an independent theologian and scholar. In 1517, Erasmus secured from Leo X a papal release from his vows and permission to live outside the monastery. By that time, Erasmus was the best known and most respected scholar in Europe, and publishers eagerly sought and often—in the absence of copyright protection—purloined his work. It is estimated that at one point as many as 20 percent of the published books in circulation were authored by Erasmus. Latin was still the common language among the educated, and Erasmus's books reached the entire Western world, from England to Italy and from Spain to Germany. He was at the peak of his power and influence.

THE *PRAISE OF FOLLY*

Erasmus conceived the idea for the *Praise of Folly* while traveling to England for the coronation of Henry VIII. He wrote the book quickly while staying with Thomas More, to whom it is dedicated. The dedication is itself a bit of folly; Erasmus notes that the project was prompted by "your family name of More, which is just as close to Moria, the Greek word for folly, as you are remote from the thing itself."[5] In fact, however, the point of the satire is that none of us is remote from folly, which is an essential and ineradicable aspect of human life, critical to human intercourse and human relationships. The acceptance and even embrace of folly, or at least the right sort of folly, is part of wisdom itself, and Erasmus attributes such acceptance to More, calling him *omnium horarum hominem agere*, a phrase from his *Adages* that means, literally, a man who is ready to act at all hours. It is rendered in the Norton Critical Edition as one who "can get along with all sorts of people at any time of day."[6] The phrase was felicitously translated in 1520 as "a man for all seasons,"[7] and that became the title of a famous (and very serious) contemporary play and movie about More's life and martyrdom. Yet, as used by the Roman historian Suetonius, from whom Erasmus lifted the phrase, it implies one who can drink all night and all day, a hail-fellow-well-met type.[8] Not exactly what Robert Bolt, the playwright, had in mind, but another ironic gift from folly that Erasmus would have appreciated.

The work takes the form of a lecture or after-dinner speech by Folly herself. She begins by noting that no one ever praises her, since everyone pretends, falsely, to dispense with folly. So she proposes to praise herself, which she acknowledges is itself the height of folly. Yet, by a curious inversion, Folly praising folly ends up looking quite a bit like wisdom, but a joyful, tolerant wisdom that finds not bitterness but amusement in our many human foibles.

Folly claims to be the daughter of Plutus (god of wealth), who controls all institutions, both sacred and profane, and drives wars, lawsuits, marriages, alliances, and even the arts. Plutus is the key to human motivation, and not even Pallas Athena (goddess of wisdom) will be able to help a man despised by Plutus. But it is she, Folly herself, who governs men's actions. Her immediate family, "with whose faithful help I maintain dominion over all things, and rule even emperors themselves," includes Self-Love, Flattery, Pleasure, Laziness, Imbecility, Self-Deception, Drunkenness, and Lust.[9]

Folly insists that folly is both ubiquitous and ineradicable in human life. Indeed, our very existence depends on her because she controls that part of the body—"so stupid and even ridiculous that it can't be named without raising a snicker"—necessary to procreation.[10] Even a Stoic sage, she notes, is willing to shave off his beard—"his special badge of wisdom (though in fact he shares it with a billygoat)"—drop his lofty expression, and talk sweet nonsense if he wants to father a child.[11] As originally printed, the text here and throughout was accompanied by woodcuts prepared by the German-Swiss artist Hans Holbein the Younger (ca. 1497–1543). Holbein's sketch of the amorous Stoic, eagerly pressing his suit on a young woman, perfectly captures Folly's point. What a Stoic might say, in his somber preaching, and what he will do, when in the grip of folly, are two very different things. Folly prefers the latter to the former.

Everything joyful and pleasant, she claims, owes its existence to folly. Folly is responsible for the ignorant, uncontrolled charms of infancy and youth and the "second childhood" that relieves the miseries of old age. If men spent their time exclusively in the company of Folly, they would enjoy eternal youth rather than prematurely sapping their animal spirits in the earnest and painful pursuit of wisdom. The pleasures of banquets—drinking games, comic songs, and charades—"those were not invented by the seven sages of Greece, you can be sure."[12] The more foolish, the more fun. Amusements of this sort dispel boredom and engender fellow feeling and friendship, which even the gravest philosophers praise and number among life's greatest goods.

Indeed, friendship would not be possible without turning a blind eye to faults and flaws, and even convincing oneself that they are virtues and attractions. Since no one is born without faults, this sort of self-deception, a species of folly, is absolutely necessary to bind people together in mutual pleasure. Such self-deception is even more vital to marriage, for "how many divorces or catastrophes worse than divorce would take place if the domestic adjustments of men and women weren't sustained and eased by flattery, jokes, yielding dispositions, mutual misunderstandings, dissimu-lations—all of them assistants to me."[13] Even if cuckolded, a husband is happier in his ignorance than he would be if, inflamed by jealousy, he turned comedy into tragedy.[14]

Folly also helps us to shut our eyes to our own vices and faults. Without self-love we could accomplish nothing. We could not give a speech, make music, act in a play, or act in the play of life. Without self-flattery—without the sense that we are playing our part well—we could not pull off any of these things. We have to esteem ourselves before others will esteem us, and what is self-esteem but a species of folly? Indeed, self-esteem often is inversely proportional to actual talent and is therefore the greatest of all gifts![15] Folly allows us to overcome diffidence, shame, and fearfulness. No project can be undertaken, no discovery made, and no battles won without self-esteem. By contrast, wisdom and self-knowledge hinder performance; states were never more poorly managed than when ruled by "some philosophaster or bookworm."[16]

The desire for praise is properly decried as foolish, but that particular folly gives rise to cities and empires, to legal and religious systems, and to all progress in the arts and sciences. Innovators "put long hours and agonized efforts into the pursuit of fame."[17] Nothing could be more inane, she admits, and yet "you can enjoy, thanks to their folly, all the good things they produce, and you don't even have to be as crazy as they are—which is the best thing of all."[18]

What is hope in the face of life's endless calamities, she asks, but more folly? Yet without hope and forgetfulness and a sprinkling of pleasure, life would be unendurable. Without the pleasure born of folly, life would be thoroughly gloomy, drab, and sullen. Philosophers preach the primacy of reason. "It's utter misery, they say, to be in the clutches of folly, to be bewildered, to blunder, never to know anything for sure. On the contrary, I say, that's what it is to be a man."[19] Reason, Folly insists, has no motivational force of its own, a contention the British empiricist David Hume would make the touchstone of his moral theory. Emotions are critical to the practice of every virtue and the performance of every good deed.[20] The purely rational man that is the Stoic ideal "is a marble statue of a man, insensitive and without a trace of human feeling."[21] We would prefer the company of anyone else over such a philosopher.[22] The truly prudent man "reflects that since he is mortal himself, he shouldn't want to be wiser than befits a mortal, but should cast his lot in with the rest of the human race and blunder along in good company."[23] Folly quotes the Roman playwright Terence to seal her argument: "*homo sum: humani nil a me alienum puto*" (I am a man: nothing human is alien to me).[24]

Folly's point is indeed profound. Folly, broadly understood, is critical to human life. It is not only unavoidable; in its more benign forms—in which "some genial aberration of the mind frees it from anxiety and worry while at the same time imbuing it with the many fragrances of pleasure"[25]— it should be embraced. We are men, not gods, and even the gods have their follies. Folly is necessary to human intercourse and fellow feeling. It is necessary to love, to friendship, and to all accomplishments. We should not therefore judge it harshly. After all, even the Stoics acknowledge that happiness depends not on things themselves but on our perception of things. There is no real difference between reality and delusion except that the latter can make one blissful at very little cost. It demands only a bit of self-persuasion.[26] Folly is an essential ingredient of true wisdom.

The first half of the *Praise of Folly* is a tour de force, a delightful inversion that has the reader looking at humanity in a new, warmer, and more amusing light. The second half is a more traditional satire. Folly walks through the various professions, occupations, and classes and points out the follies appropriate to each. She begins, naturally enough, with the foibles of orators, who pretend that carefully prepared speeches are spontaneous and off-the-cuff and who sprinkle their talks with Greek and Latin phrases as signs of their erudition (something Folly herself does frequently). She follows with incompetent doctors, shyster lawyers, grasping businessmen, pedantic teachers of grammar, would-be poets, rhetoricians, and "halfwits who expect to achieve immortal fame by writing books."[27]

She adds to her list scholars, natural philosophers, and theologians with their innumerable abstract quibbles, who "boast such mighty erudition and write such tortured prose"[28] and who threaten to have "up for a 'heretic'" anyone who does not accept their unfathomable, logic-chopping demonstrations.[29] Special scorn is reserved for monks, who "insist so vehemently on their own ceremonies and petty traditions that they think a single heaven will hardly be adequate reward for such outstanding merit."[30] But the church hierarchy comes in for its fair share of disdain, including popes, who defend their position as vicars of Christ with sword, poison, and violence of every sort, and bishops, who believe that a display of pomp and circumstance is the full extent of their required duty. After all, "teaching the people is hard work, prayer is boring, . . . poverty is degrading, and meekness is disgraceful, quite unworthy of one who barely admits even the greatest kings to kiss his feet."[31] Nor do kings and princes escape Folly's ridicule. They can find no one to speak truth to them and must therefore accept flatterers as false friends. But fools can speak truth to power, even unwelcome truth, and are greeted with laughter and presents, as if truth itself were a species of folly.

Folly claims that she is the only divinity that embraces all men as equals. We are a true democracy of fools. "I hardly know whether anyone can be found in the entire human race," she notes, "who is wise twenty-four hours a day, and who is not subject to madness in one form or another,"[32] be it the delusion that his wife is chaste, or a mania for hunting wild beasts, or a passion for building or alchemy or gambling or tales about miracles and goblins. Christians have a penchant for indulgences, pilgrimages, magic rituals, or incantations in the form of prayers, and rubbing the relics of saints: "The whole life of Christians everywhere is infected with idiocies of this sort."[33] "If you want evidence of this," Folly explains, "consider first that children, old folk, women, and simpletons are, of all people, most attracted to the services of our holy religion and are always found in closest proximity to the altar."[34] And those who have visions of their future life with God are in a state very similar to madness. Yet one person's madness is another person's cherished belief. Anticipating Don Quixote, Folly notes that the madman who takes pleasure in his delusion will not thank you for curing him of it.[35]

If the *Praise of Folly* were simply straightforward satire, however effective, the book would leave a sour taste. Satire purports to speak from an elevated position, both morally and intellectually. Satire is disdainful, and the reader is invited to join in that disdain. It is a guilty pleasure at best. But Folly freely includes herself in the laughter engendered by her self-praise. "We fools" is the subject of the book, not "you fools."[36] Folly flatters and thereby enlists her audience in challenging accepted notions, in recognizing the contradictions and absurdities of everyday existence.[37]

"Good wits," she notes, "have always been allowed the liberty to exercise their high spirits on the common life of men, and without rebuke, as long as their sport doesn't become savagery."[38] Indeed, "it's a kind of compliment to be attacked by Folly."[39]

Mikhail Bakhtin, a twentieth-century Russian Marxist philosopher and literary critic, wrote an important book, *Rabelais and His World*, which we will discuss in chapter 6. In it, Bakhtin describes the carnival interludes so important to medieval and Renaissance society, in which even the most elevated and sacred things—in fact, especially the most elevated and sacred things—are openly mocked. In this carnival atmosphere, the laughter is universal and all-embracing. "The people do not exclude themselves from the wholeness of the world," Bakhtin writes. Their satire is not delivered from a perspective of superiority and contempt; rather, it "expresses the point of view of the whole world; he who is laughing also belongs to it."[40]

Bakhtin rightly calls the *Praise of Folly* "one of the greatest creations of carnival laughter in world literature."[41] Occasionally the mask falls, and we see the venom reserved by Erasmus for theologians, monks, and high church officials, who he thinks have betrayed their calling. But, mostly, the illusion is maintained, and Erasmus (in his roles as ecclesiastic, scholar, grammarian, and writer of books) includes himself in the mockery. We recognize in this book the folly of ourselves and all of mankind. The laughter is cathartic. It embraces rather than excludes. Folly, we are told, is the only remedy for life's misery and bitterness. Folly infuses all that is good in human life: kindness, conviviality, laughter, love, innocent pleasure, and charity. No accomplishment would be possible without the energy, ambition, and hope born of folly.

The great Dutch scholar Johan Huizinga finds Erasmus's vision in the *Praise of Folly* "bolder and more chilling than Machiavelli, more detached than Montaigne."[42] We will discuss those authors in chapters 3 and 7, respectively. But a defense of Erasmus is warranted here. His vision may be bold, but it is hardly chilling, and it is far from detached. The warmth of his humor embraces our common humanity. Most important, Erasmus tried to retain that embrace even in the face of the religious disputes that would tear apart the church and western Europe. In doing so, he was perhaps himself a fool. But he was a fool for Christ's sake.[43]

THE SPIRIT OF CHRISTIANITY

In 1501, Erasmus wrote the *Enchiridion militis Christiani*, a manual or handbook for the Christian soldier. The *Enchiridion* did not attract much attention when it was first published. But a revised edition in 1513 was quickly translated into eleven languages.[44] The book is Erasmus's manifesto for religious reform. It contains the eggs that Luther hatched. Such, however, was Erasmus's reputation and temperament that his book found sympathetic readers throughout Europe, in courts, universities, and even the highest reaches of the church. The *Enchiridion* had its detractors, to be sure, particularly among the monasteries. But it did not occasion the violent reaction and counterreaction that would soon follow the writings of Martin Luther. Erasmus's book was widely welcomed as an attempt to purify and to clarify the Christian religion and to reconnect the church with its scriptural origins.

The ostensible impetus for writing the *Enchiridion* was a request by the wife of a soldier and friend of Erasmus to provide him with instruction in Christian belief and behavior. The fact that he is a soldier holds double significance. First, the violence of such a life is far removed from the peace of Christ, just as the church itself, in its secular struggles for power and wealth, has departed from Christ's original message. Second, Erasmus stresses that "mortal life is nothing but a kind of perpetual warfare" between the flesh and the spirit.[45] We all must therefore become soldiers for Christ in an allegorical sense, strengthening the spirit to conquer the temptations of the flesh and cultivating an indifference to worldly goods and worldly glory.

Erasmus has two related objectives in the *Enchiridion*: to explain the proper theory of Christianity and to outline its proper practice. In both cases, his rallying cry is *ad fontes* (to the sources). Erasmus wants to sweep aside the overlay of scholasticism and clericalism that has been interposed between us and the scriptures. The Word of God is simple, straightforward, and accessible to all—men, women, and children, educated and uneducated, noble and peasant, wealthy and poor. The Christian faith is neither exotic nor esoteric. We must focus on its most basic tenets, which unite us as Christians, rather than on abstract, artificial, and unresolvable doctrinal disputes that only divide us from one another.

Christ's teaching follows human nature and was therefore accessible, in large part, even to pagans. It accords with the best writings of antiquity, and a study of *bonae litterae* is therefore an important complement to the study of explicitly Christian works. "Literature shapes and invigorates the youthful character and prepares one marvelously well for understanding Holy Scripture."[46] Ancient writers sought a life in accord with the highest and best nature of man, an ideal foreshadowed but fully realized only in the life and teachings of Christ. Erasmus lays particular stress on the Platonists, because "in most of their ideas and in their very manner of speaking they come nearest to the beauty of the prophets and the gospels."[47] He even invokes Plato's allegory of the cave[48] to illustrate the long struggle to transcend appearances and to embrace reality. The critical Christian distinctions between the material and the spiritual, the body and the soul, the temporal and the eternal, the visible and the intelligible, are all to be found in Plato.

The same essential distinction—between surface and hidden meaning—also applies to literature. The teachings of Homer and Virgil are allegorical rather than literal. Their wisdom lies below the surface of the stories they tell about the anger of Achilles or the manifest destiny of Aeneas. So, too, with the holy scriptures, which "conceal their real divinity beneath a surface that is crude and almost laughable."[49] As for the creation story in the Bible—Adam molded from damp earth, Eve shaped from his rib, the serpent in the garden who tempts them to eat the fruit forbidden by God, and their exile from the garden with an angel posted with a flaming sword—if you take that story literally, Erasmus says, you might as well be reading about Prometheus and his theft of fire from the gods. Many of the Bible stories are even worse on their surface: the stolen birthright of Esau, David slaying Goliath, Lot coupling with his daughters, Samson losing his strength and virility from the shearing of his hair. These stories are "downright absurd, taken literally, and if understood only at the surface level, detrimental to morality."[50] We must penetrate to the "mystical spirit" of the Bible, Erasmus urges.[51] Christianity is a religion of the spirit, which can be purified only through a proper understanding of the scriptures.

This viewpoint raises a number of questions, such as why Erasmus believes that the Bible is a direct communication from God. Why, in other words, does he privilege the scriptures over the writings of the great pagan poets and philosophers? Why does he believe the former texts were inspired by God whereas the latter were written by men? What limits of interpretation are there in discerning the "mystical spirit" of the scriptures? And how does this need for interpretation mesh with the assertion that the Word of God is directly accessible to all persons?

The answer to these questions lies, for Erasmus, in the New Testament, and in particular in the life and teachings of Christ. We depend upon Christ to unlock for us the "mystical spirit" of the Bible. Christ teaches us to understand the Word of God correctly. And the message of Christ, which is embodied in his life, is indeed accessible to all. "Think of Christ," he writes, "not as an empty word, but as nothing other than love, candor, patience, purity—in brief, whatever He taught."[52] In other words, Christ himself is a living allegory, an assertion that did not seem to shock Erasmus's contemporaries, if they noticed it at all. Christ is the perfection of human nature and the embodiment of the spirit that unites us with God. Erasmus moves from the message (which he considers the perfection of human wisdom) to Christ (the perfection of human nature) to God. He believes in God because he believes in the Word of God as manifested in Christ. The Old Testament, like the writings of the pagan poets and philosophers, is just another way of preparing the soul for that message.

In understanding and elaborating upon the Word of God, we can be aided by the writings of the church fathers, as well as by careful reading of the pagan poets and philosophers. But the scriptures themselves, and especially those of the New Testament, when read with reverence and care and a proper appreciation of the distinction between the flesh and the spirit, contain all that we need to know about living our lives as Christians. Practice, not theory, is what truly matters. That is why Erasmus chose *Enchiridion* as his title, echoing the Stoic philosopher Epictetus, for whom philosophy is not a set of doctrines but a way of life. So, too, for Erasmus, Christianity is a way of life. It is a way of life based on a core set of beliefs—that God exists, that the Word of God was made manifest in Christ, and that Christ's life and message should be our constant guide—but beyond that simple core, doctrinal disputes are a harmful distraction.

Most of the *Enchiridion*, then, is devoted to articulating rules for the true Christian life. Only one of those rules deals with faith, which he calls "the sole approach to Christ" and which consists of opening oneself so thoroughly to the Word of God that it permeates one's being.[53] "While He was here in the flesh," Erasmus writes, "Christ transmitted [God's truth] in His words and expressed it in His character."[54] Accepting that truth is the essence of faith.

The rest of the rules deal with the need to follow Christ as one's only goal. In that quest, the clergy and theologians have no privileged status; all are equal before Christ and are judged not by their positions or their learning but by their hearts and their manner of life. There is no direct connection, Erasmus believes, between the spirit of Christ and the rituals, ceremonies, and practices of the church: "The practice of a spiritual life consists not so much in ritualism as in the love of one's fellow men."[55] He has no inherent objection to prayers, fasts, and the observance of holy days. They might well be useful in inculcating and reinforcing religious feeling. But when performed without understanding or spiritual engagement, they are meaningless exercises, a substitute for, rather than a path to, true piety. An obsessive focus on ritual observance, he writes, "is the common plague of all Christendom and inflicts a damage all the more pernicious for its looking so very much like piety."[56]

Erasmus has no patience for pilgrimages and the worship of saints' relics. And he is especially disdainful of attempts to strike "bargains" with God through the saying of masses, prayers for divine favor, or the purchase of indulgences. The church itself encourages and profits from these practices. As a result, Erasmus complains, "most Christians are merely full of credulous wonder, not devout, and except for using the *name* of Christ are not far removed from the superstition of pagans."[57] They might as well "offer a cock to Aesculapius that they might recover from an illness, or slaughter a bull to Neptune that they might have a safe voyage. The names have been changed, of course, but the purpose is the same."[58]

Christianity consists in imitating Christ. Going to church, reciting prayers, or even giving alms does not make you a Christian. Those activities must touch and renew your soul. The tree is known by its fruits. Erasmus wants to see in all people the fruits of Christ's spirit: love, peace, joy, patience, goodness, kindness, mildness, faith, modesty, continence, and purity.[59] This is the essence of Christianity and is the only part that truly matters.

These views animated Erasmus's publication in 1516 of the Greek New Testament with a new Latin translation on facing pages. He spent years learning Greek thoroughly and translating Greek works into Latin to hone his skills. He then gathered as many manuscript copies of the Greek testament as he could (which were not many), collated them, and applied to them the philological methods developed by humanists for editions of Homer, Virgil, and other pagan authors, correcting copying errors, resolving inconsistencies, and settling on as accurate a text as possible. Some thought it a sacrilege to treat the Bible as if it were just another text, like Plato's dialogues or Cicero's essays, to be "corrected" by scholars.

Erasmus's translation—designed to replace the New Testament portion of the Vulgate, the fourth-century Latin translation of the Bible by Saint Jerome—sparked even more outrage. Erasmus was accused of presuming to rewrite the Lord's Prayer and other staples of the church.[60] Critics complained that, in pointing out the many errors in the Vulgate, Erasmus was undermining the authority of the church.

In the foreword to the first edition, which he elaborated upon in the third edition of 1522, Erasmus defends his scholarly approach. The New Testament records the words and teachings of Christ. Nothing should be more precious to us. Knowledge of the language in which it was written is therefore the critical first step in the study of theology. Next, we must strive to make the Greek text as accurate as possible, lest we be led astray on vital matters by copying errors and other corruptions. The highest standards of scholarship—honed on the Greek and Latin classics—should be applied to the Bible above all other books. Finally, a clear and accurate translation is needed so that those who do not know Greek can still come as close as possible to hearing the genuine voice of God.

This last point, Erasmus realized, required the most defense. Erasmus wanted to bring the New Testament directly to the people. Anyone who knew Latin could read his edition. But he also urged that the Bible be translated into "all the languages of the human race" so that it could be read and studied by those who did not know Greek or Latin.[61]

> I absolutely dissent from those people who don't want the holy scriptures to be read in translation by the unlearned—as if, forsooth, Christ taught such complex doctrine that hardly anyone outside a handful of theologians could understand it, or as if the chief strength of the Christian religion lay in people's ignorance of it.[62]

Erasmus did not want the Bible to be like the holy of holies, the inner temple of Jerusalem that only the high priest might enter. He did not want theologians and foreign tongues to interpose themselves between the people and their God. His goal, therefore, was to make his Latin version as accurate as possible and then to encourage translation into the vernacular so that ordinary men and women, without education in Latin, could still have a direct relationship with the scriptures, instead of "mumbl[ing] their psalms or recit[ing] their prayers like trained parrots in a language where they don't understand what they are saying."[63] He wanted the Bible to be integrated into daily life: "I would hope that the farmer might chant a holy text at his plow, the spinner sing it as she sits at her wheel, the traveler ease the tedium of his journey with tales from the scripture."[64]

Surprisingly enough, making the Bible accessible to all was a radical idea at the time. Indeed, in 1536, William Tyndale was executed for heresy; his crime, inspired by Erasmus, was preparing and publishing an English translation of the Bible, which eighty years later became the foundation of the King James Version. Erasmus wanted to reestablish for the faithful a direct relationship with Christ. He wanted God to speak to them as directly as possible without intermediation by the church. Erasmus dismissed the elaborate scholastic theology of the Middle Ages as an arrogant attempt to project knowledge of the unknowable, as if these theologians carried the keys to heaven and only those who followed their views could find admittance there. "Very few can be learned," he stressed, "but no man is denied permission to be a Christian, no man is forbidden to be pious, and, I will add boldly, nothing prevents any man from being a theologian."[65]

To be a "theologian" in this sense is merely to read and reflect upon the words of God until they infuse one's being and determine one's character. Give your heart to the spirit of what you read, he urged. That spirit is simple. The apostles themselves knew nothing of the Immaculate Conception or the Trinity or even transubstantiation (the literal transformation of bread and wine into the body and blood of Christ during Communion). Saint Paul wrote movingly of love in his first letter to the Corinthians without academic quibbles or disputes over dogma.[66] What we cannot understand is not worth disputing, because we can understand all that is truly important. "Say to yourself: 'Things above our reach concern us not at all.' "[67]

By the time he wrote the foreword to the third edition of his New Testament, the Reformation was already underway. Erasmus included a passionate plea that the scriptures should not become a "source of quarrels, contentions, conflicts, hatreds, and even heresies."[68] But it was already too late.

LUTHER AND A CHURCH AT WAR WITH ITSELF

On October 31, 1517, Martin Luther tacked ninety-five theses to the church door at Wittenberg. This act was not quite as dramatic as it might seem. Nailing a thesis to the church door was the sixteenth-century equivalent of posting a blog on the internet and inviting debate.[69]

Nor was the subject matter of the theses themselves particularly controversial. In 1515, Pope Leo X issued a papal bull (a charter or proclamation affixed with a lead seal, or *bulla*) authorizing the sale of indulgences to pay for the building of Saint Peter's Basilica in Rome. Erasmus already had criticized the sale of indulgences and other pay-to-pray aspects of church life. Luther's text was defiantly blunt, but the substance was not new. In thesis 27, he wrote, "There is no divine authority for preaching that the soul flies out of purgatory immediately the money clinks in the bottom of the chest."[70] He attacked the whole "purgatory industry"[71] with vehemence. Luther argued that penitence does not apply to the dead but only to the living. There is, therefore, nothing the living, including the pope, can do to absolve the dead. Only God can do that. Even for the living, the pope has no power to remit sins in exchange for money. Again, only God can forgive, and a man who ignores his neighbor's plight but pays for indulgences incurs God's wrath, not his forgiveness. Let the pope build Saint Peter's with his own money, Luther concluded, "rather than with the money of indigent believers."[72]

Martin Luther was born in 1483 to a middle-class family in the Electorate of Saxony, then part of the Holy Roman Empire. He received a standard education in Latin and went on to study law at the University of Erfurt, where he was shocked by the drinking and whoring of his fellow students. In 1505, while riding back to the university from his home, a fierce thunderstorm arose, and he was nearly struck by lightning. Crying out, he vowed to become a monk if he survived the ordeal. Less than two weeks later, Luther entered the Augustinian monastery at Erfurt.

He was a troubled monk. He prayed and fasted and went to confession so often and with such minor peccadillos that he began to annoy his confessor. But he always felt sinful in the eyes of God. Try as he might, Luther could not realize in himself the Christian ideal. He was nonetheless ordained as a priest, awarded a doctorate in theology, and sent to join the faculty at Wittenberg.

Luther's "Ninety-Five Theses" would have received little note but for the printing press. Pamphlets containing them quickly spread throughout Germany and the rest of Europe. Had the pope simply ignored them, the controversy might have dissolved. But the pope instead had a heresy case prepared against Luther and summoned him to Rome. Frederick the Wise, elector of Saxony, advised Luther not to go and convinced the pope instead to have Luther examined in Augsburg during a *diet* (general assembly) of the Holy Roman Empire. The examination did not go well. Luther and the papal legatee engaged in a protracted shouting match, and Luther had to be spirited out of Augsburg at night to avoid arrest. For whatever reason, Frederick, though a devoted Catholic throughout his life, decided to protect Luther, and, as one of only seven electors of the Holy Roman emperors, he had the power to do it.

Luther's experience at Augsburg radicalized him and fed his natural intransigence. In 1520, he published three books in quick succession. In the first two, *To the Christian Nobility of the German Nation* and *On the Babylonian Captivity of the Church*, Luther not only denied the doctrine of papal infallibility, he derided the pope as the antichrist. He urged the

German people and German princes to reject the oppressive authority and financial corruption of the church in Rome and to exercise local control over religion. He also dismissed the sacraments other than baptism and Communion as having no basis in scripture. He even dismissed the doctrine of transubstantiation as a clerical conjuring trick. Finally, in *On the Freedom of a Christian*, Luther argued that good works play no part in salvation, which depends solely on the grace of God.[73] We are all worthless in the sight of God and incapable of keeping his commandments. Only our faith in God's mercy, over which we have no control and no influence, can redeem us. Our "freedom" lies in the knowledge that our salvation is completely independent of our actions and our worth.

Unsurprisingly, the pope condemned Luther for heresy. Luther publicly burned the papal bull. He was then summoned under a promise of safe conduct to the Diet at Worms in April 1521. Standing in front of the emperor and a pile of his own books, Luther was ordered to recant. He returned the next day to give his famous answer: "*Hier stehe ich, ich kann nicht anders. Gott helfe mir. Amen!*" (Here I stand, I can do no other. God help me. Amen!).[74]

The emperor, showing remarkable restraint and perhaps some sympathy with Luther's anti-Rome stance, honored Luther's safe-conduct. As Luther made his way back to Wittenberg, Frederick staged a mock kidnapping and spirited Luther away to a remote castle where he remained in safe seclusion for some months. But his movement, fueled by German resentment of money sent to Italy for the support of a corrupt church, gathered momentum in his absence. And it moved quickly out of his control. Various sects and splinter groups arose, only loosely grouped under the heading "Protestantisms." Huldrych Zwingli, John Calvin, and other theologians differed with Luther and with one another on the very sort of dogmatic quibbles against which Erasmus had warned. They all shared the same aim: to re-create the true Christianity from which the Catholic Church had departed. But with no centralized authority, there was no uniform, doctrinal guidance. Religion truly became localized, "a geographical kaleidoscope of opposing theologies," as Diarmaid Mac-Culloch, the leading historian of the Reformation, puts it.[75] Northern Europe was pockmarked with states, cities, and principalities, each with its own religion tolerating no dissent.

Meanwhile, the Catholic Church, still dominant in Spain, Italy, and most of France, launched a Counter-Reformation, aided by the Inquisition. Spanish Catholicism was particularly militant following the expulsion of Islam in 1491 and the murder, forced conversion, or exile of the Jews. Over the next 130 years, countless men, women, and children would die in religious wars and religious persecution throughout western Europe. They killed one another over doctrinal niceties that most of them did not even understand.

THE HUMANIST CONVERSATION

Where was Desiderius Erasmus during the early years of the Reformation? Conspicuously silent. He was pressed by the church to take a firm stand against Luther. He was pressed by reformers to support Luther. He did neither. He obviously was sympathetic to Luther's call for reform of church practices and for making the spiritual fundamentals of Christianity directly accessible to the people. On those issues, after all, Luther was following Erasmus. Luther even used Erasmus's Latin translation of the New Testament to prepare a German translation in 1522.

But Erasmus was repelled by Luther's militant desire to tear down a church that was 1,500 years in the making. He foresaw, correctly, that hatred, war, and misery would be the primary by-products of such uncompromising intransigence. Erasmus wanted to reform the church, not to abandon it. He also fundamentally disagreed with Luther's view of human nature. This is the issue on which Erasmus finally took his stand against Luther because it went to the heart of Erasmus's Christian humanism.

Luther, following Augustine, did not believe in free will. He thought that man was hopelessly sinful and could do nothing to ensure his own salvation. That salvation, he claimed, depends entirely on the grace of God, which lies beyond man's comprehension. Man cannot even choose to embrace God's offer of grace. God alone chooses the elect and the damned.

Erasmus, by contrast, put his faith in the fundamental freedom and dignity of man. God's grace may be beyond our comprehension, but we can choose to embrace it. As Pico della Mirandola exclaimed, in his influential lecture *On the Dignity of Man*, "O great and wonderful happiness of man! It is given him to have that which he chooses and to be that which he wills."[76] Though far less effusive, Erasmus embraced a comparable optimism. Our nature is corrupted by original sin and the fall from grace. But, through education, contemplation of the scriptures, and the application of reason, we can work our way back, not to the perfection of Christ, but at least to a state of receptivity to God's grace. In his *Diatribe Concerning Free Will*, Erasmus argued against Luther that God's truth is at least partially accessible to man. We can, by following that truth, choose to be better. On Luther's view, by contrast, there is no reason to strive for goodness because we are all sinful regardless. For Luther, God's seemingly arbitrary decision to save some and to condemn others is cruel rather than righteous. Erasmus found Luther's position both theologically and morally monstrous. He also found it sadly ironic that Luther, who had no faith in human reason to discern God's truth, was willing to split the church over doctrinal issues on which he was certain he was correct.

The title of Luther's response says it all: *The Bondage of the Will*. If we believe "that God foreknows and foreordains all things," he argues, then there can be no free will in man.[77] And if we believe that Christ redeemed men by his own blood, "we are forced to confess that all of man was lost."[78] Otherwise, Christ's sacrifice was superfluous or directed at the least valuable part of man. It follows inexorably, he thought, that man cannot choose to better himself. Luther was no Renaissance humanist. His faith lay not in the dignity of man but in the incomprehensible mercy of God.

Erasmus made two additional attempts to combat the views of Luther and other advocates of the Reformation, but no one was paying much attention by that time. His essential argument was hardly inspiring for either side: The church is imperfect, but we should remain loyal and try to make it and ourselves better. Erasmus had no patience for doctrinal disputes that he considered both unresolvable and wholly secondary to the core of faith. He preached kindness and humility over dogmatism and was appalled by the burning of so-called heretics. In a world gone mad over dogmatic disputes, Erasmus was harshly criticized for timidity by both the church and Luther.

The only major work of Erasmus's later years was his *Colloquies*. These short dialogues originally were written in his teaching days as exercises for his students to help with their Latin phrasing and expressions. But they proved so popular that Erasmus added expanded dialogues on a variety of issues and gave free reign to his humor and his acute, often sardonic, observations of human nature. The *Colloquies* joined the *Praise of Folly* as his most popular and enduring works.

Once again, he parodies all forms of hypocrisy, superstition, and corruption. In "The Shipwreck," terrified passengers make promises to the saints that they (unlike Luther) have no intention of keeping. "How devout men are made by suffering!" one interlocutor observes. "In prosperity the thought of God or saint never enters their heads."[79] In "The Abbot and the Learned Lady," Erasmus displays the willful ignorance of monks and the importance of learning for women as well as men.[80] In "A Pilgrimage for Religion's Sake," he mocks meaningless pilgrimages that take us far from home and our responsibilities to those closest to us. Gullibility is another favorite target, both those who display it and those who exploit it, whether through exorcism, or alchemy, or a fetish for phony relics, such as an alleged vial of the Virgin's milk, now turned into a chalky dust.[81] In one dialogue, rival mendicant orders clamor for donations from a dying man and engage in jurisdictional disputes with the local priest. Even when all are paid out, they go away muttering at the money wasted on the others. In another, excessive spending on building and decorating churches and ostentatious funerals is contrasted with simple Christian piety. In a very personal vein, he also condemns the pressure put upon young boys and girls to enter a monastic life for which they feel no calling.

Erasmus's hatred of war, especially wars of religion, is particularly acute. In "Charon," the ferryman of the dead is overwhelmed with the spirits of those killed when the papacy joined forces in 1525 with the king of France and various Italian city-states against the emperor, Charles V. Rome itself was sacked in the ensuing bloodbath. Priests on both sides claimed that God was with them alone and promised direct access to heaven to those killed. Charon asks, "And people believe these fellows?" "What can a pretense of religion not achieve?" is the answer. "Youth, inexperience, thirst for glory, anger, and natural human inclination swallow this whole."[82] Moreover, priests and monks don't mind the ensuing slaughter because "they make more profit from the dying than from the living. There are wills, Masses for kinsmen, bulls, and many other sources of revenue not to be despised."[83]

It is hardly surprising that the *Colloquies* met with a hostile reception from elements within the Catholic Church. The conservative and influential faculty of the Sorbonne formally censored the book in 1526. In the next edition, Erasmus added a letter to his readers, of whom there were many, arguing that the *Colloquies* serve religion and the church by exposing those who cast discredit upon both. Charlatans who "play upon the credulous minds of simple folk" are the true plague upon Christian devotion,[84] and Erasmus vows to speak out whenever and wherever "the name of religion is used as a cover for superstition, faithlessness, foolishness, and recklessness."[85] If that makes him "half a heretic," as one of his own characters announces,[86] he will bear the label proudly. The half that matters is the half devoted to the true teachings of the church.

That is the point of one of his most important colloquies, "An Examination Concerning Faith." In it, Aulus (who represents Erasmus) examines Barbatius (Luther) on the tenets of the Apostles' Creed. He finds Barbatius to be in line with church teaching on every point. Aulus exclaims, "When I was at Rome, I did not find everyone so sound in belief."[87] On the key articles of Christian faith, there is no genuine difference between them. Aulus thus asks Barbatius plaintively, "Why, then, is there such conflict between you and the orthodox?"[88] Barbatius can provide no answer. Nor, sadly, can Erasmus.

Erasmus was driven from Louvain by Catholics in 1521. He was driven from Basel by Reformation Protestants in 1529. He then settled in the imperial German city of Freiburg im Breisgau. Erasmus died on July 12, 1536, one year after his dear friend Thomas More was beheaded for refusing to acknowledge Henry VIII as the head of a separate Church of England. Erasmus was lucky to have escaped a similar fate. He was "half a heretic" to Catholics and Protestants alike. When the Catholic Church published its *Index Librorum Prohibitorum* in 1559, all of Erasmus's works were included in the ban. Over the next four hundred years, almost every significant writer, thinker, and philosopher was added to that list. It became an honor roll of Western thought. Erasmus wanted to unite Christianity with humanism.[89] But the church turned its back on Erasmus and, with him, on the modern world.

Johan Huizinga, writing in 1919, notes that Erasmus is no longer read; he has become only a name. "Erasmus is the man who is too sensible and moderate for the heroic," Huizinga writes. As a result, "his influence has ceased. He has done his work and will speak to the world no more."[90] To the contrary, we need Erasmus today more than ever. We need his carnival laughter, his ability to pinpoint and mock all forms of hypocrisy and ostentation. We need his emphasis on the softer virtues of kindness, sincerity, and simplicity. We need his innate moderation and skeptical tolerance in the face of dogmatisms of all kinds. Most of all, we need his faith in the accessibility of truth, his faith that we can, through the cultivation of reason and the thoughtful study of the great works and examples of our predecessors, approach a kind of wisdom—a fallible, human wisdom to be sure, but that is more than enough and carries with it a touch of the divine.

Chapter 3

MACHIAVELLI AND POLITICAL REALISM

Tanto nomini nullum par elogium.[1]

M achiavelli has been avidly read and vigorously condemned for half a millennium. His realistic analyses, and precepts for the exercise, of power have both shocked and intrigued thinkers and would-be masters of the universe. He is the indispensable figure in all subsequent thought about politics. No reader can remain neutral. You are for him or against him, yet even those who criticize Machiavelli the loudest often follow his precepts. Frederick the Great of Prussia, assisted by the French philosopher Voltaire, wrote a book before ascending the throne called the *Anti-Machiavel*, a chapter-by-chapter rebuttal to *The Prince*. Voltaire himself later quipped that the first thing Machiavelli would advise a new prince to do would be to write a book attacking Machiavellianism.

The very word *Machiavellian* is a term of abuse, though sometimes, in those who pride themselves on their cynicism, one of barbed praise. Machiavelli is thought to license deception, brutality, and whatever is necessary to attain and to retain power. Shakespeare called him the "murderous Machiavel,"[2] and fashioned his greatest villains, Richard III and Iago, along what he perceived as Machiavellian lines. Elizabethan drama is full of such characters.

Some apologists contend that Machiavelli, while accurate in his descriptions of contemporary politics, was savagely satirical in his prescriptions. If we accept this view, Machiavelli, though not as funny, was rather like Erasmus in the *Praise of Folly* and the *Colloquies*, exposing the wickedness and hypocrisy of the world around him while pretending to praise it. Others, with more justification, claim that Machiavelli was a closet idealist whose true love was the Florentine Republic he wanted to preserve at all costs in a Europe full of ruthless and ambitious leaders. Still others contend that Machiavelli was so eager to return to politics and the good graces of the Medicis that he wrote *The Prince* as a job application, saying whatever he thought might appeal to the new masters of Florence in order to demonstrate his own indispensability as an advisor.[3]

There is some truth in each of these views, though least in those who excuse, and thereby belittle, *The Prince* as satire. Machiavelli was a man of his time, in which the warring principalities of Italy constantly forged and broke alliances with one another, engaged in diplomatic feints and deceptions, hired *condottieri* to wage their wars, and flirted disastrously with foreign intervention by the great powers of France, Spain, and Germany. Machiavelli, as a Florentine diplomat, negotiated with princes and kings and wrote clear-eyed, incisive reports to inform and guide the Florentine government in dangerous times. The political realities described in *The Prince* he saw up close and personal, and he deplored the strategic mistakes and the failure of nerve that led to the fall of the republic and his own dismissal from office.

Yet Machiavelli was also a man of genius who transcended his time, communing with the great historians and philosophers of ancient Rome. The rise and fall of the Roman Republic—which Amsterdam professor Dominic Baker-Smith has called "the shaping myth of western political thought"[4]—was always at the forefront of Machiavelli's thinking. But his thoughts about it were filtered through the lens of contemporary politics. How power is gained, exercised, and retained was the single-minded focus of his work, and his unique combination of experience, study, and genius on that topic has never been equaled.

Augustine, in his *City of God*, argued that history is cyclical. No human civilization can endure; only the city of God provides stability and immortality. Machiavelli—who disdained religion, except as a useful tool of social stability—accepted the premise but not the conclusion. He wanted to establish conditions under which a city of man could endure as long as possible for the benefit of its citizens, even as he recognized that the wheel of fortune would eventually turn and destroy whatever men might build.

There is no indication that Machiavelli read Thomas More's *Utopia*, which was published in 1516, but, if he had, he undoubtedly would have dismissed it as pious nonsense. Indeed, he even rejected the political thought of his intellectual mentors, Cicero and Seneca, because they transferred moral values appropriate to individuals and applied them to the political realm, where they did not belong. Cicero and Seneca contended that the ideal leader must, above all, be virtuous, benevolent, generous, merciful, and honest. Machiavelli thought nothing could be more disastrous than a polity run by philosophers according to moral principles. And, certainly, nothing could be more false as a description of what actually happened in ancient Rome or was happening in the Italy of his day.

Machiavelli stressed that we must write about politics out of truth rather than idealism: "How one lives is so far distant from how one ought to live, that [a prince] who neglects what is done for what ought to be done, sooner effects his ruin than his preservation."[5] Politics has its own language, its own rules, and its own virtues. This is not to say that Machiavelli was an apologist for tyranny maintained through brutal repression. Far from it; Machiavelli was a lifelong and tireless proponent of republican liberty. But the survival of a republic or any other form of government depends on skills of leadership and strategic decisions that often have little to do with moral virtue. The political realm is autonomous and cannot be reduced to or judged by the standards of ancient morality, much less Christian morality, which Machiavelli thought had made men soft and disengaged, with its emphasis on meekness and the afterlife.

The prime quality in a leader for Machiavelli is *virtù*, a word from the Latin *virtus* that is impossible to translate. It certainly does not mean virtue in its contemporary sense. A leader with *virtù* is strong, bold, powerful, energetic, courageous, clever, resourceful, and even, when necessary, ruthless. The closest equivalent may be the ancient Greek term *polytropia*, which is what Homer calls Odysseus. It means "skilled in all ways of contending." In Machiavelli, moreover, *virtù* can be attributed to a republic (as in *The Discourses*) as well as to an individual (as in *The Prince*). *Virtù* is what allows a polity to survive and even thrive in a dangerous world, and thereby to provide a measure of peace, justice, and security for its citizens, a space within which they themselves are free to thrive.

Humans everywhere join together for mutual advantage and common defense. As Aristotle noted, only a beast or a god lives outside a body politic.[6] Yet such a collective inevitably gives rise to tensions both within the state and with other states. These inherent tensions, Machiavelli believed, cannot be eliminated and so must be channeled and controlled. Men and women are, by nature, selfish and untrustworthy, but they can also, as in the ancient Roman Republic, display the critical virtues of citizenship: courage, discipline, and fierce loyalty to their state. We must therefore be clear-eyed and realistic about human nature in constructing and preserving a society. Our own founders learned that lesson well in creating a divided government that held tensions in a dynamic equilibrium. Sometimes one faction might emerge, sometimes another. But the prospects for lasting damage were limited. Scholars generally attribute the founders' insight to the Scottish Enlightenment, but in fact it traces back to Machiavelli.

Political society is inherently problematic but absolutely critical to the well-being of all. Thus, we cannot hesitate to counter the forces that would destroy it. No civilization will endure forever, but civilized life can be prolonged through a careful balancing of competing internal forces and great skill in leadership. In our own polity, the former has so far proved sufficient even where the latter has been lacking. But, as Machiavelli's Florence showed, without both, survival is a matter of fortune, and fortune's wheel inevitably turns.

LIFE

Niccolò Machiavelli was born in Florence on May 3, 1469. His father, Bernardo, was a lawyer and dedicated humanist. Bernardo was also a member of the minor gentry, accepted in the best circles but neither wealthy nor aristocratic nor particularly successful. In order to obtain a prized set of Livy's history of Rome that he could not otherwise afford, Bernardo agreed to compile a detailed index for the printer.

Machiavelli, in keeping with his father's humanist interests, received a solid education in Latin, rhetoric, history, and moral philosophy. He copied verses from the Latin poets, particularly Virgil, Ovid, and Lucretius, in his notebooks. He read the historians, especially Thucydides (in a Latin translation), Tacitus, and, of course, Livy. He studied the political and moral writings of Cicero, Seneca, and Plutarch, and was also familiar with at least some of Plato's dialogues. The extent of Machiavelli's formal education is unclear, but most scholars believe he attended the University of Florence, where he studied with Marcello Adriani, who would later become a political colleague.

Florence in the fifteenth century was an important commercial and financial center. Bankers, merchants, and fine craftsmen made the city wealthy. Florence had been a republic for more than five hundred years, though it was often, as in the fifteenth century, dominated by prominent families, most significantly the banking house of Medici. After a brief tussle with the rival house of Albizzi that resulted in his exile, the patriarch, Cosimo de' Medici, returned to Florence in 1434. Republican formalities were maintained, but there was little doubt that the Medicis were now in charge: Cosimo, Piero, and Lorenzo de' Medici, known as Lorenzo the Magnificent, reigned successfully as princes in all but name. A 1478 plot to murder Lorenzo, along with his brother, Giuliano, during a High Mass at the Duomo fell short—Giuliano was stabbed to death; Lorenzo, though wounded, escaped. The Medicis and their supporters executed the conspirators and tightened their grip on the city.

When Lorenzo died in 1492, however, all that changed. Lorenzo's son Piero was a weak and incompetent leader. He was no match for the Dominican monk Girolamo Savonarola, who came to Florence in 1489 and lived in the monastery at San Marco in the very cell occupied half a century earlier by the painter Fra Angelico. Savonarola was an impassioned and charismatic preacher who railed against church corruption, the repression of freedom by tyrants (a not-so-subtle attack on the Medicis), the exploitation of the poor, and the decadence of secular culture. He also prophesied the coming of a foreign leader who would put the sword to Italy and reform the church. When Charles VIII of France invaded Italy to stake a claim to the Kingdom of Naples, Savonarola seized on the event as the fulfillment of his prophecy. He met with Charles and convinced him to bypass the largely defenseless Florence on his way south. The Medicis were expelled from the city, and a revived republic of the people was declared, with Savonarola's Frateschi party very much in control. The republic lasted eighteen tumultuous years before the Medicis returned in vengeful triumph; Savonarola lasted only four.

Charles VIII met with no lasting success in Italy, the church was not reformed, and an angry Pope Alexander VI excommunicated Savonarola and threatened Florence with an interdiction. The people of Florence began to tire of Savonarola, who had passed strict laws against vice and convened various bonfires of the vanities in 1497, where thousands of books—including beloved works by Dante and Boccaccio—secular paintings, and other supposedly decadent objects, such as mirrors, fancy dresses, and cosmetics, were committed to the flames. The mood turned decidedly hostile when Savonarola balked after a rival preacher challenged him to a trial by fire to test his allegedly divine sanction. Savonarola was arrested, tortured, and, in May 1498, burned at the stake, all at the instigation of the pope. His ashes were scattered in the Arno River. The Florentines were only too glad to see the last of him, and his supporters were dismissed from the government.

The fall of the Frateschi provided an ideal opportunity for the twenty-nine-year-old Machiavelli. He was appointed and confirmed secretary to the Second Chancery in 1498. The secretary to the First Chancery was his former teacher, Marcello Adriani. It was a minor bureaucratic post, but, through his talent and initiative, Machiavelli steadily turned it into something more essential during the fourteen years he held it.

With a solid position to sustain him, Machiavelli married Marietta Corsini in 1501. It seems to have been a reasonably happy union, though he was frequently traveling in the first decade of their marriage and was serially unfaithful throughout it. They had six children and remained together until the end of Machiavelli's life, despite his habit of becoming intensely, if not lastingly, enamored of other women.

Italy, at this time, was broken into five centers of power: the Kingdom of Naples (which generally included Sicily), the Papal States centered on Rome, the Republic of Florence, the Duchy of Milan, and the Republic of Venice. They existed in an uneasy equilibrium with one another, sometimes warring openly but mostly jockeying for power and influence over the satellite cities that fell within their respective spheres of influence. Each of the other four powers had strong, even tyrannical leaders. In Florence, Machiavelli's mentor, Piero Soderini, was named *gonfaloniere* (a chief administrative post) for life in 1502. Soderini was dedicated to the republic but an indecisive leader, and his weaknesses, in Machiavelli's view, ultimately led to the failure of the republic he was sworn to uphold.

Into this volatile mix in 1501 strode Cesare Borgia, bastard son of the current pope, Alexander VI. The pope named his son Duke of Romagna, a made-up title with no real territory over which to rule. Borgia, however, was the opposite of Soderini. He was bold and decisive and, since fortune favors the bold, or so thought Machiavelli, highly successful. With money and troops provided by his father, he began to add city-states to go with his title. Milan and Venice felt threatened. Borgia demanded an alliance with Florence, and the young Machiavelli was sent to Urbino to meet with him in October 1502. Machiavelli spent considerable time in his company, both in Urbino and elsewhere, and was highly impressed with

Borgia, who went out of his way to overawe the young diplomat. Machiavelli's job was to assess Borgia's character and his prospects for success. He sent detailed, and mostly laudatory, reports about Borgia back to Florence, material he later used as notes for developing his more mature political views in *The Prince* and *The Discourses*.

Unfortunately for Borgia, his father died in August 1503, and without papal patronage his budding empire soon collapsed. Alexander VI's immediate successor, Pius III, a Borgia supporter, reigned for only twenty-six days before his death. Borgia then made the fatal mistake of allowing Giuliano della Rovere to be elected as Pope Julius II. Rovere was a longtime enemy of the Borgia family. Borgia controlled a large enough block of votes to prevent the election, but he accepted Rovere's promises of money and continued support in Romagna, promises on which Julius II immediately reneged. Borgia continued his colorful career as a minor *condottiere* in Spain, until he was brutally murdered in 1507, but he was no longer a factor in Italian politics. The fox (Julius II) had outfaced the lion (Cesare Borgia), a lesson Machiavelli would take to heart.

France, England, Spain, and Germany had all built nation-states in the fifteenth century. Italy remained fractured, riven by infighting and hence vulnerable to outside conquest. Louis XII of France (following the lead of his predecessor, Charles VIII) and King Ferdinand II of Aragon each laid claim to the Kingdom of Naples, and the German emperor Maximilian coveted northern Italy. Florence was compelled to develop its own foreign policy. Machiavelli paid four separate visits to the French court. He also went to Rome in 1506 to meet with Julius II and made an extended trip to the emperor Maximilian in 1507–1508, accompanying the senior Florentine diplomat, Francesco Vettori, who became a lifelong friend and confidant. Machiavelli's face-to-face encounters with the major figures of the day—to assess their intentions, their powers, and their characters—along with the detailed reports he sent back to Florence, proved invaluable to his later writings. He needed to take a coldly realistic view of their likely actions and could not afford to be duped by soft words or lofty sentiments. Unfortunately, even Machiavelli's astute observations could not preserve the Florentine Republic, which insisted on forming an ill-fated alliance with France.

The origins of that alliance lay in Pisa, a Tuscan city once controlled by Florence, which revolted in 1502. Among the expedients Florence employed to regain Pisa was to hire the French to take it for them, using mercenaries. This was an unmitigated disaster. The mercenaries fled at the first sign of resistance, and the siege of Pisa collapsed. Louis XII nonetheless insisted on being paid, and one of Machiavelli's trips to Paris was an unsuccessful effort to convince Louis XII either to forgo the payment or to make good on his promise. The fiasco with Pisa convinced Machiavelli of the need for Florence to build up its own militia composed of citizen soldiers rather than for-hire mercenaries.

Louis XII made additional forays into Italy and called for the overthrow of the pope. In October 1511, Julius II forged an alliance against France with King Ferdinand of Spain and with Venice. The emperor Maximilian and even the king of England, Henry VIII, ultimately joined this "Holy League." Florence, faced with a choice of whom to support, stuck with the French, which proved a fatal mistake. Spanish troops ousted France from Italy and then marched on Florence, stopping to subdue the allied town of Prato. The Florentines could easily have made a treaty with Spain and retained at least the forms of the republic, but Soderini temporized and ultimately declined to treat with the Spanish. They responded with a brutal sack of Prato, and the terrified Florentines capitulated without resistance. The Medicis returned to power in 1512 following an eighteen-year absence, and the republic was dissolved. Giuliano de' Medici, the third son of Lorenzo the Magnificent, was now in charge. Machiavelli was out of a job. Worse was to come.

The following year, Machiavelli was arrested on suspicion of conspiracy against the new government. An abortive coup was uncovered, and one of the hapless participants had a sheet listing potential anti-Medici conspirators, including Machiavelli. There is no indication that

Machiavelli knew of the planned coup or the list, but he was imprisoned and tortured regardless.

On the death of Julius II in 1513, the Florentine cardinal Giovanni de' Medici, Lorenzo's second son, became Pope Leo X. Machiavelli and others not directly implicated in the coup were freed from prison as part of a general amnesty to celebrate the event. He nonetheless found it prudent to remove himself from Florence. Machiavelli settled on a family farm in nearby Sant'Andrea in Percussina. But he did not lose his interest in politics or his desire to return to that arena. Indeed, with one Medici as pope and another in charge of Florence, Machiavelli saw a unique opportunity for the Papal States and Florence to consolidate their power in the center of Italy, expel all foreign invaders, and forge a united Italy. It was a tantalizing vision that heavily influenced his first masterwork, *The Prince*, initially dedicated to Giuliano, and upon Giuliano's death to Lorenzo's grandson, also named Lorenzo. But if the book was intended to impress the Medicis with his indispensability as an advisor, it failed in that purpose. Machiavelli sent the manuscript to his former chancery colleague, Francesco Vettori, who was close to Pope Leo X. But Vettori proved unwilling to risk his own position to advance that of Machiavelli. It is unlikely that the pope or Giuliano or Lorenzo ever read the book. They did not trust Machiavelli in any event and had no intention of employing him in any political capacity.

So Machiavelli eked out a meager living from his farm in Sant'Andrea in Percussina. He also joined a group of humanist intellectuals meeting regularly in the Oricellari Gardens outside of Florence to discuss literature and politics. Mostly, though, he read and he wrote, regarding his time spent communing with ancient thinkers and historians as something close to sacred. After *The Prince* failed to secure him any patronage, Machiavelli turned back to *The Discourses*, a long-planned commentary on Livy that he turned into a detailed analysis of republican government.

In a famous letter to Vettori, Machiavelli describes a typical day on his farm, stressing with mixed humor and bitterness the mundaneness of his pursuits and the poverty of his estate. In summer, he sets snares for thrushes, which he then captures with his own hands to place in cages, presumably for sale or consumption. Come autumn, he supervises wood-cutters in his grove and squabbles with his neighbors over the price and quantity of the firewood. After that, he visits a spring and his aviary, carrying always a book of poetry in his pocket, usually Dante or Petrarch, or one of the Roman poets, such as Tibullus or Ovid. Then he repairs to an inn to discuss the news of the village and to "note the various tastes and different fancies of men."[7] He dines with his family, and they "eat such food as this poor farm of mine and my tiny property allow."[8] After lunch, he returns to the inn for games of cards and dice played for pennies but accompanied with loud disputes and colorful insults. Having deliberately steeped himself in vulgarity to "satisfy the malice of this fate of mine, being glad to have her drive me along this road, to see if she will be ashamed of it,"[9] Machiavelli himself effects a transformation:

> On the coming of evening, I return to my house and enter my study; and at the door I take off the day's clothing, covered with mud and dust, and put on garments regal and courtly; and reclothed appropriately, I enter the ancient courts of ancient men, where, received by them with affection, I feed on that food which only is mine and which I was born for, where I am not ashamed to speak with them and to ask them the reason for their actions; and they in their kindness answer me; and for four hours of time I do not feel boredom. I forget every trouble, I do not dread poverty, I am not frightened by death; entirely I give myself over to them.[10]

It is no exaggeration to say that his hours spent reading, writing, and communing with the ancients gave back the meaning to his life that he lost when his active involvement in politics ended. No longer able to meet with emperors, popes, kings, and princes, he discourses instead with the greatest thinkers of antiquity.[11]

In 1520, after completing *The Discourses*, Machiavelli, through the intervention of friends, received a formal commission from the Medicis to write a history of Florence. He spent most of the rest of his life on the work, and he used the money he received to provide a dowry for his daughter. It is not a flattering portrait, especially as it approached his own day. Machiavelli is blunt about the increasing corruption, the decadence, and the military misadventures of the city he nonetheless considered his true *patria*.

The Medicis never managed to unite Italy against foreign aggressors. To the contrary, the various city-states and principalities continued to invite foreign intervention in hopes of gaining advantage against one another. Pope Clement VII (Giulio de' Medici) formed another Holy League, this time against Charles V, king of Spain and Holy Roman emperor. On May 6, 1527, disorganized Spanish and German mercenaries sacked Rome. The pope shut himself up in the Castel Sant'Angelo and paid a heavy ransom to be left alone. Ten days later, the Medicis fled Florence, and the republic was once again restored. Machiavelli hoped for reinstatement. But it was too late, and unlikely in any event. *The Prince*, though never published, had circulated in manuscript form and made his fellow republicans wary of him. Machiavelli died on June 21, 1527, but the influence of *The Prince* has grown steadily ever since.

THE PRINCE

To understand *The Prince*, it is best to begin at the end, with Machiavelli's "Exhortation to Restore Italy to Liberty and Free Her from the Barbarians." In it, Machiavelli complains that foreign powers have looted and oppressed Lombardy, the Kingdom of Naples, and Tuscany. Only a united Italy can expel these invaders, protect itself against further incursions, and claim its rightful place among the nation-states of Europe. The time is ripe, he urges, to welcome a new prince in Italy—a Moses for the children of Israel, a Cyrus to rally the Persians, a Theseus to unite the Athenians. These strong leaders seized their opportunities and led their newfound nations to greatness, just as Romulus did in ancient Rome. Fractured, weakened Italy has waited too long for such a redeemer, and Machiavelli can barely restrain his enthusiasm in describing "the deep devotion, the dedication, the tears, that will greet him."[12] "This barbarian occupation stinks in all our nostrils!" he insists, and, in a direct appeal to the house of Medici, concludes:

> Let your illustrious house, then, take up this task with that courage and with that hope which suit a just enterprise; so that, under your banner, our country may become noble again, and the verses of Petrarch [from his famous canzone "Italia mia"] may come true:

> > Then virtue boldly shall engage
> > And swiftly vanquish barbarous rage,
> > Proving that ancient and heroic pride
> > In true Italian hearts has never died.[13]

This is laying it on a bit thick, even by the standards for dedicatory flattery in the Renaissance. But there is no reason to believe that Machiavelli was not sincere. The Florentine Republic had failed because of inadequate institutions and weak leadership. Machiavelli was ready to try something else, and he believed that only a strong leader could unite and free Italy from foreign powers seeking spoils. Cesare Borgia had tried and failed to unite Italy because the new pope was hostile to him. But perhaps the Medicis, controlling both the papacy and Florence, could succeed where he had failed. *The Prince* is Machiavelli's handbook for the Medicis to undertake such a task. Believing that "[no] time [was] more suitable than the present,"[14] Machiavelli set aside the longer work he was planning and produced *The Prince* at great speed in 1513.

There is a certain irony in this sudden change in direction. The longer work Machiavelli was planning was a set of discourses on republican government, which he clearly favored over autocratic rule. Yet Machiavelli was willing to sharpen the tools of tyranny in order to achieve his objective of a free and united Italy. It was a highly pragmatic decision, a response to circumstances of just the sort he urged on the ideal prince of his imagining. Machiavelli could not restore the Florentine Republic, but perhaps he could at least promote a strong Italian *patria*. For that to be possible, however, he had to convince the Medicis to seize an opportunity that only he saw clearly. He needed them to bend fortune to his will.

Machiavelli, in the tradition of ancient Rome, personified fortune as a goddess, *Fortuna*, with a capricious indifference to human merit and human wishes. The wheel of fortune lifts up and casts down. There is limited scope for human freedom. Machiavelli nonetheless believed, as did the Romans, that *fortuna* favors the bold. *Fortuna* presents us with the set of circumstances with which we must deal and to which we must respond.

Machiavelli stressed that there are turning points in life and in statecraft, when large consequences are at stake and fortune can be redirected by forceful and decisive action. We must seize any such opportunities and bring to bear on them the means necessary to exploit them. Shakespeare later used that same idea to motivate the conspirators who murdered Julius Caesar (ostensibly to restore the Roman Republic):

> There is a tide in the affairs of men
> Which, taken at the flood, leads on to fortune;
> Omitted, all the voyage of their life
> Is bound in shallows and in miseries.
> On such a full sea are we now afloat,
> And we must take the current when it serves
> Or lose our ventures.[15]

One such tide was presenting itself now—the opportunity to unite Italy and to expel foreign invaders—and Machiavelli wanted the Medicis to take it at the flood. Another such tide was simultaneously visible to Machiavelli personally: the opportunity for him to return to politics as an influential advisor. Machiavelli was determined not to lose either of those ventures, which is why he wrote *The Prince*. It is important to keep in mind this dual perspective, since Machiavelli's advice to the prince is exactly what he himself is following in writing the book.

The Prince accordingly is directed quite specifically to the circumstance of Medici rule; it focuses on a new, rather than hereditary, principality and the special challenges of the prince in winning the loyalty and obedience of a people accustomed to freedom but now subject to his absolute rule. Character, Machiavelli believes, is the key to success. But just what character traits will work varies from circumstance to circumstance. "A prince will be fortunate who adjusts his behavior to the temper of the times."[16] That is why the prince must be polytropic, skilled in all ways of contending. He must combine the traits of the lion and the fox: "As the lion cannot protect himself from traps, and the fox cannot defend himself from wolves, you have to be a fox in order to be wary of traps, and a lion to overawe the wolves."[17] The prince must combine the shrewdness of Julius II and the boldness of Cesare Borgia, with the good sense to know when one is called for and when the other.

Machiavelli had a fascination with the role of extraordinary individuals in shaping history, a fascination that would later be shared by the German philosopher Friedrich Nietzsche. "Specific occasions brought these happy men to power," Machiavelli notes, "and their unusual abilities [*virtù*] enabled them to seize the occasion and so to make their countries noble and prosperous."[18] New principalities are acquired and held either through the force of arms or "through the power of others and *fortuna*."[19] Francesco Sforza, the powerful warlord in Milan from 1450 to 1466, took the former path. Cesare Borgia, who depended on his father's position as pope to get his start, took the latter. But the greatness of the prince, and the greatness of his city, depends on what he does with that position once it is obtained.

The Medicis now rule Florence thanks to good fortune and the arms of Spain. But, if they want to keep it, they cannot depend exclusively on fortune or foreign arms. Even the resourceful Borgia fell from power when his father died and he uncharacteristically failed to block an enemy from becoming pope. Foreign assistance is too likely either to be fickle or to transform itself into foreign domination. A strong Florence, therefore, needs a strong leader who can consolidate his own and his city's power. And a strong leader must rely predominantly upon his own *virtù*.

Every new prince, Machiavelli notes, is beset with inherent, internal difficulties. A new prince will be opposed by those doing well under the prior regime and only half-heartedly supported by those hoping to profit from the change, who will be quick to switch allegiance if their hopes are disappointed.[20] Thus, Savonarola's followers helped to expel the Medicis twenty-three years earlier, believing they would be better off. But their economic position instead got worse, and they found themselves oppressed by his strict religious creed. Once the people ceased to believe in Savonarola's divine sanction, he had "no way of keeping the backsliders in line or of converting the doubters."[21] If the Medicis are to learn from that lesson, they must move quickly, even ruthlessly, to consolidate their power and to make the people dependent upon them for their prosperity and well-being. There is no room for sentiment in politics. Only failure will result from such weakness.

Machiavelli offers a series of lessons to the Medicis for successful rule. One might call them the seven habits of highly effective leaders. The first is immediately to suppress those most likely to cause trouble. The harm done to them must be of sufficient severity that the prince need not fear their revenge. Men will seek revenge for minor hurts, he explains, but are unable to revenge major ones. In particular, Machiavelli advises, keep your hands off the property of the citizens, for "men are quicker to forget the death of a father than the loss of a patrimony."[22] Moreover, any harm done to individuals or groups must be quick and decisive and then end, so that the rest of the people are not constantly fearing new acts of violence or oppression. A prolonged reign of terror will engender hatred and desperation; a surgical neutralization of the most problematic elements will not. In short, "when a prince takes a new state, he should calculate the sum of all the injuries he will have to do, and do them all at once, so as not to have to do new ones every day; simply by not repeating them, he will be able to reassure people, and win them over to his side with benefits" delivered slowly over time.[23]

This is a remarkable statement from a man who was thrown into prison and tortured by the new Medici regime before finally being released and retiring to his farm in Sant'Andrea in Percussina. No room for sentiment, indeed. "A new prince," Machiavelli admits, "cannot possibly avoid a name for cruelty, since new states are always in danger."[24] But the prince can use that cruelty tactically to obtain the loyalty of his people. For example, when Borgia first ruled Romagna, he set a cruel man in charge there to pacify the populace. But once the surrogate had served his purpose, Borgia had him cut in half in the public square, thereby winning the approval of the people. Such cruelty, Machiavelli insists, was "well used."[25]

But, however well used, violence must be sparing, particularly if the prince seeks honor as well as power. For "it certainly cannot be called [*virtù*] to murder his fellow citizens, betray his friends, to be devoid of truth, pity, or religion; a man may get power by means like these, but not glory."[26] A prince seeking both power and glory will resort to cruelty only when tactically necessary. Thus, Machiavelli condemns the expulsion of the Moors and the Jews from Spain. He calls it "despicable."[27] But, more to the point, it was also a political error because the Jews and Moors were important contributors to the economy, and they posed no threat to the ruling order, so their expulsion was wholly unnecessary. As Talleyrand reputably told Napoleon after Napoleon executed the Duke of Enghien—one of the few remaining relatives of the Bourbon monarchs—on dubious charges of treason, thereby sending shockwaves through the courts of Europe: "C'est pire qu'un crime, c'est une faute" (It is worse than a crime, it is a mistake).[28]

The second main lesson Machiavelli offers is to keep the citizens dependent on the prince and on the state by distributing benefits to them slowly over time—but, again, only up to a point. A prince should not be too liberal, because the money to display such liberality has to come from the people themselves in the form of taxation, which they will resent. It is better to have them think you miserly than to resent your depredations. The same is true with mercy, which can be mistaken for weakness and lead to actions that require greater cruelty in response. Making an example of the few is more merciful than allowing disorder that harms an entire community. Princes need to play the long game, and liberality and mercy can be vices rather than virtues in a leader when they lead to their opposites. As the physician of the body politic, a prince has to catch problems early, or the later cure will be much worse.[29]

A third lesson is that, while it is praiseworthy for a prince to keep his word and live with integrity, experience shows that those who succeed pay little heed to their promises. Thus, "a prudent prince cannot and should not keep his word when to do so would go against his interest, or when the reasons that made him pledge it no longer apply."[30] Such deceit is not difficult, because "a prince will never lack for legitimate excuses to explain away his breaches of faith."[31] In words that have plainly entered the playbook of all modern politicians, Machiavelli writes, "You must be a great liar and hypocrite. Men are so simple of mind, and so much dominated by their immediate needs, that a deceitful man will always find plenty who are ready to be deceived."[32]

The fourth, and perhaps most famous, lesson is that it is better to be feared than loved. "I don't doubt that every prince would like to be both," Machiavelli admits; but it is hard to cultivate both love and fear, and if you have to choose, it is much safer to be feared than to be loved.[33] "For it is a good general rule about men, that they are ungrateful, fickle, liars and deceivers, fearful of danger and greedy for gain."[34] If you serve their needs, they will profess their undying devotion. But whenever their self-interest is threatened or danger is at hand, they will forget their professed love and turn against you unless they fear you. Thus, fear is good but must stop short of hate. Fear will keep men in check; hatred will fester and, in the end, overcome fear, leading to rebellion.

Fifth, a prince should appear to have every good quality, even when he doesn't; or, rather, especially when he doesn't. "It is good to appear merciful, truthful, humane, sincere, and religious; it is good to be so in reality. But you must keep your mind so disposed that, in case of need, you can turn to the exact contrary."[35] It is impossible for anyone to possess all good qualities; human nature does not allow it. But it is particularly impossible for a prince. "To preserve the state, he often has to do things against his word, against charity, against humanity, against religion. . . . He should not depart from the good if he can hold to it, but he should be ready to enter on evil if he has to."[36] Nor should a prince be too worried if he succumbs to certain vices and indulgences, as long as they do not threaten his rule.[37] A prince need only be shrewd enough to avoid disgrace. Machiavelli clearly anticipates the modern political injunction: Sincerity is everything. If you can fake that, the rest is easy.

Sixth, a prince should focus his own and his people's attention on the art of war. If the people are united against external enemies, they will be less likely to raise any domestic disturbances. In addition, their pride in their city will translate into honor and even love for their prince. "A prince, therefore, should have no other object, no other thought, no other subject of study, than war."[38] Courage, discipline, and military leadership are not qualities a prince can dissemble; he must possess them in the highest degree. Machiavelli decries the infighting of Italian city-states; he calls for a fundamental restructuring of Italian military power, which relies too much on unreliable mercenaries and not enough on homegrown infantry. The result of such policies is that "Italy has been overrun by Charles, sacked by Louis, raped by Ferdinand, and disgraced by the Swiss."[39] An Italian state must be constructed from the bottom up, relying, as the Roman Republic did in its early years, on the pride and might of citizen soldiers and the *virtù* of remarkable military leaders.

The seventh lesson is the most important of all. A prince must be decisive. He cannot procrastinate. He cannot appear irresolute. He must act with the boldness of Cesare Borgia, for it is better to be rash than timid.[40]

"What makes the prince contemptible is being considered changeable, trifling, effeminate, cowardly, or indecisive."[41] *Fortuna* favors the bold. That is where the *virtù* of a ruler comes in, as "a kind of lucky shrewdness" in dealing with the turns of fortune.[42] An extraordinary individual, combining the character traits of the lion and the fox, can change history and achieve greatness as a leader.

In his famous letter to Francesco Vettori, to whom he entrusted *The Prince*, Machiavelli expressed his hope that "our present Medici lords will make use of me," and not leave him to become "despised through poverty."[43] They did not make use of him in any political capacity. Nor did they make use of the advice he proffered in *The Prince*. They did not "take the current when it serve[d]" and move to unite Italy. As a result, the voyage of their reign was "bound in shallows and in miseries" until it collapsed in 1527. Machiavelli himself, however, did take the tide at the flood. He was afloat on a full sea when he wrote *The Prince*. Combining the traits of the lion and the fox in his work, Machiavelli made himself the indispensable figure in all subsequent political thought. Future leaders and would-be leaders would study his work with care. Machiavelli, through his unique *virtù*, became one of those extraordinary individuals he so admired and in the process changed history.

BEYOND GOOD AND EVIL?

The question remains whether Machiavelli changed history for better or for worse. His ideal prince is cruel, deceitful, dissembling, and decisive to the point of rashness. He cultivates fear and dependency among his people and will wage foreign wars to distract from domestic troubles. Machiavelli pays lip service to admirable traits, admitting that it is good "in reality" to be merciful, truthful, humane, sincere, and religious. But the prince must be "be prepared to act immorally when this becomes necessary."[44] And it is the prince himself who makes this determination;

it is difficult not to assume that the prince will inevitably conclude that whatever perpetuates and enhances his own power and glory is also in the interests of the state and therefore necessary.[45] cf. Donald J. Trump

Having conjured such a monster, is Machiavelli himself, then, a monster of immorality, the cat's paw of tyrants? Or is he simply a realist, adopting his own injunction that a writer about principalities, like the prince himself, must be clear-eyed and without sentiment? Is Machiavelli merely describing political reality, however repulsive, or is he affirmatively prescribing a course of action?

Both and neither appears to be the answer. Politics in the sixteenth century, especially in Italy, was as ruthless and brutal as in any time in history. Machiavelli follows the Roman historians, Sallust and Tacitus, in describing both the ruthlessness and the brutality with uncanny accuracy. But Machiavelli is not a historian; he is a political thinker. He uses both historical and contemporary examples to make his points about politics. Yet he is not a political philosopher either. Despite his close study of their works, in the end he has little use for Plato's ideal state, or even the ideal ruler of Cicero and Seneca, whom they thought must be wise, just, honest, magnanimous, and driven by the desire to behave virtuously in all things. Machiavelli is a political pragmatist who accepts that a state cannot exist without the exercise of power and violence to maintain order and preserve itself against threats both internal and external.

Machiavelli draws on Aristotle and Lucretius in describing the growth of human society.[46] Man was never in a pure and innocent state of nature. In order to survive, humans gathered together in groups for mutual defense and protection. But men are by nature selfish, untrustworthy, and violent. Given the opportunity, they will prey upon one another. Men in a political society therefore had to be protected from one another as well as from outsiders. To govern these social groups, it was necessary to establish customs, which became rules, which became laws. Antisocial behavior was controlled only by the threat of collective violence.

In some respects, Machiavelli held a very Christian vision of fallen man, derived from Saint Augustine, who stressed that we are all born in a state of original sin from which only God's grace can rescue us. Christianity, however, preaches a turning away from worldly affairs to focus on the individual soul. The principal Christian virtues—faith, hope, and charity—are designed to purify that soul and make it receptive to God.

Augustine thought any city of man, even one once as powerful as the Roman Empire, was doomed to be torn apart by human strife and discord.[47] He preached instead about a city of God formed by those who shun worldly concerns and earthly pleasures and who dedicate themselves to the eternal truths of God as revealed in the Christian religion.

Machiavelli dismisses the city of God as pious nonsense, just as he dismissed Plato's *Republic* and would have dismissed More's *Utopia* had he ever read it.

> A great many men have imagined states and princedoms such as nobody ever saw or knew in the real world, and *there's such a difference between the way we really live and the way we ought to live that the man who neglects the real to study the ideal will learn how to accomplish his ruin, not his salvation.* Any man who tries to be good all the time is bound to come to ruin among the great number who are not good. Hence a prince who wants to keep his authority must learn how not to be good, and use that knowledge, or refrain from using it, as necessity requires.[48]

This is not to say, however, that Machiavelli disparages the Christian virtues. He acknowledges them, along with the pagan virtues touted by Cicero and Seneca, as "the way we ought to live." But, with the examples of the Borgia pope, Alexander VI, and his successor, Julius II, fresh in his mind, Machiavelli had a very different view of "the way we really live," even as professed Christians. Machiavelli was not interested in envisioning an ideal society. He was interested in making the society in which we actually live as secure and durable as possible.

Machiavelli was quite clear that if a man wants to embody Christian virtues, he should stay out of politics. He can join a monastery or become a desert anchorite. But he should not try to run a state or make himself responsible for the political well-being of his fellows. "For a man who desires to appear good in every respect must surely come to grief among so many who are evil."[49] Not only will he accomplish his own ruin, but the ruin of all those who depend on the state for their safety and security. Political society is inherently problematic but absolutely critical to human well-being and survival. Politics, like religion, has its own internal laws, which are often incompatible with those of Christianity. Sometimes force and violence are required. Sometimes morality must be transgressed. The effective leader cannot shrink from taking such steps. Nor can the effective thinker about politics ignore such realities. Machiavelli wants to deal with "things as they are in real truth, rather than as they are imagined."[50] Naive idealism is the worst flaw in a political thinker as well as in a prince.

Scholars frequently compare Machiavelli's views to those of Nietzsche, who also celebrated the great men of history and their willingness to transgress moral bounds. Nietzsche coined the phrase "beyond good and evil," for the moral and aesthetic space in which his *Übermensch* ("overman," commonly mistranslated as "superman") operated. And many scholars apply that same phrase to Machiavelli's exaltation of politics as "an end in itself—i.e., as something beyond the realm of good and evil."[51]

The comparison is misleading, however. Nietzsche had little concern with politics, although he vigorously condemned anti-Semitism and all forms of xenophobia (something the Nazis missed when they co-opted his "superman" rhetoric for the Aryan cause). Nietzsche's focus was on the great artists and thinkers, like Machiavelli himself, who broke with tradition to forge a new vision of human possibilities. Nietzsche was also highly critical of Christianity, which he thought cultivated a slave morality, and went so far as to call himself the Antichrist. In this regard, he is closer to Machiavelli.

Federico Chabod, an Italian historian turned politician, contends:

Nothing is further from Machiavelli's mind than to undermine common morality, replacing it with a new ethic; instead, he says that in public affairs the only thing that counts is the political criterion, by which he abides: let those who wish to remain faithful to the precepts of morality concern themselves with other things, not with politics.[52]

This, too, is misleading if by "common morality" Chabod means the Christian morality of Machiavelli's day. In fact, Machiavelli thought that Christian morality was pernicious because it made men soft and other-worldly and, therefore, poor citizens and soldiers. Machiavelli's point is that Christianity is very much like the "slave morality" later criticized by Nietzsche. Machiavelli wanted to promote a resurgence of civic virtue such as was seen in the early days of the Roman Republic. That is the prime focus of his later book, *Discourses on the First Ten Books of Titus Livius.* You cannot even be an effective citizen, he contended, much less an effective statesman, and follow Christian morality, especially not in times of crisis and turmoil. Machiavelli frankly preferred the pagan religion of ancient Rome, which promoted obedience and a love of *patria* without softening its adherents. Thus, Chabod is correct only if by "common morality" he means the ancient pagan virtues touted by Cicero and Seneca, which Machiavelli valued but was willing to sacrifice where necessary to preserve the state.

At the same time, it is not correct that *The Prince* is a how-to book for tyrants that teaches them the art of "fraud, deception, treachery, and felony," without interposing any moral point of view whatsoever.[53] Machiavelli does have a moral vision. He views the state as the essential superstructure within which human life can unfold and flourish. And he wants to maintain that superstructure even at the cost of violence and oppression because the alternative—chaos and decay—is so much worse. Machiavelli is, one might say, a pragmatic idealist. He clearly thinks a republic is preferable to a principality. But, given the inherent flaws in human nature, a well-governed principality is better than a decadent and poorly governed republic.[54] And best of all would be a strong, united Italy that could withstand the depredations of foreign powers and restore a proud sense of *patria* to its citizens. Machiavelli does not shrink from the fact (and he views it as a fact) that in order to build and maintain such a state, a ruler "often has to do things against his word, against charity, against humanity, against religion." As a matter of politics, that is the right way to act, despite its incompatibility with virtue, as narrowly understood. Indeed, we have the luxury of virtue only within the context of a secure state. There is no such thing as a perfect, ideal, static society. Conflict is inevitable, but the energy born of conflict can be directed in productive ways. This is the central point of Machiavelli's second great work, *The Discourses on Livy*.

THE DISCOURSES

Machiavelli follows Aristotle in viewing pure forms of government as inherently unstable.[55] Monarchy leads to tyranny because an absolute ruler will be unconstrained by law. Leading citizens will eventually conspire against the tyrant to preserve and protect their own positions. But aristocracy will in turn devolve into oligarchy because "the few always act in the interest of the few," and the many will eventually move to "curb the insolence of the nobles."[56] Yet democracy itself will descend to mob rule, as everyone clamors for benefits, and the people are swayed by rhetoric and false promises. A strong leader will eventually move to quell the chaos, and the cycle will repeat itself.

Machiavelli follows the historian Polybius in believing that the Roman Republic for a time transcended this cycle by incorporating elements of all three forms of government.[57] Rome was ruled first by a series of kings, starting with Romulus, who were eventually replaced by two consuls serving as chief executives. The Senate was created to serve the interests of the aristocracy. And Tribunes of the People were finally added, as citizens agitated for more say in their own affairs and as a buffer against the nobles.

The Roman Republic was not Machiavelli's answer to Augustine's *City of God*. Indeed, Machiavelli accepts Augustine's premise that no ideal state is possible that stands apart from history and is impervious to the cycles of growth and decay. But, with no perfect solution, we must look to where the greatest possibilities and fewest drawbacks lie, "because an option that is completely clear and completely without uncertainty cannot ever be found."[58] The Roman Republic lasted for almost five hundred years before it succumbed to the dictatorship of Augustus and his successors. The wonder is not that it was eventually overthrown but that it thrived for so long in the face of forces both internal and external that would have destroyed it.

What Machiavelli depicts in *The Discourses* are the features of Roman history and institutions that made such success possible. The Roman Republic, however idealized by Livy and other historians, was an actual, functioning state, subject to class tensions and external challenges, and yet it persevered through well-structured institutions and sound leadership. Machiavelli wants to understand that state, not as myth, but as it actually was so that he can draw valuable lessons from it.

> I shall boldly proclaim in an open way what I understand of ancient times and of our own, so that the minds of the young men who will read these writings of mine can avoid the errors of the present and be prepared to imitate the past whenever fortune provides them with the proper occasion.[59]

Machiavelli studies the Roman Republic, not the Roman Empire, because he believes that "governments by peoples are better than governments by princes."[60] That is true for at least four reasons. First, freedom is inherently better than tyranny and will inspire the people to become better citizens through their participation in government. Second, no government can long function without the obedience or even consent of the people. Third, in the right circumstances, "a people is more prudent, more stable, and of better judgement than a prince."[61] Fourth, and perhaps most important, a single ruler is likely to be a prisoner of his own character. Republics can change and adapt more easily to shifting circumstances than princes.

Machiavelli is engaged in an idealistic enterprise, the articulation of an enduring republican form of government. But his basic premise is starkly realistic: "It is necessary for anyone who organizes a republic and establishes laws in it to take for granted that all men are evil and that they will always act according to the wickedness of their nature whenever they have the opportunity."[62] Human nature is inherently selfish; "men are driven by two principal impulses, either by love or by fear."[63] Those passions, and their consequent aggression, must be shaped and controlled in order to make men and women into good citizens. Laws and the threat of punishment are the principal way to do that. The success of a people, like that of a prince, accordingly depends on bending one's nature to and having "respect for the laws under which one or the other lives."[64]

Laws foster discipline, but the discipline must not be so rigid as to eliminate a critical measure of freedom. A republic should fashion laws and create institutions and a governing structure in which the many are invested because it gives them opportunities to better their condition. Conflicts among classes cannot be eliminated, but they can be channeled in productive ways; "there is nothing that makes a republic so stable and steady as organizing it in such a way that the variability of those humors that agitate the republic has a means of release that is instituted by the laws."[65] Nobles and plebeians are inherently at odds with one another. The goal of the laws and institutions of a republic is to enable that tension to find productive outlets, for "those who condemn the disturbances between the nobles and the plebeians condemn those very things that were the primary cause of Roman liberty, and . . . give more consideration to the noises and cries arising from such disturbances than to the good effects they produced."[66] The tribunes, who were born of that tension, were "the guardians of Roman liberty."[67] In short, democracy is messy, and that very messiness is critical to the preservation of liberty over the long term because it provides a constructive release for energies that would otherwise tear the republic apart.

Religion also plays an important role "in controlling the armies, in giving courage to the plebeians, in keeping men good, and in shaming the wicked."[68] Religion adds the sanction of divine law to that of public law. Machiavelli calls religion "absolutely necessary for maintaining a civilized society,"[69] and concludes that "there can be no greater indication of the ruin of a state than to see a disregard for its divine worship."[70] But make no mistake. Machiavelli is talking not about Christianity. He is talking about the pagan religion of ancient Rome with its many gods and public rituals. For Machiavelli, religion should be judged by its ability to make men and women into good citizens. It should inspire them to deeds of heroism and civic virtue; it should shame cowardice and the placing of self before country.

Christianity, however, does exactly the opposite:

> Our religion has defined the supreme good as humility, abjection, and contempt of worldly things; ancient religion located it in greatness of mind, strength of body, and in all the other things apt to make men the strongest. And if our religion requires that you have inner strength, it wants you to have the capacity to endure suffering more than to undertake brave deeds. This way of living seems, therefore, to have made the world weak and to have given it over to be plundered by wicked men, who are easily able to dominate it, since in order to go to paradise most men think more about enduring their pains than about avenging them.[71]

Machiavelli is at his cynical best (or worst, if you prefer) in touting ancient religion as the bulwark of the state. There is no evidence that he believed in the pantheon of Roman gods. Instead, he believed in the efficacy of belief itself, what Plato called a "noble lie" built into the structure of the society, and essential to its stability.[72]

It is impossible to know what, if any, religion Machiavelli professed in his heart. What is clear is that he thought religion should not be a refuge from worldly struggle but a call to arms for civic virtue and the preservation of the republic. Marx would dismiss religion as the "opium of the people," intended to make them docile. Nietzsche would dismiss Christianity as a "slave morality," an excuse for weakness, born of a desire to suppress exceptional ability and to portray the exercise of strength as a species of evil. Machiavelli combines both ideas in his critique. "Although it appears that the world has become soft and heaven has been disarmed," Machiavelli concludes, "without a doubt this arises more from the cowardice of men who have interpreted our religion according to an ideal of freedom from earthly toil and not according to one of exceptional ability."[73]

Along with the rule of law and a civic-minded religion, Machiavelli believed that individuals of exceptional ability were critical to the formation and success of the Roman Republic. Machiavelli deeply admired men such as Lucius Junius Brutus, who helped to drive the Tarquins from Rome in 509 BCE and to establish the republic.[74] Similar roles were played by Lycurgus in Sparta and by Solon in Athens.[75] These lawgivers helped to organize and give coherence to the founding of a republic. They provided leadership and guidance at critical junctures. And then they let the system they established work as intended for the benefit of the people, not of the founder and his heirs. As Machiavelli explains, "the salvation of a republic or a kingdom is not . . . merely to have a prince who governs prudently while he lives, but rather one who organizes the government in such a way that after his death it can be maintained."[76]

It is a fine line. A powerful leader is needed to establish a republic, or to serve it in difficult times, but that very power may prove intoxicating and corrupting. Some leaders cannot bear to cede control. Instead, they "turn to tyranny, failing to realize how much fame, how much glory, how much honor, security, tranquility, and peace of mind they are losing through this choice, and how much infamy, disgrace, blame, danger, and anxiety they incur."[77] Others, like Cincinnatus—who, after being appointed dictator to deal with a specific threat, returned to his plow—provide a shining model for all future leaders. The Roman Republic, Machiavelli constantly reminds us, was blessed with an abundance of such leaders, until it wasn't, and the struggles for power of Marius and Sulla, of Caesar and Pompey, and, finally, of Marc Antony and Octavian destroyed the republic.[78]

Machiavelli laments "how easily men may be corrupted."[79] Once Rome obtained security against external enemies, it began an internal decline. The institutions of government fell into disrespect, and those with ability exalted power over *patria*. When men are not constrained by fear, their self-love makes them discontented and "so restless that once the smallest door is open to their ambition," they will barter their current lot for an uncertain future.[80]

To fight this inevitable decline, a republic must constantly renew its institutions and return to its beginnings, striving to "retain as much of the ancient ways as possible."[81] The same is true, Machiavelli notes, of religion. The church became corrupt through too much secular power, and it took remarkable individuals like Saint Francis and Saint Dominic to revitalize the Christian religion.[82] Secular governments "also need to renew themselves and to bring their laws back to their beginnings."[83] Patriotic fervor, like religious fervor, must be renewed in each generation. But, for that to happen, strong and decisive leaders are required, even in a republic, for the common people will not display *virtù* unless both compelled and inspired to do so.

Machiavelli has thus come full circle. Whether called a prince or a *gonfaloniere*, a strong leader is necessary. As with a principality, "the worst defect weak republics can have is to be indecisive."[84] Machiavelli believed all his life that the slaughter at Prato and the fall of the republic could have been avoided by a more pragmatic and decisive leader.[85] "Piero Soderini ... proceeded in all his affairs with humanity and patience."[86] That worked well for a time. But, when bold action was required, "he did not know how to do so, so that, along with his native city, he came to ruin."[87]

In defense of the state, no half measures are permitted. A leader must do whatever is necessary. A good man will prefer to live as a private citizen rather than to obtain or maintain power through evil means, even where his goal might be a good one. But rarely will an evil man wish to govern well.[88] What is needed is that rarest of things, a good leader willing to be "honorably bad" when the occasion requires.[89] Machiavelli gives us the following example of failure: Pope Julius II sought to oust Giovampagolo Baglioni, the ruler of Perugia. His purpose was known to all, but Julius, who always acted "with impetuosity and fury,"[90] came in advance of his own army and entered the city with only a small bodyguard. He was at the mercy of Giovampagolo and could have been killed with impunity. Yet Giovampagolo meekly allowed himself to be led away, when he could instead have "shown these priests how little there is to value in those who live and rule as they do, and he would have performed a deed the greatness of which would have surpassed all the infamy and all the danger that could possibly have come from it."[91]

In the end, Machiavelli's advice in *The Discourses* differs little from that of *The Prince*. The context is different, but the principles of leadership are the same. Fraud, deception, and even murder are necessary and acceptable means of preserving the state. Romulus killed his own brother, but "while the act accuses him, the result excuses him, and when the result is good, like that of Romulus [who founded the Roman state], it will always excuse him, because one should reproach a man who is violent in order to ruin things, not one who is so in order to set them aright."[92] In other words, the right ends successfully pursued may justify otherwise wrongful acts.

Yet everything depends on the circumstances. There is no fixed rule to govern conduct. Sometimes more can be accomplished "by a single humane act full of charity than an act which is ferocious and violent."[93] Other times, as in putting down a conspiracy, cruelty is necessary. When rulers shrink from such violence and "someone remains alive because of their lack of prudence or negligence, then they do not deserve to be excused."[94]

Machiavelli's most consistent counsel, however, remained the same throughout his life: "Above all one must avoid a middle course of action."[95] Act boldly and seize fortune by the throat, for "when she wants to accomplish great deeds, she selects a man with such spirit and such exceptional ability that he recognizes those occasions that she offers him."[96] Machiavelli was a man with such spirit and such exceptional ability.

It is not surprising that the church placed all of Machiavelli's works on the *Index Librorum Prohibitorum* (Index of Forbidden Books) in 1557. Machiavelli himself noted that all the great leaders of the past, including those he most admired, would be in the Christian hell. So much the worse for Christianity, he thought. Machiavelli made it clear that he would rather go to hell with the ancient statesmen to talk about politics than to the Christian heaven with the blessed and saintly.[97]

Chapter 4

THOMAS MORE:
THE KING'S GOOD SERVANT
BUT GOD'S FIRST

Thomas More famously declared himself "the King's good servant but God's first."[1] Machiavelli would have scoffed at the juxtaposition. Any man who tries to be good all the time, he wrote, "must surely come to grief among so many who are evil."[2] More did indeed come to grief. He spoke his words on Tower Hill, on July 6, 1535, as he prepared to place his head on the chopping block for refusing to recognize Henry VIII's marriage to Anne Boleyn and his new title as supreme head of the Church of England.

Perhaps More should have followed Machiavelli's advice: if you want to serve God, join a monastery and stay as far from court life as possible. But, although he seriously considered entering a Carthusian monastery or leading the life of a humanist scholar like his friend Desiderius Erasmus, in the end More's sense of duty and filial obligation led him into public life. He was determined, in Augustine's words, to be of "service to the earthly city" as well as to the city of God.[3]

It is ironic, therefore, that More is considered by many a woolly-headed dreamer because his most famous work, *Utopia*, depicts a socialist society in which money is abolished and all property is held in common. In fact, More was highly pragmatic and skeptical of radical reforms, both in his life and in his writing. He had no illusions about the earthly city, yet he was willing to devote himself to its service. Undoubtedly, More took pride in his steadily rising stature. Erasmus says otherwise, but pretending to view political advancement as a burden rather than a much-sought-after reward has long been a commonplace. Regardless, More's ambition was leavened with principle, which is anything but commonplace.

In 2000, More was proclaimed the patron saint of statesmen and politicians by Pope John Paul II. It was a fitting choice of titles for one who believed that, despite the fallen state of man, improvements could be made in society and that every citizen had an obligation to act as a force for good. The city of God would never be realized on earth, but the earthly city could still be improved within the limits of human nature. As an advisor to princes, he wrote in *Utopia*, "what you cannot turn to good, you may at least make as little bad as possible."[4] Again, Machiavelli would have scoffed, as does Raphael Hythloday, More's principal interlocutor in *Utopia*. And More did fail as a counselor. In an act of incredible willfulness, Henry took England out of the Catholic Church and established himself as head of the new Church of England, all to enable him to remarry and, he hoped, father a male heir. More, realizing he could not prevent those actions or even make them "as little bad as possible," took a stand that cost him his life. Yet More himself was hardly a failure. He was England's greatest humanist; he reached the pinnacle of earthly power as lord chancellor; and he died a Catholic martyr and saint. For More, all three roles were of a piece. He was indeed a man for all seasons.

LIFE

Thomas More was born in London on February 7, 1478.[5] He came from a family that was, as he himself put it, *non celebri sed honesta* (not distinguished but respectable).[6] His paternal and maternal grandfathers were, respectively, a baker and a tallow chandler (a maker of candles out of the hard fat of cattle and sheep). They were substantial merchants and members of their respective guilds, part of a burgeoning middle class accumulating wealth, property, and prestige.

Thomas's father, John More, made the transition from the merchant class into law. It was not a large jump, and he mostly represented guilds and commercial enterprises as a private lawyer. But John More rose steadily, if slowly, within the bar and eventually became a judge, first of the Court of Common Pleas at the age of sixty-six and then of the King's Bench at seventy-two. In public, he was formidable and severe but well respected among his peers. His son, who revered him, found him "an affable man, charming, irreproachable, gentle, sympathetic, honest, and upright."[7] Even after Thomas became lord chancellor of England, upon entering Westminster Hall on the way to his place in the Chancery, he would stop at the King's Bench and there kneel to ask his father's blessing.[8]

Thomas was the second of six children and manifested his talents at a young age. He attended St. Anthony's School, a short walk from the family home. Lessons began at six in the morning, and More learned to read, write, and converse in Latin as readily as in English.

At the age of twelve, More became a page to John Morton, the archbishop of Canterbury and lord chancellor of England. Morton was second only to the king in power and influence. His other pages were sons of the nobility. More's selection was a high honor, undoubtedly reflecting the growing influence and connections of his father. More continued his education in the archbishop's house with the other pages, and they performed light household duties such as waiting at table.

At the age of fourteen, More went to Oxford on a scholarship provided by Archbishop Morton. He remained for two years at Canterbury College, a predecessor to Christ Church. The medieval trivium of grammar, rhetoric, and logic was still required, along with attendance at daily mass, a habit More would retain for his entire life. The students were bound to speak with one another and with their professors in Latin. But More also studied history and moral philosophy and even began to learn Greek. It was ideal training for a lawyer as well as a humanist, and More aspired to be both.

More left Oxford in 1494, before receiving a degree, to begin his legal studies in London at New Inn, one of several associations responsible for legal education. He was then sixteen. After two years, he was accepted at the more prestigious Lincoln's Inn, where his father was governor. Despite this well-paved career path in law, More was pulled in two other directions. While at Lincoln's Inn, he forged a multiyear connection with a Carthusian charterhouse, though whether he lived there or was simply in daily attendance is unclear. More was deeply, if not morbidly, religious. From a young age to the time of his death, he wore a hair shirt that chafed and irritated his skin, and he engaged in other forms of self-mortification and penance. His religious writings—which include personal meditations, doctrinal explications, and attacks on heresy—number more than a million words. He seriously contemplated becoming a monk.

Yet More also was drawn to the "new learning" of Erasmus and other like-minded thinkers tracing back to Petrarch. Like them, More had no patience for medieval scholastic philosophy, which he found arid and artificial. He rejoiced in the rediscovery of a broader range of Greek classics, particularly the works of Plato and the second-century satirist Lucian of Samosata, along with the more standard Latin fare of Cicero, Seneca, and the Roman historians. More joined a circle of humanist scholars and continued his study of Greek in their company. He formed a close friendship with Erasmus, who first visited England in 1499.

Erasmus wrote a detailed description of the appearance and character of More, which is worth reading in full.[9] In an earlier letter, Erasmus had already remarked on the quality of More's mind:

> I do not think, unless the vehemence of my love leads me astray, that Nature ever formed a mind more present, ready, sharpsighted and subtle, or in a word more absolutely furnished with every kind of faculty than his. Add to this a power of expression equal to his intellect, a singular cheerfulness of character and an abundance of wit, but only of the candid sort; and you miss nothing that should be found in a perfect advocate.[10]

On Erasmus's initial trip to London, More took him on a casual visit to meet the royal children, including the eight-year-old Prince Henry, the future King Henry VIII. Together, More and Erasmus translated and published a selection of the works of Lucian. Erasmus wrote *Praise of Folly* at More's house outside London, dedicated the work to him, and even titled it with a pun on More's Latin name: *Morus* (fool). More, in turn, sent the manuscript of his *Utopia* to Erasmus, who edited the work, gave it a new, now immortal, title,[11] and saw it through the press. It was More who urged Erasmus to attack Luther on the subject of grace and free will, while More was penning his own polemics against the Protestant heresy. And, when he resigned his position as lord chancellor in 1533, it was Erasmus to whom More wrote explaining his reasons. Erasmus called More "the friend I love best" and explained that "no one is more open-hearted in making friends or more tenacious in keeping them."[12] The lives of the two greatest figures of the Northern Renaissance were thus deeply, inextricably intertwined.

More did not follow a career as a humanist man of letters as others in his circle did. His father did not support, and may have actively opposed, Thomas's study of *bonae litterae*. Yet More still wrote four important humanistic works. In addition to *Utopia* and the translation of Lucian that he did with Erasmus, More translated from Latin into English a biography of the Neoplatonist and Christian spiritualist Pico della Mirandola. He also wrote, in both English and Latin versions, *The History of King Richard the Third*, which heavily influenced Shakespeare's own drama of the hunchbacked tyrant some seventy-five years later. More's Richard, like Shakespeare's, is ruthless, manipulative, and murderous. When his older brother Edward dies, Richard quickly usurps the throne, imprisons Edward's two young sons in the Tower of London, and eventually orders their deaths. Yet, even so, Richard is a rounded, complex character, rather than a cardboard villain. More retains the capacity to be shocked by evil, even as he dissects its human origins. The many imagined but realistic speeches in the book provided ideal fodder for Shakespeare.

Though seldom read today, More's *History* was a key work of the English Renaissance.

More also defended the humanist agenda and his friend Erasmus in an important series of letters in 1515, the year he wrote *Utopia*. Unfortunately, consumed by religious and political controversies, More produced nothing in the humanist vein after 1520. In the end, More attained greater fame as a Christian martyr than as a secular man of letters. Yet More never did become a monk. He continued his association with the charterhouse for four years. He also gave a series of lectures in 1501 on Saint Augustine's *City of God* at St. Lawrence Jewry. And throughout his life, he sometimes thought wistfully of the small cell and ample time for prayer and contemplation he had forsaken. Erasmus said that More's sexual drive was simply too strong for a celibate life. Undoubtedly, Erasmus also told More of his own bitter experience confined to a monastery. In any event, John More expected his son to be a lawyer, and Thomas, ever dutiful, obliged.

For More, however, becoming a lawyer was not solely an act of filial piety. He had a passion for the law and relished his participation in public life. He viewed the common law of England, which had evolved over time as a result of the decisions of generations of judges, as the embodiment of collective human wisdom and a faint reflection of the mind of God.[13] Civil law aspired to natural law. Individual practitioners and judges might make mistakes, but "the law" was the perfection to which all should aspire. It is a vision that inspired lawyers and judges for centuries, until the legal realist Oliver Wendell Holmes Jr. dismissed it with the words "the common law is not a brooding omnipresence."[14] Yet for More it was precisely that: something dimly perceived but anxiously sought. More was a skilled advocate and orator. He relished the public display and the trappings of the law, which he considered vitally important to the stability of the state. As one modern biographer puts it, More "embodied the old order of hierarchy and authority at the very moment when it began to collapse all around him."[15]

More moved out of his father's home after the death of his mother in

1499 and his father's remarriage that same year. That was the same year Erasmus first visited London and the two began their long friendship. In 1505, when he was twenty-six, More married Jane Colt, the daughter of a wealthy, well-connected landowner. She was sixteen, and the couple had four children in as many years (three girls and a boy). More provided each of them a classical education, but Margaret, the oldest, was his clear favorite. She was widely acknowledged as brilliant and "undoubtedly the most learned woman of her day, at least in England."[16]

Jane died in 1511, possibly in childbirth, a common occurrence in that era. More married again a month later, seeking a mother for his children, a wife for his bed, and order for his household. His new wife, Alice Middleton, was a well-off widow. She was forty-one and therefore eight years older than her new husband. She was also very different in personality from the reserved and malleable young Jane. Dame Alice, as she was commonly called, was outspoken and at times volatile. But they seem to have been deeply attached to each other. As Erasmus wryly explained, they "lived on as close and affectionate terms as if she had been a girl of the most winning appearance."[17] She was also a devoted stepmother, and their extended household was lively and active, filled with an assortment of cousins and hangers-on as well as a menagerie of unusual pets, including a monkey, a fox, a weasel, and a ferret. Margaret married More's future biographer, William Roper, in 1521, and they both continued to live in the More household for another sixteen years.

Henry VIII had ascended the throne in April 1509, when he was but seventeen. England generally, and More in particular, had great hopes for the new king, who valued humanist learning and appeared to be a dutiful defender of the Catholic Church. More departed from his father's strictly legal path of advancement and joined the king's service. According to Erasmus, "no man was ever more consumed with ambition to enter a court than he was to avoid it."[18] But that seems unlikely. More's Carthusian belief in the emptiness of worldly affairs did not hinder his playing an active role in them. He was eager to be of service. More filled progressively more important roles in the Star Chamber and the Privy Council, as diplomat, royal secretary and confidante, as a knight of the realm, Speaker of Parliament, and, finally, lord chancellor of England.

More's hopes in Henry VIII were disappointed, however, in two main respects. First, like many English kings, Henry coveted the throne of France. He joined Pope Julius II's Holy League against France, discussed in the previous chapter, which led to the fall of the Florentine Republic, the renewed ascendancy of the Medicis, and the enforced leisure of Machiavelli. But Henry wanted to conquer France itself and imitate Henry V's military glory at Agincourt. He fell far short of his ambitions, succeeding only in depleting the treasury and imposing heavy taxes on the nobility. More was instrumental in calming the waters, and he negotiated compromises with the English nobility as well as a series of treaties with the Holy Roman emperor, Charles V, and the king of France.

The second source of dashed hopes proved far more consequential. This was the king's "great matter"[19]—his desire to set aside his marriage to Catherine of Aragon and to marry Anne Boleyn, which led Henry to break with the Catholic Church and to declare himself head of a separate Church of England.

UTOPIA

We tend to approach Thomas More's *Utopia* from the wrong end of history. We have seen the dark side of socialist and communist regimes in the twentieth century, and we project that failure onto More's great work, as if he were preaching a workers' paradise that we know is more likely to become a totalitarian nightmare. The very word *utopia* has in our language come to mean both a dreamy impossibility and a cautionary tale. Its use is laden with satire. Utopia and dystopia have become virtual synonyms.

But More's humanist exploration of the possibilities of social reform and the arguments for personal engagement in politics cannot be so smugly dismissed. More merges the fanciful and the serious in a nuanced contribution to a still-ongoing debate. Machiavelli's own contribution to that debate unfortunately was unknown to More, and vice versa. But a careful, juxtaposed reading of their respective works is a useful antidote to extreme interpretations; Machiavelli is not as cynically brutal nor More as naively idealistic as either is generally portrayed.

In *Utopia*, More adopts the dialogue form, both as a tribute to Plato and Cicero, his principal models, and as a means of dramatically exploring the very different traditions they represent. Plato's *Republic* sketches an ideal state of the philosopher's imagining. His goal is to change human nature through a radical reordering of society. Cicero's *Republic*, on the other hand, presents a grounded if idealized portrait of the Roman state as it actually existed.[20] Cicero follows the Aristotelean tradition of political thought based not on theoretical preconditions but on a close consideration of what is possible in light of human nature and existing circumstances.[21]

The two speakers in More's dialogue represent these two traditions. Raphael Hythloday (a name that, in its Latin form, means "expert in nonsense") is a seasoned traveler and uncompromising radical, who describes what he considers to be the perfect commonwealth but disdains all practical politics. More, the other speaker (not, of course, to be fully identified with More the author), is both pragmatic and skeptical of his impassioned guest but willing to engage in support of sensible reforms.

More wrote the book in reverse order. Part 2 is Hythloday's famous description of the island nation of Utopia (a pun from the Greek *ou-topos*, meaning "no place," and *eu-topos*, meaning "good place"). More composed this part first and then realized, correctly, that it was too free-floating and fantastical as a stand-alone dialogue. He then added part 1, which deals with the case for reforms in the England of his day. The interplay between the two parts, and the development of the characters in each, gives depth to the whole. The gap between the world of today and the "no place" of Hythloday's Utopia is so great as to raise fundamental questions. Are there incremental reforms that would improve the human condition short of a radical remaking of society? If so, is engagement in politics a worthwhile endeavor for a humanist thinker? Is Utopia the ideal toward which our reforms should be directed? Is Utopia even desirable in light of human nature? Part 1 deals with the first two questions; part 2 with the last two.

More and Hythloday meet largely by chance in Belgium while More is there on a diplomatic mission. More is introduced by his friend and future publisher, Peter Giles. "The stranger had a sunburned face, a long beard, and a cloak hanging loosely from his shoulders," More reports; "from his appearance and dress, I took him to be a ship's captain."[22] And, indeed, Giles reports that Hythloday was a regular companion of the legendary explorer Amerigo Vespucci. C. S. Lewis aptly compares Hythloday to the "grey-beard loon" of Coleridge's "Rime of the Ancient Mariner," who will fix the wedding guest with his "glittering eye" while he tells a story of lost innocence and bitter regret.[23] Hythloday has something of the charismatic, intransigent passion of an Old Testament prophet.

Giles promises More that Hythloday will tell him of unknown lands and peoples and their varied customs. But, in fact, they begin by discussing contemporary England, where Hythloday had spent several months in the house of More's former patron, Cardinal Morton. Giles suggests that Hythloday, with all his knowledge and experience, would be an ideal courtier, able both to entertain and advise a prince. Hythloday scoffs at the suggestion, insisting that he is temperamentally unsuited to such a position. He equates service and servitude. "As it is now," he insists, "I live as I please."[24] Moreover, he notes, any advice he offered would be quickly rejected.

As an example, Hythloday cites a discussion one evening at the cardinal's table, where one of the guests began praising the practice of hanging thieves. Hythloday strongly objects, noting that the penalty is too harsh and yet ineffective as a deterrent, since a starving man will not refrain from robbery regardless of the penalty. Moreover, if a thief is punished the same as a murderer, then "the thief will be encouraged to kill the victim whom otherwise he would only have robbed."[25] No possession or worldly fortune, he contends, can equal the value of a human life. Restitution and hard labor are ample penalties for a mere property crime. More important, society should focus on enabling each man to earn a proper living rather than pressing him to "the awful necessity of stealing and then dying for it."[26] By alleviating the causes of poverty, Hythloday insists, we will alleviate the causes of crime. This thought leads Hythloday into an attack on "enclosure," a much debated practice of the day in which once-common land dedicated to agriculture is fenced off to raise sheep and other livestock. Enclosure laws allow the rich to get richer—selling wool in foreign markets and fattening cows and pigs to sell at inflated prices—while the poor are forced off the land that once gave them a livelihood, however meager. If they steal to survive, they are hanged. If they wander the countryside, they are jailed as vagrants. The greed of the few causes the misery of the many. "Let agriculture be restored," Hythloday urges, "so there will be useful work for the whole crowd of those now idle."[27]

Hythloday notes that his diatribe against enclosure, poverty, and harsh punishments was met with hostility by the cardinal's other guests. "From this episode," he concludes, "you can see how little courtiers would value me or my advice."[28] Yet, in fact, even from Hythloday's own account, it is clear that the cardinal takes his views seriously, asks thoughtful and probing questions, and insists on hearing out Hythloday despite the outcry of others. More, accordingly, presses him on the issue of engagement, contending that it is the chief duty of a good man to provide sound advice to those in power.

"If I proposed wise laws to some king, and tried to root out of his soul the seeds of evil and corruption," Hythloday responds, "don't you suppose I would be either banished forthwith, or treated with scorn?"[29] His advice would run directly counter to what the courtiers tell the king and what the king wants to hear. They urge the king to wage foreign wars funded with ruinous taxation. They urge him to manipulate the value of currency depending on whether he is paying debts or collecting revenues. They urge him to store up gold and keep his people in poverty and dependence. Hythloday would advise the opposite of all these things. A king should let other kingdoms alone and cultivate his own for the good of his people, not himself. No king would listen to such advice, Hythloday insists: "There is no place for philosophy in the councils of kings."[30]

More responds that philosophy does have a place when it "adapts itself to the drama in hand, and acts its part neatly and appropriately."[31] A wise counselor can influence policy indirectly, through tact and skill, and "what you cannot turn to good, you may at least make as little bad as possible."[32] Just because you cannot accomplish all you would like, More insists, doesn't mean you should forgo the chance to make incremental improvements. Otherwise, idealism negates responsibility; the best becomes the enemy of the good. But Hythloday is intransigent. In a council you will lose your soul. You must go along with even the worst decisions and most vicious policies or forfeit your position. You will either become as evil as they are or "be made a screen for the knavery and folly of others."[33] The wise man should steer clear of politics altogether, preserving both his freedom and his philosophical purity.

The debate on the compromises of civic engagement is relevant to our own time as well as in the context of More's life. Within a year of finishing the book, More decided to enter the service of King Henry VIII, where he began his steady rise to the position of lord chancellor and his steady path to Tower Hill. More clearly understood how difficult it might be to keep both his soul and his head. But he was determined to enter the king's service and to make what he could not turn to good as little bad as possible.

Yet More sympathized not only with Hythloday's reluctance to serve as a courtier but also with the particular reforms and the advice he would give to the king. Indeed, by putting such advice in the mouth of Hythloday (the "expert in nonsense"), More allowed himself more freedom than he might otherwise be permitted to criticize contemporary policies dear to his king and future master.

Conversely, although Hythloday criticizes certain laws and customs, he is ultimately no more interested in progressive reforms than he is in servitude to the crown. As long as private property exists, Hythloday contends, even the most enlightened new laws are just "poultices" applied to a body beyond cure.[34] Wherever money is the measure of all things, rapacity, wickedness, and oppression will inevitably follow. The few will enjoy wealth, status, and power, while the many struggle simply to survive. Society will only be restored to good health when, as Plato urged, men live on terms of equality and all property is held in common.

More, the pragmatist, scoffs at this proposal. People cannot possibly live well, he contends, where all things are in common. Men will lose the impetus to work, relying on others to produce. And if the productive few "cannot legally protect what they have gained, what can follow but continual bloodshed and turmoil," especially if there is no respect for authority or for law?[35] Sounding like an early Adam Smith, More expanded on these views while in prison almost twenty years after finishing *Utopia*:

> People cannot ... live here in this world unless some individuals provide for many others a means of making a living. Not everyone can have a ship of his own; nor can everyone be a merchant without a stock. Not everyone can have his own plough. But such things, as you well know, must be had by somebody. ... A man with only two ducats to his name would most likely be better off if he gave them both away and left himself not a penny, if he lost absolutely everything he had, than if the rich man who puts him to work every week were to lose half of his money; for then the poor man would probably be out of work. The substance of the rich is, indeed, the wellspring of the livelihood of the poor.[36]

Yet, Hythloday insists, there is a place where everything is shared equally and yet everyone lives in plenty and in happiness. He has been there; he has seen it work.

THE ISLAND NATION

Part 2 of *Utopia* contains no abstract discussion or philosophical debate. It is a travelogue that purports to describe the people and customs of an actual island nation, which just happens to be "no place." As such, it owes as much to Lucian's *True History*—his deadpan trip to the Isle of the Blessed in which he promises the reader "many notorious lies delivered persuasively and in the way of truth,"[37]—as to anything in Plato's *Republic* or Augustine's *City of God*. Yet the inspiration is both Platonic and Christian: a community of men and women bound together by shared beliefs, shared values, and shared goods. And the description of this community is highly concrete; we get a vivid sense of the inhabitants' daily lives. The island nation of Utopia thus raises the two questions mentioned earlier, questions we must confront on a personal and emotional as well as an intellectual level: Could it actually work? Would we even want to live there?

Utopia is about the size of England, separated from the continent (we are not told which continent) by a narrow channel. It has fifty-four cities with plenty of countryside around each. The cities are identical to one another, accounting only for differences in geography. Each shares the same customs, institutions, and laws. The streets are wide and clean, the houses spacious and built on an identical plan, with large gardens behind them. There are neither slums nor mansions, neither abject poverty nor ostentatious wealth. Indeed, there is no money whatsoever. The houses are randomly assigned to extended families, and every ten years they are reassigned so that no one develops a sense of ownership. No rent is paid, and while meals can be taken at home, everyone but the sick and infirm dine in a common mess where the food is plentiful and fresh. Everyone also wears the same style of clothing, except for differences between sexes and to mark those who are married and unmarried. Each household makes its own clothes. Other goods are held in a common storeroom from which the head of each household may draw according to its needs without payment or accounting.

If any household group becomes too large, some of its members are transferred to another which has grown too small. If one city has too many people, individuals will be moved to make up shortfalls in other cities. When the population of the entire island grows too large, citizens chosen from every city are sent to the mainland to establish a colony. Any natives must join the colony and live as Utopians, or they will be driven out.

The food comes from surrounding farms, where rotating groups spend two-year stints working the land before returning to their cities. That way, no one has to do such hard work for long, though those who love farm life are allowed to stay longer. The Utopians use slaves for all the dirtiest and heaviest work. The slaves are either prisoners of war or former citizens guilty of a heinous offense. Slaves also do any butchering or hunting necessary so that the citizens do not lose their sense of compassion, a point whose irony is apparently lost on Hythloday.

In the cities, every man and woman must learn a trade, with the heavier tasks assigned to men. Boys usually learn their father's trade, but if they prefer another they can be transferred to and adopted by another family practicing that trade. Only six hours a day, however, are devoted to work. Given that no one lives off the work of others and that luxury goods are forbidden, six hours per day is more than enough to supply what the community needs. The rest of the day, aside from eating and sleeping, is generally given to learning, including daily public lectures. Education is highly valued among Utopians, and they consider a life of the mind to be true happiness. Those "who from childhood have given evidence of excellent character, unusual intelligence, and devotion to learning" may become scholars, exempted from manual labor.[38] Those not interested in learning may spend additional time at their trades. Idleness and dissipation are not tolerated.

The governance structure is simple and begins with a salutary principle: "Any man who campaigns for a public office is disqualified for all of them."[39] Each household is subject to its oldest member unless his mind has begun to fail, in which case the second oldest takes his place. Every year, each group of thirty households chooses an official called a sypho-grant. The chief job of the syphogrants is to ensure that none are idle and that everyone works hard at his trade. The syphogrants also elect the governor, who generally holds office for life. For every ten syphogrants there is a tranibor, who participates in a council that meets with the governor to advise on policy. The tranibors also handle any disputes between private parties, which are rare and quickly resolved. The laws in Utopia are simple and few; they need no lawyers to twist them under the guise of interpretation.

The Utopians trade their surplus to foreign countries and receive gold and other precious metals and gems in return. Those items serve no useful purpose within Utopia. Indeed, they show their contempt by using them as trinkets for children or to forge chains and fetters for slaves. But they are useful in the conduct of foreign relations. The Utopians detest war and engage in it only "to protect their own land, to protect their friends from an invading army, or to liberate an oppressed people from tyranny and servitude."[40] Once compelled to wage war, however, they seek to spare their own soldiers as much as possible. Indeed, only with reluctance will they kill even enemy soldiers, convinced that they go to war, not on their own accord, but at the whim of their prince. Accordingly, the Utopians will seek to assassinate any prince who causes an unjust war and, if that fails, will use their gold and silver to sow division and bribe other factions to seize the crown. Failing that, they will hire mercenaries before risking their own citizens. They do not value martial glory.

The Utopians tolerate a variety of religions, considering it "arrogant folly for anyone to enforce conformity with his own beliefs on everyone else by means of threats or violence,"[41] another deeply ironic remark considering More's later career. Their core religious beliefs are pre-Christian, drawn from the pagan philosophy of Plato, Epicurus, and the Stoics. They believe, first, that the universe is ruled by divine providence rather than by chance and, second, that the soul of each man, woman, and child is immortal and will live on after death in a realm where the virtuous are rewarded and the evil are punished. Anyone who rejects those two core principles may do so privately, but must not preach to or corrupt others on pain of death.

There are few priests, but they include women as well as men; celibacy is not required though often practiced. The priests teach the young and preside over divine worship. But churches and services are nonsectarian, with no images of the divine, no tendentious doctrines beyond the two core principles noted above, and no animal sacrifice, which they consider barbaric. "They think that the contemplation of nature, and the sense of reverence arising from it, are acts of worship to God."[42] They value natural beauty and the pleasures of the senses, especially music, but find their greatest happiness in a state of bodily and mental health and harmony. They believe it is best to "lead a life as free of anxiety and as full of joy as possible, and to help all one's fellow men toward that end."[43] Euthanasia is encouraged and facilitated for those with an incurable and painful disease. But suicides, who throw away the great gift of life, are themselves thrown into a bog to lie unburied and disgraced.

The Utopians firmly reject austerities of the sort practiced by More and various European religious orders. Yet Hythloday found them highly receptive to Christianity, particularly since Christ advocated a communal form of life for his disciples similar to their own. The Utopian way of life, Hythloday stresses, is closer to the ideals of Christianity than any existing European society. There are no pubs or brothels. The farms produce wine and cider but not beer. Gambling is forbidden, as is any adornment of the person. Citizens may travel only on a pass from the governor and must work in whatever city they visit for as long as they are there. Anyone guilty of premarital sex is punished severely and is forbidden from ever marrying unless eventually pardoned by the governor. Adultery is punished by slavery. The guilty party, upon petition by his or her spouse, may eventually be restored to freedom, but a second offense is punishable by death. Nor would it be easy to conceal such crimes. There are no locks on the doors to houses. In fact, the doors themselves swing freely, "letting anyone enter who wants to—so there is nothing private anywhere."[44] There are also no spots for secret meetings. Because the Utopians "live in the full view of all, they are bound to be either working at their usual trades or enjoying their leisure in a respectable way."[45]

Hythloday concludes by urging every society to imitate the Utopians. As long as money and private property exist, he says, a commonwealth will devolve into a "conspiracy of the rich" to advance its own interests on the backs of common workers.[46] Wealth is a burden both for those who possess it and fear its loss, and for those who lack it and resent its absence. "If money disappeared, so would fear, anxiety, worry, toil, and sleepless nights."[47] Only pride—which measures its advantage by what others lack—prevents us realizing this ideal.

It is a powerful and impassioned vision. But More is far from convinced. Though he does not express his thoughts to Hythloday, deferring discussion to another day, he tells the reader that he considered "not a few" of the particular Utopian customs and laws to be "quite absurd."[48] At the same time, he admits (without specifying) that "there are very many things in the Utopian commonwealth that in our own societies I would wish rather than expect to see."[49] This is an odd juxtaposition of comments, since most of the Utopians' practices seem to flow naturally if not inevitably from their communal living and moneyless economy. Only this basic premise ensures the radical transformation in human nature— the elimination of pride—that is essential to the Utopian way of life.

Yet it is precisely the sharing of everything in common that forms More's chief objection, which he articulates in a single sentence of considerable subtlety and irony: "This one thing alone takes away all the nobility, magnificence, splendor, and majesty which (in the popular view) are the true ornaments and glory of any commonwealth."[50] In the popular view, displays of great wealth and power—by the state and by individuals— provide a source of both pride and longing that give much of the meaning to peoples' lives. Utopian existence seems drab and colorless by contrast. More is also making a deeper, if related, point. Utopia is necessarily a static society in which departures from the norm cannot be tolerated. Much is gained by the elimination of poverty and by living on terms of equality. But a repression of the personal is a necessary concomitant. What is lost is the sense of a private life separate and apart from the commonwealth. What is lost is diversity and, with that, individual creativity and achievement. Those, too, are "ornaments and glory" of human life. Those, too, are outgrowths of human pride, and even if we could eliminate that pride we would, in so doing, impoverish our lives.

Returning to the two questions with which we started this section: Could it actually work? Would we want to live there? The answers, I think, for More (the speaker in the dialogue) are "no" and "not so sure." A city of God on earth is simply not possible in our fallen condition. We cannot eliminate the original sin of human pride. And, even if we could, the cost might be too great.

There is no closure at the end of *Utopia*. The speakers remain unreconciled.[51] *Utopia* is a Rorschach test for all its readers. When we look into it, do we see a socialist paradise or a totalitarian nightmare? Or perhaps we feel some combination of longing to belong and repulsion at conformity that are part of the human condition. The fact that we can still debate such issues five hundred years later is a tribute to the work's enduring interest.

THE HERETIC HUNTER

In 1517, Erasmus sent More a copy of the Ninety-Five Theses, or articles, that Martin Luther had supposedly nailed to the cathedral door in Wittenberg. Both Erasmus and More favored church reform, especially in ending the sale of indulgences, so they initially were inclined to view Luther's complaints in a positive light. But that changed as Luther grew increasingly hostile to the established church and as the number of his adherents swelled. More changed as well. The Reformation radicalized him. He dropped his satiric, reformist, humanist stance and adopted a new role as a fierce opponent of heresy.

Lutheran tracts and other heretical works flooded into England, brought there by German merchants. More was given a special dispensation from the archbishop of Canterbury to possess these forbidden books so that he could read and refute them. He helped Henry VIII prepare a *Defense of the Seven Sacraments* in 1521, a book that would win Henry the papal title—deeply ironic in light of future events—of "Defender of the Faith." More himself wrote a series of lengthy polemics, including *Responsio ad Lutherum* (1523) and *A Dialogue Concerning Heresies* (1529). Portions of these works make for painful reading, as More's rhetoric spins out of control, with scatological and other scurrilous epithets hurled at Luther and the "new men" who want to bring down the authority of the church.

One of the books More considered most dangerous was William Tyndale's brilliant English translation of the New Testament, which, along with his Old Testament, would later become the foundation for the King James Version of the Bible. Given Erasmus's and More's own erstwhile support for vernacular scripture, the opposition to Tyndale's Bible seems surprising. But Tyndale, who fled England in 1524, was a passionate and uncompromising Lutheran, and he used his translation to promote Lutheran doctrines and undermine church hierarchy by, for example, translating *ecclesia* as "congregation" rather than "church," and substituting "senior" or "elder" for "priest." In More's mind, the very idea of ordinary people reading the Bible on their own and forming opinions as to the nature and requirements of faith without being guided by the authority of the church became increasingly heretical. Tyndale's New Testament was seized and burned at every opportunity, as was Tyndale himself by agents of the church outside Brussels in 1536.

The death of Tyndale was more than a year after More's own death. But More himself played an active part in combatting heresy, and not just with words. He prepared a list of forbidden heretical works. He employed a network of spies to seek out and destroy those works and to arrest the people who distributed them. He even participated personally in the interrogation, prosecution, and ultimately the murder of unrepentant heretics, calling one such "well and worthily burned."[52] More's defenders note that he never engaged in torture and that a mere "half a dozen" heretics were burned at the stake during the two and a half years he was lord chancellor.[53] But that is still six too many, and even if More neither conducted nor ordered the torture of suspected heretics, he knew that it occurred and took no steps to prevent it.

More defended the burning of heretics, if they would not recant, as necessary to preserve the souls of others from eternal damnation:

> For I think no reasonable person will have it that when the heretic, if he went at large, would with the spreading of his error infect other folk, the bishop should have such pity on him that he would, rather than allow other people to punish his body, allow him to kill other people's souls.[54]

There was also a more personal revulsion at work, as he admitted in a letter to Erasmus after resigning as lord chancellor:

> I find that breed of men absolutely loathsome, so much so that, unless they regain their senses, I want to be as hateful to them as anyone can possibly be; for my increasing experience with those men frightens me with the thought of what the world will suffer at their hands.[55]

We can neither excuse nor defend More's persecution of heretics. But we can make an effort to understand how this otherwise humane man, dedicated to peace and equality before the law, came to such an extreme, in an age when extremes became the norm.

In some respects, More was prophetic. He feared greatly that the protestant heresy would spread, as of course it did, and that it would lead to an overthrow of the existing order he was sworn to defend. More believed civil disorder was an inevitable consequence of religious disorder, a point Machiavelli had already recognized. For More, "sowing schisms and seditions" were one and the same.[56] Heresy was by its nature an attack on existing social and political as well as religious institutions. Wherever heresy had reared its head, civil unrest had followed, starting a century before with the Peasants' Revolt of 1381, which was in part stirred by John Wycliffe and the Lollards. So, too, in Germany, where that country's own Peasants' War of 1524–25 was inspired by Luther's antiauthoritarian teachings. More considered heresy a challenge to both royal and ecclesiastical authority. Combatting heresy was thus a "communal war" in defense of the existing order.[57]

More's conservative impulse was not, however, purely reactive. His reverence for the church mirrored his reverence for the common law. Both embodied what he considered the accumulated, communal wisdom of the centuries. In the case of the church, that was the wisdom of the church fathers in building on the teachings of Christ. That does not mean More believed that the church as an institution, including the papacy, was infallible. To the contrary, More was in favor of many incremental reforms starting with the papacy itself. But he believed that the faults of individual clergymen could not detract from the cumulative, collective truth of the church, just as the errors of individual judges did not detract from the collective wisdom of the common law. The church brings men and women together in common worship and belief. More considered the church as an institution greater than the mistakes of any priest or even pope and worthy of our collective devotion. Without the doctrinal structure and the rituals and sacraments provided by the church, More thought that religion was too insubstantial and abstract a matter to unite people. A revolt against the established church would thus lead to many untethered doctrinal variations, as the Reformation was itself demonstrating. One common doctrine was not being replaced by another common doctrine. Instead, the community of believers was being splintered by doctrinal disputes driven by individual, charismatic leaders.

More saw the essence of the Reformation as a challenge not just to the pope or the church as an institution; each man and woman was being encouraged to forge his and her own personal relationship with God unmediated by the traditions and teachings of the church. The fundamental dispute was between inner conscience, private prayer, and individual grace and revelation on the one hand, and the formalities, rituals, sacraments, and authorized teachings of the church on the other. In his deepest heart, More himself recognized the importance of the former and the often artificial aspects of the latter. But he no longer allowed himself to think in those terms. More, the subtle ironist and gentle reformer, clung all the more fiercely to the doctrinal consensus and to the rituals and trappings that he thought essential to communal belief and the maintenance of order. More, ever the dutiful son, hated disorder, anarchy, chaos, and lack of respect for traditional institutions. Protecting the church and the existing social-political order became the twin foci of his public life. When those two came into conflict with each other, as they soon would, More would have to choose between them and to accept the consequences of his choice, as the heretics he prosecuted accepted the consequences of theirs.

THE KING'S GREAT MATTER

Catherine of Aragon, daughter of Ferdinand and Isabella of Spain, was just fifteen years old when she came to England to marry Prince Henry's older brother, Arthur. Arthur died less than six months after the ceremony. It is unclear if the marriage was ever consummated; Catherine claimed not. Regardless, Henry received a special dispensation from Pope Julius II in December 1503 to marry his brother's widow. The wedding itself did not take place, however, until 1509, shortly after the death of his father, Henry VII.

The royal couple had one daughter, Mary, after several male children

were lost to miscarriage or stillbirth or died in infancy. Additional mis-
carriages and stillbirths followed. Henry, who was serially unfaithful,
developed an obsession for Anne Boleyn, his wife's maid of honor, after
an earlier affair with her sister, Mary. Henry decided he wanted Anne as
his new queen and mother of the next king. Anne wanted it even more.
She even obtained livery for her servants inscribed "*Ainsi sera, groigne
qui groigne*" (Thus it will be, grudge it who will).[58] Anne was ambitious,
manipulative, and fully aware of her power over the king.

Henry sought to have his marriage to Catherine annulled so that he
could marry Anne and father a male heir. He instructed his chancellor,
Cardinal Wolsey, archbishop of York, to make it happen. Henry claimed
that his marriage to Catherine was void *ab initio* because the Bible forbade
marriage with a dead brother's wife: "And if a man shall take his brother's
wife, it is an unclean thing: he hath uncovered his brother's nakedness;
they shall be childless."[59]

Cardinal Wolsey arranged for a papal legate to come to London and
convened a legatine court at Blackfriars in May 1529 to examine the
matter. But the current pope, Clement VII, was very much under the
thumb of the emperor, Charles V, whose troops had recently sacked Rome
and virtually imprisoned the pope in the Castel Sant'Angelo. As noted
in the previous chapter, this event led to the overthrow of the Medicis
and to the restoration of the Florentine Republic. It would also have
repercussions as far away as London. Since Catherine was Charles's aunt,
the emperor was not going to allow the pope to dissolve the marriage.
The legatine court dragged on through the summer of 1529. Catherine
defended her claims with passion and swore (likely correctly) that she
was still a virgin at the time of her marriage to Henry. Eventually matters
ground to a halt. In July 1529, responding to a direct petition from Catherine, Pope Clement ordered the proceedings in England to cease and the
legatine court to reconvene in Rome.

Wolsey had failed the king, who did not tolerate failure. Wolsey was
fired as lord chancellor, his possessions were seized, and he ultimately was

charged with treason. The devastated and enfeebled Wolsey died before trial. Remarkably, the king chose Thomas More as his new lord chancellor and delivered to him the Great Seal of England, used as a stamp for the approval of formal state documents. Even more remarkably, More accepted. The lord chancellor, generally a member of the clergy, was traditionally the king's closest advisor on both secular and spiritual matters. He was known as the keeper of the king's conscience. More, a layman, had already advised the king privately that he believed Catherine's claim that she was a virgin when she married Henry and that her former marriage to Henry's brother was not, in any event, grounds for annulment. Yet Henry wanted, and convinced, More to take the job. As More reported the conversation, Henry assured More "that [he] should first look unto God and after God unto him."[60]

Those assurances did not last. More was lord chancellor for two and a half years. Heretics aside, More was extremely efficient and fair in his judicial duties. He believed that the rule of law and its impartial application and prompt administration were crucial to a well-functioning society. But Henry's frustration with the lack of progress in his annulment steadily increased. Henry arranged for a lengthy letter to be sent to Pope Clement in 1530 explaining why his marriage to Catherine was invalid. It was signed by a large array of distinguished English clerics and scholars. Thomas More declined to sign the letter. The pope did not bother to respond.

In 1531, the king took matters into his own hands. He declared himself supreme head of the Church of England and demanded that a convocation of English bishops recognize him as such. They did so, but with the cautious proviso "so far as the law of Christ allows," which of course, from the perspective of the Catholic Church, was not very far at all. Henry stormed, bullied, and threatened. And on May 15, 1532, the cowed bishops agreed to articles for the "Submission of the Clergy" to the crown. This act effectively made Henry, without qualification, supreme head of the English church and made the church subordinate to the crown. More, who vigorously opposed the law, resigned the next day and personally delivered the great seal to Henry. At that time, the two men reached an implicit bargain: More would remain silent, and Henry would leave him alone. More accordingly explained his resignation in a letter to Erasmus without mentioning the king's marriage or his bid for supremacy over the church:

> It has been my constant wish almost since boyhood, dearest Desiderius, that some day I might enjoy the opportunity which, to my happiness, you have always had, namely, of being relieved of all public duties and eventually being able to devote some time to God alone and myself; at long last this wish has come true, Erasmus, thanks to the goodness of the Supreme and Almighty God and to the graciousness of a very understanding Sovereign.[61]

More pared down his household staff after finding them positions elsewhere. Although his income was much reduced and his family's standard of living would have to be adjusted accordingly, he jokingly reassured them that some standards would be maintained: "We will not therefore descend to Oxford fare, nor to the fare of New Inn, but we will begin with Lincoln's Inn diet," descending as need be from there.[62] More also adjusted quickly to the lack of pomp and circumstance. When he and Dame Alice attended church, they always sat in separate sections for men and women. Hitherto, when More was ready to depart, a servant would go to Dame Alice's pew and announce, "Madame, my lord is gone." Now, More himself would appear at her side and state in a solemn tone, "Madame, my lord is gone."[63]

More, however, could not remain silent on issues of religion. Nor could Henry tolerate anything less than affirmative support. He dispensed with papal authorization and married a pregnant Anne Boleyn on January 25, 1533. Their daughter, Elizabeth, the future queen, was born less than eight months later. Catherine's appeal to Rome was rendered illegal by Act of Parliament, which asserted that the pope had no jurisdiction or authority in England. A few months later, another Act declared Henry's marriage to Catherine invalid and his marriage to Anne legitimate. On June 1, Anne was crowned as queen of England. Henry's great matter was finally resolved without foreign interference. Henry was eventually excommunicated by the pope, but it was a futile gesture, since Henry had already left the Catholic Church and taken the Church of England with him. The pope might as well have excommunicated the grand sultan or the chief rabbi for all the effect it had.

More's friends urged him to attend the coronation, but he declined to do so, citing a story from Tacitus. Under the emperor Tiberius, Roman law forbade a virgin from being condemned to death for a given crime. A virgin committed that particular crime, and the emperor was nonplussed, since he wanted to enforce the law in question but without violating the proscription. One of his advisors in council offered a simple solution: "Why make you so much ado, my lords, about so small a matter? Let her first be deflowered, and then after may she be devoured."[64] As More explained to his friends, "It lieth not in my power but that they may devour me; but God being my good lord, I will provide that they shall never deflower me."[65] He might, that is, suffer the ultimate penalty of execution, but he would keep his conscience clear and not be seen publicly to condone, even tacitly, the annulment, the new marriage, or Henry's hostile takeover of the church.

More probably sealed his fate by shunning Anne's coronation. She nursed her grudge and inflamed Henry against him. But More made his opposition clear in more overt ways. Throughout the course of his great matter, Henry had received support from some Lutherans, who saw a chance to challenge the authority of the pope. A prominent lawyer and ally of the king, Christopher St. German, published several books in which he attacked the ecclesiastical courts and the treatment of heresy cases. He also argued that the common law is supreme over canon law, the state over the church, and the king over the pope. These were all critical positions of the king. But, implicit understanding or no, More could not remain silent. He responded with several counterattacks of his own. St. German published his works anonymously, which allowed More to maintain the pretense that he did not know their authorship, but in fact it was widely known, and the books were published by the king's own printer. More's dueling tracts were thus read as direct opposition to the king, and the king would not tolerate opposition.

Henry had come increasingly to rely on Thomas Cromwell as an advisor and enforcer of the king's will. Cromwell, despite obscure beginnings, had made his fortune on the continent and returned to London as a prosperous merchant and banker. He married well and became a protégé of Cardinal Wolsey. Cromwell remained loyal to Wolsey to the end, which is to his credit, but he was ready enough to serve the king when the occasion arose. Where Wolsey failed, Cromwell did not. He bullied bishops, maneuvered acts through Parliament, and conducted interrogations of those suspected of treason. Cromwell was in many respects More's doppelganger, or Machiavellian twin, and it is fitting that their magnificent portraits by Hans Holbein the Younger hang opposite one another at the Frick Collection in New York.[66] Holbein's More is thoughtful and steadfast. His Cromwell is a man of undeniable talent but also of relentless ambition and unbendable will.

Robert Bly's play *A Man for All Seasons* and the movie based upon it present More as a gentle man of kindly wit and profound wisdom, at peace with himself and ready to die rather than compromise his beliefs. His Cromwell is a lurking, devious presence, a flatterer and scoundrel, a sort of Renaissance Uriah Heap. Hilary Mantel, by contrast, in her splendid novel *Wolf Hall*, which covers the years from 1500 to 1535, makes Cromwell her hero and offers a very sympathetic account of a gifted, complex, and pragmatic servant of the king. Her More is a less admirable character, vicious in his pursuit of heretics. Readers may take their choice, but viewers of the Holbein portraits are likely to get the best sense of their respective characters. Holbein also painted remarkably revealing portraits of Henry VIII and Erasmus.

There was considerable underground ferment against the king and his new queen. Many subjects remained sympathetic to Catherine and loyal to the Catholic Church. More played no active part in these rumblings, but his resistance helped inspire others. In 1534, More was summoned by Cromwell and questioned about his dealings with one Elizabeth Barton, known as the Holy Maid of Kent, who claimed divine visions and foretold divine punishment for Henry's sinful divorce. Barton was executed for treason, and several alleged associates faced similar charges. More was initially named in, but ultimately dropped from, an indictment. When his daughter Margaret offered her congratulations, More responded, "In faith, Meg, *Quod differtur, non aufertur*" (What is put off is not put aside).[67]

The king, through Cromwell, sought to buy More's acquiescence by promising a return to riches and high position if he would publicly approve the divorce. More refused. Cromwell, who was Anne's ally in the divorce, became the instrument of her revenge, just as he would become the instrument of her own death in two years' time, once she failed to produce a male heir and the king's impatient eye settled on Lady Jane Seymour.

Cromwell arranged for passage of an Act of Succession that required subjects to swear an oath recognizing the offspring of Anne and Henry as the legitimate heirs to the throne. All the members of Parliament and most of the clergy duly swore the required oath. More was summoned to do so in April 1534. He declined. More had no objection to recognizing Elizabeth and any future children of Henry and Anne as the royal successors. He was indifferent to such a purely political matter. But the preamble of the oath affirmed the legitimacy of the marriage and hence of the annulment as well as Henry's sovereignty over the church.

More's family urged him to swear the oath regardless, contending that God regards the heart not the tongue. But More would accept no such evasion. He refused to sign as a matter of conscience and took refuge in silence, declining to explain his reasons or openly question the authority of the king. He was arrested on April 17 and sent to the Tower of London.

It was not a strict confinement. More was at liberty to walk in the garden and around the Tower. And he joked with Margaret that he had finally obtained his wish for a monk's cell and time for prayer and contemplation. But it was still uncomfortable, and the cold, the damp, and the poor food took a steady toll on his health. Margaret visited him there as often as she was allowed to do so. More was also in constant contact with his fellow prisoner and future saint, John Fisher, the bishop of London. Eventually Dame Alice was permitted to visit as well, and she reproached him heartily for putting himself and his family in such straits.

More remained in his Tower cell for more than fourteen months. He had access to books and writing materials and sent out a succession of letters and tracts containing his meditations on death, the importance of the sacraments, the transitory nature of worldly pleasures and possessions, the temptations of pride, Christ's suffering and death, and the actual presence of Christ in the Eucharist. His writings from prison have been compared to those of Boethius, who wrote his *Consolation of Philosophy* from prison in the year 523 while awaiting his execution, and to the conversations of Socrates before he was instructed to drink the hemlock that killed him.

More was brought from his Tower cell on several occasions to be interrogated by Cromwell and his colleagues. We have detailed accounts of these sessions, written by More himself and given to Margaret for later publication. The interrogators alternately cajoled and threatened More, leading him to retort at one point, "My lords, these terrors be arguments for children, and not for me."[68] More was steadfast in his refusal to swear any oath legitimizing the king's marriage or his position as head of the Church of England. Yet More was careful never to deny those claims either. A new Treasons Act provided that anyone who "maliciously" denied the king's absolute sovereignty over the church was guilty of treason and therefore to be hanged, cut down before death, revived, disemboweled while still alive, and then dismembered. Cromwell sought to trap More in such a denial, but More was too good a lawyer and thwarted every such attempt. He deflected all their efforts, noting that he had once stated his views directly to Henry as his advisor but that now he refused to have anything to do with political affairs.

> I do nobody harm, I say none harm, I think none harm, but wish everybody good. And if this be not enough to keep a man alive, in good faith I long not to live. . . . And therefore my poor body is at the King's pleasure; would God my death might do him good.[69]

Eventually the king's patience, and that of Anne and Cromwell, was exhausted. More was tried on four counts of treason on July 1, 1535. He argued in his own defense, contending that his silence on the subject of supremacy and succession could not properly be taken as treason. More invoked the common-law presumption, *Qui tacet consentire videtur* (He who is silent appears to consent). Three of the four charges against him were rejected by the jury, even though the jury had been specifically chosen by Cromwell to condemn him. In the end, Cromwell was forced to rely on the perjured testimony of Richard Rich, an ambitious young lawyer in Cromwell's employ. Rich claimed that, when removing books from More's cell, he heard More state affirmatively that the king had no authority over the church. More vehemently denied the statement and was perfectly prepared to swear an oath that he had said no such thing. It is impossible to believe that so careful a lawyer would have made so foolish a statement. But he was found guilty regardless.

At that point, knowing he was to be condemned, More dropped his silence and directly challenged the constitutionality of any

> act of Parliament directly repugnant to the laws of God and His Holy Church, the supreme government of which, or of any part whereof, may no temporal prince presume by any law to take upon him. . . . This realm, being but one member and small part of the Church, might not make a particular law disagreeable with the general law of Christ's universal Catholic Church, no more than the City of London, being

but one poor member in respect of the whole realm, might make a law against an act of Parliament to bind the whole realm.[70]

In short, God's law, as recognized by the church, is supreme over the laws of men. More added, in a calculated dig at the hypocrisy of the entire proceeding, that it was not because he denied the supremacy of the king that they sought his blood: "I know well that the reason why you have condemned me is because I have never been willing to consent to the King's second marriage."[71]

More was taken to the scaffold on Tower Hill on the morning of July 6, 1535. The king had commuted his sentence in that he was to be beheaded rather than suffering the full array of tortures for treason. More's final speech was brief. He said, echoing the promise Henry had made to him when he became lord chancellor, that he would die "the King's good servant but God's first."[72] And so he did, by his own lights and by those of the church he loved.

Chapter 5

CASTIGLIONE: A GENTLEMAN IN URBINO[1]

Machiavelli and Castiglione were born only nine years apart. But in some ways, they are men of different eras as well as different sensibilities. Machiavelli came of age in an early Renaissance of brutal power struggles throughout Italy, struggles into which popes and foreign rulers alike readily interjected themselves. Italy was somewhat more settled in Castiglione's day, though the sack of Rome in 1527 by the troops of Charles V of Spain is a notable exception. The great nation-states in France, Spain, and England were solid, established monarchies. And even in Italy, princes ruled as autocrats over their city-states in Venice, Milan, Florence, Urbino, and elsewhere, and they prided themselves on the cultural as much as the military and diplomatic accomplishments of their courts. *Condottieri*—the mercenary warriors needed to maintain power—had increasingly become courtiers. Just as Machiavelli wrote a handbook for the new or would-be prince, Castiglione wrote his handbook for "a gentleman living at the courts of princes."[2]

The Book of the Courtier is not just a how-to manual, however, though it was often viewed in that light over the ensuing centuries. Following in the tradition of Plato and Cicero, Castiglione was trying to define an ideal type, one that does not exist in the real world but to which one can nonetheless aspire and take as a model. This dual aim gives the work its creative tension: the vision of the courtier is ideal, but his code of behavior must work within a system of despotic rule. His virtues must be chosen carefully and balanced to incite the admiration, delight, and trust of his sovereign.

There is a decided measure of calculation factored into this ideal type. But, then, calculation is critical to all success, whether in Renaissance Italy or in contemporary America. The techniques for making an impression and for gaining and retaining the favor of a powerful patron have not changed very much in the intervening five hundred years. But the most important and lasting ideal presented by Castiglione is not courtiership *per se* but self-fashioning—making oneself a work of art through education and imitation; playing a role to perfection. That ideal of self-fashioning was a defining feature of what is now known as the High Renaissance—the period of Leonardo da Vinci (1452–1519), Michelangelo (1475–1564), and Raphael (1483–1520)—and it had a profound impact on Montaigne, Shakespeare, and many others.[3] As the great Renaissance scholar Jacob Burckhardt explained:

> [Castiglione's courtier] was the ideal man of society, and was regarded by the civilization of that age as its choicest flower; and the court existed for him rather than he for the court. ... The inner impulse which inspired him was directed, though our author does not acknowledge the fact, not to the service of the prince but to his own perfection.[4]

Castiglione's portrait of the ideal courtier—a master of language, literature, manners, art, music, and humor; a master, in short, of life itself—is every bit a match for those of Leonardo and Raphael in its beauty, complexity, and historical importance.

LIFE

Baldassare Castiglione was born on December 6, 1478, on the family estate at Casatico, outside Mantua, in Lombardy. Both his father and grandfather had been military commanders in the service of the Gonzaga family, and the Castigliones were connected by marriage to the then-current marquis of Mantua, Ludovico Gonzaga.

Castiglione was sent to Milan at the age of twelve to live with relatives and to pursue his education. In 1494, he also became connected with the court of Ludovico Sforza, the Duke of Milan, known commonly as Ludovico il Moro, who was a patron of Leonardo da Vinci and commissioned *The Last Supper*.

Castiglione's father died in 1499, and that same year Ludovico il Moro was driven out of Milan by the French. Castiglione returned to Mantua, where he took over as head of the family and entered the service of Francesco Gonzaga, the new marquis of Mantua. He spent five years in Francesco's service, going on frequent diplomatic missions and even participating in a military campaign against the Spanish in Naples. On a mission to Rome, Castiglione met Guidobaldo da Montefeltro, the Duke of Urbino and brother-in-law to Francesco Gonzaga.

In 1504, Guidobaldo and Castiglione prevailed on Francesco to permit Castiglione to leave Mantua and to take up residence at the court of Urbino, then considered one of the most sophisticated in all of Italy. Guidobaldo was crippled and rendered impotent by gout. But the court was presided over by his beautiful wife, the duchess Elisabetta Gonzaga, and her sister-in-law, Emilia Pia. Distinguished courtiers from all over Italy gathered for music, games, pageants, and, most of all, conversation. Raphael, a native of Urbino, painted portraits of Elisabetta, Emilia, and a number of their guests and courtiers. Raphael was one of the great Italian masters of this period, along with Leonardo and Michelangelo—a trinity of artists to match the three pillars of Italian literature of an earlier era: Dante, Petrarch, and Boccaccio.

Castiglione participated happily in the entertainments at Urbino, writing songs and sonnets in honor of Elisabetta and even a pastoral play to be performed at the court. But he was often absent on diplomatic missions. He traveled to Rome in 1505, and in 1506 he was sent to England to receive the Order of the Garter on behalf of Guidobaldo. But Castiglione was present in Urbino when Pope Julius II, along with his substantial entourage, visited for a week at the beginning of March in 1507. Castiglione would set the fictional date for the first of the four successive conversations that make up *The Book of the Courtier* on March 8, the day after Julius's departure.

When Guidobaldo died in 1508, Castiglione stayed on at Urbino in the service of Guidobaldo's nephew and adopted son, Francesco Maria della Rovere. He fought in a series of military campaigns with Rovere, at the behest of Julius, between 1509 and 1512. In reward, he was made a count and was given a castle in Novilara, near Pesaro. In 1513, he was sent to Rome as the resident ambassador from Urbino. Castiglione greatly enjoyed his time there, associating with numerous artists, including Michelangelo, who was busy with the ceiling of the Sistine Chapel, and deepening his friendship with Raphael, who had moved there permanently and was hard at work on the "Raphael Rooms" in the Vatican, including his masterpiece, *The School of Athens*. It was at Rome, not Urbino, that Raphael painted the famous portrait of Castiglione that now hangs in the Louvre. It was also at Rome that Castiglione began working on the *Courtier*, an undertaking that would engage him off and on for the next two decades. The *Courtier* was Castiglione's *School of Athens*.

When Pope Julius died in 1513, he was succeeded by Cardinal Giovanni de' Medici, who served as Pope Leo X. Leo, eager to install his nephew Lorenzo as Duke of Urbino, excommunicated Rovere and exiled him to Mantua. Castiglione, ever the loyal courtier, followed Rovere into exile. But Mantua had its consolations. In 1516, Castiglione married the young Ippolita Torelli, who was descended from another noble Mantuan family. They had a son, Camillo, and two daughters, Anna and Ippolita. Castiglione returned alone to Rome as ambassador of the new marquis of Mantua, Federico Gonzaga. Two letters survive from Castiglione revealing the deep love and passionate affection he felt for his wife. But she died in 1520 while giving birth to their third child.

Castiglione remained in Rome as ambassador, and, since Lorenzo de' Medici had died in 1519, he tried unsuccessfully to have Urbino restored to Rovere. Battered by the death of his wife, Castiglione moved in an increasingly religious direction. The death of Raphael in 1520 was an added loss, and Castiglione wrote an elegy in his memory. In 1521, he received the "first tonsure" from Pope Leo X, a ritual shaving of a portion of the back of the head as a necessary introduction into clerical orders.

Castiglione remained in Rome until 1524, when he was appointed papal nuncio to the court of the emperor Charles V in Spain. He was still there in 1527 when Spanish troops sacked Rome and held Pope Clement VII hostage for a time. The pope at first blamed Castiglione for not keeping him apprised of the emperor's intentions. Castiglione responded, in a famous letter, chastising the pope for his temporizing policies and provocations. The pope, surprisingly enough, acquiesced in the criticism. Charles V soon thereafter made Castiglione bishop of Avila.

Castiglione finished his *Courtier* and published it in early 1528. The duchess Elisabetta Gonzaga had died a widow in 1526. Many other members of the Urbino court had also died by this time, and a pall of melancholy and nostalgia reigns over his final revisions to the work. Emilia Pia died in 1528, shortly after she received a copy of the *Courtier*. Castiglione himself was not far behind. He died of the plague the following year in Toledo at the age of fifty. He is buried in the cathedral there. The emperor himself attended the service and stated, "I tell you that one of the best *caballeros* of the world is dead."[5] A monument designed by a pupil of Raphael was erected near his birthplace outside Mantua. The inscription reads:

> Baldassare Castiglione of Mantua, endowed by nature with every gift and the knowledge of many disciplines, learned in Greek and Latin literature, and a poet in the Italian (Tuscan) language, was given a castle in Pesaro on account of his military prowess, after he had conducted embassies to both great Britain and Rome. While he was working at the Spanish court on behalf of Clement VII, there he drew up *The Book of the Courtier* for the education of the nobility; and in short, after Emperor Charles V had elected him Bishop of Avila, he died at Toledo much honored by all the people. He lived fifty years, two months and a day. His mother, Luigia Gonzaga, who to her own sorrow outlived her son, placed this memorial to him in 1529.[6]

THE IDEAL COURTIER (BOOK 1)

Plato's *Symposium* recounts the speeches made at a drinking party that occurred in 416 BCE, when Athens was at the height of its glory. But the account was written many years later, after Athens had lost the Peloponnesian War, had been stripped of its empire, and had emerged from a brutal tyranny into a brittle democracy that condemned Socrates, the dialogue's principal protagonist, to death. The fictional narrator, moreover, is someone who was not even present at the event itself but has had to construct it from the accounts of others. The narrative frame marks what follows as an urgent attempt to re-create a lost golden age and to recapture, in idealized terms, the wisdom of those participants and particularly that of Socrates, the grandfather of Western philosophy.[7]

The effect of the frame narrative in Castiglione's *Courtier* is similar. The conversations reported in the four books purportedly occurred over those four nights in Urbino following the festive visit of Julius II in 1507. But the book was not published until twenty years later. Duke Guidobaldo's heir has been driven from Urbino, and most of the participants, including the beloved duchess, are dead. A golden glow suffuses the narrative that accentuates this sense of loss. Castiglione's announced goal is to "preserve this bright memory from mortal oblivion, and make it live in the mind of posterity through my writing."[8] Curiously, however, Castiglione claims to have been in England at the time of the conversations. In fact, he had returned from England the prior year and was definitely present in Urbino for the papal visit. His claimed absence is merely a literary device that allows him to restrict his own purported role to reconstructing and narrating the conversations as accurately as possible based on accounts he has heard from others. This conceit allows the author, in an age of absolute monarchs, to present and explore controversial views without the hazard of voicing them directly. Thomas More achieved the same effect in *Utopia* by making Hythloday his main speaker. In the *Symposium*, Socrates's final speech is plainly intended to embrace and transcend all that went before.[9] In the *Courtier*, as in *Utopia*, definitive statements are attempted but not achieved. We must base our understanding instead on the structure of the dialogue and the back-and-forth among the participants.

In a dedicatory letter to Don Michel de Silva, the bishop of Viseu, Castiglione compares his task to that of a painter: "I send you this book as a portrait of the Court of Urbino, not by the hand of Raphael or Michelangelo, but by that of a lowly painter and one who only knows how to draw the main lines, without adorning the truth with pretty colors or making, by perspective art, that which is not seem to be."[10] In other words, he claims his book is simple and artless; in fact, of course, it is a consummate work of art and anything but simple. But Castiglione's modest, self-deprecating claim—which nonetheless manages to put himself in the same sentence with Raphael and Michelangelo—is of a piece with his advice to "a gentleman living at the courts of princes." Castiglione displays in his narration what is described in the conversations: "What manner of man he must be who deserves the name of perfect Courtier, without defect of any kind."[11]

The participants in the conversations are all historical figures at the court of Urbino, each intimately known to Castiglione. They have individual personalities, but the group portrait is idealized, like the recognizable but idealized figures in *The School of Athens*, and each plays his or her part in the harmony of the whole. Castiglione, despite his protestations, is "adorning [his] truth with pretty colors" and making "that which is not seem to be."

Guidobaldo assumed the throne at Urbino in 1482, when he was only ten years old. His father, the renowned *condottiere* Federico da Montefeltro, was known as "the light of Italy" for his promotion of the arts and humanities. Great hopes were placed in Guidobaldo, and Castiglione praises his judgment and ability. But Guidobaldo met with adversity in every undertaking and, by the time he was twenty, was crippled and deformed. He nonetheless gathered a distinguished court at Urbino and presided over jousts and tournaments and hunts, distributing praise and criticism as an observer rather than a participant.

But Guidobaldo is a factor in the conversations that make up the *Courtier* only through his absence. Each evening, he retires immediately after dinner, while everyone else repairs to the rooms of the duchess, and it is she, with Emilia Pia as her lieutenant, who presides over the nighttime entertainment: music, dancing, and conversation. The small group of noblemen and noblewomen—reminiscent of Boccaccio's *brigata* from the *Decameron*[12]—gather together like brothers and sisters bound by love to one another and to the duchess. Each is free to speak or jest or contest up to a point, limited always by "a rule of fine manners from the presence of so great and virtuous a lady."[13]

The nighttime world of the *Courtier* is thus an inversion of the daytime world, and yet the goal of each is the same. During the day, the courtiers vie with one another in physical displays to be thought worthy of the duke and his company. At night, the courtiers vie with one another in cultural displays to be thought worthy of the duchess and her company. Yet both realms are slightly off-kilter and disconnected from each other. The duke has absolute power over his subjects but is helpless against his crippling disease. Even the critical connection of physical intimacy between the duke and the duchess is broken. The realm of the duchess is divorced from that of the duke. And although Castiglione calls her rooms "the very abode of joyfulness,"[14] the confinement of the space and the "rule of fine manners" eventually impose feelings of claustrophobia and sterility that one of the courtiers, Pietro Bembo, tries to transcend in the final book, though with limited success.

Thus, Castiglione's *brigata*, which, like Boccaccio's, has also separated itself from a daytime world gone awry, is operating within a very restricted set of circumstances. This constraint is evident even in the games they choose to pursue. As they gather on the first evening, Emilia calls on each gentleman present to suggest a game. Most of the suggestions prove unsuitable because they would violate the rule of fine manners: identifying defects in one's beloved; confessions of individual folly; exploring the causes of anger among lovers. All such games would probe beneath the surface refinement and expose fault lines of cruelty, folly, self-deception, and hostility that are better kept hidden. As we shall see, there is plenty of aggression among the courtiers, but that aggression, for the most part, is cloaked in fine manners and thereby rendered acceptable to social discourse.

Emilia accordingly chooses a game proposed by Federico Fregoso: "forming in words a perfect Courtier."[15] Emilia will designate the speakers, but everyone has a right of objection and interjection to ensure a genuine dialogue and exchange of views. Indeed, when she selects Count Canossa to begin, she laughingly suggests that everyone will disagree with him, which will make the conversation livelier. Her apparent barb is disarmed by humor, a perfect example of the fine manners expected of the group.

In the same spirit, Canossa declines an offer to wait until the next evening to prepare his presentation. "I do not wish to be like the man who stripped to his doublet and jumped less far than he had done in his great-coat," he explains. Speaking spontaneously, he will be excused the lack of forethought, and "so, free of censure, I shall be permitted to say whatever comes first to my lips."[16] He then embarks on a bravura performance, perfectly illustrating the principal qualities of the courtier he describes.

Yet Canossa is interrupted almost before he can begin. Canossa suggests that the ideal courtier will be noble born because the virtues of a nobleman will shine all the brighter, and he would be ashamed not to attain a prominence at least as great as his ancestors. Beauty of countenance and person are inborn, Canossa insists, as well as a certain grace "we call an 'air,' which shall make him at first sight pleasing and lovable to all who see him."[17]

Gaspar Pallavicino, a frequent objector and controverter, counters with some force that a noble birth guarantees neither virtue nor beauty, just as a humble birth does not preclude them. It is an awkward truth to voice amid a group of privileged nobles, particularly when their own duke is so ill formed and unprepossessing. Accordingly, Canossa quickly brackets the issue, noting that they must contend with the realities of their society, in which a lowborn person is held in less esteem and must work harder to make a good impression. He will thereby seem less a gentleman, for what appears in a noble as simply assuming his proper station will be put down to vulgar ambition in an upstart. Canossa is not going to challenge the social and political hierarchy of Renaissance Italy.

The first concern of the courtier, Canossa explains, must be military prowess, improved by constant exercise and the refinement of martial skills. A courtier must never fail his prince on the field of battle. Any disgrace in that regard, whether through cowardice or incompetence, can never be overcome. With that said, however, Canossa quickly moves on. Although military skills are necessary and highly valued, they form but a small part of his portrait of the courtier. He offers no thoughts on the art of war; the refined arts of manner and culture are more to his taste.

Indeed, Canossa quickly cautions that a courtier cannot always be swaggering around like a mighty warrior.[18] The place for ferocity is on the battlefield or at least on the practice grounds, not at court. Canossa offers a comic anecdote of a lady at court bidding a courtier to dance and being told that such trifles were not his business; fighting was his business. She responded by suggesting that when he is not in battle he should be greased all over and stored in a closet with his armor. The true courtier must show extreme adaptability to his circumstances: "Let the man we are seeking be exceedingly fierce, harsh, and always among the first, wherever the enemy is; and in every other place, humane, modest, reserved, avoiding ostentation above all things as well as that impudent praise of himself by which a man always arouses hatred and disgust in all who hear him."[19]

Canossa does not, however, object to all self-praise. Indeed, a courtier should have a proper sense of his own worth. But self-praise, paradoxically, must be modest to be effective and not invite envy or disgust; it is the art of "saying things in such a way that they do not appear to be spoken to that end, but are so very apropos that one cannot help saying them; and to seem always to avoid praising one's self, yet do so."[20] One could object—though none of the courtiers do—that self-praise under the guise of modesty makes the courtier a hypocrite and a dissembler. But that is not quite fair. We all want to be thought well of, especially by our peers and superiors. And it is natural to turn the conversation to subjects that put one in a flattering light. Those who are effective do so subtly and praise themselves by indirection, such as through self-deprecating remarks. Again, think of Castiglione's comparison of his own artless portrait to the great paintings of Raphael and Michelangelo. A man who wishes to accomplish much must presume much, and some of that confidence will demand display.

Canossa expects his ideal courtier to accomplish a great deal indeed. He is agile, well built, and light on his feet but strong. He is an expert rider, hunter, and swordsman. He excels at swimming, wrestling, jumping, and running. He even plays tennis well and dances with style. In short, he excels in all activities of the body where a good name is to be won.

His mind and manners are as well tuned as his body. He possesses all the conventional virtues: honor, integrity, prudence, goodness, fortitude, and temperance. He knows Latin and Greek and all the major works of the poets, orators, and historians in those languages. He is equally versed in the vernacular. He draws and paints, having learned to see what is in the world and to discern its beauty. He can read music, sing, and play various instruments *con bella maniera* (in a beautiful style), and is even skilled in improvisation.

Signor Gaspar objects that music is unmanly and would render the courtier effeminate. But Canossa will have none of that. Music is a sacred thing, he insists, that "not only makes gentle the soul of man, but often tames wild beasts."[21] A man who does not feel the richness and pleasure of music has something lacking in his soul, like that courtier whose only professed business is fighting.

Canossa's courtier is by turns thoughtful and witty in conversation as the occasion demands. He is self-deprecating and mildly ironic. In short, he is thoroughly civilized and entertaining short of folly: "Let him laugh, jest, banter, frolic, and dance, yet in such a manner as to show always that he is genial and discreet; and let him be full of grace in all that he does or says."[22]

This last concept, *grazia* (or grace), is critical. The courtier works hard to shine in an impossible range of activities.[23] But he does not let the effort show. All of his actions and words are tempered with good judgment and *una certa grazia* that make them seem natural and unstudied, as if inborn.

But if not born with such grace—and most are not—how does one acquire it? Canossa's advice is to keep before one's eyes with respect to every skill and virtue "those men who are known to be most perfect in these matters."[24] A good pupil, moreover, seeks to imitate not only his own master, but also to gain exposure to other masters, "taking from each the part that seems most worthy of praise."[25] In picking and choosing what to imitate, good judgment must be his guide. This may seem circular, but, as Aristotle pointed out, it is exactly what we do in acquiring any form of excellence.[26] We begin by imitation, and through constant practice, exposure to good examples, and the gradual acquisition of judgment, we gain our own mastery and develop our own particular style. We act in the right manner and at the right time, not according to abstract rules (as Plato envisioned) but by internalizing and perfecting the values and norms of an existing practice. It is a virtuous circle.

The courtier mimics and absorbs standards of conduct from others until they become second nature (i.e., disguised art). But there is a fine, almost imperceptible line between grace born of study, which perfects any performance, and affectation, which spoils all it touches. In the most famous single passage in the *Courtier*, Canossa explains:

> I have found quite a universal rule which in this matter seems to me valid above all others, and in all human affairs whether in word or deed: and that is to avoid affectation in every way possible as though it were some very rough and dangerous reef; and (to pronounce a new word perhaps) to practice in all things a certain *sprezzatura* [graceful ease; studied nonchalance], so as to conceal all art and make what-

ever is done or said appear to be without effort and almost without any thought about it. And I believe such grace comes of this: because everyone knows the difficulty of things that are rare and well done; wherefore facility in such things causes the greatest wonder; whereas, on the other hand, to labor and, as we say, drag forth by the hair of the head, shows an extreme want of grace, and causes everything, no matter how great it may be, to be held in little account.[27]

The cult of *sprezzatura*—and it did indeed become a cult after the publication of the *Courtier*—is subject to an immediate objection. Like "modest self-praise," it seems to imply deception. One strives to appear that which one is not. But of course one does. That is what learning every art entails: to achieve a mastery one does not yet possess. And when one attains that mastery, the effort that went into the process disappears into the performance. Thus, the paradox that "we may call that art true art which does not seem to be art."[28] It does not mean the artist is dissembling but rather that he has fully internalized his craft. Those familiar with the art in question know how much effort is behind the performance; but the effort itself must not show, only the results. Mastery makes the difficult look easy and hints at powers held in reserve, like a good actor playing Lear or Othello.

Castiglione (and it is appropriate to substitute the author for the speaker in this context) does not advocate an affectation of ease. Quite the contrary. He believes that affectation is even more off-putting than a display of effort without skill. *Sprezzatura* is not affectation; it is an effortless mastery by one who appears "almost incapable of making a mistake."[29] *Sprezzatura* is the perfection to which every activity aspires, whether it be writing a poem, playing a sonata, arguing a case in court, or teaching a class. These are all difficult activities requiring enormous preparation to be done well, but when done well the performance itself seems effortless and natural. Think of Roger Federer playing tennis or Joshua Bell the violin. Such ease causes "the one who listens to believe that with little effort he too could attain to such excellence—but who, when he tries, discovers that he is very far from it."[30] As Horace noted, a great poet will "make it look like child's play, / Although, in fact, he tortures himself to do so."[31]

Renaissance thinkers freely understood and embraced the idea that all activities are performances. Today, we may resist that idea, but the reality remains. We are all of us performing; we simply have lowered the standards for acceptable performance. We grudgingly accept that some activities such as playing tennis or the violin require constant practice. But in everything else we believe we must act naturally and spontaneously, avoiding any design in our behavior and such elitist mannerisms as refined speech and elaborate courtesy. But what Castiglione understood was that acting naturally and spontaneously is the most difficult performance of all. The proper courtier must work hard to attain "that pure and charming simplicity which is so appealing to all."[32] Our standards of affectation, like our standards for acceptable behavior, may have changed, but Castiglione's fundamental insight remains. True mastery and *sprezzatura* are one and the same, across the entire range of human conduct.

To be sure, standards evolve over time. Castiglione uses the example of language to make this point. Language is not static; it is a living instrument. Words come into and fall out of use. Petrarch and Boccaccio were masters of the Italian language, but they used Tuscan words appropriate to their time and location. Imitating their language in the sixteenth century would be stilted and affected, whether in speech or in writing. We should indeed imitate good writers and speakers, but adapted to the language of our day. That is not to say that any sloppy usage or slang phrases now in fashion should be adopted uncritically. Good usage comes from those "who have talent, and who through learning and experience have attained good judgment, and who thereby agree among themselves and consent to adopt those words which to them seem good; which words are recognized by virtue of a certain natural judgment and not by any art or rule."[33]

Again, we follow the virtuous circle of Aristotle. We learn what is good by imitating those who are good and by developing good judgment. Castiglione's brilliance lies in extending this insight to all aspects of human life and behavior. He is crafting an educational program for the ideal person, sound in body and mind. The goal of the courtier is to turn himself self-consciously into a work of art, but with such mastery that the self-consciousness drops away. He is both artist and subject, shaping his personality and his skill set based on the various exemplars around him.[34] To be sure, *sprezzatura* is an elitist concept. The courtier performs only for a select group of like-minded individuals, all part of the inner circle of the court. And he is judged by criteria of excellence that very few share or even fully understand. But anyone, noble born or not, can, "with care and effort,"[35] seek to excel as a human being over the full range of human activities.

THE DARKER SIDE OF COURTIERSHIP (BOOK 2)

Book 1 of the *Courtier* articulates a Renaissance version of the Greek ideal of *paideia* (education). With proper training and good examples, a man may become at ease with himself and his world, dignified but charming, multitalented but unassuming, ambitious but honorable, learned but unaffected. It is a beautiful vision of a fully realized human being—the proverbial Renaissance man—that would exercise a strong influence on writers and thinkers from Shakespeare to Nietzsche.

But Shakespeare and Nietzsche also saw a darker side to human nature. And so did Castiglione. He sets a very different tone in the preface to book 2. He notes that we praise bygone times not because they were objectively better but because we were young. The passing years have taken from us both loved ones and vitality. The years of our early adulthood in retrospect seem all the sweeter, and so we tend to idealize them, as Castiglione has idealized the court at Urbino. But, he stresses, "there is no contrary without its contrary,"[36] no good without evil, no justice without injustice, no health without sickness, no truth without falsehood, no happiness without misfortune. We cannot escape the latter, however much we embrace the former.

Book 2, while it purports to continue the discussion of the ideal courtier in book 1, recasts everything in this darker light. However perfect the courtier may seem in his own right, he depends on the favor of the prince for his very existence.[37] As Federico Fregoso, the main speaker in the first half of book 2, explains, we can converse as if the prince and the courtier are equals, but the reality is otherwise—one is "a lord" and the other "a servant."[38] All the power rests with the prince, and that fact inevitably shapes the norms of the courtier's behavior.[39]

The virtues praised in book 2 are therefore carefully calculated to obtain and retain the favor of the prince. This pragmatism cannot be acknowledged directly, since a good courtier is never obvious in his calculation. But Federico makes it clear where he is heading when he promises to explain how the courtier can make the most of his good qualities "to win praise deservedly, and a good opinion on the part of all, and favor from the prince whom he serves."[40] Federico clings to the word "deservedly," but, in an autocratic world where advancement depends on the whims of the prince, virtue and grace may not be enough. As Federico explains, "our Courtier must be cautious in his every action and see to it that prudence attends whatever he says or does."[41] Suddenly, the Renaissance version of the Greek ideal begins to seem like sycophancy. Cunning and dissimulation are necessary traits in an age of despotism.[42] The virtuous circle of Aristotle meets Machiavelli.

Federico "would have the Courtier devote all his thought and strength of spirit to loving and almost adoring the prince he serves above all else, devoting his every desire and habit and manner to pleasing him."[43] The courtier must "bend himself to this," Federico twice repeats.[44] The successful courtier must like what by nature he dislikes; he must never be ill-humored or presumptuous or the bearer of bad news. His primary trait is *mediocritas*, which means not mediocrity but balance. His qualities soften one another so as to maintain flexibility and to accommodate the changing moods of the prince. Aggression and ambition are concealed behind gentleness and modesty. Youth is tempered with judiciousness, and age with vigor. In private, he will lay aside the seriousness of daily affairs in order to amuse his prince with pleasant conversation and to charm him with humor and wit.

Federico has taken the courtier from merit to marketing. Aristotelian contextualism (learning to act in the right way, in the right circumstances, for the right reasons) receives a more calculated focus on display: "Let him consider well what he does or says, the place where he does it, in whose presence, its timeliness, the reason for doing it, his own age, his profession, the end at which he aims, and the means by which he can reach it."[45] The courtier is now concerned less with genuine excellence than with a performance that will attract the eyes of spectators. Engage in acts of courage, Federico advises, only when the right people are watching. Otherwise, hold back from the fighting. Even in sport, by no means wrestle or contend with persons of low birth at county fairs unless absolutely sure of winning, "because it is too unseemly and too ugly a thing, and quite without dignity, to see a gentleman defeated by a peasant."[46] Indeed, a courtier should associate only with noble companions and should dress in a manner to convey his station. He might, for a masquerade, adopt the attire of a rustic shepherd to emphasize his charming simplicity, but his noble status must never be in doubt. He may dance and sing with grace or play tennis with skill. But, however much he prepares for such displays, it must appear that all is done on the spur of the moment. "I would have him dissimulate the care and effort that is required in doing anything well," Federico explains, "and let him appear to esteem but little this accomplishment of his, yet by performing it excellently well, make others esteem it highly."[47] As for matters where he doesn't excel, Federico adds, the courtier should avoid them or touch on them only casually and in such a way to suggest to others that he knows more than he claims to know.

When Gaspar protests that Federico is advocating deceit, he demurs. It is merely "circumspect dissimulation," he insists, and then adds that, "even if it be deceit, it is not to be censured."[48] Indeed, before we ourselves censure Federico's version of the courtier, we need to be honest about contemporary strategies for gaining advancement and winning esteem. In almost any profession—business, law, politics, teaching, art—crafting the right impression with the right people is critical to success. A "circumspect dissimulation" of talent sometimes works better than the real thing. And even true talent has to be packaged and presented in a compelling way to break through in highly competitive environments with many others vying for favor and preferment. In social settings, the jockeying may be less obvious but no less intense.

We don't need Machiavelli to tell us that the reality of sixteenth-century court life was even more ruthless than your standard faculty meeting or Washington, DC, cocktail party. Absolute monarchs held power of life and death over their subjects. A courtier, once entered into service, could not easily withdraw. It was hazardous to lose the favor of the prince, and even worse to incur his disfavor. "We must pray God," one participant interjects, "to grant us good masters, for, once we have them, we have to endure them as they are."[49]

Princes, no less than their modern counterparts, do not always perceive merit. Some value flatterers. Others respond to presumptuous self-promotion. Still others seek out those who will do their bidding regardless of morality. To what extremes must one go to obtain and retain the good opinion of such a prince? Is courtiership inherently corrupting?[50] Such questions are not explicitly raised or answered in book 2. But they rest just below the surface, like dangerous reefs on which the entire enterprise might founder. The *brigata* wants to explore the features of the ideal courtier, not to call the position itself into question.

It is not true that "the princes of our day are all corrupt and bad," Federico insists; "there are *some* who are good."[51] But that is faint praise, indeed. For if only some are good, then many must be corrupt and bad. So Federico cannot avoid the awkward question raised by Ludovico Pio, "namely, whether a gentleman who serves a prince is bound to obey him in all that he commands, even if it is something dishonorable and disgraceful."[52] Federico quickly answers that the courtier must never do evil, even if it appears good to his master. But that facile response simply leads to a further challenge: how to distinguish what is really good from what appears to be good. Federico now begs off entirely: "I do not wish to go into that, for there would be too much to say; but let the whole question be left to your discretion."[53] In other words, that is an issue for philosophers to contemplate, not courtiers. Courtiers are neither philosophers nor saints, and they must get on with their lives as best they can, making whatever compromises they find necessary and can justify to themselves.

Not all the advice given by Federico is cynical. In a debate on the hazards of placing too much trust in other people, Federico contends that friendship "yields all the good that life holds for us."[54] And while he insists that public performance is a young man's game and that old men cannot *cantare alla viola* (sing to the viola) in public without appearing ridiculous, he adds, "let them do so in secret and simply in order to relieve their spirits of the troubling thoughts and great vexations of which our life is full, and to taste that something divine in music."[55] It is interesting to note that Castiglione himself, having suffered many losses, still loved to play the viola and sing.

But, despite these moments of grace, Federico has refashioned the portrait painted by Canossa, or at least has added a strong element of chiaroscuro to it. The charming *sprezzatura* of book 1 is replaced by the "circumspect dissimilation" of book 2. There is no longer anything pure about the courtier's performance, however polished and beautiful it might appear. But, then, life itself shares that inherent and terrible ambiguity. Castiglione did not write a treatise; he wrote a dialogue in which the perspectives of the various speakers sometimes harmonize and sometimes clash with one another. That dissonance continues in book 3, where the ideal court lady is introduced.

THE IDEAL COURT LADY (BOOK 3)

On the third night, the conversation turns away from the ideal courtier to the ideal court lady. The Magnifico Giuliano de' Medici is the main speaker, though there are even more interjections than usual from Gaspar, the resident misogynist. Gaspar's chauvinism is in part a way of teasing the ladies and displaying his wit, but his raillery, and that of a few others, is more barbed than usual. Women held prominent positions in every court society, but nowhere more so than in Urbino, where the prince was infirm and largely absent. Courtiers were already moving away from their historical role as *condottieri* and into the more domestic sphere of polite society, where the women must be served and pleased as well as the prince. But, in Urbino, the usual hierarchy is wholly inverted in the evenings. The duchess and her lady-in-waiting, Emilia Pia, hold sway over the courtiers. The men may do most of the talking, but the two women control the range of topics, select the speakers, and police the "fine manners" that set bounds on frankness. In effect, the men are competing for the favor of the women, as they ordinarily would for the prince, under rules set by the duchess and Emilia. Gaspar is unusually blunt in voicing his resentment at this emasculation. Indeed, indirect reference is made to the prince's literal emasculation by disease when one of the courtier's, in praising continence, indelicately notes that the duchess "has lived with her husband for fifteen years like a widow."[56]

The Magnifico soundly routs the misogynists in argument. His court lady is the equal of any courtier in virtue and talent. Some qualities befit a woman more than a man, and vice versa. She need not pursue bodily exercise or learn to handle weapons. The courtier's manliness is replaced in the court lady by tenderness and sweetness. Her conversation is marked above all by "a certain pleasing affability."[57] And beauty is more necessary for her than for the courtier. But the virtues of the mind are similar, and women deserve the same education as men. "I say that women can understand all the things men can understand and that the intellect of a woman can penetrate wherever a man's can,"[58] a proposition Shakespeare would illustrate repeatedly in his plays. Thus, the court lady, like the courtier, should have "knowledge of letters, of music, of painting, and know how to dance and how to be festive."[59] Her good qualities will also balance one another, a blending of seeming contraries such as a "quick vivacity of spirit," yet also "a certain gravity, tempered with wisdom and goodness."[60]

The Magnifico goes beyond purely social and intellectual graces, however, and claims that women could rule cities and command armies as well as men do.[61] This change of focus is interesting. During the first two evenings, when describing the perfect courtier, nothing beyond the vaguest generalities was offered about the serious business of helping the prince run the state and fight off its enemies. But the Magnifico piles up example after example of women whose wisdom, cunning, and courage either have rescued a state from the defects of its male rulers or have stood up to tyranny. Men write history, he notes; otherwise, women would play an even more prominent role. Even so, it is beyond dispute that they "have undertaken wars and won glorious victories, governed kingdoms with the greatest prudence and justice, and done all that men have done."[62]

The Magnifico starts with Alexandra, wife of Alexander, king of the Jews.[63] Upon his death, the people were full of rage at the dead tyrant and threatened to kill his two children in revenge for his cruelty. Alexandra forestalled them by having Alexander's dead body thrown into the middle of the town square and telling the citizens that they should take their justified revenge on the body of the dead king but have mercy on her children, who were wholly innocent of their father's wrongdoing. The crowd was so moved and appeased that it not only spared the children, but chose them as their rulers.

The Magnifico follows with the story of Epicharis, a freed Roman slave who suffered unspeakable tortures in silence rather than reveal a plot against the tyrant Nero. He mentions the siege of Chios, in which the attacking ruler promised freedom and their masters' wives to any slaves who would escape the city and join the attacking army. The women were so outraged that they themselves donned armor and fought fiercely on the walls until the besiegers were driven off. Similarly, when Cyrus routed a Persian army in battle, so that the fighters fled toward their city, the women met them outside the gate and so upbraided them for cowardice that they turned and defeated the enemy.

These anecdotes, as well as others presented by the Magnifico, illustrate Machiavellian *virtù* rather than the anodyne virtues of the courtier articulated in the first two books.[64] Court life may be elegant, refined, and civilized. But that veneer cannot fully disguise the brutality necessary to maintain it or the abuses inherent in absolute power. It would have been impolitic to introduce such themes in the discussion of the courtier. But, by focusing on the sometimes ruthless courage of women in historical examples, Castiglione, through the Magnifico, can make the same point obliquely.[65] The world is a dangerous place, and in extreme circumstances the courtier (or the court lady) must call upon Machiavellian *virtù*.

The Magnifico quickly steers away from such a conclusion, however, turning back instead to the domestic sphere and a discussion of courtly love. Yet, here, the parallels between the prince and the court lady are equally pronounced. For the courtier must pay court to his lady in the same way as his prince. A courtier gains favor "by loving and serving her and by being worthy, valiant, discreet, and modest."[66] If anything, the Magnifico places more value on the favor of the court lady than of the prince. For without women, he insists, we find no pleasure or satisfaction, and our lives would be devoid of all sweetness.[67] In a beautiful passage, he sings the praises of women "*che detengono nel loro sguardo e parole e ogni movimento tutti avvenenza, tutte le maniere gentili, tutte le conoscenze e tutte le grazie che ha portato insieme—come un unico fiore composto da tutte le eccellenze nel mondo*" (who hold in their countenance and words and every movement all comeliness, all gentle manners, all knowledge, and all the graces brought together—like a single flower composed of all the excellences in the world).[68]

The court lady, too, must behave with the greatest circumspection, like a prince. She should not be easily persuaded that she is loved, for those who are glib about being in love seldom are. She must be as chary of her trust as a prince is of his. And some of her machinations are also those of the prince. In the face of an importunate courtier, she can pretend not to understand or take it all in jest and thus deflect requests for favors she cannot or does not wish to grant. Most of all, before she gives any sign of her favor, she must ensure that the courtier wishes only to serve her and to make her wishes his own, and to find his highest happiness in such union of desire and will.

The courtier, then, alternates between a master (the prince) and a mistress (the court lady), to each of whom he must demonstrate his devotion. But is there not more to being a courtier than a life of service and subjection to the will of others? Is there not more than an endless series of tournaments, dances, witty conversations, and even lovemaking within the constraints imposed by "fine manners?" Signor Ottaviano Fregoso, the brother of Federico, insists that there is, and he is charged to make good on that promise the following night.

THE COURTIER AS PHILOSOPHER-EDUCATOR (BOOK 4)

Book 4 is intended to elevate courtly life and to avoid what Renaissance scholar Wayne Rebhorn has aptly called "the problems of deception and triviality" that weigh on the first three books.[69] The courtier of those books is a master of display. With his grace and his *sprezzatura*, he creates the illusion of omnicompetence, of someone who will never put a foot wrong. But to what end? To entertain and amuse, of course. And to secure his own advancement. But, really, the display is an end in itself. That is simply what the courtier is—a walking, talking, dancing display of perfect courtiership. Ottaviano, for one, finds that profoundly unsatisfying. If "the Courtier were to bring forth no other fruit than to be what he is," he explains, "I should not judge it right for a man to devote so much study and labor to acquiring this perfection of Courtiership as anyone must do who wishes to acquire it."[70] In that single sentence, the first three books are summed up and dismissed as unworthy of a thinking, morally responsible human being.

By all accounts, however, Castiglione originally had planned to include only the first three books. What led him, then, to add a fourth night of conversation? His prefaces, which he wrote after the various books were completed, contain at least a partial answer. In them, he speaks of his deep sense of loss and longing. The court gathered at Urbino has been dispersed. Many of its brightest lights, including the duchess, have been extinguished. Mutability and death are the only constants.[71] Castiglione, in his word portrait, can try to recapture that lost world and rescue it from oblivion. But if the world itself is trivial and devoted to illusion, then what is the point? Castiglione needs to find a deeper meaning in it; he needs to explain why that world mattered and somehow redeems "human miseries and . . . vain hopes."[72]

It is hazardous to attribute artistic decisions to personal biography, but the death of his wife and his own religious turn, though unmentioned in the prefaces, may well have played a part in this shift. Book 4 explores two avenues by which courtiership might be elevated to a higher level. The first, presented by Ottaviano, is political. The second, presented by Pietro Bembo, is philosophical and mystical. Ultimately, neither is dispositive; neither wholly transcends deception or triviality. But both broaden the discussion beyond the "fine manners" that have threatened to stifle the entire enterprise.

Ottaviano arrives late on the fourth night, after the others have given up on him and turned to dancing. The interruption signals that something out of the ordinary course will be discussed; and Ottaviano's delayed arrival has pushed the time for discussion to the late hours when, by a tradition dating at least from Plato's *Symposium*, the deepest truths will be revealed.[73] It is with some disappointment, then, that the reader realizes that Ottaviano's thoughts are in fact fairly pedestrian and, in a post-Machiavellian era, strikingly naive.

Ottaviano's central thesis is that the courtier must use his accomplishments to win the favor and trust of the prince in order to educate him about his responsibility to rule for the benefit of his people. If the courtier has gained the affection and goodwill of the prince, he can dissuade him from unjust actions and keep him on the path of virtue. He can show the prince how much honor and profit is to be won by justice and liberality rather than by selfish despotism. He will then fulfill his true role as a courtier, for "it is certain that a man aims at the best end when he sees to it that his prince is deceived by no one, listens to no flatterers or slanderers or liars, and distinguishes good from evil, loving the one and hating the other."[74] He can, in short, speak truth to power, and power will listen.

Erasmus presented a similar argument in his *Education of a Christian Prince*. In a hereditary monarchy, he noted, the prospects for reform are limited. There is no power to select the next prince, but that simply means that the man who is to educate the prince must himself be selected with the greatest care. Plato had contended that men will be governed justly only when philosophers become kings. Erasmus was willing to settle for having philosophers educate kings, and he offered himself as an ideal candidate. He thought he could convince a future ruler to govern justly and benevolently by means of a classical, liberal education and a deep grounding in philosophy, history, and Christian thought. Erasmus's educational program could not have been more different from Machiavelli's *Prince*. It is ironic, therefore, that both works were written as respective bids for employment, and both failed utterly in that regard. Each in his own way was ready to speak truth to power, but power wasn't interested.

Yet Ottaviano's courtier faces an even tougher problem than did Erasmus. Courtiers take their princes as they find them. They don't get to mold them from a tender age and to build a long relationship of trust and respect. They must stand out from the crowd of sycophants through a dazzling array of talents that the prince will find both an ornament to his court and grounds for his trust. A courtier must, in short, be someone like

Thomas More: an ornament to the court of Henry VIII, with his deep learning, and a sound advisor who, by special dispensation of the king, was allowed always to advocate for the right course of action. And where did that get Thomas More? It got him to Tower Hill on July 6, 1535.

Sometimes, to be frank, power will not tolerate truth. Ironically, Ottaviano—ostensibly speaking in 1507—cites "Henry, Prince of Wales," as a future monarch of the greatest promise, just the sort of ruler his courtier is intended to advise and keep on the path of virtue. The murderous example of Henry VIII is not necessarily a repudiation of Ottaviano's passionate plea for a courtiership that transcends flattery and complicity. But it certainly fits better with Machiavelli's darker view of the world. Even Ottaviano rather plaintively admits at one point that, if he were to speak freely to most princes, he would lose whatever favor he had with them.[75] He advocates out of hope rather than experience.[76]

The little group continues the debate, discussing standard Renaissance questions initially posed by Plato and Aristotle, such as whether virtue can be taught, whether men do wrong knowingly or through ignorance of the good, and whether monarchy is a better form of government than a republic. But there is, at this point in the evening, a certain *pro forma* stating of respective positions without any real prospect of their resolution. The energy has definitely gone out of Ottaviano's attempt to raise courtiership to a higher level through political engagement.

Pietro Bembo, then, tries a different tack, focusing on the individual courtier and building upon the discussion of courtly love from the night before. Here, he echoes Socrates's speech from the *Symposium* about the ladder of love.[77] Love, he contends, is a longing to enjoy beauty. It initially takes the form of a desire for physical intimacy with another individual, particularly among the young. But such sensual desire eventually leads either to tedium and even disgust or to an endless cycle of yearning and anguish. It is inherently unstable and unsatisfying because it remains focused on the body rather than the soul. External beauty is but a reflection of internal goodness. The lover who values beauty only in the body misses the happiness of a union of souls and inevitably suffers loss when his love is absent.

In order "to escape the torment of this absence and to enjoy beauty without suffering, the Courtier, aided by reason, must turn his desire entirely away from the body and to beauty alone, contemplate it in its simple and pure self, in so far as he is able, and in his imagination give it a shape distinct from all matter."[78] That is quite a statement; for what does it mean, we might ask, to give beauty "a shape" that is "distinct from all matter?" Pietro is advocating a mystical vision of the divine light that "holds sway over material nature" and gives all things the "gracious and sacred beauty" that is their supreme adornment.[79]

Just as we can move from loving the physical beauty of an individual to love of that person's soul, he insists, so can we move from the beauty of the physical world to love of the divine goodness that is at the center of all that exists, for "beauty springs from God and is like a circle, the center of which is goodness."[80] The lover must ascend from the particular to the universal, from contemplation of the beauty of a single person to the beauty of all that exists and ultimately to the source of that beauty in God. Dazzled by this greater light, he will no longer hold in esteem what he first prized so greatly.[81] It is an inward turn, as well as an ascent, for the lover will learn to contemplate beauty with the eyes of his mind alone. In the highest stage of perfection, this beauty will guide his soul "from the particular intellect to the universal intellect" and from there to "a very keen perception of heavenly things."[82] The beauties of the everyday world will drop away like the faintest of shadows before the light of the highest good. Pietro ends his rapt monologue with a prayer:

Accept our souls which are offered to thee in sacrifice; burn them in that living flame which consumes all mortal ugliness, so that, being wholly separated from the body, they may unite with divine beauty in a perpetual and most sweet bond, and that we, being outside ourselves, may, like true lovers, be able to become one with the beloved, and, rising above the earth, be admitted to the banquet of angels. . . .[83]

Pietro falls silent, with his eyes turned toward heaven, until Emilia shakes the hem of his robe and cautions him not to let his soul, along with his thoughts, forsake his body. It is gentle raillery and a reminder that they are not yet admitted to the banquet of angels but still exist very much in the physical world. However exalted the discussion may get, it will not fundamentally change their lives. Indeed, they are already planning the next topic of discussion for that very evening, for when they open the windows they see that a beautiful dawn has arisen over Mount Catria in the distance.

It was also dawn when Socrates left the drinking party at which all the other revelers had drifted off to sleep. Socrates performed his ablutions and then proceeded with his day. Plato was making the point that only the lover of philosophy is truly awake to the realm of truth and goodness. Pietro makes a similar assertion—that only one who contemplates the spiritual and intellectual life is "wakened from deepest sleep" and opens his eyes to a true image of heavenly things.[84]

Yet as dawn breaks, our courtiers and court ladies return to their chambers to sleep. Pietro has not transformed them into Platonic philosophers. But he has, like Ottaviano, expanded the scope of their discourse and concerns. There is something profoundly reassuring in this lack of transcendence. Castiglione does not promise what he cannot deliver. But what he delivers is a growing consciousness of self and the roles one plays in the world. The little *brigata*, through its evening conversations, seeks to know itself, to live an examined life. But while that effort in self-understanding may push the boundaries of "fine manners," ultimately it reaffirms those boundaries as a necessary condition of civilized discourse and social interaction.[85]

Machiavelli thought that human aggression could not be suppressed or channeled in less destructive directions. As a result, every society is inherently unstable and dangerous.[86] Thomas More, or at least his main speaker, Hythloday, thought it possible to extirpate human aggression through the suppression of individual freedom. Whether the result of such suppression is utopia or the gulag continues to be debated. But Castiglione takes us in a third, more optimistic direction. Aggression and ambition don't have to be endured or extirpated; they are a vital force that can be channeled by law, by custom, and by mutual respect and affection.[87] Wisdom need be neither cynical nor transcendent.

Within the confines of polite conversation, there is a place for the idealism of Canossa, the cynicism of Federico Fregoso, the contentious interjections of Gaspar Pallavicino, the feminist defense of the Magnifico Giuliano de' Medici, the earnestness of Ottaviano Fregoso, and even the philosophical heights reached by Pietro Bembo. None of them breaks the circle. The lasting lesson of the court at Urbino is that social discourse and a growing level of self-consciousness can make civilization both possible and delightful. Like a Bach fugue, beauty is born from constraint. Even in a world ruled by tyrants and despots, there is room for grace and *sprezzatura*. As Virginia Woolf would later write, "This is our triumph; this is our consolation."[88]

Chapter 6

RABELAIS AND THE
WISDOM OF LAUGHTER

Mieulx est de ris que de larmes escripre,
Pour ce que rire est le propre de l'homme.[1]

The second book of *Gargantua and Pantagruel* opens with a prologue from its putative author, Alcofribas Nasier (an anagram of
François Rabelais). Alcofribas cites Plato's *Symposium*, in which Alcibi-
ades compares Socrates to a statue of Silenus, companion of Dionysus—
a statue ugly on the outside but inside filled with tiny gold figurines of
the gods. Socrates was notoriously ugly, rustic in manners, and comic in
bearing. But, inside, he was a man of "superhuman understanding, mirac-
ulous virtue, indomitable courage, unparalleled moderation, assured con-
tentment, perfect confidence and an unbelievable contempt for all those
things for which human beings wake, run, toil, sail and battle."[2]

My books are just like that, Alcofribas insists. They may appear to be
full of crude jests and wild fictions. They may seem frivolous and ugly.
But the reader must "scrupulously weigh what is treated within."[3] Like
a dog patiently and painstakingly cracking open a marrowbone in order
to savor its contents, these books require "careful reading and frequent
meditation" in order to reveal "the highest hidden truths and the most
awesome mysteries touching upon our religion as well as upon matters of
state and family life."[4]

Having seduced the credible reader with this plea for deeper understanding—a reader he has just compared to a dog—Alcofribas immedi-

ately makes fun of him. You don't really think Homer had in mind all the allegories that have been attributed to him by overly enthusiastic interpreters, he asks, or that Ovid was anticipating the Gospels in his *Metamorphoses*, as some idiots have tried to prove? Of course not, Alcofribas insists, and so too here: "I was no more thinking of such things when I wrote them than you were."[5] My books, he claims, smell more of wine than of midnight oil. That is, they are the product of inspiration, not scholarly toil. Make of them what you will and "enjoy yourselves . . . happily reading what follows for your bodily comfort and the good of your loins."[6]

The prologue is of a piece with the work itself. Rabelais's books really do contain treasures of wisdom about religion, matters of state, and family life, among other topics. And his principal character, Pantagruel, does develop over time the virtues of a Socrates. But there is no esoteric message hidden beneath a comic exterior. The serious and the comical are both on the surface, inextricably intertwined with each other. The message, to the extent one exists, *is* the intermingling of the serious and the comical, the lofty and the grotesque, for such is the human condition.[7] Thus, Rabelais often seems at his most comical when he is most serious, and the reader—like Gargantua on the death of his wife, Badebec, and birth of his son, Pantagruel—does not know whether to weep out of grief or to laugh out of joy. Gargantua does both. But the laughter ultimately dominates, for laughter is *le propre* (in the sense both of what is natural and what is best) for man.[8]

Rabelais—a monk turned doctor, turned author, who was ultimately condemned by the church—wrote his books between the initial phases of the Reformation in the 1520s and the French Wars of Religion, which began in 1562, a decade after his death. He was heavily influenced by Erasmus's writings on the value of a humanist education, the need for religious reform, and the moral imperatives of statecraft. Rabelais's succession of giants—Grandgousier, Gargantua, and Pantagruel—grow through multiple volumes from cardboard cutouts into embodiments of classical and Christian wisdom on these issues.

Rabelais was a Neoplatonist in the manner of the great Christian philosopher of the Renaissance Marsilio Ficino. Ficino believed in a hierarchy of being, guided by a divine intelligence. Man is close to God in that hierarchy by virtue of his immortal soul. Thus, Ficino stressed the centrality of religion to human experience.

But Rabelais was even more strongly influenced by the comic works of Erasmus, his *Colloquies* and his *Praise of Folly*, as well as by their shared love of the Greek satirist Lucian. Despite his Christian Neoplatonism, Rabelais was not one to ignore the material and materialistic side of human experience. As a doctor and the father of three illegitimate children, he understood that man's pressing need for food, drink, and sex is also central to his humanity. If we ignore those needs, we attain no self-knowledge. And, if we suppress them, we distort our own natures. Rabelais chose instead to celebrate the body. He wanted to embrace the world in all its variety, free from religious and doctrinal restrictions. He also realized, of course, that bodily functions are an endless source for jokes and humor. Rabelais delights in pulling back the curtain on humankind at its most private business; his comedy is broad and frequently crude, sometimes hilariously and sometimes, for the modern reader, uncomfortably so. "Nothing is sacred and no one is spared," as one scholar notes.[9] Or perhaps, more accurately, nothing is either too sacred or too profane for laughter and no one too lofty or too lowly to be the butt of fun.

Thus, the spiritual and the material are uniquely conjoined in Rabelais's work. He can be high-minded and in the gutter in the same sentence. The health of the spirit and the health of the body are both to be cherished and enjoyed, for they are both part of the human condition. Life is not an illness from which we hope to be cured, as many Neoplatonists taught. Life is a gift to be savored and relished in all its manifold and glorious absurdity. A rich and full life should acknowledge no limits, hence our term *Rabelaisian*, ordinarily (if misleadingly) applied only to orgies of food, drink, and sex, but properly extended to learning and friendship as well. Above all, Rabelais thought that life should be full of laughter and joy, triumphing over tears and grief. Not even death can block the endless regenerative power of life. Rabelais, for all his celebration of excess, strikes a remarkable balance between the bestial and the divine. As the English novelist and critic John Cowper Powys concluded, "Rabelais is the sanest of all the great writers, perhaps the only sane one."[10]

LIFE

François Rabelais was born in Chinon, a town in the Loire Valley that played an often pivotal role in the Hundred Years' War between France and England, though it is known today mostly for its medieval castle and its Cabernet Franc wine. Rabelais likely was born in 1483, the same year as Martin Luther. His father, Antoine, was a prominent lawyer and modest landowner.

Rabelais and his two brothers must have received a good education, though little is known of the specifics. His school friends, Jean and Guillaume du Bellay and Geoffroy d'Estissac, achieved considerable prominence—Jean and Geoffroy as bishops, and Guillaume as a statesman—and they would prove invaluable patrons in his later life.

Rabelais studied law at some point before joining the Franciscan monastery in Fontenay-le-Comte in 1510 or 1511. It was an odd choice for one who—despite his protestations—burned a great deal of midnight oil studying Latin and Greek and eventually Hebrew so that he could read the Bible and the classics in their original languages. The Franciscans—a mendicant order founded by Francis of Assisi—were indifferent if not actively hostile to education. They favored the spirit and were suspicious of intellect as inclined to lead one astray.[11]

While Rabelais toiled in the monastery, François I became king of France in 1515. He continued the "Italian Wars" of his predecessors, even capturing and controlling Milan for a time. But the cultural conquest ran the other way, with ideas from the Italian Renaissance pouring into France, starting, of course, with Petrarch and continuing through the three-year residence of Leonardo da Vinci at the court of François I in Amboise. François was an active patron of Renaissance artists and writers. It is said that the king himself cradled Leonardo's head in his arms as he died. Horace's words about Greece and Rome could readily be applied to Italy and France: "Captive Greece took its Roman captor captive, / Invading uncouth Latium with its arts."[12] Without this prolonged invasion of Italian arts and letters into France, neither Rabelais nor Montaigne—the twin crowns of the French Renaissance—would have been possible.

Yet it was a northerner, Erasmus, who exercised the most direct influence on Rabelais. In a famous letter, Rabelais wrote to Erasmus: "Whatever I am and am worth, I have received from you alone."[13] In religion, Rabelais advocated the same significant reforms urged by Erasmus. His sympathies lay with a group known in France as the Evangelicals, who believed in the primacy of the scriptures, which should be read whenever possible in their original languages but otherwise in accurate vernacular translations. The Evangelicals rejected the Latin (Vulgate) Bible and the authority of the Catholic Church in matters of biblical interpretation. Each man and woman, they urged, should read and meditate directly upon the word of God without the mediation of clerics.

Rabelais and the Evangelicals were also hostile to the sale of indulgences, monasticism, the worship of saints and their relics, and the making of pilgrimages to the shrines of saints. They believed only in the sacraments mentioned in the Gospels (baptism and the Eucharist) and discarded the other five, including confession, the ordination of priests, and even matrimony, as anything other than a secular ceremony of no religious significance (the last quite convenient for the father of three illegitimate children).[14] They were also antipapists, particularly insofar as the pope claimed divine authority to dictate specific articles of faith. The Evangelicals believed in the goodness and power of God, the obligations of charity and love, and very little else. They wholly rejected the vast and, in their view, arid constructions of medieval scholastic theology.

They also adamantly rejected the use of force in matters of religion, something that set them apart from the Catholic Church and its often equally authoritarian opponents.

Rabelais, like Erasmus, nevertheless remained a Catholic. In particular, he rejected Luther's belief that man lacks free will and can play no part in his own salvation, which depends solely on the grace of God. Yet he was constantly at war with the conservative theology faculty of the University of Paris at the Sorbonne, which harshly condemned his books for departing from the faculty's approved orthodoxy. It was a time of rapidly growing religious intolerance in which people, including friends of Rabelais, were hanged, burned, or both for alleged heresies. Rabelais, like Erasmus, was fortunate to escape such a fate.

In 1523, the Sorbonne banned the study of Greek in France precisely so that citizens could not read the New Testament in the original language. Rabelais's library of Greek books was temporarily seized. In 1524, he was allowed by papal dispensation to transfer, along with his books, from the Franciscan to the Benedictine order, which was less rigid and encouraged scholarship. Eventually, however, Rabelais left monastic life altogether. He studied medicine at Paris and Montpellier from approximately 1526 to 1530. The pope gave his retroactive approval to this unusual arrangement in 1536, permitting Rabelais both to practice medicine and to remain a nominal member of the Benedictine order. The patronage of the du Bellay family and of Bishop Geoffroy d'Estissac was critical in obtaining both these dispensations.

While he was studying in Paris, Rabelais fathered two children, François and Junie, likely by the same woman. A third child, Theodule, was born in 1535, the same year Rabelais's father died. But Theodule died in infancy, and Rabelais took the loss very hard. The other two children were eventually legitimized by the pope in 1540.

Rabelais was appointed as physician at the Hôtel-Dieu in Lyons in 1530. He began to lecture and translate Greek medical texts. He published his first book, *Pantagruel*, in 1532. The prequel, *Gargantua*, followed two years later. Although he was accomplished in Latin and an admirer of Erasmus, Rabelais chose to write in everyday French, though always with a heavy sprinkling of neologisms derived from Hebrew, Greek, and Latin. His writings, and those of Montaigne, were critical in the development of modern French prose.

Rabelais's first two books were censured by the faculty of theology at the Sorbonne. This is unsurprising, since Rabelais ridicules the Sorbonne, its logic-chopping scholastic theology, and its outmoded gothic education in both books. Aside from the Sorbonne's condemnation, however, there was no serious short-term consequence to Rabelais's evangelical and humanistic challenge to conservative thought. It helped that the king himself, François I, was a fan.

François I was, of course, a Catholic king and aspired (unsuccessfully) to be crowned as Holy Roman emperor, losing out to Charles V of Spain in 1519 and eventually spending a year as the latter's prisoner after the ill-fated battle of Pavia in 1525, in which the French were routed by the Spaniards in Italy. But François was sympathetic to moderate religious views. His sister, Marguerite of Navarre, to whom Rabelais dedicated his *Third Book of Pantagruel*, was a pronounced Evangelical. Such sympathies almost cost François his life and his crown at the hand of hard-line Catholic reactionaries. Yet he still read Rabelais—or, rather, had Rabelais read to him by the bishop of Macon—with the greatest enjoyment. As M. A. Screech remarks in his exhaustive study of Rabelais, "It is a nice conceit to imagine Rabelais's Chronicles read aloud to his king by a bishop."[15]

That easy tolerance began to change after the so-called Affair of the Placards on the night of October 17, 1534, when Huguenot posters attacking papal authority and the Mass appeared in Paris and several other French cities. One such poster was even affixed to the bedchamber door of the king in Amboise. The posters were apparently inspired by the views of the Protestant reformer Ulrich Zwingli, whose heresies included rejecting transubstantiation, the literal transformation of the bread of the Eucharist into the body of Christ during communion. From that time forward, François I began to align himself more and more with conservative orthodoxy and to remove his protection from Protestant reformers. It was also in 1534 that Thomas More was confined to the Tower of London; that Luther finished his German translation of the Bible; and that the Society of Jesus, known commonly as the Jesuits, was founded by Ignatius of Loyola as a vanguard of the Counter-Reformation, though not formally approved by Pope Paul III until 1540.

Rabelais waited twelve years before publishing another book. He taught and practiced medicine, ministered to plague victims, and traveled several times to Rome and other parts of Italy, remaining there for extended periods as part of the entourage first of Jean and, later, of Guillaume du Bellay. When Rabelais published the *Third Book of Pantagruel* in 1546, he had the king's express permission do so. He published the book under his own name. But neither the king's blessing nor the royal dedication to Marguerite of Navarre saved the book from immediate and harsh condemnation by the increasingly reactionary Sorbonne, and Rabelais found it prudent to leave the country, settling first in Metz, in what is now northeast France, and later traveling again to Rome.

In 1547, François I died, and his son Henri II succeeded to the throne. Through the intercession of another patron, Cardinal de Châtillon, Henri II granted Rabelais a royal privilege to reprint his earlier books, providing him with a degree of copyright protection. Thus emboldened, Rabelais revised the earlier books and published a *Fourth Book of Pantagruel* in 1552. Despite the royal privilege, the book was promptly condemned by the Paris Parliament at the behest of the Sorbonne. But Rabelais, who had less than a year to live in any event, was unmolested, despite widespread rumors that he had been imprisoned.

In 1553, Rabelais resigned two benefices at Meudon and Saint-Christophe-du-Jambet that he had obtained in 1551 with the help of Cardinal de Châtillon. He died in early April and was buried in the cemetery of Saint Paul's Church in Paris. In 1562, the Council of Trent listed Rabelais among "heretics of the first class." A supposed *Fifth Book* was published under his name in 1564, though how much, if any, of it was actually written by Rabelais is a matter of scholarly dispute. Rabelais's vast reputation rests on the four books published during his lifetime.

PANTAGRUEL

Rabelais did not invent his family of giants. He was preceded by a popular chapbook (an inexpensive, illustrated volume—the Renaissance equivalent of a penny dreadful) called *The Great and Inestimable Chronicles of the Great and Enormous Giant Gargantua*. There of course had always been folktales of giants, dating back to Goliath in the Bible, the titans of Greek mythology, and the Cyclops of Homer's *Odyssey*. But the giants of the *Gargantua Chronicles* were comic rather than frightening figures, and, as Rabelais's anagram author notes in the prologue to *Pantagruel*, "the printers have already sold more of them in two months than bibles will be bought in nine years."[16] Scholars once speculated that Rabelais himself was their anonymous author, but most reject that view today. Rabelais seems simply to have capitalized on the popularity of the chronicles and, in the process, transformed them in ways that likely surprised even Rabelais himself.

Rabelais's *Horrifying and Dreadful Deeds and Prowesses of the Most Famous Pantagruel, King of the Dipsodes, Son of the Great Giant Gargantua*, was published in 1532. It, too, was immediately popular. As noted, Rabelais chose to write in the French vernacular, which restricted the book's initial circulation to French speakers but, among those, made it accessible to a much broader cross section than the community of scholars and clergymen who still knew Latin. The book was read by or to wide audiences. Even today, *Pantagruel* is the most accessible of Rabelais's four volumes. Despite its episodic structure, the narrative is coherent, and modern readers will find it funny even without understanding the numerous references to scripture, to Latin and Greek works, to contemporary political events and religious controversies, and to the entire gamut of Renaissance learning that his books increasingly incorporated. Nothing kills a joke more quickly than an explanatory footnote.

Pantagruel opens, as tales of heroes generally do, with a lengthy genealogy. It begins with Chalbroth and proceeds through fifty-nine biblical "begats" before it reaches Pantagruel, son of Gargantua and grandson of Grandgousier. One of these early giant ancestors, Hurtaly, lived through the great flood, and the narrator, eager to establish the credibility of his account, explains how it is that Hurtaly survived in addition to Noah and the handful of others in the ark. Hurtaly was not in the ark, Alcofribas admits. He was too big. Instead, he sat astride it, like a child on a hobbyhorse, with his legs dangling on either side. And a good thing he did, because without Hurtaly propelling the boat with his legs and using his foot as a rudder, the boat would surely have foundered. Those inside, recognizing the help he provided, sent up food to him through a funnel.

This opening chapter sets the tone for what follows. The author makes deliberate fun of biblical/heroic genealogies and the scriptural account of Noah's ark. He offers a deadpan recital of wholly absurd events. In his hands, the ridiculous will become mundane and the mundane ridiculous. Small wonder that conservative reactionaries hated the book and that the general populace loved it. As the Soviet scholar Mikhail Bakhtin pointed out in a highly influential study, Rabelais capitalizes on the "culture of folk carnival humor," in which all that is official and somber—particularly ecclesiastical dogmatism and rigid social hierarchy—is turned upside down and transformed by laughter.[17] The only law of the carnival is joyous freedom, which mocks pomposity and celebrates the abundance of earthly existence. Rabelais's first two books are just such carnival feasts.

And yet, that is not to say that Rabelais is not serious. As we shall see, even in *Pantagruel*, he writes passionately on the subject of humanist education, the limitations of language, and the proper mode of prayer. Over several volumes, Pantagruel himself will become a model of the Christian-Stoic sage and ideal ruler. But the seriousness is never narrow-minded, authoritarian, or dogmatic; it is always broad enough to embrace humor and to accommodate doubt. The laughter crowns rather than undercuts the serious. Bakhtin explains that, in contrast to the modern viewpoint according to which "that which is important and essential cannot be comical,"

> the Renaissance conception of laughter can be roughly described as follows: Laughter has a deep philosophical meaning, it is one of the essential forms of the truth concerning the world as a whole, concerning history and man; it is a peculiar point of view relative to the world; the world is seen anew, no less (and perhaps more) profoundly than when seen from the serious standpoint. Therefore, laughter is just as admissible in great literature, posing universal problems, as seriousness. Certain essential aspects of the world are accessible only to laughter.[18]

We saw such profound, life-embracing laughter in the plays of Aristophanes, in Boccaccio's *Decameron*, Chaucer's *Canterbury Tales*, and Erasmus's *Praise of Folly*. We will see it again in Cervantes's *Don Quixote* and the comedies of Shakespeare before it largely dissolves into satire and domestic comedy during the rational, enlightened, neoclassical eighteenth century. It will rise again in James Joyce's *Ulysses*. But Rabelais was the apotheosis of philosophical laughter.

After these genealogical preliminaries, Rabelais begins his first book by intertwining death and birth. That remains his theme throughout the four volumes. In keeping with the carnival atmosphere, images of destruction, dissolution, and decay are always countered with those of fertility, generation, and renewal. Badebec dies giving birth to the enormous Pantagruel. Gargantua is full of miserable doubt: should he weep for his lost wife or laugh out of joy for his son? He notes that he has good dialectical arguments for both sides. On the one hand, he reproaches God for Badebec's death, for leaving him alone, and for not taking him in her place. On the other, he praises God for giving him a son so big and fair, so happy, so laughing. But the *pro et contra* of scholastic debate, he knows, is useless and never leads to resolution or any form of wisdom. Our reactions to the contradictory unity of life and death cannot be worked out syllogistically. Having swept away the whole of medieval scholasticism, Gargantua affirms life without ignoring, or blaming God for, its pain. He simply cannot help himself because of his abundance of vital spirits and love for his son. It has always been thus. It will always be thus. No quantity of tears will break this cycle. He composes an epitaph for Badebec's tomb noting her virtues and concluding, "She died on the day death came: That is all."[19] Then he embraces his newborn child, as well as an array of other women.

Like all legendary heroes, Pantagruel performs remarkable feats while still in his cradle. These feats are actually just a function of his enormous size and even more enormous appetite, but, like all good fathers, Gargantua finds them remarkable. Pantagruel's education, mimicking Rabelais's own, is both eclectic and peripatetic. Gargantua's kingdom is known as Utopia—a somewhat satirical tribute to Thomas More and a nod to political, educational, and religious reform—but the first two books are clearly set in Rabelais's own France.

Pantagruel goes to Montpellier to study medicine but finds it too tedious. Besides, the physicians stink of enemas. After being drawn away by his tutor from Avignon (too many loose women) and Angers (the plague), he settles for a time to read law, first in Bourges and then in Orléans. He loves his Roman law books, which seemed to him "like a beautiful golden robe, triumphant and wondrously precious, which had been hemmed with shit."[20] That is, he finds intolerable the medieval glosses that befoul the pure classical texts.

Pantagruel learns to play bowls and royal tennis and to carouse with his fellow students. But he does not tax his brain by overmuch studying lest it weaken his sight, especially after seeing one fellow with "scarcely more learning than he could lug," who made up for it by being very good at tennis and dancing and thus received his academic hood.[21] When Pantagruel arrives in Paris, the state of education is, if anything, worse. He finds those who ape learning by so liberally sprinkling their French with bastardized Latin that they are all but incomprehensible. He visits the library of the Abbey of Saint-Victor, famous for its collection of medieval books of scholastic philosophy and theology. Rabelais pillories the library mercilessly with a five-page listing that includes the following titles:

The Apparition of Saint Geltrude to a Nun of Poissy during her Child-birth;
On the Art of Discreetly Farting in Company;
Nine Enneads on Profits to be Milked from Indulgences;
The Comforts of the Monastic Life;
The Shackles of the Religious Life;
The Manacles of Devotion;
On the Deposability of a Pope by the Church.[22]

It is clear from the list and from the descriptions of Pantagruel's education to date, that Rabelais saw little virtue in medieval scholasticism and much to reform in the current church. His own program for reform—passionately advocated but suitably exaggerated for comic effect—is set forth in a letter from Gargantua to his son.

Gargantua makes three points in the letter: one dynastic, one humanist, and one evangelical. All three owe their debt to Erasmus. First, Gargantua extols God's blessing in allowing men and women—despite the sin of Adam and Eve—to obtain a species of immortality through their lineal descendants: "what was lost to the parents remains in their children and what perished in the children remains in the grandchildren."[23] Thus, life will overcome death until the final judgment, when all generation and corruption will cease. This line of succession imposes on parents, particularly rulers, an obligation to see their children "fully perfected in virtue, honor and wisdom,"[24] an injunction earlier laid down by Erasmus in his *Education of a Christian Prince*. One of the most important tasks of the king is to produce a suitable heir, a basic necessity that—as Mark Hansen demonstrates in his remarkable and fascinating book, *The Royal Facts of*

Life: Biology and Politics in Sixteenth-Century Europe—proved beyond the power of most of the royal houses, leading to war and chaos.

Second, Gargantua urges Pantagruel to take advantage of the new humanist learning that was unavailable in Gargantua's own youth:

> The times were still dark, redolent of the disaster and calamity of the Goths, who had brought all sound learning to destruction; but, by the goodness of God, light and dignity have been restored to literature during my lifetime: and I can see such an improvement that I would hardly be classed nowadays among the first form of little grammar-schoolboys, I who (not wrongly) was reputed the most learned of my century as a young man.[25]

Gargantua's thirst for knowledge and appetite for learning are nothing short of gargantuan. Pantagruel must acquire a perfect command of Greek, Latin, and Hebrew, as well as Chaldean and Arabic. He must mold his Greek style after Plato and his Latin after Cicero. "Let there be no history which you do not hold ready in memory," Gargantua continues.[26] Master geometry, arithmetic, music, and astronomy, but leave astrology and scholastic debate alone as "abuses and vanities."[27] In a rush of enthusiasm, Gargantua enjoins Pantagruel to apply himself with curiosity to all natural phenomena: "let there be no sea, river or stream the fishes of which you do not know. Know all the birds of the air, all the trees, bushes and shrubs of the forests, all the herbs in the soil, all the metals hidden deep in the womb of the Earth, the precious stones of all the Orient and the South: let none remain unknown to you."[28] Study also the texts of civil law and the ancient medical writers, "and by frequent dissections acquire a perfect knowledge of that other world which is Man."[29]

"In short," Gargantua concludes, "let me see you an abyss of erudition."[30] It is a course of study suitable for a giant or a new Aristotle. Yet it is the course of study that Rabelais himself largely followed, and he incorporated as much of it in his books as he could. Rabelais's excitement at the vast horizons of humanist learning available to his generation is palpable. It is the spirit of the Renaissance itself.

Yet Rabelais does not forget religion. His humanism is secular and freed from the restraints of religious dogmatism, but his faith is unswerving. That is the third point of Gargantua's great letter. Knowledge without conscience, he writes, is but the ruin of the soul. Thus, Pantagruel should love and serve God, place all his hopes in him, and "by faith informed with charity," live a life conjoined with God and never cut off from him by sin.[31] That faith must be "informed with charity" is an important emendation of Luther, who thought faith alone was required and that sinful man could not hope to win God's grace through good works. Rabelais wanted man to meet God more than halfway. It is the only doctrinal item on which Rabelais insists. He otherwise shows his evangelical leanings by urging Pantagruel to study the scriptures—the Gospels and Epistles in Greek and the Old Testament in Hebrew—for several hours each day.

Rabelais refined and expanded upon his three principles but never swerved from the basic outline established in Gargantua's letter to his son. Pantagruel, struck to the heart by his father's advice, studies with renewed dedication, and "his mind was so tireless and keen among his books that it was like a flame among the heather."[32] He vows to preach the Gospel purely and simply without the doctrinal accretions imposed upon it by "a load of bacon-pappers and false prophets."[33] Most important of all, he becomes a wise and benevolent king who seeks peace and prosperity for his people.

Once Pantagruel's education is complete, however, the focus of the book shifts to a new character named Panurge. Panurge is a classic trickster. He is cunning, boastful, amoral, and linguistically facile. When Pantagruel first encounters him, Panurge has recently escaped from Turkish captivity and is battered and starving. But Panurge perversely asks for help in thirteen separate languages (three of them wholly invented) before finally making his needs known in his native French. He is the embodiment of the Shrovetide (i.e., pre-Lent) carnival spirit, with his constant pranks, his overflowing energy, and his self-proclaimed sexual and martial prowess. He exists to make Pantagruel, and Rabelais's audience, laugh. The modern reader must judge for herself whether his antics are still funny.

One Panurge episode warrants special mention, however, both because even the modern reader—in fact, especially the modern reader—will find it genuinely funny and, separately, because it connects with Renaissance concerns about the limitations of language in communicating matters of the greatest importance. Pantagruel becomes famous for his erudition on all manner of subjects after he posts, at the crossroads of Paris, 9,764 theses dealing with the greatest controversies in all the disciplines. He is even called upon to resolve a legal dispute so obscure and so buried in pleadings and cross pleadings that no one can understand it. He dismisses the mountains of paper as "nothing but subversions of justice and ways of prolonging the process,"[34] which shows that the legal system has not changed much in over four hundred years. After hearing directly from the incoherent parties, Pantagruel renders a judgment that satisfies both sides and leaves the assembled counselors and doctors of law in a rapture of amazement.

Pantagruel's reputation for wisdom attracts from England a great scholar named Thaumaste, who searches out Pantagruel to discuss certain texts of philosophy, magic, alchemy, and the Kabbalah (ancient Jewish, mystical interpretations of the Bible) about which Thaumaste is in doubt. But Thaumaste does not want to debate *pro et contra* as "the scoundrels" at the Sorbonne do, because such scholastic debates are not a search for truth but a pointless matching of thesis and antithesis. Nor does he want to proceed by rhetorical declamation, which is merely a means of showing off. "I want to dispute by signs alone with no talking," Thaumaste insists, "for the matters are so arduous that no words of Man would be adequate to settle them to my satisfaction."[35]

Renaissance thinkers were fascinated by the distinction between conventional signs (assigned their meaning by custom) and natural signs (which conveyed their inherent meaning). In particular, scholars sought biblical sanction for certain esoteric signs that could convey mystical meanings that eluded mere words. Thaumaste is such a scholar, and Rabelais's portrayal of him is sympathetic. But, as always, Rabelais does not shrink from finding comedy even in what he admires. Panurge presents himself as Pantagruel's disciple and offers to debate Thaumaste. But whereas the earnest Thaumaste employs signs from the esoteric tradition, Panurge responds with a series of obscene and vulgar gestures, such as forming a circle of his index finger and thumb and repeatedly thrusting into it the index finger of the other hand, or making absurd faces by pulling his mouth apart with his fingers and his eyelids down with his thumbs. Thaumaste, like the doctors of law after Pantagruel's judgment, is utterly vanquished. He extols Pantagruel's virtue before the assembled company:

> You have seen how one sole disciple of his has satisfied me, telling me more than I ever asked for, and has in addition both revealed and solved for me other incalculable doubts. In that way he has, I can assure you, broached for me the true well and abyss of the encyclopedia of erudition—of such a sort that I, indeed, never thought I could find any man who knew merely the first elements of it—namely when we disputed by signs without uttering one word, nay, half a word.[36]

Thaumaste promises to write a treatise documenting and explaining the entire exchange—itself a comical notion since the meaning of the signs is supposed to lie beyond words—and Pantagruel takes him off to dinner where they drink "guts to the ground" until they are slurring, a fitting end to a trial of the limits of language for conveying the profoundest truths.[37] The Thaumaste episode—with its charitable humor and comic wisdom—is Rabelais at his best.

Pantagruel departs Paris when he learns that Utopia has been invaded by the neighboring Dipsodes. A similar incident is developed more fully in *Gargantua*, and we will deal with issues of war and peace in discussing that book. But one particularly famous episode warrants mention because it perfectly illustrates Rabelais's genius for making the familiar seem grotesque and the grotesque familiar. The episode is known as "The World in Pantagruel's Mouth" after the essay of that title in Erich Auerbach's *Mimesis*. Pantagruel is of course a giant. But the reader—and seemingly Alcofribas—often forgets that fact as Pantagruel studies medicine, meets with doctors of law, and entertains visiting scholars. Yet his giant stature is always available for comic exaggeration. Thus, Pantagruel, given a diuretic by Panurge, pisses so copiously that he drowns the enemy camp, and their king escapes only by being carried away on the shoulders of his own giants. Pantagruel then—after a perfectly serious evangelical prayer commending himself to God—kills the largest of those giants, Loup Garou, in single combat, and uses his body to batter the others. It is a mock-heroic epic of gross proportions.

Pantagruel then decides to invade the land of the Dipsodes with his army to put an end to their aggression. But they are confronted with a deluge of rain. Pantagruel, of course, can see above the clouds. He realizes that it is only a passing shower and, gathering his army at close quarters, puts out his tongue—"only half-way"—to shelter them from the downpour. Alcofribas, who interjects himself into the narrative, finds it too close packed under Pantagruel's tongue. "I therefore clambered up as well as I could," he explains, "and journeyed for a good two leagues over his tongue until I entered his mouth."[38] There he finds an entire land, bearing a distinct resemblance to France, with mountains, wide meadows, great forests, and spacious cities. He meets peasants planting cabbages or trapping pigeons to be sold at market. Alcofribas considers it a new world, but the peasants insist it is certainly not new, though they have heard rumors of "some new-found earth outside, with a sun and a moon, and full of all sorts of fine things."[39] Alcofribas enjoys himself so much—despite a plague caused when Pantagruel consumes too much garlic sauce—that he stays there for four months. When he finally climbs out, passing through Pantagruel's beard to his shoulder and then sliding to the ground, the land of the Dipsodes has been conquered and peace restored. Pantagruel asks Alcofribas how he survived there, and Alcofribas explains that he "exacted a toll on the most delicate morsels that passed through your lips." "But where did you shit?" Pantagruel asks. "In your gorge, my Lord," is the answer, which causes Pantagruel the greatest merriment.[40]

As Auerbach explains, "everything goes with everything" in Rabelais.[41] The natural and the fantastic, the familiar and the grotesque, the comical and the serious, all flow seamlessly together; coarse jokes are conjoined with great erudition, obscene stories with philosophical insight, adolescent pranks with spiritual elevation. Man—with his bodily functions and physical dissolution—is comical in comparison with his ideals, but the ideals can be held no less deeply for all that. A good Pantagruelist, as Rabelais notes, lives "in peace, joy and health, always enjoying good cheer,"[42] yet nonetheless fixes his thoughts on God and, "by faith informed with charity," is never to be cut off from him.

GARGANTUA

Gargantua was published in 1534, a mere two years after *Pantagruel*, which is a tribute both to the popularity of the first book and to its author's productivity. With this prequel—for although *Pantagruel* was written first, Gargantua obviously precedes his son Pantagruel—Rabelais established the first blockbuster franchise. The next two installments were called, in essence, *Pantagruel III* and *Pantagruel IV*; there was even a fifth, largely ghostwritten volume that appeared ten years after the author's death.

Gargantua has the same basic plot as *Pantagruel*. We learn about the giant's childhood and education; a secondary character, or sidekick, is introduced for comic relief and to propel the plot; and the giant ultimately takes his rightful place as a good Christian king and defender of his people. Both books are even located for the most part in the same area near Chinon where Rabelais was born, and they share the same frank treatment of those basic bodily functions that connect the Platonic spirit with the world in a constant cycle of regeneration and decay: eating, drinking, farting, defecating, urinating, expectorating, and copulating, to name a few. The Florentine Neoplatonism derived from Marsilio Ficino and carried over into Castiglione's *Courtier* still wallows happily in the muck of the family farm at La Devinière. Rabelais will not let the reader forget that man—to his joy and sorrow—shares more with the beasts than with the angels.

Despite the parallels in subject matter, the treatment is sufficiently different in each volume to retain the reader's interest. Rabelais espouses a more direct humanistic and evangelical message in *Gargantua*, and sharply satirizes the Sorbonne and monasticism. That sense of intellectual and satirical freedom would change in late 1534 when the Affair of the Placards led to a conservative backlash and a re-ascendant Sorbonne. It would be twelve years before Rabelais—busy in any event with his medical career and extensive travels in the entourages of the du Bellays and Geoffroy d'Estissac—felt comfortable publishing another volume; even then, the tone of the work would change significantly from the innocent, carnivalesque humor of the first two.

We will skip over Gargantua's childhood—in which he demonstrates his remarkable abilities in a search for the perfect ass wipe—as well as his initial "gothic" education, which leaves him ignorant, dirty, lazy, and boorish. Ultimately, as outlined in chapters 21 and 22, Gargantua casts off the "Sorbonagres" and "Sorbonists" and receives a humanist education fit for a Renaissance prince or even a courtier from Urbino. We will also skip the delightful incident in which he takes the great bells from the Cathedral of Notre-Dame in Paris and hangs them around the neck of his mule. We will limit ourselves instead to discussing two episodes: the Picrocholine war and the founding of the Abbey of Thélème, both of which are set in or near La Devinière.

The Picrocholine war occupies the bulk of the book, from chapter 23 through chapter 49. It starts innocently enough. Local shepherds are guarding the vines to prevent starlings from eating the grapes when a group of bakers from a nearby town pass by with cartloads of freshly baked *fouaces* (flat cakes). Since there is no better breakfast than fresh *fouaces* and grapes, the shepherds politely ask to buy some of the *fouaces* at the market price, but the bakers rudely decline. A scuffle ensues, and the shepherds, along with some nearby peasant farmers, thrash the bakers and help themselves to a few dozen *fouaces* for which they pay the going rate.

The shepherds and their shepherdesses then enjoy a bucolic breakfast, while the bakers repair to the neighboring capital to complain to their king, Picrochole. Picrochole (whose name means "bitter bile") flies into a rage, launches a surprise attack on the shepherds, and lays waste the surrounding area. His disorganized troops even attack the vines of the nearby abbey at Seuilly. The monks huddle in the chapter house and offer up utterly useless prayers for relief; all but one, that is—Frère Jean— who is "young, gallant, lively, lusty, adroit, bold, daring, resolute, tall, slim, loud-mouthed, endowed with an ample nose, a galloper through of matins, an unbridler of masses: in short, a true monk if ever there was one since the world first monked-about."[43] Frère Jean casts off his habit, grabs a cross, and rushes to the defense of the grapes, crying out: "Harken to me, Gentlemen: He who loves wine, by God's body let him follow me! For bluntly, may Saint Anthony's fire burn me if any of those taste the wine who never succoured the vine. Guts of God! It's church property!"[44] Frère Jean lays about so lustily with the shaft of the cross that he kills or scatters the attackers. Some of the wounded are confessed by the other monks before Frère Jean dispatches them straight to paradise.

Grandgousier does his best to calm the enraged Picrochole. As he explains in a letter to his son, Gargantua, "My intention is not to provoke but appease; not to attack but defend; not to make conquests but to protect my faithful subjects as well as my hereditary lands."[45] He sends Picrochole five cartloads of *fouaces* as well as money for the most seriously injured of the bakers. But Picrochole takes Grandgousier's overtures as a sign of weakness: "By God, Grandgousier is shitting himself, the poor old soak."[46] He seizes the money, the *fouaces*, the carts and oxen, and resolves on a war of conquest. Grandgousier, concluding that "there was no hope of bringing them to make peace save by war, quick and strong,"[47] calls Gargantua and his men home from Paris.

The resulting Picrocholine war unfolds on a number of levels: comical, philosophical, religious, and historical. It parodies the *chanson de geste*, a medieval "song of heroic deeds," of which the *Song of Roland* is the most notable surviving example.[48] It also mimics the typical carnival pageant of the uncrowning, thrashing, and debasing of the king, here Picrochole.

But Grandgousier is not a comic figure. He represents the ideal Christian prince praised by Erasmus and More who seeks peace but will fight a just war when no other choice remains. The bread (*fouaces*) and wine (grapes), as well as the cross with which Frère Jean defends the latter, place Grandgousier on the side of Christ. Picrochole, by contrast, indulges his own passions and spreads misery among his own subjects and beyond. Bread is not sacred to Picrochole; it is merely a *casus belli*, an excuse for war.

On an historical level, Grandgousier is clearly intended to represent François I, the wise and just Christian ruler of France. Small wonder he enjoyed the book! Picrochole represents the notoriously choleric emperor Charles V of Spain, who constantly sought to encroach on France and who fancied himself a modern Alexander the Great. Picrochole's advisers counsel him to divide his army, throwing one part at Grandgousier while the other part rolls up towers, towns, and cities on both sides of the Mediterranean (soon to be renamed the Picrocholine Sea), from Majorca to the Pillars of Hercules. They acknowledge no possibility of setback or reversal and treat the planned conquests as already accomplished and as bases for further expansion of the Picrocholine empire. Picrochole quaffs it all like vintage wine.

But Picrochole's army can no more withstand Gargantua, Frère Jean, and their companions than the Dipsodes could stand up to Pantagruel, Panurge, and company in the first book. This time, however, it is Gargantua's mule who pisses so copiously as to drown numerous of the enemy. And Gargantua fashions a staff of his own out of a large tree with which he razes the Picrocholine towers and fortifications. He is no more bothered by the enemy's cannon balls, which he brushes from his hair, than he would be by grape seeds. Picrochole tries to steal a miller's mule to make an escape, but he is beaten by the millers, who take his fine clothes and leave him with only a smock. He ends up as a penny laborer in Lyons.

In sharp contrast to the example set by Charles V—who imprisoned François I, exacted a huge ransom, and kept François's children as surety for its payment—Grandgousier treats the defeated Picrocholines with Christian mercy, sending the soldiers home with a protective escort and money in their pockets, and leaving the kingdom in the control of Picrochole's young son, with "the older princes and scholars of his realm as regents and tutors."[49] "The time has passed," explains Grandgousier cum Erasmus, "for such conquering of kingdoms to the harm of our Christian brothers and neighbors."[50] Any attempt to imitate Alexander the Great and other ancient heroes—as Charles V wished to do—"is contrary to the teachings of our Gospel, by which we are each commanded to guard, save, rule and manage his own realms and lands, and never aggressively to invade those of others."[51]

As a reward for Frère Jean's service, Gargantua decides to build him a monastery. But it will be an order "flat contrary to all others,"[52] for Gargantua has nothing but contempt for monks, at least the lazy ones. A monk "never ploughs like the peasant, never guards the land like the soldier, never cures the sick like the physician, never expounds sound doctrine like the good evangelical preacher and tutor, never transports goods and commodities vital to the kingdom like the merchant."[53] The monk is utterly useless and lives off the labor of others. Grandgousier mildly interjects that monks do pray to God for us. But the well-educated Gargantua will have none of it. He insists that their mumbled prayers are not for us but "for fear of losing their wheaten loaves and thick bread-and-dripping"; they are a "mockery of God."[54]

It is a harsh condemnation but not atypical of humanistic and evangelical views in this period. The great monasteries—built and sustained by donations from the rich hoping to store up their treasure in heaven—were under both intellectual and physical attack, particularly in England, where they were looted and closed by Cromwell at the bidding of Henry

VIII. But Frère Jean, of course, is exempted from Gargantua's condemnation. He is good company, works hard, drinks copiously, and is loyal to his friends and not afraid to fight when called upon, in the tradition of Archbishop Turpin from the *Song of Roland*.

Frère Jean's monastery will therefore be the antimonastery. It will have no walls or gates. It will not be ruled by Hours, to which the inhabitants are called by the sound of bells. Women as well as men will be welcome in equal numbers, and all will be handsome, well formed, and well-endowed by nature. They are free to leave and marry if they wish; no one is constrained by vows to remain. The building is to be magnificent and richly furnished, and both the men and the women will dress elegantly and colorfully. Education and enjoyment are their primary pastimes. Most important of all, the traditional monastic virtues—poverty, chastity, and obedience—are replaced by their opposites. There is but one clause in the rule of the abbey: *Faictz ce que vouldras* (Do what you will), for people are basically good, and, with proper education, training, and examples, will naturally choose the good.

> People who are free, well bred, well taught and conversant with honorable company have by nature an instinct—a goad—which always pricks them towards virtuous acts and withdraws them from vice. They called it Honor.[55]

The monastery of Thélème reminds, and is intended to remind the reader, of the country estates of the *brigata* from Boccaccio's *Decameron* or the elegant court of Urbino from Castiglione's *Book of the Courtier*. It is a Renaissance Utopia, yet far removed from the drab and colorless island of Thomas More. It is a beautiful vision, reflecting Rabelais's optimism about human nature, an optimism that will be sorely tested in the years to come. Indeed, even at the end of *Gargantua*, a darker tone is sounded. Among the foundations of the new abbey is discovered a huge bronze plaque with an enigma inscribed upon it. That enigma appears to foretell a coming time of persecution and darkness for those who uphold God's truth.

Yet nothing is ever exactly as it seems in Rabelais, and even serious forebodings become fodder for comedy. Frère Jean, cherry-picking words and phrases, interprets the "enigma" in a wholly different and lighthearted manner:

> "By Saint Goderan," said the Monk, "I think it is the description of a tennis-match and that the 'round globe' is the ball; the 'guts' and the 'innards' of the 'innocent beasts' are the rackets; and the folk who are het up and wrangling are the players. The end means that, after such *travails*, they go off for a meal! And be of good cheer!"[56]

With that injunction, the book ends. Why be depressed, it seems to ask, when only God knows the future and good cheer is ready to hand?

THE THIRD AND FOURTH BOOKS

The *Third Book of Pantagruel*, commonly known as *Le Tiers Livre*, was published in 1546, twelve years after *Gargantua*. Unlike the prior volumes, the listed author is not an anagram; "Maître Franç. Rabelais, Doctor of Medicine," is proudly noted on the title page. The new book is dedicated to the king's sister, Marguerite of Navarre, and is accompanied by a "King's privilege," which calls the first two volumes "no less useful than delightful,"[57] and awards Rabelais sole rights to reprint those volumes and any subsequent ones for a period of six years.

Yet, despite the royal patronage and the protection it appeared to offer, the *Third Book* is considerably more sober than its predecessors. The tone struck in the prologue and throughout the volume is less an irreverent romp than an earnest, and at times didactic, display of Christian Stoicism. In part, this is surely a reflection of a more troubled religious climate. But one must also recognize that Rabelais was now sixty years old. *Le Tiers Livre* and its companion volume, *Le Quart Livre*, are still funny but without the uninhibited exuberance of the first two books.

Pantagruelism is redefined in their respective prologues as never taking badly anything that "flows from a good, frank and loyal heart,"[58] and as "a certain merriness of mind pickled in contempt for things fortuitous."[59] The message is clear: enjoy what you can, endure what you must.

Pantagruel and Panurge are once again the principal characters. But they have little in common with their namesakes from the first volume.[60] Pantagruel is no longer portrayed as a giant, except in moral and religious authority. Nor will he play the straight man for Panurge's antics. He is a wise, sober, Christian monarch and, as a consequence, rather boring and at times censorious. Panurge has changed even more dramatically. He is never boring, but his frenetic energy is now channeled into distorted rhetoric and specious reasoning to advance his own selfish interests. He has become not only a hypocrite but a pious one as well, who frequently hurls the epithet "heretic" at others. As a measure of how far he has fallen, Panurge actually invokes the Sorbonne as authority! It is such a relief when Frère Jean appears toward the end of the volume that the reader happily ignores the chronological incongruity that Frère Jean was a contemporary and companion not of Pantagruel but of Pantagruel's father, Gargantua. Indeed, even Gargantua himself—who had been translated to the land of the fairies at the end of the first book—reappears in the *Third Book* no worse for the wear.

Following the war with the Dipsodes, Panurge has been given charge of a wealthy estate that he quickly dissipates on banquets and women and foolish investments. He is already deeply in debt when he is counseled by Pantagruel on the virtues of thrift. In response, Panurge launches a fantastical tribute to debt, misciting both classical and scriptural sources in defense of the indefensible. He distorts Ficino's Platonic/Christian theme of mutual love as binding the universe and its inhabitants in harmony by claiming that it is actually mutual obligation (i.e., borrowing and lending) that binds us together. God and nature alike created men to depend on and to help one another, and thus Panurge is performing his Christian and moral duty by allowing others to lend to him.

Always owe somebody something, then he will be forever praying God to grant you a good, long and blessed life. Fearing to lose what you owe him, he will always be saying good things about you in every sort of company; he will be constantly acquiring new lenders for you, so that you can borrow to pay him back, filling his ditch with other men's spoil.[61]

Pantagruel silences Panurge's fatuous display of rhetoric and dialectic by properly citing the scriptures: " 'Owe no man anything,' said the holy Apostle, 'save mutual love-and-affection.' "[62] Panurge is advocating a form of self-love that is destructive of civil society and religious obligation alike.

The main conceit of the *Third Book*, which extends over almost forty chapters, is Panurge's indecision about whether to marry. He very much wants to and yet fears it will end badly, with him cuckolded, beaten, and robbed. Much of the book involves Panurge's search for an authoritative answer to his doubts. Pantagruel will offer no such comfort. In standard Stoic fashion he advises that the only thing we control is our own will: "All the rest is fortuitous and dependent on the destined dispositions of Heaven."[63] Matrimony is a personal choice as to which no assurance is possible. Once Panurge makes it his will to marry, he should do so without trying to foretell the future but simply by commending himself to God.

Yet Panurge insists on subordinating his own will to some external authority. And so they embark on a quest for revealed wisdom. Panurge tries Homeric and Virgilian lots (i.e., opening volumes of Homer and Virgil to random passages); he casts dice; he seeks divination from his dreams; he consults, among others, a sybil, a poet near death (and hence at the apogee of his inspiration), a master of the occult, and a deaf-mute who communicates with signs. In each case, the forecast seems clear: he will be cuckolded, beaten, and robbed. Yet in each case, Panurge distorts the prediction into its opposite.

A theologian offers a more optimistic view. Find a woman from a good family, he instructs, one who fears God, is well instructed in virtue, is schooled by moral company, and will be inspired by the wise and loving example of her husband. Never saw such a person, is Panurge's only response. So he continues his quest, consulting a misogynist physician, a judge (who, after the most careful and exhaustive study, decides his cases by throwing dice), a skeptical philosopher ("I'd as soon undertake to get a fart out of a dead donkey as a decision out of you," Panurge quips.),[64] and a fool (who proves far wiser than Panurge).

At one point, when the conceit is growing rather thin, Frère Jean reappears and ratchets up the energy and the comedy. For a brief period, we are back in the bawdy world of *Pantagruel*. Of course you should get married, Frère Jean tells Panurge. Come the day of judgment, "do you really want them to find you with your balls full?"[65] Just make sure you plough the field regularly. "I've seen it experienced by many a man," he added. "They wouldn't when they could, so couldn't when they would. As the law clerks say: All privileges are lost by non-usage."[66]

When Panurge reiterates his fear that he will be cuckolded, Frère Jean scoffs. If you marry a young and beautiful wife, of course you will be cuckolded, since eventually you will not be able to satisfy her. Everything grows soft in time. "Even if you're not there yet, in a few years' time I shall hear you confessing that some folk we know have balls dangling down for lack of a game-pouch."[67] He then, in the abundant fashion of the early volumes, offers over 150 different synonyms for "wilted bollock."[68] Anyway, what of it? Frère Jean concludes. "If you are a cuckold, *ergo* your wife will be beautiful; *ergo* she will treat you well, *ergo* you will have many friends."[69] And if you are lucky, you will never even know. The only way to avoid cuckoldry for sure, Frère Jean explains, is to wear the ring of Hans Carvel, to whom the devil appeared in a dream and promised to appease his jealous torments by giving him a ring that, as long as it remained on his finger, would guarantee his wife was never known carnally by another man. Hans Carvel awoke full of joy, only to find "his finger up his wife's thingummy."[70]

In essence, what Frère Jean is saying in his Rabelaisian way is that we all, eventually, become carnival figures of fun: uncrowned, mocked, and debilitated. Panurge's desire to avoid such a fate is a desire to avoid the human condition, which means eschewing its joys as well as its sorrows.

The *Third Book* is a thoughtful as well as humorous meditation: Who has moral authority? How is truth to be determined? How are we to make decisions? Law, medicine, philosophy, divination, and even the Bible cannot answer Panurge's question. In such a choice, as Pantagruel explains, "each man must be the arbiter of his own thoughts and seek counsel from himself."[71] That sentence encapsulates the new Pantagruelism and the spirit of the late Renaissance. Only God knows the future, but he isn't talking, or at least his signs are themselves subject to interpretation. Man must meet him more than halfway. The *Third Book* thus ends with an ode to human ingenuity and all that can be accomplished, with even the simplest of materials, through hard work and creative thought.

In the *Fourth Book of Pantagruel*, Pantagruel, Panurge, and Frère Jean embark on a voyage of discovery to seek the word of the *Dive Bouteille* (Divine Bottle). Their adventures echo the fantasy voyages of Lucian's *True History* and channel the Renaissance fascination, evident in More's *Utopia* and Montaigne's *Essays*, with newly discovered lands and their strange inhabitants and varied customs. Like good Renaissance explorers, they even gather specimens of new animals, plants, birds, stones, and other curiosities, which Pantagruel sends back to his father. But there is also a deeper resonance with Dante's Ulysses, who urged his men to visit "lands beyond as yet by none surveyed" and thus "to follow valor's lure and wisdom's quest."[72] Ulysses's desire to go beyond the bounds of human knowledge, without acknowledging the limits imposed by faith, ended in disaster. But Pantagruel's voyage will end in triumph of a sort.

The *Fourth Book* was first published in a truncated and probably unauthorized version in 1548, but reached its final form in 1552, with a renewed royal privilege signed by King Henri II (François I having died while Rabelais was in Metz). We will spend very little time on the *Fourth Book*. It is heavy with literary, philosophical, religious, and political allusions, most of which will be lost on a modern reader without detailed footnotes or the exhaustive exegeses of M. A. Screech and Donald Frame.[73] Undoubtedly, most readers of Rabelais's own day were equally at a loss, but almost all of the episodes are enjoyable on their own terms. At the island of Medamothi (meaning "nowhere," like More's Utopia), the three travelers buy paintings of Plato's ideas and the atoms of Epicurus. They visit an island of those who live only on wind (which is surely true of many politicians, lawyers, and pundits today). They encounter a storm of frozen words that crash upon the deck, releasing the voices of men and women from long ago (surely a reference to the power of writing to conquer time, for what is a book but a collection of words frozen in time and space, awaiting a reader to thaw them out and let them speak again). In a direct attack on papal authority—typical of evangelical reformers— Rabelais has them visit the land of the Papimanes, who make an idol of the pope and worship not the Bible but the sacred Decretals (papal decrees). And, in a moving episode, Pantagruel retells the story, from Plutarch, of the death of the great god Pan, which he interprets as an allusion to the Savior: "for in Greek he can rightly be called *Pan*, seeing that he is our *All*, all that we are, all that we live, all that we have, all that we hope, is in him, of him, by him."[74] When he finishes the story, Pantagruel remains in silent contemplation, shedding tears the size of ostrich eggs. Suddenly, Pantagruel is a giant again. It is a comical image but a moment of genuine pathos. In Rabelais, the one never excludes the other.

It is this simple faith, moreover, that allows the voyagers to survive the storm that eventually descends on all epic heroes at sea, from Odysseus to Aeneas to Dante's Ulysses. While Panurge cowers in fear and makes promises to God that he never intends to keep, Pantagruel, Frère Jean, and others face the danger with prayer and action. They meet God halfway and are "workers together with him."[75] Rabelais's faith is not, as in Dante, a limited horizon beyond which man's search for knowledge must not venture. It is a sturdy vessel running before the wind that sustains and supports any and all forms of humanistic inquiry.

RABELAISIAN WISDOM

Rabelais died in 1553. A *Fifth Book of Pantagruel* was printed in 1564. How much of it was actually composed by Rabelais or derived from his detailed notes is unclear. Screech declines to discuss the *Fifth Book* at all in his otherwise comprehensive book. Frame, by contrast, accepts twenty-six of the forty-seven chapters as authentic or at least "largely so."[76]

We will focus here only on the ending, which, as Frame notes, is too wonderful not to be by Rabelais.[77] Our explorers eventually make it to the island of La Bouteille, where they meet the high priestess Bacbuc (derived from the Hebrew word *bacbuc*, meaning bottle or pitcher). She leads them through a magnificent temple to a fountain whose waters taste of whatever wine the drinker has in mind. Ultimately, Panurge alone is led to the oracle itself, which consists of a single word, *Trinck* (drink). The prologue to *Gargantua* proclaimed that to laugh is proper to man (rire est le propre de l'homme). That is no longer adequate; as Bacbuc explains, "icy maintenons que non rire, ains boyre est le propre de l'homme" (here we maintain that it is not laughing which is the property of man, but drinking).[78]

Yet the word *drink* has to be understood in a special sense. All words require a gloss, Bacbuc explains. Here, to drink is "to flood the mind with all truth, all knowledge and philosophy."[79] It is to drink in the wonders of the world—physical, spiritual, and intellectual—in all their richness and variety.[80] It is Gargantua's "abyss of erudition," the Renaissance ideal encapsulated in a silver book shaped like a demijohn that even Panurge eagerly quaffs.

But this ideal is inherently personalized. Like the waters of the fountain that taste of whatever wine the drinker is thinking of, the world will appear to each individual according to his or her own lights. "Be ye yourselves the interpreters of your enterprise," Bacbuc enjoins.[81] There is no set path that absolves us of the need for thought, for choice, and for exploration. In other words, we must liberate human consciousness from medieval categories and strictures that preclude a frank and free encounter with the world.[82] And yet, Bacbuc concludes, at the same time we act "under the protection of that Intellectual Sphere, whose center is everywhere and whose circumference nowhere, whom we call God."[83] A paradox to be sure, but the essence of Rabelaisian wisdom is that religious belief imposes no limits on human inquiry or human responsibility, just as a spiritual life is not incompatible with the full physical enjoyment of our earthly existence, however absurdly grotesque that existence might sometimes appear in comparison to our spiritual ideals.

We can embrace life even as we embrace God, Rabelais seems to say. Indeed, the one is in keeping with the other, for life itself is the manifestation of God. "As a part of nature," Auerbach explains, Rabelaisian "man rejoices in his breathing life, his bodily functions, and his intellectual powers, and, like nature's other creatures, he suffers natural dissolution."[84] Rabelais affirms the inevitable cycle of birth, fertility, decay, and regeneration, even if at times he doesn't know whether to laugh with joy or shed tears in sorrow.

Panurge, finally shaken out of his self-love, recognizes his need for a mutual connection with others in order to live a full life. Setting all doubts aside, he resolves to marry and have children, as does Pantagruel. Only Frère Jean is blocked from full humanity by his monkish vows. Celibacy—like asceticism or self-mortification—is an affront to, and a repudiation of, nature and hence of God and man alike. The all-embracing, all-enduring, life-affirming wisdom of Pantagruelism triumphs in the end.

Mikhail Bakhtin rightly places Rabelais among the creators of modern European writing, along with Dante, Boccaccio, Shakespeare, and Cervantes.[85] But, as we will see in the next chapter, Bakhtin should have added to the list that most un-Rabelaisian of men, Michel de Montaigne, whose largely unacknowledged debt to Rabelais pervades the *Essays*.

Chapter 7

MONTAIGNE AND THE
WISDOM OF EXPERIENCE

*It seemed to me as if I had myself written the book, in
some former life, so sincerely it spoke to my thought and
experience.*[1]

Read him in order to live.[2]

*The fact that such a person has written has truly enhanced
the joy of living in this world.*[3]

*This talking of oneself, following one's own vagaries, giving
the whole map, weight, color, and circumference of the
soul in its confusion, its variety, its imperfection—this art
belonged to one man only: to Montaigne.*[4]

The list of major figures in philosophy and literature offering such
praise for Michel de Montaigne could be extended indefinitely.
His influence as a thinker and a writer is incalculable. Unfortunately,
though, Montaigne is taught today neither in philosophy departments
nor in classes on creative literature. Some precious few colleges and universities still offer Western civilization sequences, and he will be found
there, albeit greatly excerpted. Otherwise, he is left to upper-level French
courses or to the private reading of inquisitive students.

This is, or should be, a scandal.[5] Montaigne is a pivotal figure in the history of Western thought. He has a better claim than Petrarch to be called the first modern man. In him, the last vestiges of medievalism, Scholasticism, and all forms of religious and philosophical dogmatism are shed in favor of a direct, unimpeded encounter with the world. Yet neither the self that experiences nor the world that is experienced is treated as something fixed and absolute. Both are known, fitfully and imperfectly, only through their changing interactions over time. In the stream of his own consciousness, Montaigne finds a wisdom that eludes abstractions, a wisdom that cannot be condensed into precepts. Paradoxically, Montaigne teaches us how to live by deliberately undermining the ethical, social, and religious structures by which most of us do live but which falsify and thereby disguise *la condition humaine*.[6]

In the *Republic*, Plato presented his own celebrated allegory of the human condition. We are like prisoners in a cave, with legs and neck fettered, observing only the shadows of things cast upon the wall by a weak fire. The philosopher is the one who can break those fetters, stand up and turn around, and recognize that what he has been seeing, what he has taken for reality, are mere images and shadows. Yet he must go farther, up the steep path and out of the cave, where he will at first be blinded by the dazzling light but will gradually come to know not the images of things dimly perceived, but the things themselves and even the sun itself, the eternal form of the Good. And he will then recognize how inconsequential are the shadow images known to the prisoners.

Montaigne accepts the allegory but rejects the solution. There is no way to break our fetters and exit the cave in which we exist. We cannot know things in themselves. There are no fixed, eternal forms that cast their shadows on the world. Indeed, the very concept can have no meaning for us since our words (even our abstract words) derive their meaning from the experience of our senses, and we have no experience of the absolute. We have no knowledge of a metaphysical essence that underwrites the outer world. Montaigne extends that insight to religion. We can have faith in divine providence, but we can know nothing about God. All the deadly disputes between Catholics and Protestants that led to civil war in Montaigne's France are but dueling illusions. Even the soul is a problematic concept. We have no direct knowledge of our own metaphysical essence. We know ourselves only imperfectly, through the passing and ever-changing array of our thoughts, feelings, and actions.

Without the aspirational tyranny of absolutes, however, Montaigne is free to value experience on its own terms. As Virginia Woolf puts it, in a deliberate paradox, for Montaigne "movement and change are the essence of our being."[7] That is to say, there is no essence for the philosopher or the theologian to discover. We can know only movement and change. If we cannot know things in themselves, but only the appearance of things, then we should dedicate ourselves to the appearances, celebrating what we can, lamenting what we must. Appearance is our only reality. And so Montaigne dedicated himself to such ephemeral knowledge, seeking to enrich everyday experience through close attention and to maintain his balance through the exercise of an admittedly all-too-human judgment. In the process, he learned to know himself. It is not an exaggeration to say that the whole literature of self-exploration, from Cervantes and Shakespeare to Proust and Joyce, finds its greatest predecessor in Montaigne.

LIFE

Michel Eyquem de Montaigne was born on February 28, 1533, at the family château outside Bordeaux. The Château de Montaigne had only been in the family for three generations. It was purchased by Michel's great-grandfather, Ramon Felipe Eyquem, a wealthy merchant. The family name, d'Yquem, would become—and still is—famous for its magnificent Sauternes. But Michel dropped that name in favor of the honorific title "de Montaigne."

Montaigne was the third of ten children, but the two oldest died, leaving him as the principal heir. There were wide age gaps among siblings.

Montaigne was twenty-seven when the youngest, Bertrand, was born. Montaigne's father, Pierre Eyquem, was a gentleman soldier who fought briefly in Italy and later became the mayor of Bordeaux. Along with the château, Montaigne would inherit the kidney stones that plagued his father for years.

Montaigne's mother was Antoinette de Louppes de Villeneuve. Her father's family were likely Spanish Jews, driven out of Spain in 1492 by Ferdinand and Isabella. The Jews were not particularly welcome in France either. Most converted to Christianity and tried to assimilate as inconspicuously as possible. Michel's maternal grandmother was a French Catholic from Gascony. Some *conversos* (converted Jews) managed to remain in Spain at the fringes of society. Miguel de Cervantes may have descended from that group. It is interesting to contemplate that these two great figures of the sixteenth century, both revered today as national treasures by their respective countries, may have shared the same outcast Marrano origins.

The Guyenne region where Montaigne was born had been an English province from 1154—when Eleanor of Aquitaine married the soon-to-be King Henry II of England—until the end of the Hundred Years' War in 1453 when it was annexed by France. It was by and large a Catholic region, but there were many Protestants, and the civil wars of religion that would devastate France were particularly acute here. The Eyquem family itself had its share of Protestants, and Montaigne himself was broadly tolerant in an era and area of intolerance.

Montaigne had a highly unusual upbringing. His father, Pierre, received only a basic education but revered learning and consulted the greatest humanists of his day on the proper upbringing of his son. Three aspects of this Renaissance-inspired education stand out. First, Montaigne was sent to live with peasants while he was still nursing and even beyond. His father wanted to give him a familiarity with, and empathy for, "the humblest and commonest way of life."[8] The result, or so Montaigne would claim, was a natural compassion that inclined him always to the side of the poor and lowly. Yet anyone schooled in modern theories of child rearing cannot but wonder if the bond with his own parents suffered in the process. Although Montaigne revered and felt immense gratitude toward his father, he remained aloof from his mother, and they had a fraught relationship in later years when Montaigne inherited the family estate.

Second, once he was back in the château, Montaigne was treated with remarkable gentleness. His father believed (or his advisors convinced him) that knowledge should be freely acquired, without rigor or restraint, in the form of amusement and exercise. The same advisors assured Pierre that "it troubles the tender brains of children to wake them in the morning with a start, and to snatch them suddenly and violently from their sleep."[9] As a result, Montaigne was awakened each morning by music played on one instrument or another. Montaigne extols the goodness and affection of a father who took such pains for his son.

Third, and perhaps most remarkable, Montaigne's first language—his mother tongue, so to speak—was Latin. His father hired a German tutor with excellent Latin, and no French, who spoke with Montaigne exclusively in that language. Other servants were specifically hired for their ability to speak Latin. The rest of the household, including his parents, either learned Latin words and phrases or stayed silent in his presence. As a consequence, Montaigne spoke Latin with a native fluency no scholar could match, at a time when Latin was still common in the law and the civil service, and when a facility with Latin and an intimate knowledge of the great Latin authors was considered the pinnacle of humanistic education.

In 1539, however, when Montaigne was six, Pierre had run out of newfangled ideas and sent him to the Collège de Guyenne in Bordeaux. It was a prominent school, though the teachers were overawed by Montaigne's command of Latin. He acted in Latin plays and, through the connivance of an understanding tutor, was given the freedom to read the Latin classics at his leisure. "He went about it cleverly," Montaigne later explained. "Pretending to see nothing, he whetted my appetite, letting me gorge myself with these books only in secret, and gently keeping me at my work on the regular studies."[10] Montaigne devoured Ovid, Terence, Plautus, and Virgil, among others. But for all that, Montaigne concludes, it was still school, and his Latin had sorely degenerated by the time he left there at the age of thirteen in 1546 or perhaps early 1547.

François I, the king of France and patron of Rabelais, died in 1547 and was succeeded by his son Henri II. Henri II would rule for twelve years—continuing the Italian Wars of his father and trying unsuccessfully to suppress the rapid growth of the Huguenots (French followers of Calvin)—before he was killed in a freak accident at a jousting tournament.

Montaigne's father was mayor of Bordeaux when, in 1548, the city rioted over stricter enforcement of a salt tax that had long been evaded through smuggling. Twenty tax collectors were killed before the riots were harshly repressed by French troops. The city was disarmed, fined, and had its parliament suspended by a furious Henri II. More than a thousand people were sentenced to death. But the salt tax was quietly dropped and an amnesty declared the following year, by which time an attack of the plague, though fortunately limited, had further sobered the city.

Montaigne appears to have been still in Bordeaux for these events. But little is known of his life during the next decade. He presumably studied law, but where and for how long is unclear. In 1557, at the age of twenty-four, he became a member of the restored Bordeaux parliament. This was not a legislative position. He was a magistrate in a lower chamber helping to decide an array of civil and criminal cases. He spent thirteen years in that position, gaining the respect of his colleagues but no particular renown.

It was a difficult time in France. Henri II was succeeded seriatim by his three young sons, François II (r. 1559–1560), Charles IX (r. 1560–1574), and Henri III (r. 1574–1589). All were weak leaders who died without direct heirs. The first two were dominated by their mother, Catherine de' Medici. A series of wars of religion (often called simply "the troubles," a term adapted to the Irish Catholic and Protestant struggles of the twentieth century) began in 1562, after the slaughter of dozens of Protestants at Vassy by the Catholic firebrand François de Guise. De Guise himself was assassinated in 1563. The civil wars blazed intermittently through the rest of Montaigne's life and beyond. It was a time of brutality, treachery, and intolerance. While Spain and, later, England were building empires in the New World, France was busy tearing itself apart.

Montaigne offers little insight into these political events. But he does record a series of personal shocks closer to home. The first was the death of his dear friend Étienne de La Boétie, who died of dysentery in 1563 at the age of thirty-two. As colleagues in the parliament and fellow literary aspirants, they had formed a deep friendship that made up in intensity what it lacked in longevity. That friendship was both celebrated and mourned by Montaigne throughout his life, and immortalized in the *Essays*.

In 1568, Montaigne's father died at the age of seventy-two, probably from complications caused by kidney stones. Montaigne took over the estate, which needed a great deal of work to complete improvements begun by Pierre. His siblings received their respective shares without complaint. But Montaigne's own inheritance created friction with his mother, who complained bitterly that the terms governing her marital property had not been properly observed. After some jockeying, they reached a legal settlement in August of that year that spelled out in somewhat chilling detail their respective rights and the terms on which they would coexist.

The following year, Montaigne's brother Arnaud died after playing tennis. It was a shocking event. He was struck in the head with a tennis ball, suffered no apparent ill effects, went home, and promptly died, presumably as a result of a cerebral hemorrhage. The fragility of life and the suddenness of death were further impressed on Montaigne when he himself was almost killed in a riding accident.

More happily, in 1565 Montaigne married Françoise de La Chassaigne, from an established Catholic family. The marriage seems to have been content enough if not passionate. Indeed, as we shall see, Montaigne decidedly disapproved of passion in marriage. Despite that, the couple had six children, all of them girls. Five, however, died in their first few months of life. Only one, Léonor, lived to adulthood. She died in 1616, at the age of forty-five. Montaigne's wife lived until 1627, surviving her husband by almost thirty-five years.

Buffeted by these changes, tired of the religious and political disputes that were growing increasingly deadly, and blocked from a promotion to the highest chamber of parliament, Montaigne seized on that rebuff as an occasion to retire in 1570. He sold his magistracy and retreated to the Château Montaigne, which formed a courtyard with twin towers at the front corners. He turned the top floor of one of the towers into a library and study. The library had a thousand volumes held in curving wooden shelves. Six months after his retirement, in celebration of his birthday, Montaigne had a Latin inscription placed outside the library:

> In the year of Christ 1571, at the age of thirty-eight, on the last day of February, anniversary of his birth, Michel de Montaigne, long weary of the servitude of the court and of public employments, while still entire, retired to the bosom of the learned Virgins, where in calm and freedom from all cares he will spend what little remains of his life now more than half run out. If the fates permit, he will complete this abode, this sweet ancestral retreat; and he has consecrated it to his freedom, tranquility, and leisure.[11]

Montaigne added numerous quotes from classical authors that were burned into the crossbeams of his library. The tower, the library, and the inscriptions still exist in their original form, though the rest of the château had to be rebuilt after a fire in 1885.

Time began to hang heavy on Montaigne's hands. He did not truly share his father's zeal for estate improvements. He began many projects but finished few. Instead, he preferred the company of the muses (the "learned Virgins" of his inscription). He had already translated a lengthy theological work by Raymond Sebond at the behest of his father, finishing it just as his father died. He now edited and published several works of

La Boétie. Yet he still found his mind wandering and his thoughts darkening. As he explained in an early essay, with a characteristic mixture of candor and false modesty:

> Lately when I retired to my home, determined so far as possible to bother about nothing except spending the little life I have left in rest and seclusion, it seems to me I could do my mind no greater favor than to let it entertain itself in full idleness and stay and settle in itself, which I hoped it might do more easily now, having become weightier and riper with time. But I find . . . that, on the contrary, like a runaway horse, it gives itself a hundred times more trouble than it took for others, and gives birth to so many chimeras and fantastic monsters, one after another, without order or purpose, that in order to contemplate their ineptitude and strangeness at my pleasure, I have begun to put them in writing, hoping in time to make my mind ashamed of itself.[12]

Montaigne rounds out this account in a later essay:

> It was a melancholy humor, and consequently a humor very hostile to my natural disposition, produced by the gloom of the solitude into which I had cast myself some years ago, that first put into my head this daydream of meddling with writing. And then, finding myself entirely destitute and void of any other matter, I presented myself to myself for argument and subject.[13]

These two passages provide invaluable insights into the origins of the *Essays* and the character of their author. Montaigne sought refuge in solitude. But, beset by melancholy and aimlessness, he took up writing in order to better understand himself and how to live. Yet he was almost embarrassed to be seen as a professional man of letters. A nobleman, after all, practiced arms, rode at horseback, and tended to his estate. Even Castiglione advocated, at most, a general patina of learning and polish for his ideal courtier. Thus Montaigne, at least at first, affected a casual disdain for his own work and the deep learning he displayed. Initially, he sought his answers on how to live in precepts and examples from classical sources. But he quickly found that traditional approach unsatisfying. He was not content to regurgitate Plutarch or Seneca. Moreover, he found that every precept could be met with its opposite, seemingly as wise. The very titles of his chapters show that everything depends on context: "By diverse means we arrive at the same end" (1.1); "One man's profit is another man's harm" (1.22); "Various outcomes of the same plan" (1.24); and the highly Rabelaisian "How we cry and laugh for the same thing" (1.38).

Eventually, Montaigne devised an entirely new method of writing in pursuit of self-understanding. He coined the term *essais* (attempts) to capture the tentative nature of his explorations. He tried out various ideas and approaches, making a series of sketches rather than a finished painting. Montaigne started writing these essays in 1572. The first edition (consisting of books 1 and 2) was published to wide and immediate acclaim in 1580. Even the then-current king, Henri III, read them. Montaigne continued to revise the first two books through the years, rarely deleting but instead interpolating substantial additional material: a few words here, a sentence there, at times whole paragraphs. He eventually added a third book as well, generally considered his most mature work. The essays were written and revised over a twenty-year period, from 1572 to 1592.

Following the publication of the first edition, Montaigne set out from home in June 1580 on what would prove a seventeen-month trip to Switzerland, Germany, Austria, and Italy. He traveled with his youngest brother, a widowed brother-in-law, two friends, and several servants. Montaigne had many motives for the journey: he wanted to escape the civil wars; he was bored with domestic life; at the many baths and spas he visited, he hoped to find relief if not a cure for the kidney stones that had begun to plague him in 1578; and, most important, he had a restless desire to see Rome and Venice and to experience other cultures, customs, and climates. According to the calculations of his principal biographer, Donald Frame, Montaigne and his small entourage covered close to three thousand miles on horseback, traveling between twenty and twenty-five miles per day on average. That is the equivalent of riding his horse across the United States. He kept a journal, though often his valet wrote the entries. Even Frame admits that the travel journal, which was not discovered until 1774, "is neither polished nor profound."[14] But it is highly revealing of Montaigne the man and his sheer love of travel. Montaigne was something of a celebrity at this point, welcomed by officials and literary figures in the cities he visited. Yet he also made a point of spending time with common people, sharing their food and following their customs. The trip reinforced his views on both the mutability of human nature and the importance of habit in forming character. Amusingly, Montaigne's own copy of the *Essays* was seized by the authorities when he first entered Rome and finally returned with various suggestions for improvements, some editorial and some religious. He politely ignored them all.

The trip was cut short in November 1581 when Montaigne was notified in Rome that—in his absence—he had been elected mayor of Bordeaux. Montaigne may have been pleased with the honor. His government career to date had been rather lackluster, and he was now being asked to fill the post his father had held. Nonetheless, he was inclined to say no, until he learned that the king, Henri III, wished him to take the job. So Montaigne made his way back to France and to duty. He was reelected to a second term, and thus served as mayor from 1581 to 1585.

During these years and beyond, Montaigne was swept up in national events. He served as a mediator during what historians call the "War of the Three Henris":

- Henri III, the Catholic king, who tried to chart a middle course, made complicated by the shifting allegiances of his mother, Catherine de' Medici
- Henri of Navarre, a Protestant and closest heir to the throne of France, whose 1572 marriage to the king's sister, Margaret of Valois, sparked the St. Bartholomew's Day massacre, in which almost five thousand Huguenots were murdered in Paris alone

- Henri de Guise, son of the assassinated François, who controlled the radical Catholic faction known as the Holy League

The three Henris, hovered over by the queen mother, all maneuvered, and Montaigne was often in the middle as a go-between. He was once kidnapped and imprisoned by Henri de Guise before being promptly released at the behest of the queen mother. As Montaigne later explained, "I incurred the disadvantages that moderation brings in such maladies. I was belabored from every quarter; to the Ghibelline I was a Guelph, to the Guelph a Ghibelline."[15]

Henri III finally had Henri de Guise killed, and he himself was assassinated by a radical monk not long after. Montaigne helped to convince Henri of Navarre to embrace Catholicism in order to succeed to the throne as Henri IV in 1589. Henri IV was finally able to end the religious wars, after Montaigne's death, by reuniting France in opposition to Spain in 1595. His Edict of Nantes in 1598 guaranteed freedom of conscience and loosened restrictions on Protestant worship. Henri IV was assassinated in 1610 by a Catholic fanatic. Montaigne himself had died quietly in his bed at the château on September 13, 1592, at the age of fifty-nine.

STOICISM

There are very few personal revelations in Montaigne's early essays.[16] Often, they are simply glosses on his extensive reading. Montaigne offers propositions from philosophers (such as Seneca and Cicero) or poets (especially Lucretius, Virgil, and Horace) and then, like a good lawyer, uses "case studies" drawn from historians (Livy, Tacitus), biographers (Plutarch), and even natural philosophers (Pliny) to build up his evidence for or against them. Occasionally, he will cite his own experience or what he has been told by others, but not in the form of personal revelations. His goal—the traditional goal of the Hellenistic philosophers and their

Roman counterparts—is to develop and refine a set of general precepts and moral exemplars to serve as guides to life.

Montaigne's method is in keeping with Renaissance humanism, which seeks wisdom through a careful reading of classical authors, while shunning the logical abstractions of medieval Scholasticism. "Away with all those thorny subtleties of dialectics," he urges, "by which our lives cannot be amended."[17] Montaigne's matter, however, is a rather conventional Stoicism.[18] He wants to cultivate indifference to fortune, a condition known in the Stoic literature as *ataraxia*. Fortune is neither good nor bad, Montaigne writes. It merely provides the raw material "which our soul, more powerful than she, turns and applies as it pleases, sole cause and mistress of its happy or unhappy condition."[19] It is up to us how we react to the twists and turns of everyday life, of which there were many in sixteenth-century France. We are as well-off or as badly off as we choose to think. "Let us no longer make the external qualities of things our excuse; it is up to us to reckon them as we will. Our good and our ill depend on ourselves alone."[20] Given the vicissitudes of fate, we cannot rule events. We can only rule ourselves. The sovereign good, accordingly, lies in tranquility if not active indifference to the material and social conditions of life. "The worth and value of a man is in his heart and his will; there lies his real honor."[21]

This cultivation of *ataraxia* is nowhere more evident than in Montaigne's treatment of dying, which he calls "the greatest task we have to perform."[22] He suggests, in standard Stoic fashion, that to philosophize is to learn how to die. Our existence is preceded and succeeded by nothingness.[23] To fear death is to presume to know something we cannot know. Peasants meet death with brave indifference; philosophers should do no less. Indeed, death can even be welcomed as a release from the ills of the world, a useful reminder that itself breeds indifference to those ills. "It is no great thing to live—your valets and the animals live—but it is a great thing to die honorably, wisely, and with constancy."[24]

It is a rather bleak message, in keeping with the "melancholy humor" that led Montaigne into writing. But, over time, he will write himself into a more optimistic mind-set. And, although Montaigne never wholly abandons his emphasis on self-reliance and tranquility, he will come to view the rigid Stoicism of his early essays as emotionally impoverished and intellectually untenable. Ideals of heroic constancy and stability will give way to a more nuanced perception of man's inherent fallibility in the face of a changing world. The encapsulated wisdom of the ancients and the potted biographies of past figures can provide only so much guidance. Indeed, as often as not, Montaigne will conclude, the "heroic" actions of Stoic exemplars were driven by delusion, insensibility, and fanaticism rather than virtue. He will likewise conclude that fixed precepts are inadequate to govern our lives. Circumstances are too varied and change too rapidly. Man is not one thing but an ever-shifting amalgam. There is no single path to virtue. Knowledge is never certain. Judgment and experience will become his new lodestars. Living, not dying, is our greatest task.

SKEPTICISM

Montaigne's growing dissatisfaction with Stoicism is paralleled by a growing fascination with skepticism. A central tenet of traditional Stoicism was that the natural world is governed by divine providence and that, through the application of reason alone, man can both determine and live a life in accordance with the divine intention manifested in nature. Montaigne, however, came to doubt that reason can unveil divine intention or anything else beyond the scope of human experience. Montaigne thus bracketed and dismissed with a sweep of his pen much of philosophy and all of theology. Metaphysics, Scholasticism, and even the standard Catholic doctrines challenged in the Reformation are not suitable subjects for dispute. One might have faith, but knowledge in such matters is beyond our powers.

In 1568, at the request of his father, Montaigne translated a lengthy work of natural theology by Raymond Sebond, a Catalan scholar and theologian. The work was written in a sort of bastardized Catalonian Latin that his father found difficult to read, and Montaigne dutifully worked on a translation whose eventual publication unfortunately coincided with his father's death. Sebond's central premise—derived from traditional Stoicism but going well beyond its original scope—was that all the truths of the Christian religion about God, about man, and about their relationship to one another can be deduced by the application of reason to nature. In Sebond's view, natural reason and faith are perfectly compatible because the proper use of the former leads to the latter.

It seems clear that working on the translation helped Montaigne to define his own thinking in opposition to that of Sebond. Montaigne's most substantial essay, which occupies almost half of book 2, is called the "Apology for Raymond Sebond." It purports to defend Sebond, but, as one scholar aptly puts it, Montaigne supports Sebond " 'as the rope supports the hanged man.' "[25] Montaigne's central premise is the opposite of Sebond's: that through the application of natural reason, we cannot learn any truths about God, about the world, or even about ourselves. "*Que sçay-je?*" (What do I know?) asks Montaigne.[26] And his answer: not very much at all.

Montaigne starts from the premise that "all knowledge makes its way into us through the senses; they are our masters."[27] We are dependent upon what they tell us. Yet the knowledge they impart is itself uncertain. "The first consideration that I offer on the subject of the senses," Montaigne explains, "is that I have my doubts whether man is provided with all the senses of nature."[28] In many respects, we are inferior to animals in their perception of and adaptation to the external world. Our senses readily mislead us; we are easily deluded by the appearance of things. Indeed, "our senses are not only altered, but often completely stupefied by the passions of the soul."[29]

Regardless of their fallibility, the senses provide the only raw material on which our knowledge is based. "The senses are the beginning and the end of human knowledge."[30] They circumscribe the scope of human knowledge. Reason can help us to make general statements, but only statements grounded in the particulars that we experience through our senses. That is the ultimate touchstone. "Whoever can force me to contradict the senses has me by the throat; he could not make me retreat any further."[31] Divorced from that context, reason is worse than useless because it leads us to think we know things that we cannot know. The pro and contra of medieval disputation does not attain knowledge. "It is a two-handled pot, that can be grasped by the left or the right."[32] At that level of abstraction from human experience, one proposition is as good as another. "There is no reason that does not have its opposite."[33] There are as many opinions as there are people. "I think my opinions are good and sound; but who does not think as much of his?"[34] Confidence and even certainty are marks of dogmatism, not guarantors of correctness.

In short, man cannot raise himself above his own humanity, "for he can see only with his own eyes, and seize only with his own grasp."[35] Montaigne's thinking on this issue is astonishingly modern and anticipates the great eighteenth-century German philosopher Immanuel Kant, who sought to chart the limits of human knowledge from within. Kant, too, would argue that all knowledge begins with the senses. We can construct images of God and the metaphysical essences that underlie all things, including the self. But these are man-made metaphors and are limited as such. They are in no sense the truth. Or, rather, we have no idea wherein the truth lies. We do not know essence, only accident. We do not know things in themselves, but only the appearance of things. In Kantian terms, having reached the limits of knowledge, we must turn back to the world of appearances. We cannot transcend our own limitations.

This is the background assumption that circumscribes Montaigne's essays: "man can be only what he is, and imagine only within his reach."[36] Our very language is tied to and derives its meaning from the senses. "Philosophy," he concludes, to the extent that it seeks to transcend those bounds, "is but sophisticated poetry."[37] And the same must be said of religion. "Reason does nothing but go astray in everything, and especially when it meddles with divine things."[38] God is inaccessible to us. We cannot grasp his essential being. It is beyond our powers.

> Our overweening arrogance would pass the deity through our sieve. And from that are born all the delusions and errors with which the world is possessed, reducing and weighing in its scales a thing so far from its measure.[39]

Understandably, though, Montaigne is somewhat guarded on the subject of religion. He does not expressly dismiss theology as "sophisticated poetry." That would have been dangerous to state too explicitly. But it is the clear implication of what he has to say. Montaigne claims, as Kant would do in all sincerity, that he denies knowledge to make room for faith. His skepticism is designed to counter dogmatism, not to undermine faith. And Montaigne, rather blandly and ambiguously, asserts that faith: "We must either submit completely to the authority of our ecclesiastical government, or do without it completely. It is not for us to decide what portion of obedience we owe it."[40] In other words, if we are going to believe, we should simply accept the traditional tenets and practices of the Catholic Church. The doctrinal disputes raised by Luther, Calvin, and others—disputes over which men were furiously killing one another—have no basis in knowledge. They are simply assertions countering assertions, and there is no reason to adopt them in place of the status quo. It is a deeply conservative approach; not quite the rope with which he supports Sebond, but not so very different either, as the Catholic Church would itself conclude when it placed Montaigne's *Essays* on the index of forbidden books in 1676, where it remained until the list was finally abolished in 1966.

The basis for Montaigne's religion is at most a general fideism not far from pagan Stoicism: a belief in some sort of divinity underlying the world. The rest is poetry, and, while poetry is important, it is not worth killing one another over it. Those who profess religion "should avoid all contentions and dialectical argumentations and fall back purely on the prescriptions and formulas of faith established by the ancients."[41] Montaigne has nothing to say about Christ, the afterlife, or redemption. Indeed, he shows flashes of hostility to any such doctrines, though thinly masked as a dismissal of other religions:

> Is there any opinion so bizarre—I leave aside the gross impostures of religions, with which so many great nations and so many able men have been seen to be besotted, for since this matter is beyond the scope of our human reason, it is more excusable for anyone who is not extraordinarily enlightened by divine favor to be lost in it; but of other opinions is there any so strange—that habit has not planted and established it by law in the regions where she saw fit to do so?[42]

We adopt our religion the way we adopt the many other customs and practices of our time and place. "We pray out of habit and custom, or to speak more correctly, we read or pronounce our prayers. All in all, it is only an act."[43]

By the end of the "Apology," as the great French scholar Jean Starobinski notes, "Montaigne leaves man at the center of an unknowable universe, confronting an inaccessible divinity about which nothing at all can be asserted."[44] But, paradoxically, for Montaigne this absence of knowledge is a source of liberation and even optimism. With God distant and inaccessible, with knowledge limited to the world of experience, he has been freed to explore and embrace the richness and variety of that experience, just as Rabelais wallowed happily in the muck of the family farm at La Devinière.

No essential reality warrants denigration of mere appearance. That is not to say that no such essential reality exists. We cannot say definitively "I know" or "I do not know." We must doubt even our doubt, for we cannot partake of the absolute. We must accept our innate limitations. In this sense, skepticism validates appearance. It grants it legitimacy. Thus, Montaigne brackets and dismisses all metaphysical and theological questions in his essays. They are irrelevant to his project of learning how to live. Any form of dogmatism distorts experience and therefore keeps us from wisdom. Montaigne, like Rabelais, will not let the reader forget that man—to his joy and sorrow—shares more with the beasts than with the angels.

SELF-KNOWLEDGE

In Rabelais's *Third Book of Pantagruel,* Panurge wants to learn how to live—more specifically, he wants an answer to the question whether he should marry. He seeks guidance from multiple sources to which he hopes to subordinate his will. But all external authority fails him. As Pantagruel finally explains, "each man must be the arbiter of his own thoughts and seek counsel from himself."[45]

Montaigne makes a similar turn in the *Essays.* He has found wanting the claims to knowledge made by philosophy and theology. The precepts of the Stoics, toward which he has a natural affinity, have proved too simplistic to match the complexity of actual experience and too harsh and life-denying to allow human nature to flourish. Even Stoic exemplars—those great moral figures from the past—must be handled with care. We know too little of their actual circumstances and motivations, and their heroics are too extreme to make them reliable models for our own behavior.

Montaigne thus turns inward to become the arbiter of his own thoughts and to seek counsel from himself. "I would rather be an authority on myself than on Cicero," he explains. "In the experience I have of myself I find enough to make me wise, if I were a good scholar."[46] Thus begins what Erich Auerbach rightly calls "the first work of lay introspection."[47] Montaigne wants to be at home in the world but recognizes that he must orient himself "without fixed points of support."[48] That means he must start with himself. Just as all knowledge begins with the senses, all wisdom begins with the self. "I study myself more than any other subject. That is my metaphysics, that is my physics."[49]

But, just as we cannot perceive whatever metaphysical reality under-lies appearances, we cannot study the self or the soul directly. The self is not a fixed mark. It is an elusive Proteus, subtle and ever changing.[50] It can be observed only obliquely in the constant tumble of our thoughts, beliefs, sensations, emotions, and actions. We cannot grasp its essence, but only describe its passing existence. We must lie in wait for ourselves, observing and overhearing, in order to know ourselves. Self-knowledge is a process of peripheral investigation that never ends. "I have no busi-ness but with myself; I continually observe myself, I take stock of myself, I taste myself."[51] Montaigne offers no abstract definition of man but only an ever-shifting portrait of one particular man.

> I cannot keep my subject still. It goes along befuddled and staggering, with a natural drunkenness. I take it in this condition, just as it is at the moment I give my attention to it. I do not portray being: I portray passing. Not the passing from one age to another, or, as the people say, from seven years to seven years, but from day to day, from minute to minute.[52]

The pitfalls in such an approach are many. The two most signifi-cant—to which Jean-Jacques Rousseau will often succumb in his *Con-fessions*—are mawkish self-absorption and artful dissimilation. Mon-taigne largely avoids them both. He neither sentimentalizes his subject nor seeks to make himself appear more admirable than he is. "Now, I am constantly adorning myself," he admits, "for I am constantly describing myself."[53] Description is inherently adornment since the self can never be displayed directly. Montaigne recognizes and respects the gulf between a man's inner self and what he projects to the world. He constantly strives for unvarnished honesty about the former. Yet his object is not confes-sion but self-knowledge. He writes to know himself in all his variety and inconstancy. He will not impose on his narrative a false consistency and stability beyond the reach of man. Since the self is ever changing, so too is his description.

> This is a record of various and changeable occurrences, and of irreso-
> lute and, when it so befalls, contradictory ideas: whether I am different
> myself, or whether I take hold of my subjects in different circumstances
> and aspects. So, all in all, I may indeed contradict myself now and then;
> but truth . . . I do not contradict.[54]

Montaigne recognizes that the record of one person's truth—his
account of his changing passions and beliefs—will be a jumble of con-
tradictions. But truth is more important than consistency. As Walt
Whitman would say, echoing Montaigne: "Do I contradict myself? /
Very well then I contradict myself, / (I am large, I contain multitudes.)."[55]
Nothing about the human condition is unambiguous. Since Montaigne
is constantly changing, his description of himself must change as well.
Movement in time becomes the elusive "essence" he seeks to know.

> It is a thorny undertaking, and more so than it seems, to follow a move-
> ment so wandering as that of our mind, to penetrate the opaque depths
> of its innermost folds, to pick out and immobilize the innumerable flut-
> terings that agitate it.[56]

All he can do is be as faithful and as accurate as language will allow
in describing himself as he appears at each moment in time. Montaigne
is not making progress toward a finished portrait of some Stoic or other
moral ideal. He does not hold himself out as an exemplar but simply as
one man. "Others form man," he explains. "I tell of him, and portray a
particular one, very ill-formed."[57]

To accommodate his subject, Montaigne adopts a style as fluid and
fluctuating as the self he seeks to understand. Digressions are not digressions; they are an essential part of the enterprise as the mind flows seamlessly from topic to topic. "If my mind could gain a firm footing, I would
not make essays, I would make decisions; but it is always in apprentice-
ship and on trial."[58] Montaigne is never finished but constantly evolving,
and the book is part of that process. He is thus liberated from the rhe-

torical restraints and established standards of finished prose. That is why *Essais* (attempts) is such a perfect title for his enterprise.

> I take the first subject that chance offers. They are all equally good to me. And I never plan to develop them completely. For I do not see the whole of anything; nor do those who promise to show it to us.[59]

Montaigne lets his mind wander from topic to topic, rarely following a single thread. He speaks directly to us, like an intimate friend. Montaigne's free-flowing conversations with the reader are some compensation for his lost conversations with his friend La Boétie. As Auerbach notes, you can all but hear Montaigne's voice and see his gestures in his prose.[60] "Cut these words, and they would bleed," Ralph Waldo Emerson says admiringly; "they are vascular and alive."[61]

Montaigne comes to exist most truly in his book, in the stream of his recorded consciousness, in his judgments and interpretations, and in his efforts to make sense of his life and the world around him. The only unity is provided by the "I" that is both present and absent in experience and that provides the voice that marks change and passing. It is a tenuous unity because this "I" changes over time, from day to day and even minute to minute. But the very process of chasing it through all the vagaries and digressions of life gives it a stronger, firmer shape.

> And if no one reads me, have I wasted my time, entertaining myself for so many idle hours with such useful and agreeable thoughts? In modeling this figure upon myself, I have had to fashion and compose myself so often to bring myself out, that the model itself has to some extent grown firm and taken shape. Painting myself for others, I have painted my inward self with colors clearer than my original ones. I have no more made my book than my book has made me—a book consubstantial with its author, concerned with my own self, an integral part of my life; not concerned with some third-hand, extraneous purpose, like all other books.[62]

Yet Montaigne's focus is neither selfish nor self-absorbed. He attempts to understand human experience directly from his own life, the only life to which he has such privileged access. But in the process, he is seeking to understand humankind more generally, since we all share a common form. Montaigne is presenting a particular life, but one that contains the seeds of man's estate.

> I set forth a humble and inglorious life; that does not matter. You can tie up all moral philosophy with a common and private life just as well as with a life of richer stuff. Each man bears the entire form of man's estate.[63]

"Chaque homme porte la forme entière de l'humaine condition."[64] That is the justification for Montaigne's entire enterprise. A common, ordinary life can become an exemplary life, a mirror into which others can look. That is why Montaigne seems so remarkably close to us. He offers us a representative life, not in the sense of the heroic Stoic exemplars, but because each and every life is representative of what it means to be human.

A word of caution is in order, however. Despite Montaigne's frequent tone of self-deprecation, his pretense that his prose artlessly follows his thoughts, and his insistence that he is not teaching but merely reporting, the *Essays* reflect enormous intelligence, are carefully crafted, and are full of hard-won wisdom. In a famous aside, Montaigne asks, "When I play with my cat, who knows if I am not a pastime to her more than she is to me?"[65] The reader requires similar caution, for Montaigne is often playing with us, despite his moral seriousness. I would not go as far as Barbara Bowen, who suggests that "Montaigne's whole attitude to himself, his book, and his reader is tongue in cheek."[66] But there is some truth to her claim that Montaigne loves ambiguity for its own sake and relishes the spell he casts over his readers.[67]

T. S. Eliot complained that Montaigne was impervious to counterargument: "You could as well dissipate a fog by throwing a hand grenade into it." It is a nice touch that Eliot, in his early poem "The Love Song of J. Alfred Prufrock," compares fog to a cat slinking through "Streets that follow like a tedious argument / Of insidious intent."[68] Both Eliot and Bowen see a sort of "insidious intent" in the fact that Montaigne offers us not a fixed self or clear, refutable arguments, but an ungraspable fog that curls around us and lulls us to sleep. What I see instead is an author who refuses to falsify experience through simplifications and who is content to live "without fixed points of support." Moreover, like Pantagruel, he often finds reason both to laugh and to cry, but largely and courageously chooses laughter over tears. He considers constant cheerfulness the surest sign of wisdom.[69]

> I, who boast of embracing the pleasures of life so assiduously and so particularly, find in them, when I look at them thus minutely, virtually nothing but wind. But what of it? We are all wind. And even the wind, more wisely than we, loves to make a noise and move about, and is content with its own functions, without wishing for stability and solidity, qualities that do not belong to it.[70]

THE SELF AND OTHERS[71]

Montaigne's study of the self does not preclude a focus on other people. To the contrary, the self cannot be studied in isolation. Our interactions with family, friends, lovers, colleagues, and even strangers help to define us, albeit always in a fluid, rather than fixed, manner. If we want to know ourselves, we must understand ourselves in relation to others. For "he who lives not at all unto others, hardly lives unto himself."[72]

There is, perhaps, in this turn to others, a flavor of the old joke, "Enough about me. Let's talk about you. What do you think of me?" But such relationships, Montaigne insists, not only help to define us, they are essential to human happiness. "There is nothing to which nature seems to have inclined us more than to society."[73] We have a pressing need to interact with and to care about other people. Such communication is vital both to our mental and moral well-being. Montaigne calls conversation "the most fruitful and natural exercise of our mind,"[74] and adds that "no pleasure has any savor for me without communication."[75]

As a consequence of this need for communication in order to forge connections with others, Montaigne has an aversion to lying, which he calls "an accursed vice."[76] Truth is critical both to public life and to personal identity. Language cannot fix anything in place and is an imperfect instrument of communication, but it is the only such instrument we have. Whether speaking or writing, we must constantly strive to reveal rather than to conceal, to describe rather than to adorn, even as Montaigne acknowledges that every description is necessarily, to some extent, an adornment. Complete communication with others, like complete knowledge of ourselves, may lie beyond the reach of language, but the aspiration is our most urgent moral imperative.

As a politician and critical go-between during the civil wars, Montaigne knew the dangers of deliberate falsehood. Even on a more personal level, we cannot connect with others if we dissimulate.

> Since mutual understanding is brought about solely by way of words, he who breaks his word betrays human society. It is the only instrument by means of which our wills and thoughts communicate, it is the interpreter of our soul. If it fails us, we have no more hold on each other, no more knowledge of each other. If it deceives us, it breaks up all our relations and dissolves all the bonds of our society.[77]

Communication will never be perfect. Truth will never be absolute. But the case for both has never been more powerfully stated.

That said, as always in Montaigne, there is a balance to be struck. We should not give ourselves wholly to others. For if we disappear into a tangle of familial, social, and political connections with others, we will lose ourselves. "We must reserve a back shop all our own, entirely free,

in which to establish our real liberty and our principal retreat and solitude."[78] While we may lend ourselves to others, "we must husband the
freedom of our soul and mortgage it only on the right occasions; which
are in very small number, if we judge sanely."[79]

There is, then, a deliberate distance in Montaigne and at times a
chilling reserve, or at least a reserve at odds with our modern sensibilities.
This is perhaps most apparent in his discussion of his own family. In an
early remark, from his Stoic phase, he negligently comments on the death
of his infant children with apparent indifference: "I have lost two or three
(but while they were still nursing), if not without grief, at least without
repining. Yet there is hardly any accident that touches men more to the
quick."[80] Did the losses, which he says he bore without repining, nonetheless touch him to the quick? He seems to imply as much, but it was an
era in which infant mortality rates were extremely high, and parents were
cautious of too great an attachment.

Less understandable, perhaps, is Montaigne's reserve about marriage. "Of my own choice," he explains, "I would have avoided marrying
Wisdom herself, if she had wanted me." But choice has little to do with
marriage, for "the custom and practice of ordinary life bears us along."[81]
Montaigne, in a Rabelaisian moment, quotes Socrates on whether it is
preferable to take or not to take a wife: "Whichever a man does, he will
repent it."[82] Yet he says that if one marries well and takes it rightly, "there
is no finer relationship in our society."[83] Again, there is deliberate ambiguity here because life itself is ambiguous. We taste nothing pure, as the
title of one middle essay announces. "Whoever supposes," Montaigne
adds, "to see me look sometimes coldly, sometimes lovingly, on my wife,
that either look is feigned, is a fool."[84]

Although Montaigne does not believe that good marriages are built
on amorous desire, he is quite frank on the subject of sex. "What has the
sexual act," he asks, "so natural, so necessary, and so just, done to mankind,
for us not to dare talk about it without shame and for us to exclude it
from serious and decent conversation?"[85] In his anti-Platonic late essay

"On some verses of Virgil," he argues that sexual attraction is not a step on the ladder of love that must be surmounted and sublimated in favor of a purely intellectual and spiritual passion. Sex is highly pleasant in its own right. Man is a mixture of mind and body, and neither should be sacrificed to the other, since both are necessary to good health, high spirits, and a balanced life. But he qualifies this remark by suggesting that sex with one's spouse should be approached more soberly and "circumspectly."[86]

The only relationships Montaigne discusses without ambiguity are those with his father and with his friend Étienne de La Boétie. Montaigne clearly loves and admires his father. But the father-son relationship is not one of equals or of unfiltered disclosures. Montaigne's love for his father, however deeply felt, is formal rather than intimate. Only with La Boétie did Montaigne achieve, at least in retrospect, what he considers a pure and perfect connection. "In the friendship I speak of, our souls mingle and blend with each other so completely that they efface the seam that joined them, and cannot find it again."[87]

Montaigne offers us perhaps the most powerful tribute to friendship ever written. His treatment is schooled by earlier writers, particularly Aristotle and Cicero, but is more moving than either because it is filtered through his personal experience with La Boétie. Most of what we call friendships, he notes, are merely acquaintances formed by chance for our advantage and convenience. Such relationships are natural and pleasurable, but true friendship is not a matter of convenience or self-interest; it is a relationship that fulfills the self in union with another. Despite the inherent imperfections of language, Montaigne and La Boétie achieved a connection in which their innermost selves were shared and became one. Each cared for the other more than himself, or rather as an extension of himself. "All associations that are forged and nourished by pleasure or profit, by public or private needs, are the less beautiful and noble, and the less friendships, in so far as they mix into friendship another cause and object and reward than friendship itself."[88] True friendship is a relationship in and for itself. It lies beyond the power of language to explain. "If you press me to tell why I loved him, I feel that this cannot be expressed, except by answering: Because it was he, because it was I."[89]

The death of La Boétie was certainly the single most devastating event of Montaigne's life. As we have discussed, much of the impetus of the *Essays* is as a substitute for his conversations with his friend. He discloses himself to his readers as he once disclosed himself to La Boétie. In his travels, moreover, Montaigne increasingly sought out others for social engagement and the pleasures of conversation. But a deep loneliness hovers behind the later essays. The compensation Montaigne found in writing and in social interactions was no substitute for the loss of his friend.

> For in truth, if I compare all the rest of my life—though by the grace of God I have spent it pleasantly, comfortably, and, except for the loss of such a friend, free from any grievous affliction, and full of tranquility of mind, having accepted my natural and original advantages without seeking other ones—if I compare it all, I say, with the four years which were granted me to enjoy the sweet company and society of that man, it is nothing but smoke, nothing but dark and dreary night.[90]

LIVING WITH IMPERFECTION

Philosophy fails to provide us with any knowledge beyond experience. We have no insight into the metaphysical underpinnings of this world, much less into some other world that will succeed it. But, along with vain hopes for such knowledge, we can shed the "philosophical scorn for transitory and mundane things."[91] Appearance is our only reality, and muddling through as best we can is the only sensible response to that reality. With no determined end, the journey becomes the goal. "Life should be an aim unto itself, a purpose unto itself."[92]

Montaigne is adamant, moreover, that we cannot live that life according to abstract principles. We have no more knowledge of moral absolutes than we do of metaphysical ones. Even tentative moral precepts too often ignore context and nuance. "There is no way of life so stupid and feeble as that which is conducted by rules and discipline."[93] Where reason fails, we fall back on experience. We must rely on our own judgment in making sense of, and navigating through, a changing world. But our judgment is inherently fallible, and the better part of wisdom lies in understanding that fact. Here, the influence of Erasmus as well as Rabelais comes to the fore. "Our life is part folly, part wisdom. Whoever writes about it only reverently and according to the rules leaves out more than half of it."[94]

We are often vain, frivolous, wayward, and absurd. Learning to live with such imperfection—in ourselves and in others—is part of the human condition.

> All contradictions may be found in me by some twist and in some fashion. Bashful, insolent; chaste, lascivious; talkative, taciturn; tough, delicate; clever, stupid; surly, affable; lying, truthful; learned, ignorant; liberal, miserly, and prodigal: all this I see in myself to some extent according to how I turn; and whoever studies himself really attentively finds in himself, yes, even in his judgment, this gyration and discord.[95]

Understanding our shortcomings allows us to strive to improve our minds, our bodies, and our characters within the limits of human nature. It also permits us to be tolerant of, and to have compassion for, others. Montaigne professes a morality cut to the cloth of human nature. Its catchwords are kindness, flexibility, sociability, curiosity, and acceptance.

> If others examined themselves attentively, as I do, they would find themselves, as I do, full of inanity and nonsense. Get rid of it I cannot without getting rid of myself. We are all steeped in it, one as much as another; but those who are aware of it are a little better off—though I don't know.[96]

The tentative, skeptical note—"though I don't know"—remains. There are no guarantees, no fixed points of support. But Montaigne tries to find a way of living that will enrich his experience and that of others.

Among Montaigne's cardinal virtues are moderation and mindfulness. Moderation, or *mediocritas*, as Rabelais termed it, is the ability to exist within the limits of our needs and our strength. The happiest life is an ordinary one: a life of order, consistency, and tranquility, both in our thoughts and in our actions. "Greatness of soul," Montaigne writes in a seeming contradiction, "shows its elevation by liking moderate things better than eminent ones."[97] Anyone can summon the resolve to shine on the public stage; but imposing order on our thoughts and emotions, and on our private and personal actions, is far more difficult.

> Order is a dull and somber virtue. To win through a breach, to conduct an embassy, to govern a people, these are dazzling actions. To scold, to laugh, to sell, to pay, to love, to hate, and to deal pleasantly and justly with our household and ourselves, not to let ourselves go, not to be false to ourselves, that is a rarer matter, more difficult and less noticeable.[98]

Like the Stoics or religious fanatics, we seek extremes that we cannot sustain. But those who attempt to rise above human nature invariably fall below. "They want to get out of themselves and escape from the man. That is madness: instead of changing into angels, they change into beasts; instead of raising themselves, they lower themselves."[99] Our only business is living appropriately within the limits of human nature.

Prosochē, the Greek word for mindfulness or attention, signifies an attempt to be present in experience, to observe closely and feel keenly the passing array. Too often, fear, desire, and hope lead us to anticipate the future or regret the past and thus steal us from the present. "We are never at home," Montaigne warns, "we are always beyond."[100] We always reach for more than we can hold and are rarely content with what we have. We sacrifice rest, health, and life to phantoms such as wealth, power, and reputation. We thereby lose ourselves in trivialities that do not engage our being. "Among our customary actions there is not one in a thousand that concerns ourselves."[101] We are already richer than we think, if only we savor the pleasures and joys in everyday life. In one of many beautiful passages in his final essay, "Of experience," Montaigne writes:

> When I dance, I dance; when I sleep, I sleep; yes, and when I walk alone in a beautiful orchard, if my thoughts have been dwelling on extraneous incidents for some part of the time, for some other part I bring them back to the walk, to the orchard, to the sweetness of this solitude, and to me. Nature has observed this principle like a mother, that the actions she has enjoined on us for our need should also give us pleasure; and she invites us to them not only through reason, but also through appetite.[102]

OLD AGE AND DEATH

Montaigne was thirty-nine when he retired to his library and began to write. He already considered himself old, with his best days behind him. His early essays show a standard Stoic preoccupation with death, personalized by the deaths of his infant children, his father, his brother, and his dear friend La Boétie, as well as by the riding accident that left Montaigne himself in the anteroom of death for some days. But it is understandably in the great essays of his third book, particularly "On some verses of Virgil," "Of vanity," "On physiognomy," and his masterpiece, "Of experience," that Montaigne truly comes to grips with old age and the prospect of death. By then, he has firmly rejected the Stoic idea that life is but a preparation for death. "Death is indeed the end," he writes, "but not therefore the goal, of life; it is its finish, its extremity, but not therefore its object. Life should be an aim unto itself, a purpose unto itself; its rightful study is to regulate, conduct, and suffer itself."[103] The wisdom of these late essays may be the wisdom of autumn, but, with the possible exception of his beloved Horace, no one has ever written more beautifully and profoundly about the last phase of life than Montaigne.

Montaigne's account of old age is not sugarcoated as in Cicero, his main prose rival on the subject.[104] Montaigne frankly admits that body and soul alike decay with age, however gradually and imperceptibly at first. The mind grows less supple, the body begins to break down, and amorous passion justly becomes an object of ridicule. Old age would be a cause for celebration if it occasioned an increase in wisdom. But, too often, the opposite is the case.

> Besides a silly and decrepit pride, a tedious prattle, prickly and unsociable humors, superstition, and a ridiculous concern for riches when we have lost the use of them, I find there more envy, injustice, and malice. Old age puts more wrinkles in our minds than on our faces; and we never, or rarely, see a soul that in growing old does not come to smell sour and musty. Man grows and dwindles in his entirety.[105]

Yet Montaigne has neither tears for the past nor fears for the future. Old age is natural and inevitable. "I have seen the grass, the flower, and the fruit; now I see the dryness—happily, since it is naturally. I bear the ills I have much more easily because they are properly timed."[106] Indeed, life is to be cherished even in old age as long as some semblance of health can be preserved. Montaigne's painful but steadfast battle with kidney stones underscores this point.

> Health is a precious thing, and the only one, in truth, which deserves that we employ in its pursuit not only time, sweat, trouble, and worldly goods, but even life; inasmuch as without it life comes to be painful and oppressive to us. Pleasure, wisdom, knowledge, and virtue, without it, grow tarnished and vanish away; and to the strongest and most rigorous arguments that philosophy would impress on us to the contrary, we have only to oppose the picture of Plato being struck with a fit of epilepsy or apoplexy, and on this supposition defy him to call to his aid these noble and rich faculties of his soul.[107]

There are pleasures available to each phase of life. Those appropriate to old age include, first and foremost, companionship. Montaigne, the reclusive sage, increasingly descended from his tower to enjoy the conversation and company of people from all walks of life. "The sweetness of harmonious and agreeable company cannot be bought too dearly."[108] Montaigne knows he will never recapture the intense friendship he had with La Boétie. He is now content with more superficial, yet still pleasurable and enriching, connections. In his old age, Montaigne cultivated what Samuel Johnson would later call a disposition to be pleased. "I love a gay and sociable wisdom," Montaigne writes, "and shun harshness and austerity in behavior, holding every surly countenance suspect."[109] Particularly in the calamity of old age, we should, as Horace advised, mingle a dash of folly with our wisdom.[110] Indeed, the happiest and most adventurous among the elderly have more than a dash.

Reading is another consolation dear to his heart. Montaigne rejects the Renaissance assumption that all wisdom is to be found in the books of classical authors. He does not worship books or slavishly absorb their contents. He retains from them only what he has made his own, the thoughts and ideas by which his judgment has profited.[111] But reading is nonetheless "the best provision I have found for this human journey."[112] Books are always at hand and ready to serve. They provide consolation in old age and solitude; they banish boredom and divert us from sorrowful thoughts. And they never object to being set aside or sought out "only for want of those other pleasures, that are more real, lively, and natural."[113]

Travel is yet another profitable exercise for mind and body. Exposure to new lands and unknown customs keeps us flexible and alert. It takes us out of the narrow world in which our own habits have imprisoned us. "I know no better school, as I have often said, for forming one's life, than to set before it constantly the diversity of so many other lives, ideas, and customs, and to make it taste such a perpetual variety of forms of our nature."[114] There is also the sheer joy of movement, of trying different foods, and of meeting new people. Travel gives us a more acute awareness of the passing days.

So too, of course, does death, which paradoxically may be the greatest consolation of old age. Death need not cast its shadow over life. It can instead heighten our awareness and joy in each day of life. "My plan is everywhere divisible," Montaigne explains; "it is not based on great hopes; each day's journey forms an end. And the journey of my life is conducted in the same way."[115] As we age, we relinquish desires—for riches, for reputation, for power—that interposed themselves between us and life.

Montaigne's attitude toward death is neither Stoic nor Christian. He does not consider death the great event of life for which we must constantly steel ourselves. "If you don't know how to die, don't worry," he wryly explains. "Nature will tell you what to do on the spot, fully and adequately. She will do this job perfectly for you; don't bother your head about it."[116] Yet neither does Montaigne view death as a passage to another, better life. Those who resort to prayer and piety are simply distracting themselves from the reality of death instead of facing it. "They avoid the struggle; they turn their consideration away from death, as we amuse children while they are being lanced."[117]

Death is something individual to each of us, and Montaigne wants to face his death in his own way, as he led his life in his own way. "Death is frightful to Cicero, desirable to Cato, a matter of indifference to Socrates."[118] Montaigne came agonizingly close to death as a young man and found it far from frightful. But neither does he consider it desirable. Suicide throws away our most precious gift to hurry a death that is, of all events, the most inevitable. Nor does Montaigne treat death as a matter of indifference; he even chides Socrates for choosing death over banishment, as if one could enjoy life only among the "community of climate or of blood" into which one is born.[119]

Montaigne treats death with acceptance but not resignation. It is part of the natural order of things. Attempting to flee death is pointless. We must use our awareness of death to enhance life. We live on borrowed time, but that time is all the more to be cherished. "I want a man to act, and to prolong the functions of life as long as he can; and I want death to find me planting my cabbages, but careless of death, and still more of my unfinished garden."[120] Montaigne wants to die as he has lived: without heroics. He is neither an angel nor a beast. He is a human being, and in Montaigne's case that is saying a great deal.

> The most beautiful lives, to my mind, are those that conform to the common human pattern, with order, but without miracle and without eccentricity. Now old age needs to be treated a little more tenderly. Let us commend it to that god [Apollo] who is the protector of health and wisdom, but gay and sociable wisdom:
>
> > Grant me but health, Latona's son,
> > And to enjoy the wealth I've won,
> > And honored age, with mind entire
> > And not unsolaced by the lyre.
> >   Horace[121]

I would only add "and not unsolaced by Montaigne's *Essays*."

Chapter 8

CERVANTES: LIFE AS LITERATURE

Montaigne, echoing Horace, enjoins his readers to mix a little folly with their wisdom. Montaigne is already post-Renaissance. He does not worship classical learning, perhaps because his own is so extensive. Books are no substitute for experience and may lead us astray as often as not. He also lacks the Renaissance faith in the perfectibility of man. A cheerful acceptance of our flawed humanity is, for him, the beginning of wisdom. Those who aspire to be angels, he warns, frequently end as beasts. The excesses of neither the Reformation nor the Counter-Reformation are to his taste. He does not aspire to tragedy.

Cervantes is also post-Renaissance. He mocks the follies of his age. But his irony is, if anything, gentler and even more humane than Montaigne's. It is sweet, never bitter, despite the fact that few men had more cause for bitterness than Miguel de Cervantes. The publication of *Don Quixote*—which the philosopher Miguel de Unamuno has called "the Spanish Bible"—was contemporaneous with the first performance of *King Lear*, another work about self-delusion in a godless world. Harold Bloom claims that "Cervantes, like Shakespeare, gives us a secular transcendence."[1] Yet the two works could not be more different. *Lear* is unrelievedly bleak: "All's cheerless, dark, and deadly."[2] In a world abandoned by God, human ties are too fragile, too fraught with misunderstanding, and human goodness too ineffective to keep us from tearing each other apart for the sheer joy of exercising power and asserting dominance. "Humanity must perforce prey on itself, / Like monsters of the deep."[3] I find no transcendence in *Lear* aside from the language in which our lack of transcendence is presented; that is to say, only the art is transcendent. When the loyal Kent exits the stage to commit suicide—

I have a journey, sir, shortly to go;
My master calls me. I must not say no.[4]

—it is a judgment upon the universe. We, as spectators, are devastated, not inspired to acts of love or feats of courage.

Cervantes makes no such judgment. He mingles more than a dash of folly into his noble knight. Don Quixote speaks wisely on every subject but one: he believes that the novels of chivalry he reads so obsessively are historically true and that it is therefore possible and necessary for him to take up the abandoned mantle of knight errantry and to right the wrongs of the world. Instead of the classical ideal of *mimesis*—art imitating life— Cervantes adopts a more modern notion: life imitating art. The Don is inspired to genuine acts of love and feats of courage by what he has read. His literary ideal repeatedly clashes with a very different reality. Therein lies the humor of the book. But therein lies more than humor. Erich Auerbach, in a rare blunder, finds in *Don Quixote* only farce and comedy. But Auerbach does not appreciate pathos. He wants the greater notes of tragedy.

Cervantes, like Montaigne, does not aspire to tragedy. The human comedy in all its pathos is enough for him, and we as readers mingle tears with our laughter. We come away from reading the book with a greater sense of our common humanity and the possibilities of being human. *Don Quixote* bears more resemblance to Shakespeare's late romances than to his middle-period tragedies. That seems appropriate given that Cervantes was fifty-eight when he published part 1 of *Don Quixote*, ten years older than Shakespeare was when he wrote *The Tempest* and *The Winter's Tale*, in which anger and bitterness have given way to gentle tears. Don Quixote is saved by his love, his courage, and, above all, his friendship with his squire, Sancho Panza. In the end, we are all inspired to add a bit of folly to our wisdom and to find transcendence in our connections with one another.

Like all great works of literature, *Don Quixote* should be read at least three times: first, in the bloom of idealistic but untested youth; second, amid the successes and setbacks of adult engagement; and, third, in old age, a time when one disengages from the concerns of the broader world and focuses on the memory—or, if one is lucky, the continuation—of essential human connections. The exact mix of laughter and tears will change over those three readings. But both are present at every point. Therein lies its claim to be not only the first modern novel, but the greatest as well.

LIFE

Miguel de Cervantes, as one biographer has noted, led a "harassed and vagabond life."[5] He fled Spain as a young man to evade arrest; enlisted as a marine and was badly wounded at the famous Battle of Lepanto; was captured and held for ransom for more than five years by Barbary pirates; and, when he returned finally to Spain, was unable to secure any preferment in recognition of his service. He met with little success as a poet and playwright and even less as a procurement officer for the Spanish Armada. He moved frequently and was jailed at least once for debt, once on suspicion of embezzlement, and once as part of an errant murder investigation. His family circumstances were irregular to say the least. That he became the father of the modern novel at the age of fifty-eight and, by consensus, wrote the greatest of all novels seems nothing short of a miracle. Yet he was the right person at just the right place and time. His Don Quixote sits astride his horse Rocinante, lance in hand, at the crossroads where the clarity of the Renaissance faded into the chiaroscuro of the Baroque; where Cervantes's own youthful ideals met with the harsh reality of an indifferent world; and where the euphoria of the golden age of Ferdinand and Isabella gave way to widespread *desengaño*—an untranslatable Spanish word that means not so much disengagement, disappointment, or even disillusion as it does awakening to a more sober reality.

Miguel was born in September 1547 in Alcala de Henares, a university town about twenty-five miles from Madrid. That was the same year in which two powerful monarchs, François I of France and Henry VIII of England, both died. Charles V was the Holy Roman emperor. He ruled over much of Spain (including Castile and Aragon) and parts of Italy and France, as well as the Low Countries (Belgium and the Netherlands), Bohemia, and Austria. Spanish conquistadors had already pushed aggressively into the New World.

Miguel's grandfather, Juan de Cervantes, was a prosperous attorney for the Inquisition who settled in his native Córdoba. Miguel's father, Rodrigo, did not fare so well. He was partially deaf, and his education was limited, particularly after his own father, Juan, abandoned the family for a mistress. Suddenly forced to make a living, Rodrigo became a surgeon in Alcala. In those days, a surgeon was one step up from a barber and indeed sometimes shaved his customers as well as bled them. It was frequently a Jewish profession, a fact which, along with Miguel's inability to find favor in the rigid Spanish social order, has led scholars to speculate that Miguel, like Montaigne, had *converso* roots.[6] Ferdinand and Isabella had expelled the Jews from Spain in 1492, but many converted, whether nominally or in reality. These *conversos* were allowed to remain but were definitely a disfavored group in an increasingly orthodox Catholic country. Also in 1492, the Reconquista was completed with the fall of Granada. Any Moors who wanted to stay in Spain also had to convert. These Moriscos were even more disfavored and were banished altogether between 1609 and 1614. The expulsion of the Jews and Moors, many of whom were active in trade and finance, proved to be an economic disaster for Spain, exacerbated by crippling taxation, rampant inflation, drought, famine, and outbreaks of plague.

Rodrigo married Leonor de Cortinas in 1542. It appears that Leonor's parents, who were rural landowners, considered the marriage a mistake and shunned the young couple. Rodrigo's mother, who received no support from her former husband, was in no position to help either. Six children survived infancy: three daughters (Andrea, Luisa, and Magdalena) and three boys (Miguel, Rodrigo, and Juan). The young and growing family spent fifteen years moving from place to place, barely making a living. Their household goods were seized, and Rodrigo was jailed for debt at one point, just as his own father had once been jailed in a political dispute. The Cervantes men, despite their hidalgo (minor nobility) status, were all acquainted with Spanish prisons.

Juan de Cervantes finally provided financial support and a house to the family in Córdoba. Undoubtedly, the fact that the youngest child, born in 1554, was named after his grandfather reflects this rapprochement. But the elder Juan died in 1556, the same year that Charles V abdicated in favor of his son Philip II and retired to a monastery, where he himself died two years later.

Miguel began his formal education in Córdoba, probably at the hands of the Jesuits. But the family moved to Seville in 1564—the year Shakespeare was born—and on to Madrid in 1566, five years after Philip II made that fledgling city the capital of Spain. Miguel's formal schooling was limited, and though he learned Latin, he was largely self-taught through his wide and deep reading.

In Madrid, Miguel developed a fascination with the theater. He also developed a fascination for a young barmaid, but their planned elopement was blocked by the girl's father, who forbade her to see the impecunious student from such a dubious background. In any event, Miguel was forced to flee Spain in 1569 after he wounded another young man in a duel. To avoid arrest, he traveled first to Seville and then to Italy. He was sentenced *in absentia* to ten years of banishment and to have his right hand publicly severed. The sentence proved uncannily prophetic in light of subsequent events.

Miguel entered into the service of various church officials in Italy. To do so, he had to obtain a purity-of-blood certificate indicating that none of his ancestors were Jews, Moors, or converts. The fact that he could readily do so, however, is apparently no indication that the certification was true. It was more a formality than a searching inquiry into his background. Miguel made the most of his time in Rome, reading widely in Italian literature.

In 1571, Pope Pius V called for a "Holy League" to counter the Ottoman Empire's aggressive expansion in the Mediterranean. The key members of the League were the Venetian Republic, the Papal States, and the Spanish Empire, whose ruler, Philip II, relished his title as "Most Catholic King" and his role as a defender of the faith against Muslim incursions. The Spanish Empire provided most of the money. Venice, whose dominance of Mediterranean trade was at risk, provided most of the ships. The pope mostly provided prayers and blessings. The fleet was led by Don Juan of Austria, in whose service both Miguel and his brother Rodrigo enlisted.

The crucial encounter occurred in the Gulf of Lepanto on October 7, 1571. It was the last great battle of ships powered entirely by rowers. The hitherto invincible Turkish fleet was soundly defeated, and that glorious victory has been compared to the Greek defeat of the Persian Empire at Salamis in 480 BCE, another sea battle that preserved the independence of Europe. Miguel fought with great courage as his ship grappled with and boarded a Turkish galleon. He was wounded three times, twice in the chest, followed by a harquebus shot that forever cost him the use of his left hand. Despite his wounds, he relished the memory of his service. The intensity of a comparable capstone military experience would be beautifully captured by Shakespeare in the speech Henry V gives before the Battle of Agincourt on the feast of Saint Crispin in 1415:

> He that shall see this day and live old age
> Will yearly on the vigil feast his neighbors,
> And say "Tomorrow is Saint Crispian."
> Then will he strip his sleeve and show his scars,
> And say "These wounds I had on Crispin's day."
> . . .
> This story shall the good man teach his son,
> And Crispin Crispian shall ne'er go by
> From this day to the ending of the world,
> But we in it shall be remembered.[7]

Alas, as we shall see, Miguel's service was largely forgotten in Spain, but it was a source of fierce pride for a writer who praised a life of arms over one of letters.

After a long convalescence, Miguel returned to active service and took part in at least two subsequent engagements, despite his useless left hand. He spent a total of four years as a soldier in the uniform of the Spanish Empire before deciding to return home with letters from Don Juan and another officer testifying to his exemplary service. Miguel hoped to parlay those letters into a comfortable sinecure in Spain, but they played a very different role in his life.

The flotilla in which he was returning was scattered by a storm. Miguel's ship was in sight of his homeland when it was assaulted and captured by Barbary pirates. Miguel and others, including his brother Rodrigo, were carried off to Algiers. His letters of recommendation served only to convince his Moorish captors that he was a man of importance, and they demanded a large ransom for his freedom. The downside of this was that his impoverished family could not possibly raise such a sum. The upside was that he was treated as a valuable commodity rather than being enslaved and sent off to work under harsh conditions. Algiers was at this time a city of 150,000, whose wealth depended largely on piracy. As many as twenty-five thousand captives were there awaiting ransom or serving as slaves.

Miguel was held in Algiers for five years before finally being able to arrange a ransom. He tried four times to escape, and throughout showed great courage and leadership. When one of his plots to free more than a hundred captives was betrayed at the last minute, he took full responsibility. Luckily, on this and other occasions, he escaped severe punishment. He later arranged for his brother Rodrigo to be ransomed first, despite Miguel's own rights as the eldest son.

Miguel was finally freed in October 1580, ransomed by a group of Trinitarian monks. He returned to Spain after an eleven-year absence and without a functioning left hand. Recall the sentence he had received *in absentia*. It took some doing, but in honor of his service the warrant for his arrest was finally annulled. The sentence, after all, had already been carried out by adverse fortune.

Miguel's attempts to find a comfortable sinecure in his home country were met with indifference. He repeatedly stressed his "Old Christian" background and his military service in letters seeking preferment. It was a time of growing religious intolerance. The Inquisition was in full swing. Perhaps a *converso* background explains his lack of patronage. More likely, the great Battle of Lepanto was now a distant memory. Miguel had missed his moment. And it was a time of economic collapse, which made opportunities scarce. Miguel's brother Rodrigo had returned three years earlier and, unable to find any employment, rejoined the military in Flanders. The Spanish Empire was still intact but had already begun its steady decline. As historian J. H. Elliott explains, "The crisis of the late sixteenth century cuts through the life of Cervantes as it cuts through the life of Spain, separating the days of heroism from the days of desengaño."[8]

Miguel tried to make a living both as a poet and as a playwright. His pastoral romance, *La Galatea*, attracted favorable attention when it was published in 1585. He also wrote a number of plays that met with modest success. But Lope de Vega was the wildly popular playwright of his day, and Miguel disdained what he viewed as de Vega's modern, slapdash style. His own plays were more formal and classical, which seems ironic in light of the stunning innovations in *Don Quixote*. Unable to attract patronage or to support himself with his pen, Miguel all but abandoned writing for almost two decades.

In 1584, at the age of thirty-seven, Miguel fathered an illegitimate child with Ana Franca de Rojas, a Morisco who ran a tavern with her much older husband. That same year, about two months after the birth of his daughter Isabel, he married Catalina de Salazar y Palacios, a young woman not yet twenty who had just lost her father. Her family had a small estate in the village of Esquivias, near Toledo, in the region of La Mancha; the estate was encumbered with debts, but it appeared to support the widowed mother, her three children, and even her new son-in-law at first. For reasons unknown, however, the restless Miguel left this home and his young wife after three years. The opening of *Don Quixote* reads: "Somewhere in La Mancha, in a place whose name I do not care to remember ..." One biographer has suggested that Esquivias is the place he no longer wanted to recall.[9]

Over the next ten years, Miguel filled a variety of minor government posts in Andalusia, mostly in the areas around Seville and Córdoba. He started as a requisitions officer for the Spanish Armada. Later, after the disastrous collapse of the seemingly invincible Armada, Miguel served as a tax collector, an equally unpopular position. He was an honest official but not very good with the accounts, which he sometimes mistook to his own disadvantage. Twice he was excommunicated for perfectly legal requisitions of church property, though both sentences were ultimately overturned by the archbishop of Seville. He was also jailed briefly at one point until his accounts were reconciled. He was imprisoned again in Seville for as much as six months, in 1597–1598, following the bankruptcy of a financier to whom he had entrusted state funds. Philip II ordered him freed before his own death in September 1598. Philip also signed a peace treaty with Henri IV of France and restored the autonomy of the Low Countries (where Miguel's brother Rodrigo had died in the fighting). Spain still had a substantial empire in the New World, but its empire in Europe was crumbling fast.

While he was in prison, Cervantes conceived the idea for *Don Quixote* and may even have begun writing it there. He had reconciled with his wife, Catalina, at some point, and they began living together again, first in Seville, and later in Valladolid and Madrid. Miguel's household included two of his sisters, Magdalena and Andrea. Upon the death of Ana Franca, Magdalena adopted Miguel's daughter, who took the name Isabel de Saavedra. For unknown reasons, Miguel had taken Saavedra, the name of a distant cousin, as his second surname and bestowed that name on his only child. It was an irregular household to say the least. Magdalena and Andrea had multiple affairs, generally with nobles who falsely promised to marry them; in each instance, cash settlements were made. Some suitors may have skipped the promises and proffered only cash. Miguel's daughter Isabel and Andrea's daughter Constanza would largely follow the same pattern. Indeed, shortly after Isabel married, she gave birth to a daughter who was not her husband's. And when that husband died soon thereafter, Cervantes arranged another marriage for her with the help of a substantial dowry paid by her lover.

Out of this turmoil and chaos, *Don Quixote* emerged. Published in 1605, the book quickly spread throughout Spain and was translated into English, French, and other European languages. Miguel de Cervantes Saavedra was suddenly famous, though not rich, having sold the manuscript for a flat fee.

We have no reliable portrait of Cervantes. But, in the prologue to a book of *Exemplary Stories* he later published, Cervantes offers his readers a verbal self-portrait and brief autobiography. Imagining a frontispiece portrait that the volume lacked, he tells the reader what it would have shown:

> The man you see before you, with aquiline features, chestnut-colored hair, smooth, unwrinkled brow, bright eyes, and curved though well-proportioned nose, silver beard that not twenty years ago was golden, large moustache, small mouth, teeth neither large nor small—since he boasts only six of them, and those he has are in poor condition and even worse positions, for not one of them cuts against another—of medium build, neither tall nor short, a healthy color in his cheeks, fair rather than dark complexion, slightly stooping, and not very light on his feet. This, then, is a description of the author of *La Galatea* and *Don Quixote of la Mancha* ... and other works which have gone astray, perhaps without their owner's name upon them. He is commonly known as Miguel de Cervantes Saavedra. He was for many years a soldier and a prisoner for five and a half after that, during which time he learned to cultivate patience in adversity. He lost his left hand in the naval battle of Lepanto to a blunderbuss shot, and although the injury is ugly he

considers it beautiful because he incurred it at the most noble and memorable event that past centuries have seen or future generations can ever hope to witness, fighting beneath the victorious banners of the son of that thunderbolt of war, Charles V of happy memory.[10]

THE FIRST SALLY

Don Quixote, the most famous of all novels, begins and ends quietly. Alonso Quixano is a fifty-year-old hidalgo of modest means. He lives with his niece and housekeeper in a small, unnamed village somewhere in the region of La Mancha, in southcentral Spain. The aging bachelor leads an uneventful and celibate existence. His two friends are the village priest and the barber. To while away the many hours of leisure, he reads books of chivalry. They become his obsession. He reads day and night and even sells off acres of arable land to buy more books.

Quixano, like most of us, longs to step outside the drab conventions that define and confine him. He dreams of himself as another person altogether, a heroic man of arms like those about whom he reads. He wants to live in the world of Amadís of Gaul, Orlando, and other celebrated knights. He wants to remake himself and his world according to his longings.

The Renaissance ideal, as Stephen Greenblatt reminds us in his groundbreaking work, is all about self-fashioning, about reinventing oneself in accordance with classical ideals.[11] Machiavelli prepared a handbook for the prince. Castiglione urged his ideal courtier to turn himself into a work of art. Renaissance painting idealized its subjects. Even the skeptical Montaigne, though with more irony and self-deprecation, thought we could remake ourselves through close attention to experience.

It is perhaps natural, therefore, that Alonso Quixano believes he can reinvent himself as Don Quixote de la Mancha, a knight errant dedicated to truth and justice and the righting of wrongs. Accordingly, the book does not begin with the birth of Alonso Quixano. We know nothing of his early life and experience. It begins with his rebirth, literally his *renaissance*, as Don Quixote. The Don renames his horse Rocinante and reenvisions the tired, skinny nag as a warhorse of great stamina and blazing speed. And, in a remarkable bit of sublimation, he reenvisions a robust, sexually charged peasant girl, Aldonza Lorenzo, as his lady love, the imperious and peerless Dulcinea del Toboso.

We all spin fantasies. As passionate readers, we enter vicariously into the lives of fictional characters and place ourselves at the heroic center of their stories. And we all project on loved ones virtues that a more dispassionate observer might find wanting. As Montaigne noted, each man and woman interprets the world differently depending on background, status, experience, and desire. The stories we read, and the stories we invent, are part of that process. Everyone has their own narrative, which they impose on the world. That is how we give meaning to our lives in a world abandoned by God, once thought to be the omniscient narrator of our individual destinies. We are each of us, to some extent, compelled to be the author of our own fictional universe.

The key words, of course, are "to some extent." For at what point does fantasy turn into madness, or playacting into outright schizophrenia? That is a question raised throughout the book, and it is one that can never clearly be resolved since the line between the two is blurry at best. Certainly, though, Alonso Quixano seems to cross that line when he patches together an ancient set of armor with a pasteboard helmet held together with ribbon, mounts his horse, picks up his lance, and sets off in search of adventure. As he rides along, the freshly minted Don Quixote even begins to narrate his own story, as he imagines a future historian will do, adopting the language of chivalric romances:

> "No sooner had rubicund Apollo spread over the face of the wide and spacious earth the golden strands of his beauteous hair, no sooner had diminutive and bright-hued birds with dulcet tongues greeted in sweet, mellifluous harmony the advent of rosy dawn, who, forsaking the soft

couch of her zealous consort, revealed herself to mortals through the door and balconies of the Manchegan horizon, than the famous knight Don Quixote of La Mancha, abandoning the downy bed of idleness, mounted his famous steed, Rocinante, and commenced to ride through the ancient and illustrious countryside of Montiel."[12]

"And it was true that this was where he was riding," the actual narrator (which is, as we shall see, a complicated story in its own right) wryly remarks.[13]

The Don continues riding all day, dreaming of the day when his great deeds will win him immortal fame and letting Rocinante determine their direction, for therein he thinks lies the essence of adventure. Finally, hungry and tired, he comes upon a ramshackle inn, which in his mind is a magnificent castle complete with towers and a deep moat. He greets two whores standing in the courtyard as if they were noble ladies, provoking gales of laughter. He mistakes the innkeeper for the lord of the castle, and the innkeeper—who is a bit of a rogue but not unkindly—decides to play along with his mad guest, even to the point of offering to dub him a knight; for Don Quixote has realized, to his horror, that he cannot legitimately engage in adventures until he receives the official order of knighthood.

What follows, of course, is a parody of the ceremony of knighthood, as Don Quixote stands watch through the night over his armor (which is hanging on a trough in the courtyard because, inexplicably, the castle has no chapel), does battle with two muleteers who cast aside the armor to water their mules, and receives his knighthood from the innkeeper-cum-castellan, who strikes him on the shoulders with a sword, murmuring prayers while pretending to read from an old account book. The two whores assist at the ceremony, dress the new knight in his armor, and graciously accept his offers of service.

The entire scene is undeniably and even riotously comic. But it is not only comic. There is considerable pathos in the account of the dignified, if deluded, Alonso Quixano pacing beside his armor and, through an incredible act of creative will, transforming everything and everyone he encounters into what he dreams and wishes them to be. His collisions with reality simply make him cling all the more fiercely to his fantasy, for "everything that our adventurer thought, saw or imagined seemed to him to be done and to happen in the manner of the things he had read."[14] The two whores and the innkeeper are amusing themselves, but not at Don Quixote's expense. They are pulled, despite themselves, into Don Quixote's imaginative orbit. One man, with a strong enough narrative, however fantastic, can alter the trajectory of other narratives. And this is what Don Quixote de la Mancha does throughout part 1. In the new Copernican universe, he becomes a sun around which others revolve.

In the sixteenth century, it was still commonplace to find humor in those who were mentally and physically disabled. Dwarfs were kept at court as objects of fun. The scales for us tip more toward pathos; but we can still appreciate the comedy, just as Cervantes's original readers must have felt an ache in their hearts for the would-be Don Quixote. As Rabelais and Montaigne were at pains to remind us, both laughter and tears are essential to the human condition. The Don is sublime as well as ridiculous. He is Miguel de Cervantes, clinging to the glory of Lepanto and dreaming of literary fame and fortune. He is Spain itself, clinging to its golden age and dreaming of an expanded Catholic empire even as its Invincible Armada is decimated by bad weather, bad planning, and the long-range guns of the English. He is all of us. And the person he dreams himself into being is admirable. He is committed to truth and justice and shows great courage and perseverance even though the results of his endeavors are so often slapstick failures.

The last adventure of his first sally is a case in point. He accosts a group of merchants on the road and demands that they confess that in the entire world there is no one more beautiful than Dulcinea del Toboso. One of the merchants—who, like the innkeeper, appreciates a good joke—responds that they have never seen the woman in question and that the Don should first show her to them and then they would be happy to do what he asks. "If I were to show her to you," he responds, "where would the virtue be in your confessing so obvious a truth? The significance lies in not seeing her and believing, confessing, affirming, swearing, and defending that truth; if you do not, you must do battle with me, audacious and arrogant people."[15]

The merchant then makes a common mistake with Don Quixote, which is to push the joke too far. He asks at least to see a portrait of the lady in question and promises that, even if she is blind in one eye with discharge flowing from the other, they will praise her as much as he wishes. Infuriated at this blasphemous insult, Don Quixote lowers his lance and charges. It would have gone badly for the merchant, except that Rocinante trips and falls, and the Don is cast to the ground where, due to the weight of his armor and other accoutrements, he cannot stand. One of the mule drivers, incensed by the insults hurled by Don Quixote, beats him soundly with his own lance until it shatters.

In this scene, as in most of part 1, comedy conquers over pathos at first, despite the beating. Somehow the reader knows that the Don is never in serious danger. And the setbacks he suffers are merely physical; his spirit is undaunted: "And still he considered himself fortunate," the narrator explains, "for it seemed to him that this was the kind of mishap that befell knights errant, and he attributed it all to his horse's misstep, but his body was so bruised and beaten it was not possible for him to stand."[16]

When he is left battered and bruised and unable to stand, the scales shift, and one sees on the ground not Don Quixote but Alonso Quixano, helplessly spouting the chivalric ballad of a wounded knight from one of his books. And it is Alonso Quixano who is discovered, still lying there, by a kindly neighbor, Pedro Alonso, who lifts him up, puts him gently on his own donkey, and leads him and Rocinante home. Pedro tries gently to convince Quixano that he is not a hero from one the books of chivalry, but the would-be Don will have none of it. "I know who I am," he replies, "and I know I can be not only those I have mentioned but the Twelve Peers of France as well, and even all the nine paragons of Fame, for my deeds will surpass all those they performed, together or singly."[17] In a nice touch of delicacy, Pedro waits until dark to bring his neighbor home, "so that no one would see what a poor knight the beaten gentleman was."[18] Thus ends the first sally.

SANCHO AND THE DON: THE SECOND SALLY

A number of scholars believe that Cervantes's initial conception did not extend beyond the return home of Alonso Quixano. There is a very funny scene in which the priest and the barber, urged on by the niece and the housekeeper, make a bonfire of the books of chivalry that turned Quixano's brain and, at the niece's urging, even add to the pile certain pastoral works, lest Quixano, cured of knight errantry, will "want to become a shepherd and wander through the woods and meadows singing and playing, and, what would be even worse, become a poet, and that, they say, is an incurable and contagious disease."[19] In a parody of the Inquisition— the niece even calls the books "heretics" that must be burned—the priest and the barber debate the virtues and vices of the various books, sparing some and condemning others. Cervantes's own *Galatea* barely escapes the flames after the priest notes that the author is "better versed in misfortunes than in verses."[20] But they decide to withhold judgment pending an expected second part of a book that, so far, "proposes something and concludes nothing."[21] Significantly, there are no religious books in the library: no books of devotion or pious biographies of saints. Alonso Quixano may be a devout Christian, but God plays no part in the world of Don Quixote.[22]

Perhaps Cervantes did intend the Don's first sally, with or without the book burning, to be a stand-alone novella, like those in his sadly neglected *Exemplary Stories*. Indeed, with Don Quixote as the sole focus, it is hard to see what else Cervantes could have done with the tale without it becoming tedious, as the Don suffers one collision after another with a nonchivalrous world. Like *La Galatea*, it would propose something and conclude nothing.

But, in an act of pure genius, Cervantes decided to give his woeful knight a companion, a neighboring farmer named Sancho Panza, "a good man—if that title can be given to someone who is poor—but without much in the way of brains."[23] The "buddy movie" was thus born out of the greatest, funniest, and most moving friendship in all of literature. The two are, of course, polar opposites. The Don is a hidalgo; Sancho is a peasant. The Don is well-off; Sancho is poor. The Don is educated; Sancho is illiterate. The Don is tall and thin; Sancho is short and round. The Don can live on "sweet memories"[24] of the golden age of chivalry; Sancho requires a steady diet of sausage and wine. The Don is an idealist, full of books and classical learning; Sancho is a realist, who can spout commonsense proverbs until the proverbial cows come home.

Don Quixote, while still on his sickbed, talks to Sancho at such length about the world of chivalry and the life of adventure that Sancho agrees to go with him and serve as his squire. Despite the combined efforts of the priest, the barber, the niece, and the housekeeper, the Don has not given up his belief "that what the world needed most were knights errant and that in him errant chivalry would be reborn."[25] The greatest lure for Sancho is Don Quixote's assurance that one day the Don might have an adventure that would gain him an *insula* (the Latin word for *island* used in books of chivalry) and that he would make Sancho its governor. The governorship of this hypothetical *insula* becomes an idea fixed firmly in Sancho's brain.

The presence of Sancho adds variety and complexity to the adventures. Sancho and the Don see the world completely differently. They embrace conflicting narratives that are in constant dialogue with one another. Don Quixote sees a number of giants ready to do battle; Sancho sees windmills. Don Quixote sees the famous helmet of Mambrino; Sancho sees a barber's basin. Don Quixote sees two warring armies and narrates the course of their battle, even to the point, in Homeric fashion, of reciting the names, arms, and standards of the various famous knights; Sancho sees nothing but the dust cloud stirred up by two flocks of sheep. Don Quixote is the imagination run amok; Sancho is the bellwether of reality.

Repeatedly, of course, the Don's imagination collides with Sancho's reality, often to the detriment of both. Such incidents are a constant subject of dispute between them. Yet Sancho's reproaches are always met by the Don's insistence that their setbacks are contrived by an evil enchanter who is worried that the Don's deeds and fame will eclipse those of some other, more favored knight. Sancho receives these explanations— which by definition can never be refuted—with a delicious combination of skepticism and credulity.

Their "adventures" are all variations on a theme, but they continually expand our understanding of and affection for the two characters, just as they expand Sancho's and the Don's understanding of and affection for each other. They grow together over the course of the novel. The Don is the dominant member of the pair, to be sure, at least in part 1; but they are a pair. Starting with the second sally, the entire focus of the novel is on the two of them, as opposed to the single hero of the chivalric tradition or the antihero of the picaresque novels then sweeping Spain. It is as if their world is indeed shaped by an enchanter—which of course it is, by the benign enchanter Miguel de Cervantes—to test and deepen their relationship, a tendency that will become even more pronounced in part 2, when other characters literally become the planners and authors of adventures for the pair. Over the course of the novel, they reach terms of more or less equality based on their common humanity. Their relationship transcends barriers of rank, fortune, and education. Sancho transforms the Don as much as the Don transforms Sancho. Indeed, without Sancho, Don Quixote would be just a madman and a fool. Sancho's belief in him, qualified as it is, makes him something more. "No doubt about it," Sancho says to himself when the Don routs a group of men carrying torches, "this master of mine is as courageous and brave as he says."[26] The Don has to be validated in the eyes of at least one other. It is perhaps true that no man is a hero to his valet, but in his own way Don Quixote is a hero to his squire, Sancho Panza. The Don, too, insists that despite Sancho's flaws, "I would not trade him for any other squire."[27]

Sancho and the Don do not idealize one another. They quarrel like an old married couple, yet they love and are loyal to each another. One complaint to which Sancho frequently reverts is that he was tossed in a blanket by a group of ruffians, and the Don did not intervene—that evil enchanter again had rendered him powerless. The Don's most frequent complaint about Sancho is that he is "not well-versed in the matter of adventures"[28] and regularly presumes beyond his proper role as squire. Their conversations are invariably ironic. The reader sees the limitations on both sides. But the irony is always gentle. Their respective views of the world are totally incompatible, yet they coexist. They expand the realm of each other's thoughts and hence the realm of their discourse. And they both become better human beings as they learn from one another.

Obviously, their friendship is not on the high intellectual plane of Montaigne and La Boétie. There is even a fair amount of toilet humor that owes much to Rabelais. Yet Sancho's own explanation as to why he stays with the Don sounds not so different from Montaigne's "because it was he; because it was I."[29]

"If I were a clever man, I would have left my master days ago. But this is my fate and this is my misfortune; I can't help it; I have to follow him: we're from the same village, I've eaten his bread, I love him dearly, he's a grateful man, he gave me his donkeys, and more than anything else, I'm faithful; and so it's impossible for anything to separate us except the man with the pick and shovel."[30]

FROM THE ROMANCE TO REALISM

It is a commonplace that *Don Quixote* is a book about books. Its ostensible purpose, Cervantes claims, is to warn against books of chivalry, which tell

275

the most outrageous lies under the guise of truth and thus poison the minds of those who read them, as they poisoned the mind of his eponymous hero. Yet the critique is also a form of homage, for, like any good parody, *Don Quixote* adopts the conventions of the genre even though, as Don Quixote himself admits, "all things having to do with knights errant appear to be chimerical, foolish, senseless, and turned inside out."[31]

Cervantes purports to be merely the editor of a history of the adventures of the Don and his squire compiled by a Moorish scholar, Cide Hamete Benengeli. This fact is dramatically revealed in the middle of Don Quixote's epic battle with a Basque mule driver, when each has raised his sword, intent on striking a fatal blow. But they sit there frozen in time atop their mounts, for "at this very point and juncture," Cervantes reports, "the author of the history leaves the battle pending, apologizing because he found nothing else written about the feats of Don Quixote other than what he has already recounted."[32] Confident that so great a knight would not lack a wise man to record not only his great deeds but also his "slightest thoughts and fancies, no matter how secret they might be,"[33] Cervantes devotes himself to finding the rest of the history. And, of course, he does, when he comes across a boy in the market in Toledo hoping to sell some notebooks and old papers. Among them is a lengthy work in Arabic, and, after Cervantes prevails on a Morisco to read it for him, translating on the fly, he quickly realizes that it is the lost history of Don Quixote. Cervantes buys the notebooks and sets the Morisco the task of preparing a proper written translation into the Castilian language.

The history of Don Quixote is thus written by a Moor, translated by a Morisco, and edited, with narrative commentary, by a Castilian. Cervantes vouches for its truth, with the caveat that Arabs "are very prone to telling falsehoods" and are also "great enemies of ours," which might lead Cide Hamete Benengeli to understate the virtues of so good a Castilian knight.[34] Truth, Cervantes stresses, is the ultimate touchstone of value:

Historians must and ought to be exact, truthful, and absolutely free of passions, for neither interest, fear, rancor, nor affection should make them deviate from the path of the truth, whose mother is history, the rival of time, repository of great deeds, witness to the past, example and adviser to the present, and forewarning to the future.[35]

It is an idealized Renaissance view of history, as applied to a work of complete fiction. But what Cervantes is implying is that fiction has its own standards of truth that are every bit as rigorous as those of history.

Don Quixote, of course, is not really a cautionary tale about the pernicious absurdity of books of chivalry. Although such novels were popular under Charles V, they were already out of fashion by the time Cervantes was writing, and there was no pressing need to discredit them further. Pastoral novels—combining prose and verse like Cervantes's *Galatea*—were more in vogue, and picaresque novels—the episodic adventures of a clever rogue interspersed with moralistic sermons—were the latest rage for their colorful portrayal of the lower, seamier side of life: they could titillate and condemn all at once.

In *Don Quixote*, Cervantes combines elements of all three genres in a deeper meditation on the uses and abuses of fiction. He is striving for something new. Chivalric idealism, pastoral romance, and the picaresque underworld are all present at the birth of the modern novel. But each has its own set of conventions that define and confine it. Cervantes wants to go beyond those conventions and, in the process, reenvision the novel as a more flexible tool for understanding reality. Cervantes is indeed dedicated to truth: not the truth of history but the higher truth of fiction, fiction that is faithful to experience and even to the "slightest thoughts and fancies, no matter how secret they might be." Cervantes views the novel, as Montaigne did his *Essays*, as a means of exploring experience and obtaining a new level of self-knowledge and self-understanding. Cervantes, like Montaigne, seeks wisdom as well as entertainment, and he provides both in his characters' encounters with the world and with one another.

Yet Cervantes, again like Montaigne, understood that the written word creates, as well as describes, the world. Fiction doesn't just imitate reality; it transforms reality through the act of representing it. No single representation can ever claim to be definitive. The novel, like the essay, is never through with its work of redescribing and re-creating. Our attempt to understand is never at an end. We are never frozen in place like the Basque and Don Quixote, waiting to deliver their final blows.

All knowledge may come from experience, but reading is part of our experience. It changes us. It transforms us. It creates new ideals and new longings, which are then tested in the crucible of experience as the Don's chivalric visions are tested. Reality can be a harsh teacher, but we cannot go back to a preliterary experience. Auerbach suggests that, in *Don Quixote*, reality is always right, and the Don's ideals are repeatedly exposed as absurd, even mad. But that is too simplistic a dichotomy. Reality is not totally intractable; ideals and desires are essential to life itself, and the key question is to what extent we can shape reality to accord with those ideals and desires. We might even say that every attempt at realism is a new form of romanticism; indeed, that seems a perfect description of *Don Quixote*.

Part 1 of *Don Quixote* contains a number of interpolated novels. One of them is found in a traveling bag left behind at an inn and is read aloud to the other characters by the priest. Another is delivered by a former prisoner of the Moors, like Cervantes himself, who recounts his life and adventures to the assembled company at the same inn. A pastoral novella about a beautiful, well-off young woman who decides to become a shepherdess and shuns all contact with men is integrated somewhat better in the story, although still at odd angles from the main plot. Cervantes also briefly hints at the picaresque adventures of Ginés de Pasamonte, one of the galley slaves the Don frees from captivity.

It is worth noting that the encounter with the galley slaves is one of the few incidents in part 1 where the Don does not misperceive what is happening. Indeed, it marks a turning point in the first volume. The Don does not transform the situation in his mind into an adventure from the books of chivalry. He understands that these men are convicted criminals sentenced to serve as rowers in the king's ships, where they will be chained to their oars, whipped, underfed, and as likely as not die before tasting freedom. The Don carefully questions each man to understand "the particular reason for each one's misfortune."[36] Most of them are more pathetic than venal, at least according to their own accounts. One has only "confessed" under torture. Another was convicted because he had no money to bribe the judge. But Ginés, who is weighed down with double the usual shackles, has allegedly "committed more crimes than all the rest combined."[37] He has also written his own history, which he predicts will overshadow the most popular of picaresque novels because it is true.

> "What I can tell your grace is that it deals with truths, and they are truths so appealing and entertaining that no lies can equal them."
>
> "And what is the title of the book?" asked Don Quixote.
>
> "*The Life of Ginés de Pasamonte*," Ginés replied.
>
> "And is it finished?" asked Don Quixote.
>
> "How can it be finished," he responded, "if my life isn't finished yet? What I've written goes from my birth to the moment when they sentenced me to the galleys this last time."[38]

Cervantes is again parodying a popular genre of his day. But he is also insisting that the best books are true to life, because such "truths [are] so appealing and entertaining that no lies can equal them." Ginés notes that he will finish his book, and by implication his life, in the galleys of Spain. But the Don, sounding like a modern civil rights activist, decries the severity of the punishment, the perversion of justice, and the oppression of the weak. He spurs Rocinante to the galley slaves' defense and, with the help of the slaves themselves, routs the four guards escorting the convicts. Instead of expressing gratitude they shower him, Sancho, and their mounts with stones after the Don seeks to compel them to carry their chains to Toboso, where they can deposit them at the feet of Dulcinea and tell of his great deeds. The galley slaves then scatter, and, in a passage of great pathos, the picaresque interlude concludes:

> The donkey and Rocinante, Sancho and Don Quixote, were left alone; the donkey, pensive, with bowed head, twitching his ears from time to time, thinking that the tempest of stones had not yet ended and was still falling around his ears; Rocinante, lying beside his master, for he too had fallen to the ground in the shower of stones; Sancho, in his shirt sleeves and afraid of the Holy Brotherhood; Don Quixote, grief-stricken at seeing himself so injured by the very people for whom he had done so much good.[39]

The most extended and important of the novels within the novel are the intertwining stories of Cardenio and Luscinda and Dorotea and Don Fernando. The Don and Sancho first encounter them in the Sierra Morena, where the Don has gone to imitate Amadís of Gaul and other knights who went mad and lived in a remote wilderness after being rejected by their beloveds. Sancho points out that Don Quixote, unlike Amadís and the others, had not been rejected and has no reason to do penance. But the Don will not be deterred from his preplanned bout of madness. He explains as he sends Sancho away with a plaintive letter for Dulcinea del Toboso that "a knight errant deserves neither glory nor thanks if he goes mad for a reason. The great achievement is to lose one's reason for no reason, and to let my lady know that if I can do this without cause, what should I not do if there were cause?"[40]

In the mountains, Don Quixote encounters someone who has truly gone mad for love, one Cardenio, a wealthy young noble secretly betrothed to Luscinda but betrayed by the man he thought was his best friend. Don Fernando, the younger (and therefore impecunious) son of Duke Ricardo, has already seduced Dorotea, the daughter of wealthy peasants, with false promises of marriage. He then convinces Luscinda's father—who is dazzled by the prospect of an aristocratic son-in-law—to require Luscinda to marry him instead of Cardenio. The intertwining plots are intricate and drawn out. Yet, once again, Don Quixote plays a clear-eyed role in helping to reconcile Don Fernando and Dorotea and thereby free Cardenio and Luscinda to fulfill their earlier vows to each other. But, as Jane Austen would perfectly appreciate, the denouement owes as much to class and money as to romance. Dorotea, as she herself admits, succumbed to Don Fernando because she was ambitious to rise "from a humble to a noble estate";[41] Don Fernando just as surely recognizes that her family's fortune will cure his primogeniture problem. Social and economic forces were also present at the birth of the novel.

Cervantes was clearly hedging his bets with these interpolated novels, uncertain whether a steady focus on Sancho and the Don would retain his readers' interest. He had many diversions in the traveler's bag of tricks he left at that inn. Yet he insists that the stories added to the history of Don Quixote are "no less agreeable and artful and true than the history itself."[42] Cervantes remains faithful in his commitment to verisimilitude, just as his knight remains faithful to the ideals and principles of chivalry. That commitment transcends the conventions of individual genres.

These stories also highlight a change in Don Quixote himself. He is no longer the author of his own fiction. His individual perceptions are more grounded in reality; he himself seems more solid and real than the fictions that swirl around him. And on all subjects but one he speaks sanely, even soundly, befitting his rank and education. The Don is now deluded not so much because he sees giants where others see windmills; he is deluded by the machinations of other characters who play upon his belief that books of chivalry have the truth of history and provide an accurate description of events in the world. The priest and the barber, aided by Dorotea and Cardenio, develop an elaborate fiction regarding a princess and the evil giant who threatens her kingdom in order to trick Don Quixote into returning to his own village. "Isn't it strange," asks the priest, "how easily this unfortunate gentleman believes all those inventions and lies simply because they are in the same style and manner as his foolish books?"[43]

But who is mad and who is sane? The priest and the barber have also left their village and their responsibilities to go in search of Don Quixote in order to playact in his fantasies, as they conceive them. These characters don ludicrous disguises, assume outlandish identities, and profess utter nonsense—all, ostensibly, in order to lure a madman back to his home. The various intertwining stories—of, among others, Dorotea and Don Fernando, Cardenio and Luscinda, and the captive and the Moorish beauty who saved him—reach their largely happy denouement in a single raucous evening at the inn when Don Quixote, in a dream, successfully slays the evil giant in the form of several large wineskins hanging in his room. He then does battle with the Holy Brotherhood, which has a warrant for his arrest for having freed the galley slaves.

The men of the Holy Brotherhood are convinced by the others that arresting a madman is futile. But left still with the problem of what to do with Don Quixote, the assembled characters disguise themselves as phantoms sent by an enchanter and lock Don Quixote in a cage. Accompanied by prophecies of Don Quixote's future greatness and his impending marriage to Dulcinea del Toboso, they place the cage in a cart and drive the Don home, accompanied by Sancho on his mule. The novel ends (for, at the time, no second part was planned) with Don Quixote at home, lying in his bed and staring uncomprehendingly ahead of him. Yet before he lapses into this state, he reaffirms the value of books of chivalry that improve the spirits and drive away melancholy:

> For myself, I can say that since I became a knight errant I have been valiant, well-mannered, liberal, polite, generous, courteous, bold, gentle, patient, long-suffering in labors, imprisonments, and enchantments, and although only a short while ago I saw myself locked in a cage like a madman, I think that with the valor of my arm, and heaven favoring me, and fortune not opposing me, in a few days I shall find myself the king of some kingdom where I can display the gratitude and liberality of my heart.[44]

These are truths so appealing and entertaining that no lies can equal them.

THE ENCHANTMENT OF LITERATURE

The publication of *Don Quixote* in 1605 made its author famous, even if it did little to alleviate his poverty. The work circulated widely in Spain and beyond. Shakespeare read an English translation in 1612 and even cowrote a lost play about Cardenio, one of the pastoral characters in what is now part 1. The popularity of part 1 becomes a plot device in part 2 of the novel as Don Quixote and Sancho repeatedly encounter people who have read of their earlier adventures. This fiction within the fiction, paradoxically, makes the pair seem all the more substantial.

Cervantes, however, initially had no intention of writing a sequel. He worked on various novellas, plays, and long poems. But Don Quixote and Sancho were not destined to remain back in their unnamed village in La Mancha for long. The Don retained his determination "to revive and bring back to the world the forgotten order of chivalry";[45] Sancho still dreamt of his promised governorship; and surely Cervantes himself hoped finally to translate his talents into ready cash, something his contemporary Shakespeare was so adept at doing.

Cervantes began work on a sequel in 1611 and spent four years on it. He was forestalled, however, by a bogus sequel published in 1614 under the pseudonym Alonso Fernández de Avellaneda. The imposture is by all accounts tedious: its Sancho is never more than a gluttonous, drunken buffoon, and its Don Quixote never rises above slapstick. Worse, the "author," in a prologue, mocks Cervantes himself for his old age and his useless left hand.

But Cervantes deftly and definitively disposes of Avellaneda. Addressing his readers in his own prologue, Cervantes ostensibly declines to engage in the expected reprisals: "You would like me to call him an ass, a fool, an insolent dolt, but the thought has not even entered my mind: let his sin be his punishment, let him eat it with his bread, and let that be an end to it."[46] But Cervantes does take offense at the disparagement of his wounds, acquired at the Battle of Lepanto, "the greatest event ever seen in past or present times."[47] As for his age, he retorts that "it should be noted that one writes not with gray hairs but with the understanding, which generally improves with the years."[48]

In the course of part 2, Don Álvaro Tarfe, a character in Avellaneda's book, encounters the real Sancho and Don Quixote and recognizes at once that Avellaneda's characters were gross imposters. He even signs a testimonial to that effect and apologizes to the knight and the squire for his mistake. It is a comic masterstroke of dismissal. Don Quixote, too, having learned of the false news published by Avellaneda, changes the course of his travels to give the lie to his ersatz historian.

But the role of Avellaneda's book in part 2 is tiny compared to the role of part 1. Don Quixote has not even risen from the bed to which he has been confined before he learns from a local student—Sansón Carrasco, honorifically titled "Bachelor" in recognition of his learning—that a history of his adventures has already been written by a Moor, translated from the Arabic into Castilian, and widely distributed. Many of the characters in part 2 are readers—if often misreaders—of part 1. They have their own expectations about how Don Quixote and Sancho ought to behave, and they are eager to play a part in driving the narrative. They are drawn out of their own lives and into the ever more powerful orbit of Don Quixote and Sancho.

Most critics find part 2 to be superior to part 1.[49] But, along with Thomas Mann, I miss "the happy freshness and carelessness" of the first part,[50] even as I recognize the literary brilliance of the second. Part 2 is an extended meditation on the role of imaginative literature in shaping life. As Roberto Echevarría aptly explains, "in Part II, Part I plays the role that the romances of chivalry play in Part I."[51] Don Quixote is so intoxicated with the romances of chivalry that he "can almost say I have seen Amadís of Gaul with my own eyes."[52] Don Quixote and Sancho have become as real to the readers of part 1 as Amadís of Gaul is to Don Quixote. We can quite literally say that we have seen them with our own eyes.

Statues of Don Quixote and Sancho stand in the Plaza de España in Madrid. Picasso's line drawings are instantly recognizable. These two characters have become part of the history of their country. They are as important as, if not more important than, Charles V or Philip II in Spain's developing identity. We have nothing quite comparable in the United States, despite statues of Mary Richards in Minneapolis and Rocky in Philadelphia. Even Tom Sawyer and Huck Finn, or Melville's Captain Ahab, the darker cousin of Don Quixote, have not etched themselves in our collective consciousness to the same extent. But the point remains: fiction is part of our history, both personal and collective.

As we have seen, a key theme of part 1, echoing Montaigne, is that we are all, to some extent, the authors of our existence. We impose our imaginative will upon the world. The comedy and pathos of part 1 is that the world is not as malleable a material as we might wish. We can only go so far in our fantasies before we run smack into an intransigent reality. In part 2, Cervantes introduces the additional complexity of how the dreams and imaginings of other people intersect with our own, particularly when those dreams and imaginings are themselves the product of fiction. If everyone is a character in the fiction we create or the fictions we have absorbed, we are also characters in other people's fiction. In part 2, Don Quixote and Sancho have become so absorbing to the people who read part 1 that those readers become mini-Avellanedas and attempt to construct new narratives for the pair of their own devising. Yet, just as reality formed a check in part 1, so too the fictional reality of Don Quixote and Sancho constantly confounds the expectations and manipulations of the would-be authors in part 2.

This process begins with the Bachelor Sansón Carrasco, who is eager to play along with, and even encourage, Don Quixote's madness, greeting him as the "flower of errant chivalry" and the "honor and paragon of the

Spanish nation."[53] He offers some common criticisms of part 1, particularly of the interpolated novels that have nothing to do with the story of Don Quixote. And, like a typical scholar, he fastens on some inconsistencies in the narrative, which Sancho dismisses as errors by the historian or the printer. Mostly, though, Sansón praises the work, if somewhat condescendingly, as "the most enjoyable and least harmful entertainment" ever seen:

> Children look at it, youths read it, men understand it, the old celebrate it, and, in short, it is so popular and so widely read and so well-known by every kind of person that as soon as people see a skinny old nag they say: "There goes Rocinante."[54]

When it is clear that Don Quixote is determined to set forth again, Sansón decides that he himself should be the author and hero of the next sally. He plans, with the connivance of the priest and the barber, to confront Don Quixote on his journey disguised as another knight and to challenge him to a joust, with the loser bound to do the bidding of the winner. Sansón, after defeating the elderly knight, will require Don Quixote to return home and give up knight errantry for a full year. In his guise as the Knight of the Mirrors, Sansón is going to show Don Quixote who he really is and cure him, once and for all, of his fantasies.

But, as with Avellaneda, Sansón's planned sequel goes awry. He stops his horse midfield because Don Quixote is not yet ready. And, what with trying to get his recalcitrant mount restarted and fumbling to secure his lance in its socket, Sansón is helpless in the face of Don Quixote's own furious charge. The Don knocks Sansón backward over the haunches of his horse, and he crashes to the ground. Sansón learns in part 2 what he should have learned from reading part 1: when fantasy encounters reality, the one nursing the fantasy is likely to end up battered and bruised. The reality Sansón encounters here is the true Don Quixote, who knows very well who and what he is—the "flower of errant chivalry" and the "honor and paragon of the Spanish nation." Sansón goes off to plaster his broken ribs after making a solemn promise to travel to Toboso and, there, to place himself at the service of the Lady Dulcinea—a promise, it is worth noting, he does not keep. Sansón, despite his playacting, is no Don Quixote.

Sancho, too, shapes the narrative of part 2 by relying on Don Quixote's credulity. Recall that, in part 1, Sancho pretended to travel to Toboso to deliver a letter to Dulcinea. He tells Don Quixote that he found her sifting wheat, all sweaty and smelling sour. She received him gracefully enough, however, accepting the proffered devotion of Don Quixote and commanding that the Don present himself before her. Naturally, therefore, Toboso is the first place to which Don Quixote turns his horse in part 2, directing Sancho to bring him before his Lady Dulcinea.

Sancho, having made up the story, is now in a dilemma: he has no idea even where Aldonza Lorenzo lives, much less Dulcinea del Toboso. He therefore resorts to the explanation that Don Quixote so often invoked in part 1 when reality intruded on illusion: enchantment. Sancho picks out three peasant girls coming toward them on jackasses and tells Don Quixote that it is Dulcinea and her two ladies-in-waiting coming to greet him, richly dressed, adorned with jewels, and riding the finest palfreys. Don Quixote, like Sancho in part 1, insists on the banal reality before them, while Sancho insists just as fiercely that this round-faced, snub-nosed peasant girl, who smells strongly of garlic and greets them with coarse oaths, is a peerless and elegant beauty. The crestfallen Don Quixote accepts that malicious enchanters have deprived him of the greatest happiness in seeing his lady in her rightful person. He now begins to live within the fiction created by Sancho, and the need to rescue Dulcinea from her enchantment remains a motif throughout part 2.

Sancho at least feels guilty about his deception. As he explains to the squire of the Knight of the Mirrors, who has admitted that his own master, the disguised Sansón Carrasco, is a scoundrel:

> "Not mine," responded Sancho. "I mean, there's nothing of the scoundrel in him; mine's as innocent as a baby; he doesn't know how to harm

anybody, he can only do good to everybody, and there's no malice in him: a child could convince him it's night in the middle of the day, and because he's simple I love him with all my heart and couldn't leave him no matter how many crazy things he does."[55]

The tables are truly turned when Sancho loves the Don for being simple. The master-squire relationship has been replaced by a purely human and equal one based on love and friendship, particularly when the Don becomes dependent on Sancho to counter the enchantment. Indeed, Sancho, though the inventor of the fiction, comes close to believing it himself in the end.

The characters in part 2 have varying reasons for creating new fictions for Don Quixote to act within. Sancho is trying to avoid being caught in one lie by telling a greater one. Sansón, despite his ostensible desire to "cure" Don Quixote, is really playing out his own fantasy. Ginés de Pasamonte, who reappears in part 2 disguised as the puppet master Don Pedro, sweeps Don Quixote into his tale of a gallant knight rescuing his wife from her Moorish captors simply as an unfortunate by-product of his theatrical verisimilitude.

Only the duke and duchess, into whose clutches Sancho and Don Quixote innocently wander, manipulate the pair purely for their own amusement. Although they resolve outwardly to treat Don Quixote "like a knight errant with all the customary ceremonies found in the books of chivalry,"[56] they instruct their butler to contrive a series of further "adventures" for the pair that are often distasteful in their cruelty and always cruel in their mockery. The duke and duchess live in extravagant luxury; their idle and frivolous existence is propped up by loans from a wealthy peasant upon whom they are dependent. They stand in sharp contrast to the various low-life characters in parts 1 and 2, who—at least when they are not provoked into delivering blows—treat Don Quixote and Sancho with innate kindness and consideration, even as they enjoy the joke of playing along with Don Quixote's madness. The one saving grace of the duke and duchess is that they give Sancho, briefly, the governorship he has long coveted and in which he surprises all concerned with his wisdom and compassion. Sancho's display of natural reason—uninfected by the corruption of the aristocracy—prefigures the Enlightenment.

THE MADNESS OF DON QUIXOTE

Before he encounters the duke and duchess, Don Quixote has an adventure that Thomas Mann considers the climax of the novel for "its peculiarly moving, magnificently ridiculous contents."[57] Sancho has wandered off to buy curds from a group of shepherds when his master calls urgently to him. Sancho quickly places the curds in the helmet he has been carrying and rushes back. He no sooner arrives than Don Quixote seizes the helmet and places it firmly on his own head, causing the whey to drip down the sides of his face and into his beard. Don Quixote—at first concerned that his brains are melting—soon discovers the curds. Sancho, of course, blames enchanters, noting that if the curds were his own they would be in his stomach, not in Don Quixote's helmet. It is, somehow, the perfect setup for what follows.

Don Quixote, after returning the now smashed curds to Sancho, wipes his face, calls for his sword, grasps his lance, and steadies himself in his stirrups as he awaits an approaching wagon bearing royal banners. In the wagon are two cages, each containing a lion. The lions have been sent from Oran as a present for the king. Don Quixote insists that the lion keeper open the cages and release the lions so that he may test his might and his courage against them. The lion keeper protests, noting that the lions are hungry because they have not yet eaten. So does Sancho, who peeks into one of the cages and assures Don Quixote that there is no enchantment here: it is a real lion, large and fierce, with huge claws. A local gentleman, Don Diego, who had recently fallen into step with Don Quixote and Sancho as they were traveling in the same direction, also tries to dissuade him, but to no avail. The wagon owner unyokes his mules and flees, as does Sancho on his donkey and Don Diego on his horse, all convinced that Don Quixote will be torn to pieces.

Don Quixote dismounts to confront the lions on foot, tossing away his lance and standing before the wagon with his sword in one hand and a shield in the other. The lion keeper then unlocks the first cage and throws open the door. The male lion stretches, yawns, unsheathes his claws, and puts his head out of the cage to look around, "with eyes like coals, a sight and a vision that could frighten temerity itself."[58] But the lion proves indifferent to Don Quixote's bravado, shows the Don his hindquarters, and placidly returns to his cage. Don Quixote calls upon the lion keeper to hit the lion and provoke him into coming out. But the lion keeper, fearing for his own life, assures Don Quixote that this is unnecessary:

> The greatness of your grace's heart has been clearly demonstrated: no brave warrior, to my understanding, is obliged to do more than challenge his opponent and wait for him in the field; if his adversary does not appear, the dishonor lies with him, and the one left waiting wins the crown of victory.[59]

Don Quixote's perceptions of reality may be distorted by his literary infatuation, but his courage is real. So is his kindness, his sense of honor, and his devotion to justice. In part 2, he performs a number of genuinely good deeds, including defending the honor of a widow and her daughter and protecting a young couple in love. Even in his failures, Don Quixote never loses his innate dignity. Even with curds in his helmet and whey streaming down his face, he retains a certain nobility if not a touch of the sacred. He somehow transcends the absurdity of his circumstances. And the remarkable thing is that we, as readers, can both enjoy the absurdity and be awed by the transcendence. If either were missing, it would be a lesser book.

As long as Don Quixote is facing a reality at odds with his ideals, he is unwavering. He will hold to those ideals, however humiliating the setbacks. "Find strength in weakness," he advises Sancho, "and I shall do the same."[60] Yet, when reality is not pushing back, when Don Quixote can give free rein to his imagination, doubts begin to creep in and undermine the self he has chosen to present to the world. As Sancho earlier said to him, "Maybe you go looking for one thing and find another."[61]

What Don Quixote goes looking for is the famous Cave of Montesinos. In the spirit of Odysseus, Aeneas, and Dante, Don Quixote undertakes a journey to the underworld to encounter death and ultimately his own self. It begins and ends prosaically enough. He is lowered by ropes into the depths of the cave and is pulled out less than an hour later profoundly unconscious. When he finally is brought back to the world, he tells of his several-day encounter with the chivalric heroes of Spain's golden age and how he was honored there and took his rightful place among them, somewhat as Dante took his rightful place in the anteroom of the underworld among the great poets of antiquity.[62]

Don Quixote describes his vision in vivid if sometimes banal detail. He even claims to have encountered his Lady Dulcinea in her still enchanted state as a peasant girl. At this point, he loses a crucial member of his audience. Sancho, who "had been the enchanter and had invented the story, . . . recognized beyond the shadow of a doubt that his master was out of his mind and completely mad."[63] Yet that is not what we take away from this episode. To the contrary, it is the beginning of Don Quixote's unfortunate return to sanity. The world he encounters in the cave is exactly what he dreams. And yet he himself begins to doubt it even as he first recounts it. Paradoxically, the Don needs his clashes with reality to confirm his fantasy. In the cave, he encounters nothingness. There is no check on his imagination. As one critic correctly notes, "The novel's entire machinery, built on the opposition between fantasy and reality, is suspended on this sole occasion."[64]

Don Quixote desperately wants to believe that his dream vision is true, but doubts remain, calling into question his entire enterprise. He knows how to combat giants and knights and enchanters. But he doesn't know how to combat his own doubts. His descent into the Cave of Montesinos is more corrosive and sobering than any other adventure. Don Quixote begins to lose his grip on his fantasy. He seeks reassurance from others, even absurdly from the soothsaying monkey of Don Pedro and the talking bust of Don Antonio Moreno. He now needs others to believe in him as Don Quixote de la Mancha in order to validate his own belief. Most of all, he needs Sancho. So when Sancho narrates his own fantastic journey aboard the flying horse, Clavileño, the Don is prepared to cut a deal. "Sancho," he whispers, "just as you want people to believe what you have seen in the sky, I want you to believe what I saw in the Cave of Montesinos. And that is all I have to say."[65]

But it is too late. Desengaño has already taken root in his soul. And when he encounters the Knight of the Moon—Sansón Carrasco in a fresh disguise—this time the outcome is inevitable. Don Quixote, knocked ignominiously from his horse, is compelled by the laws of chivalry to return to his village and to give up arms for a full year. Sansón believes it is a cure. But, of course, it is a death sentence. As the great Spanish philosopher and critic José Ortega y Gasset notes, Don Quixote lives in the gap between heroic ideals and earthly reality.[66] When that gap closes, Don Quixote is no more. "May God forgive you for the harm you have done," Don Antonio tells Sansón.[67]

Is it mad to want to play a noble part in life and to pursue that ideal with great courage and persistence in the face of a hostile reality? Is it mad to want to pass beyond a dreary and uneventful life into a world of adventure and glory? If so, Don Quixote is mad, but his very madness is sublime. Sancho calls him "the conqueror of himself; and, as he has told me, that is the greatest conquest anyone can desire."[68] We all do battle with nothingness, and nothingness always wins in the end. "Thou art an O without a figure," the Fool says to Lear; "thou art nothing."[69] The fiction of life closes with life itself, but, as Sancho wisely insists, "Everything's life until we die."[70] And something of what we built remains. We are not "nothing," and our enemies are not enchanters. Our enemies are disenchantment, disillusion, and desengaño.

We have lingered in the chambers of the sea
By sea-girls wreathed with seaweed red and brown
Till human voices wake us, and we drown.[71]

By the time Cervantes came to write his masterpiece, Spain had lost the high ideals of its golden age. The Battle of Lepanto was a distant memory. Setbacks against the Turks, the French, and in the Low Countries were the new reality. What more Quixotic act could there be than sending the Invincible Armada to circumnavigate England to its own destruction, without inflicting any genuine harm on anyone but itself. Did Spain recognize itself in Don Quixote? Clearly it did, even as it laughed at his misadventures. Catharsis can be found in comedy as well as tragedy.

Cervantes, of course, recognized himself as well in his famous hero. The reality of his life was often shabby after Lepanto and was riddled with failures as a writer, as a husband, and even as a protector of his sisters, his daughter, and his niece. And yet he pursued his own ideals with courage and persistence. He refused to relinquish his grasp on glory and adventure. He wrote at the end of his great work: "For me alone was Don Quixote born, and I for him; he knew how to act, and I to write; the two of us alone are one."[72]

Cervantes died in Madrid on April 22, 1616, one day before Shakespeare. He has been revered ever since as the "flower of errant chivalry" and the "honor and paragon of the Spanish nation."

Chapter 9

SHAKESPEARE

The applause, delight, the wonder of our stage!
. . . He was not of an age but for all time!—Ben Jonson[1]

"There can be little doubt," wrote the eighteenth-century critic and essayist William Hazlitt, "that Shakespear was the most universal genius that ever lived."[2] Stephen Greenblatt is somewhat more modest in his claim, suggesting that the thirty-six plays preserved in the First Folio constitute "the most important body of imaginative literature of the last thousand years."[3] Even so qualified, that assessment would place the histories, comedies, tragedies, and romances of Shakespeare above Dante and on a par with the greatest works of antiquity. Harold Bloom boldly contends that Shakespeare invented what it is to be human. Extravagant, perhaps, but we can hardly dispute that, together with Montaigne and Cervantes—both of whom he read—Shakespeare created our modern consciousness and opened the way to Goethe, Austen, Dickens, Proust, and Joyce, among others. Rankings may be pointless, but however short a list one might make of the greatest figures in Western thought, Shakespeare is surely on it. I would follow Hazlitt in placing him at the top.

At the close of Plato's *Symposium*, as the other revelers drop off to sleep, Socrates attempts to demonstrate that the most skilled tragic dramatist should also be a comic poet, thus capturing the full range of human experience. Shakespeare is that dramatist, and trying to assess the measure of his achievement is both an immense joy and an impossible challenge. The critical literature is larger than any ten scholars could read in a lifetime. And the quality of that criticism—from Hazlitt and

Samuel Johnson, through Harold Goddard and G. Wilson Knight, to A. D. Nuttall and Harold Bloom—is unmatched. Yet I can safely say, quoting Prospero, that Shakespeare's creative genius still lies "deeper than did ever plummet sound."[4] In the pages that follow, we will make our own attempt, however inadequate, to sound one play each among the histories, comedies, tragedies, and romances of William Shakespeare.

LIFE

Shakespeare was baptized on April 26, 1564, in Stratford-upon-Avon, a smallish market town about a hundred miles northwest of London. We do not know the exact date of his birth, but it was likely on or around April 23, which is also the date on which he died, fifty-two years later. He is lucky to have survived at all. Stratford's already small population of about two thousand was ravaged in 1564 by the plague, which would play a decided if intermittent role throughout Shakespeare's life. Almost two-thirds of the babies born in Stratford that year died before their first birthdays.

Shakespeare was baptized a Protestant, a member of the Church of England, but thereby hangs a tale. He was born thirty years after the break with Rome precipitated by Henry VIII's "great matter." There had been a brief, and bloody, return to Catholicism under Mary I, the child of Henry VIII and his first wife, the pious Catherine of Aragon. Mary succeeded her younger half brother Edward VI—the only son of Henry VIII and Jane Seymour—in 1553 and promptly married Philip II, the Catholic king of Spain. But the marriage was childless, despite a well-publicized and much mocked false pregnancy. So, when Mary died in 1558, she was succeeded by her half sister, Elizabeth I, the daughter of Henry VIII and Anne Boleyn. England reverted to Protestantism, this time for good, during the forty-four years of her reign.

Many adherents of the "old faith" remained, however, including, apparently, Shakespeare's father, John. They were known as recusants because they declined to attend Protestant services, and they often celebrated Catholic Masses in private and retained Catholic books and relics. Elizabeth, unlike Mary, was at first inclined to tolerance: *video et taceo* ("I see but say nothing") was her motto. But, after Pope Pius V purported to release her subjects from obedience in 1570 and Pope Gregory XIII openly invited her assassination in 1580, she understandably began to see plots and conspiracies everywhere. Catholicism and treason became virtually synonymous, and remaining Catholics burrowed deeper into their closets. Priests and Jesuits coming from the continent to minister to the faithful were hunted down and executed as would-be assassins. Some scholars have suggested that William Shakespeare was himself a hidden Catholic, and they scour his plays and poems for hints to that effect. But that is only speculation, with no basis in the known facts of his life, and his writings demonstrate no particular faith beyond what Aristotle termed the higher truth of poetry.

Shakespeare's father, John, made and sold gloves. He was born in 1531, the son of a tenant farmer in nearby Snitterfield. His wife, Mary Arden (born 1540), was the daughter of the owner of the land John's father had farmed. She came from the lesser branch of a more distinguished family, which owned the nearby "Forest of Arden," to be immortalized as the pastoral setting of *As You Like It*. Mary's father left her both money and his choicest farm. By the time Shakespeare was born, the couple had a fine double house on Henley Street; one portion was used for the glove shop, the other was reserved for the family. They also owned and leased out farmland in surrounding areas. John sold wool on the side, though he was not licensed to do so, and may have been a moneylender, which was also illegal. But, in addition to his private ventures, John had a successful public career. He started as an ale taster, to ensure the quality of the brews. Successively, he served as constable, affeeror (one who fixes fines for offenses), burgess, chamberlain, alderman, and finally bailiff, the equivalent of the mayor. He even applied, although unsuccessfully, for a coat of arms, which would have conferred on him the status of a gentleman. The Shakespeares were one of the handful of families that ran Stratford.

John and Mary had eight children, five of whom, four boys and one girl, lived into adulthood. Shakespeare, who came third, was the oldest of the surviving children and was the more precious on that account. He attended an excellent local grammar school, named the King's New School after Edward VI. There, he received an immersive education in Latin and the Latin classics. The students even performed Latin plays. Various traveling companies of players visited Stratford and nearby locales while Shakespeare was young. Given his father's position as bailiff—who had to grant licenses and arrange payments for the performances—it is likely that the young Shakespeare attended many of these plays. Presumably he showed great promise in school and was marked out for further education at Oxford.

But in the late 1570s, about the time Shakespeare would have finished grammar school, things began to go awry for John Shakespeare and his family. He was absent from meetings of the aldermen starting in 1576. He was kept on the rolls, which suggests he was well liked, despite his struggles. He was also exempted from various levies and assessments. But, after years of nonattendance, he was finally dropped in 1586. By then, his financial condition had deteriorated greatly. He had mortgaged lands left to his wife and couldn't repay the loans, leading to the loss of the property. He was charged at least two times each for illegal wool sales and for usury (which probably stemmed from selling wool on account with interest for the delayed payment). One biographer, Stephen Greenblatt, speculates that John Shakespeare, like his son's beloved character Sir John Falstaff, was too fond of beer and other hard liquors. But we really don't know the cause of his economic and social collapse or its psychological effect on the young Shakespeare.

What we do know is that there is a several-year gap in the record of public documents for Shakespeare between the late 1570s, when he would have left school, and 1582, when he had to be present in Stratford in time to have impregnated his neighbor, Anne Hathaway. Some suggest, on tissue-thin evidence, that he spent time as a private tutor in Catholic Lancashire. Others believe he studied law, based only on the fact that he shows considerable facility with legal concepts and arguments in his plays. Most plausibly, he stayed at home and tried to help his father straighten his tangled financial affairs. Regardless, we do know that, in late November or early December 1582, the eighteen-year-old Shakespeare married the twenty-six-year-old, already pregnant Anne Hathaway. It was a hurried affair, with a special dispensation to allow a license before all the typical banns were read on three successive Sundays. Anne was recently orphaned and likely illiterate but was left with independent means. Two of her late father's friends posted a substantial bond against any legal impediments, and they presumably rode herd on the young Shakespeare to secure his acquiescence, if not enthusiastic participation, in the nuptials. In *Much Ado About Nothing*, there is a reference to "wooing, wedding, and repenting."[5] Whether that was an accurate digest of Shakespeare's own experience is anyone's guess. Snippets from the writings are a hazardous substitute for biographical facts.

Anne gave birth to a daughter, Susanna, in May 1583. Twins Hamnet and Judith followed in early 1585. The couple had no further children, perhaps due to complications from the birth of the twins or perhaps the result of some estrangement. We simply do not know. They were married for thirty-four years, but Shakespeare spent much of that time in London, where he had moved sometime in the mid-to-late 1580s.

Just why Shakespeare moved to London, like most else about his life, is unclear and therefore the subject of speculation based on questionable evidence. He may have been caught poaching deer from a local lord's park. He might have had a more serious involvement with Catholic recusants. Or he may simply have seized on an opportunity to fill in with a traveling troupe of actors who lost one of their players in a brawl. Perhaps all three.

What we do know is that in the late 1580s, Shakespeare was employed in London—a crowded, smelly, frenetic city of two hundred thousand—

as an actor and writer with a troupe known, after their patron, as Lord Strange's Men. It was the beginning of the greatest age of London theater, ushered in with the two parts of Christopher Marlowe's *Tamburlaine the Great* in 1587 and 1588. Marlowe, the son of a shoemaker, was the same age as Shakespeare and was also born in a provincial town. But he managed to attend Cambridge on a scholarship and also worked as a spy for the Queen's secret service. In addition to *Tamburlaine*, he wrote *The Jew of Malta* and *Doctor Faustus*. His premature death in a barroom brawl at the age of twenty-nine has led to endless, if idle, arguments as to whether his mature works would have equaled those of Shakespeare.

The defeat of the Spanish Armada in 1588 was a pivotal event in English history, perhaps as critical—though not as unlikely—as the Athenian defeat of Persia at Marathon in 490 BCE, and more so than the Spanish-led rout of the Turks at Lepanto. It inspired an outpouring of patriotic pride and made English history plays a good bet in attracting audiences. Shakespeare, at first in collaboration with others, quickly penned three plays on Henry VI, which were received with great acclaim. This series covered the Wars of the Roses and culminated in a fourth play, *Richard III*, in which the competing claims of the House of York and the House of Lancaster were finally resolved when the Machiavellian, hunchbacked, nephew-murdering Richard III was defeated at the battle of Bosworth Field in 1485, and the first of the Tudors took the throne as Henry VII. The tetralogy not only was good business, it was smart politics as well, since it promoted what became known as the "Tudor myth," which confirmed the royal status of Elizabeth I, granddaughter of Henry VII. As we saw, Thomas More was an early propagator of that myth, when he wrote his darkly colored biography of Richard III under the patronage of Elizabeth's father, Henry VIII.

Shakespeare also contributed two early comedies, *Two Gentlemen of Verona* and *The Taming of the Shrew*, as well as an apprentice Roman tragedy, *Titus Andronicus*. He even played minor parts as an actor. But this promising beginning to his stage career was interrupted when the theaters were shut down for almost two years from 1592 to 1594, first due to a riot over labor conditions and permissive immigration, and later by a virulent outbreak of the plague, which killed almost 14 percent of the population of London.

It is unclear whether Shakespeare remained in London during these two years or whether he retreated to the relative safety of Stratford. He was not idle, however. He wrote two narrative poems for publication. The first was *Venus and Adonis*, developed from a story in Ovid's *Metamorphoses*; the second was *The Rape of Lucrece*, which had as its sources both Ovid and Livy's *History of Rome*. Both poems were dedicated to the Earl of Southampton, the first rather cringingly so, the latter with more confidence after the great success of *Venus and Adonis*, which quickly went through six editions. During this period, Shakespeare may also have started the early group of sonnets, which are likely addressed to that same Southampton, urging him to marry and produce an heir. Shakespeare may have written these sonnets at the behest of Southampton's guardian, Lord Burghley, who was insisting that Southampton marry Burghley's granddaughter. If so, they failed in their desired effect. But the world has been enriched by their composition even if Shakespeare was not.

When the theaters reopened in the summer of 1594, Shakespeare joined with many of his former colleagues to form the Lord Chamberlain's Men. It was a joint stock company, and Shakespeare was an original shareholder, a reflection of his already perceived value to the company as its chief playwright. He would remain with this same troupe, despite occasional changes of patron and once of theater, for almost twenty years and would write all of his greatest plays with them. They performed at first in Shoreditch at a venue known simply as The Theatre. It was open to the elements, and plays were performed in the afternoon to take advantage of natural light. "Groundlings," who stood in the pit, paid a penny to attend and got soaked if it rained. For another penny, the better-off could sit on benches under cover, and one penny more even bought them a cushion to sit upon. The actors—all of whom were male, with boy apprentices playing the female parts—were protected from the rain by a painted astronomical covering known as "the heavens." The authorities were suspicious of theaters as potential breeding grounds of dissension as well as plague. The so-called Master of Revels had to approve and license all plays. But it was a wildly popular form of entertainment, which was fortunate, since the Lord Chamberlain's Men, like other troupes, needed to attract as many as two thousand people a day in order to turn a profit.

While in London, Shakespeare lived in a series of temporary lodgings. How often he visited Stratford is unknown. It was a long two days on horseback, or four on foot. Surely he returned for the burial of his son Hamnet, who died at the age of eleven in 1596. It is generally believed that he made the journey at least once a year. He may have returned for longer periods, since the theaters were closed in 1603–1604, briefly again in 1605, and then for almost four years from 1606 to 1610, with a brief hiatus in 1608. Throughout this time, however, Shakespeare continued to write plays for royal and other private performances. It is possible that he moved back to Stratford more or less full time as early as 1606. We know from cast lists that his last part as an actor was likely in Ben Jonson's *Sejanus* in 1603. So a constant presence in London was not required, and he could have written his greatest tragedies from home, traveling to London every six months or so with a new script to be produced.

Anne and the children apparently lived with his parents until 1597, when Shakespeare purchased and refurbished a large residence known as New Place. Unlike his father, Shakespeare "knew how to put money in his purse and to keep it there."[6] He continued through the years to make substantial investments in land and farm buildings in the Stratford area. Shakespeare even completed an unfinished bit of business for his father, reviving his application and securing the Shakespeare coat of arms in 1596. The design shows a falcon and spear with the motto *Non sanz droict* (Not without right).[7] Ben Jonson, Shakespeare's other great rival in the theater, gently mocked this bit of pretention. A character in one of his plays, written in 1599 for the Lord Chamberlain's Men, acquires a coat of arms depicting a boar without a head and the motto *Not without mustard.*

Shakespeare's theatrical career encountered a bump in December 1598, when the Puritan landowner, who did not approve of such frivolous pursuits, declined to renew the lease on the Theatre in Shoreditch that was the home of the Lord Chamberlain's Men. Taking matters into their own hands, the entire troupe went to the theater in the dead of night, pulled down the building, loaded the timbers on wagons, and drove them across the frozen Thames to their new home, which would become the Globe Theatre. It could hold three thousand spectators. *Julius Caesar* was the first play put on there on September 21, 1599. Over the next twelve years, *As You Like It, Hamlet, Twelfth Night, Measure for Measure, Othello, King Lear, Macbeth, Antony and Cleopatra*, and Shakespeare's late romances were all performed there. As Bill Bryson has noted in his brief biography, "no theater—perhaps no human enterprise—has seen more glory in only a decade or so than the Globe during its first manifestation."[8]

Shakespeare and the Lord Chamberlain's Men ran into trouble of a different sort in 1601, when they were commissioned by followers of the Earl of Essex to put on a command performance of *Richard II*, in which the rightful but ineffectual king is deposed by Henry Bolingbroke, who seizes the throne as Henry IV. The following day, Essex, who was out of favor with the queen, tried to provoke an uprising to "rescue" her from bad advisers. The incipient rebellion was met with indifference by the populace and failed miserably. Essex slunk back to his home, where he was arrested and soon thereafter executed as a traitor. Southampton was caught up in it as well and spent two years in the Tower of London. An inquiry fortunately determined that the Lord Chamberlain's Men bore no responsibility for the uprising and played an unwitting role. But their favor at court waned decidedly until James VI of Scotland, son of Mary Stuart, Queen of Scots, and cousin of Elizabeth, took the throne two years later as James I. His mother had been championed by Catholic England and ultimately executed on suspicion of treason by Elizabeth I, thus precipitating the war with Spain. But James I was a solid member of the Church of England and even became the patron of what became known as the King James Bible, one of the greatest feats of translation and the foundation of the modern English language. He also turned the Lord Chamberlain's Men into his own company, the King's Men. An attempt by Guy Fawkes and other Catholic fanatics to blow up the King, his court, and Parliament was exposed and thwarted on November 4, 1605. The failure of the Gunpowder Plot marked the end of Catholic attempts to retake England.

The Globe burned down in 1613, when a prop cannon set the roof thatch on fire. A "New Globe" was constructed by the troupe at the same location,[9] but by then Shakespeare had stopped writing, and he sold his shares to avoid having to pay for the reconstruction. If this was a planned retirement, he had only three years to enjoy it. Shakespeare died, probably of typhus, on April 23, 1616, the same week, if not the same day, as Miguel de Cervantes. His three younger brothers had all predeceased him, as had both parents. Shakespeare's will famously gave to his wife only his "second best bed," along with the linens and hangings. Most everything else went to his beloved daughter Susanna and her issue, with separate, smaller provisions made for his other daughter, Judith—which he attempted to secure from her ne'er-do-well husband—and his sole surviving sibling, Joan.[10]

A folio edition of *Mr. William Shakespeare's Comedies, Histories, and Tragedies* was published in 1623. This labor of love by two longtime friends and theater colleagues, John Heminges and Henry Condell, collected thirty-six of his plays, many of which would otherwise almost certainly have been lost. Less than twenty years later, the English Civil War led to the execution of Charles I and to the rise of the Puritans under Oliver Cromwell. They shut down the theaters as a godless and unholy form of entertainment. Bearbaiting and public executions, however, continued. London theaters would not reopen in earnest until the Restoration in 1660, by which time Shakespeare was out of fashion.

THE EDUCATION OF A PRINCE

Shakespeare's initial historical tetralogy consisted of the three parts of *Henry VI* and *Richard III*. The first three plays were largely prentice work, but the fourth showed flashes of his later genius in characterization, and the entire series was popular enough to establish him firmly with Lord Strange's Men. His second tetralogy was even more popular and reflected his growing mastery. It begins with the deposition and subsequent murder of Richard II. The two middle plays cover the reign of the usurper, Henry IV, and his efforts to solidify his rule. But their real focus—to the extent they are not altogether hijacked by the comic character of Falstaff—is Prince Hal, the heir apparent and future Henry V, whose stirring, if ephemeral, conquest of France forms the subject of the final play.

The two tetralogies fit together snugly enough, covering nearly a century of English history and two civil wars. Peter Saccio, in his indispensable book *Shakespeare's English Kings*,[11] explores the actual history behind the stage history of Shakespeare's plays. But, frankly, it is the dramatic history that remains in our minds and has conquered our hearts: the feckless but hauntingly eloquent Richard II; the brittle grip on power of Henry IV; the wayward youth and galvanizing kingship of Henry V; the saintly but ineffective Henry VI; and the twisted yet charismatic villainy of Richard III, whose defeat by Henry VII at Bosworth Field in 1485 began the Tudor dynasty that continued in Shakespeare's day with Elizabeth I.

It may well be that the first-composed-but-later-in-time tetralogy was intended to promote the Tudor myth and to curry favor with the Queen. Indeed, any counter-narrative would have been extremely dangerous. But those who see an overall arc and theory of historical development running through all eight plays are imposing a confining structure that the stand-alone plays simply will not bear. We don't know Shakespeare's political and historical views, any more than we know his religious views. It is evident from the plays that he thought very deeply about history, religion, philosophy, and morality, among other topics. But, as the poet John Keats noted, Shakespeare in his work displayed "negative capability"—that is, an openness to experience without the distortion of a preconceived ideological framework. That is precisely what Montaigne advocated in his most famous late essays. Shakespeare's characters express and embody an astonishing variety of perspectives and philosophies. But Shakespeare himself, in Keats's words, seems to have been "capable of being in uncertainties, Mysteries, doubts, without any irritable reaching after fact & reason."[12] Shakespeare gives authentic voices to all his characters, but none can claim to be the authentic voice of Shakespeare.

This is perhaps nowhere clearer than in the acknowledged masterpiece of his English history plays, *Henry IV, Part 1*. Prince Hal stands between three other characters: his father, the insecure and easily angered king; his rival, the honor-drunk Hotspur; and Falstaff, the mentor and companion of his youthful follies. He survives and transcends each of them to become a successful king; he has "mastered there a double spirit / Of teaching and of learning instantly."[13] Yet no one would suggest that Hal is Shakespeare's ideal of a human being, even if Henry V is, as one scholar suggests, a "machiavel of goodness" and therefore an ideal king for the times.[14]

Erasmus wrote his *Education of a Christian Prince*, at least in part, as a rebuttal to Machiavelli's *The Prince*. According to Erasmus, a solid classical education infused with Renaissance, humanist values and imparted by a Christian scholar such as himself is the best guarantor that a future king will put the interests of his people before those of himself. Prince Hal has a very different upbringing and imbibes (quite literally) a very different set of lessons. But he cannot escape the power politics articulated by Machiavelli and exercised by Hal's father.

With the deposition and murder of Richard II, the myth of the divine rights of kings is necessarily shattered. Richard cannot quite believe, despite his flaws as a leader, that he will be deposed—as if an army of angels might descend to prevent such sacrilege. Yet providence proves indifferent to majesty. "Time is broke," says an imprisoned Richard.[15]

Without the linear succession of kings and hence the linear progression of history, nothing is left of majesty but an endless jockeying for power and advantage. Richard, unkinged, has lost his identity. I "am nothing," he complains.[16] But Henry IV is not thereby made something. In Richard's view, a counterfeit king has assumed the throne, and those who helped him to it will demand more than he is prepared to give them.[17] The usurper has delegitimized kingship itself and must suffer the consequences. "Uneasy lies the head that wears a crown," Henry admits.[18]

But what about the future heir to that ill-gotten crown? Does he carry the burden of his father's guilt? Does he feel the precariousness of his own position? Or will the passage of the crown from Henry to his firstborn son—this "lineal honour" due from "thy place and blood"[19]—enable the prince to establish his identity as a rightful king? Henry has his doubts. He envies the rebel Northumberland, whose son, Hotspur, "is the theme of honour's tongue."[20] He even fantasizes that Hotspur and his son were exchanged at birth. For "riot and dishonour stain the brow / Of my young Harry."[21] Prince Harry, or Hal, compensates for the burden of expectations by carousing with a dissolute knight, Sir John Falstaff, and his companions.

The tavern scenes in *Henry IV, Part I*, are a festival of language, wit, and irreverence. The eating, the drinking, and the whoring are decidedly secondary, at least from the playgoer's perspective. William Hazlitt felt obliged to caution, not altogether convincingly, that "the heroic and serious part of these two plays . . . is not inferior to the comic and farcical."[22] The Boar's Head Tavern in the Eastcheap section of London is set apart from the time that Richard II considered "broke." It is set apart, like the Forest of Arden in *As You Like It*, from affairs of state and all such sober concerns. Hal and his companions, as Hotspur dismissingly notes, have "daffed the world aside / And bid it pass."[23] When Falstaff asks the time of day, Hal responds with mock fury:

What a devil hast thou to do with the time of the day? Unless hours were cups of sack, and minutes capons, and clocks the tongues of bawds, and dials the signs of leaping-houses, and the blessed sun himself a fair hot wench in flame-coloured taffeta, I see no reason why thou shouldst be so superfluous to demand the time of the day.[24]

Falstaff is on permanent holiday. He is, or claims to be, "the true and perfect image of life" in all its untrammeled vitality.[25] He is the embodiment of fellowship, freedom, and outrageous excess. "I live out of all order, out of all compass," he boasts.[26] He also lives happily outside any moral compunctions. Falstaff doesn't just admit his vices, he revels in them. Indeed, he exaggerates them for the sake of humor. Samuel Johnson is appropriately censorious: "He is a thief, and a glutton, a coward, and a boaster, always ready to cheat the weak, and prey upon the poor; to terrify the timorous and insult the defenseless."[27] Falstaff is all those things, and he freely confesses it. And yet, even Dr. Johnson has to admit that "his licentiousness is not so offensive but that it may be borne for his mirth."[28] Falstaff is rendered not merely tolerable but delightful "by the most pleasing of all qualities, perpetual gaiety, by an unfailing power of exciting laughter, which is the more freely indulged, as his wit is not of the splendid or ambitious kind, but consists in easy escapes and sallies of levity, which make sport but raise no envy."[29] We embrace Falstaff because he views himself and everyone else in a humorous light. But we also embrace him, contrary to what Johnson claims, because his wit is both splendid and ambitious. His goal is nothing less than subversion of the established order. He is the Lord of Misrule.

Harold Bloom calls Falstaff "the Socrates of Eastcheap."[30] It is a brilliant and telling sally. Socrates was himself a highly subversive figure. He exposed those with power and authority as frauds. They claimed to be virtuous but, under his questioning, could not even give a coherent account of piety, or courage, or justice, or temperance. They threw such words about in a pompous display of their righteousness without ever sounding their true meaning. Socrates revealed the emptiness of their rhetoric to the delight of his young followers. But these Socratic dialogues were aporetic—that is, they ended in doubt and uncertainty. No positive knowledge replaced the deflated claims of his interlocutors. Socrates corrupted the young by teaching them to question received social norms. He could also drink them under the table.

Falstaff, too, punctures the pretension of high rhetoric. His weapon is not logic but wit. He exposes the absurdity and hypocrisy of so much of our speech. He mocks piety, courage, honor, the law, and all the trappings of state. He even mocks war and death. The Socrates of the early dialogues was a nihilist, but with a purpose: to clear the ground of false claims about virtue in order to make way for true knowledge. Falstaff, too, is a nihilist with a purpose: to clear the ground of platitudes and make way for life. It is a nihilism without pessimism, a nihilism in the service of life.

No wonder Hal delights in his company. The Boar's Head is a necessary tutorial. If the old values no longer hold and there is no discernable providence to guide us, then where is meaning to be found? In public life and the obligations of time and power? Or outside time in the free exercise of the imagination and the appetites? For Falstaff, meaning lies in life itself. He is the embodiment of play—irresponsible, spontaneous, and full of a humor that acknowledges no bounds and no restraints. He says what we often think but cannot publicly admit. Hazlitt rightly called Falstaff "the true spirit of humanity, the thorough knowledge of the stuff we are made of."[31] As Erasmus, Montaigne, and Cervantes each taught in turn, wisdom requires a significant admixture of folly, though perhaps none had in mind so gross an admixture as embodied in Falstaff.

But Hal is the heir apparent. He is destined for the world of time, and there is only so much folly he can tolerate without sacrificing his position and becoming another Richard II. He therefore plays a double game. Despite the appearance of dissolution, he has himself under control and is fully calculating:

I know you all, and will awhile uphold
The unyoked humor of your idleness.

Yet herein will I imitate the sun,
Who doth permit the base contagious clouds
To smother up his beauty from the world,
That, when he please again to be himself,
Being wanted, he may be more wondered at
By breaking through the foul and ugly mists
Of vapours that did seem to strangle him.[32]

Hal steps out of time to revel with Falstaff and to learn the ways of common men. "I wasted time, and now doth Time waste me," Richard II bemoaned.[33] But Hal will redeem his seemingly wasted time and even turn it to his advantage. Indeed, as king he "weighs time / Even to the utmost grain."[34] Part of life may be play, but it cannot be the whole, and already the rebels are gathering. Richard accurately predicted that those who helped Bolingbroke to power would turn on him when he was king, unsatisfied by their share of the spoils.

Owen Glendower, Harry Hotspur, and Lord Mortimer, Richard's appointed heir, now plot their own rebellion. But they fall to quarreling over the future division of the kingdom, as if Henry IV were already defeated. The scene has a delicious parallel at the Boar's Head, where Falstaff and his companions decide to rob some travelers carrying gold coins, and Hal and Poins elect to hang back and, in disguise, rob the robbers simply to hear "the incomprehensible lies that this same fat rogue will tell us when we meet at supper: how thirty at least he fought with, what wards, what blows, what extremities he endured; and in the reproof of this lives the jest."[35] And so it plays out: the robbers are robbed, and Falstaff returns with a tale that grows ever more fantastic in the telling of being set upon by fifty men in buckram, with whom he fought at least two hours before giving way and leaving the coins behind. He even shows the sword thrusts in his clothes and the hack marks on his sword—all of which he counterfeited before returning to the tavern. Yet, when Hal confronts him with the lie, Falstaff deftly turns the joke around:

By the Lord, I knew ye as well as he that made ye. Why, hear you, my masters: was it for me to kill the heir apparent? Should I turn upon the true prince? Why, thou knowest I am as valiant as Hercules, but beware instinct. The lion will not touch the true prince; instinct is a great matter. I was now a coward on instinct.[36]

The Boar's Head crew never divides their projected spoils; Hal has the crowns returned to the travelers, or so he says. Neither will the rebels divide England; Henry IV retains his unitary crown.

The culmination of the play lies in the encounter between Hal and Hotspur at the battle of Shrewsbury to determine the rightful heir of the usurper king. Hotspur is a remarkably compelling character. He is the embodiment of feudal honor, quick to quarrel and eager to shine. Even Prince Hal acknowledges his virtues:

> I do not think a braver gentleman,
> More active-valiant or more valiant-young,
> More daring or more bold, is now alive
> To grace this latter age with noble deeds.[37]

Hotspur is no courtier and no diplomat. He displays a gruff, if genuine, affection for his wife, Kate. But he cannot forbear insulting even his ally, the Welshman Owen Glendower, who boasts of his magical powers and claims that the earth shook and the heavens were on fire at his birth:

> GLENDOWER: I can call spirits from the vasty deep.
> HOTSPUR: Why, so can I, or so can any man,
>   But will they come when you do call for them?[38]

The rebels are heavily outnumbered. Glendower sulks in Wales, claiming he cannot gather his troops in time to join the coalition. And Hotspur's father, Northumberland, "lies crafty-sick" at home with his forces.[39] But Hotspur is undaunted. His cause is just, or so he believes, and the poor odds will simply add a greater luster to the enterprise:

> An if we live, we live to tread on kings;
> If die, brave death when princes die with us.[40]

Falstaff again provides a deliberate contrast. He leads a ragtag group of pressed men into battle. Originally, he recruited sturdy yeomen but let them buy themselves out of service. What remains are pitiful rascals, nothing but "food for powder," he admits. Still, they will "fill a pit as well as better."[41] In his famous speech on honor—the most memorable prose soliloquy in all of Shakespeare—Falstaff questions, in a mock Socratic dialogue with himself, the values that have led both sides to Shrewsbury:

> FALSTAFF: I would 'twere bedtime, Hal, and all well.
> PRINCE: Why, thou owest God a death. [*Exit.*]
> FALSTAFF: 'Tis not due yet. I would be loath to pay him before his
> day. What need I be so forward with him that calls not on me?
> Well, 'tis no matter; honour pricks me on. Yea, but how if honour
> prick me off when I come on? How then? Can honour set to a
> leg? No. Or an arm? No. Or take away the grief of a wound? No.
> Honour hath no skill in surgery, then? No. What is honour? A
> word. What is in that word "honour"? What is that "honour"? Air.
> A trim reckoning. Who hath it? He that died o'Wednesday. Doth
> he feel it? No. Doth he hear it? No. 'Tis insensible then? Yea, to the
> dead. But will it not live with the living? No. Why? Detraction will
> not suffer it. Therefore I'll none of it. Honour is a mere scutcheon.
> And so ends my catechism.[42]

We can admire Hotspur's ebullient courage and yet sympathize with Falstaff's counterargument. Why, after all, should Falstaff give his life in a sordid struggle over the spoils of kingship? Arguably, Falstaff even does England a service by preserving its sturdy yeoman. And he certainly does himself (and all playgoers) a service by counterfeiting death to preserve his life. "Die all, die merrily," says Hotspur, and so he does. "Give me life," cries Falstaff, and grants his own wish.

Prince Hal can permit himself no Socratic doubts about the demands of duty, honor, and patriotism. When he saves his father's life and later kills Hotspur in single combat, he will prove himself his father's true heir. The crown will pass to him by rightful succession. "You won it, wore it, kept it, gave it me," Hal will say with chilling clarity. "Then plain and right must my possession be, / Which I with more than with a common pain / 'Gainst all the world will rightfully maintain."[43]

Indeed, Hal will rightfully maintain the crown even against Falstaff. In the world of time that Hal has rejoined, there is no place for the fat, jolly, irreverent knight. A ruler must impose order and project majesty and legitimacy with ceremonies "creating awe and fear in other men."[44] Hal is no more concerned for morality than Falstaff or Hotspur or Henry IV. But he will hold to power.

Before Shrewsbury, at the Boar's Head, Hal is summoned to a reckoning with his father. He prepares with a mock interview: "Do thou stand for my father," he tells Falstaff, "and examine me upon the particulars of my life."[45] But Falstaff does not speak like a king, and Hal quickly switches places, excoriating Harry for keeping company with "a devil [that] haunts thee in the likeness of an old fat man."[46] Falstaff, as Hal, seeks to defend himself in a tone of pleading desperation:

FALSTAFF: No, my good lord, banish Peto, banish Bardoll, banish
   Poins, but for sweet Jack Falstaff, kind Jack Falstaff, true Jack Falstaff,
   valiant Jack Falstaff, and therefore more valiant being as he is old Jack
   Falstaff, banish not him thy Harry's company, banish not him thy
   Harry's company. Banish plump Jack and banish all the world.
PRINCE: I do; I will.[47]

The foreshadowed repudiation of Falstaff awaits a second play. Clearly, Shakespeare (and his audience) could not bear to part with him sooner. But part with him we must, for Falstaff's role as surrogate father to the scapegrace prince could no longer be tolerated for the new, now fatherless king.

Indeed, once crowned, Henry V turns the repudiation of Falstaff into a public ceremony of sorts, announcing to the world and not just to Falstaff:

> Presume not that I am the thing I was,
> For God doth know, so shall the world perceive,
> That I have turned away my former self;
> So will I those that kept me company.[48]

To make himself an effective king, Hal must sacrifice much of his own humanity. As Henry V, Hal has become his father, invading France to "busy giddy minds / With foreign quarrels," and thus to unite his subjects and "waste the memory of the former days,"[49] meaning both his own youthful excesses and, even more important, his father's unjust seizure of the crown. Whether Henry V is a "machiavel of goodness" is debatable, but he is certainly a successful king, and the country will thrive under his leadership without civil war.

One hopes he feels more than a twinge of regret for his old companion and teacher. Harold Bloom dismisses any such suggestion, but Bloom detests the hypocritical and calculating Prince Hal and has effectively commingled Falstaff's image with Bloom's own. The fact is that Hal must reject both Hotspur and Falstaff in order to become his father's son and rightful heir. In their charismatic attraction, both men are shoals that the young king avoids.

Death in battle is the apotheosis for Hotspur, the only form of transcendence he knows. Falstaff finds transcendence in life itself but cannot survive his rejection by Prince Hal, whom he truly does love as a son. Socrates, convicted of corrupting the young, chose death over banishment. So does Falstaff. As his companion Pistol notes, "his heart is fracted" by Hal's rejection.[50] Socrates drank hemlock, and the poison worked its way up his body, turning each part cold and numb in turn. So, too, Falstaff. The bile of his rejection steadily robs him of the life he so cherished. Mistress Quickly reports in her inimitable fashion:

> A bade me lay more clothes on his feet. I put my hand into the bed, and felt them, and they were as cold as any stone. Then I felt to his knees, and so up-peered and upward, and all was as cold as any stone.[51]

Falstaff reveals us all as counterfeits in our many comings and goings through time. We all, more or less, sacrifice humanity to calculation. In the process, we counterfeit life itself. Falstaff may not be "the true and perfect image of life," but he embodies its disordered freedom and vitality. As Bardolph laments for us all: "Would I were with him, wheresome're he is, either in heaven or in hell."[52]

HEAVENLY ROSALIND

As You Like It is the purest and most sunlit of Shakespeare's comedies. But it is not less profound on that account. Indeed, in that regard, it will not yield even to *Hamlet*, which it immediately preceded. As Nietzsche said of the Greeks, they were superficial—out of profundity:

> They knew how to live. What is required for that is to stop courageously at the surface, the fold, the skin, to adore appearance, to believe in forms, tones, words, in the whole Olympus of appearance.[53]

As You Like It is a play of forms, tones, and words; and Rosalind, who keeps bravely to the surface, may lay better claim than Falstaff to be "the true and perfect image of life." Certainly, she has a better claim than the melancholy Prince Hamlet, who disdains life because it does not accord with his ideals.

The time is out of joint in Denmark, and Hamlet is charged to set it right. The time is also out of joint in *As You Like It*. But Rosalind, daughter of the banished duke, resolves to "show more mirth than I am mistress of."[54] And when she and Celia flee the court for the Forest of Arden, they step aside from time every bit as much as Falstaff and Hal did at the Boar's Head—but to very different purpose. Rosalind will test whether it is possible to be wise and happy; whether it is possible to be wise and neither melancholy nor cynical; most of all, whether it is possible to be wise and in love, that greatest of all follies and yet the most essential. For without love, life is a bleak and barren thing. Rosalind chooses to be foolishly in love, and therein she is wise. Hamlet, like Jaques, chooses otherwise, and life delights him not.

Charles, the usurping duke's wrestler, refers to the Forest of Arden as a place where young gentlemen flock to Ferdinand, the true duke, and "fleet the time carelessly as they did in the golden world."[55] We are meant to think of Arden, sight yet unseen, as a new Eden, far from the intrigues of court. "Here feel we not the penalty of Adam," claims Ferdinand.[56] Arden also calls to mind the pastoral Arcadia of Greek and Latin poetry, where shepherds wooed shepherdesses with sophisticated verses celebrating the simple life, and the Tuscan villas where Boccaccio's *brigata* retreated from plague-ridden Florence to entertain and distract one another with stories. Harvard philosopher Stanley Cavell even finds echoes of Arden in the Connecticut countryside of films such as *Bringing Up Baby*. And, indeed, those echoes are faithful to Shakespeare's play, in which the pastoral tradition is both gently mocked and richly embraced.

Arden is far from idyllic. The duke and his men know "the icy fang / And churlish chiding of the winter's wind."[57] They frighten the animals and kill them "in their assigned and native dwelling-place."[58] And they bring their courtly artfulness to bear on artless nature, purporting to find "tongues in trees, books in the running brooks, / Sermons in stones, and good in everything."[59] "Sweet are the uses of adversity," claims the duke, for they "persuade me what I am."[60] That is to say, they reduce him to his essentials. The forest is not cosseting, but it is nonetheless a place for restoration and reconnection with the natural order of things and with our place within it. In the end, all the characters are drawn to it, even Orlando's brother, Oliver, who seeks to kill him for no other reason than that Orlando is "of all sorts enchantingly beloved."[61]

Rosalind and Orlando make their separate ways to the Forest of Arden, already infatuated on the slightest of acquaintance and yet unaware of each other's movements. Rosalind is disguised as a young man and takes the name Ganymede, after the cupbearer beloved of Jupiter. The cross-dressing and gender fluidity of the lead character, who was of course played by a boy actor, nearly derail Orlando, whose attraction to Ganymede would seem unfaithful to Rosalind were Ganymede not in fact Rosalind. The shepherdess Phoebe also falls for the "peevish boy" who chides her.[62] And Celia, well before Rosalind dons manly dress, acknowledges a bond dearer than sisters:

> We still have slept together,
> Rose at an instant, learned, played, ate together,
> And whereso'er we went, like Juno's swans,
> Still we went coupled and inseparable.[63]

Rosalind, as boy and as girl, is enchanting to all. She "conjure[s]" men and women alike,[64] and the ensuing complications—which rival those of the forest scenes in *A Midsummer Night's Dream*, but without any need for fairy magic beyond that provided by Rosalind/Ganymede themselves—seem very modern indeed.

Another highly modern touch is the exploration of multiple perspectives, as in Kurosawa's now-classic film *Rashomon*. Each character, even the native inhabitants, reacts to the golden world of Arden in his or her own way. Only Rosalind maintains a clear-eyed consciousness of the whole, though always colored by her love for Orlando. She has the wit, intelligence, and spirit to encompass and transcend the others.

Silvius, a shepherd, loves the shepherdess Phoebe. His love is both shaped by and expressed in conventional verses from the pastoral tradition, which he adopts without a hint of irony:

> If thou rememb'rest not the slightest folly
> That ever love did make thee run into,
> Thou hast not loved.
> Or if thou hast not sat as I do now,
> Wearing thy hearer in thy mistress' praise,
> Thou hast not loved.
> Or if thou hast not broke from company
> Abruptly as my passion now makes me,
> Thou hast not loved.
> O Phoebe, Phoebe, Phoebe![65]

Silvius is enslaved by his passion for Phoebe. The extravagant language is comical, but the pain of love unrequited is no less genuine for being artificially induced. Silvius has learned that love is abject devotion. He is in love, ergo . . . This is the love sentimental.

Touchstone, the court fool who has accompanied Celia and Rosalind to the Forest of Arden, is the epitome of urban sophistication and courtly corruption. "I have trod a measure," he boasts; "I have flattered a lady; I have been politic with my friend, smooth with mine enemy; I have undone three tailors; I have had four quarrels and like to have fought one."[66] He is out of place in Arden and compares himself to Ovid, the sophisticated court poet, banished to live among ignorant Goths. "When I was at home I was in a better place," he announces.[67] Touchstone carries a small sundial, thereby introducing the element of time's decay into the timeless world of the pastoral:

> from hour to hour we ripe and ripe,
> And then from hour to hour we rot and rot,
> And thereby hangs a tale.[68]

But even Touchstone is not immune to sexual attraction. The shepherdess Audrey is the object, not of his admiration exactly, but, certainly of his lust. In a send-up of pastoral poetry, he wishes that she were "poetical" because poetry is dishonest, and her claims to chastity might then be feigned. But Audrey does not even understand the term, so Touchstone will marry her—at least in a dubious ceremony. "Come, sweet Audrey," he says. "We must be married, or we must live in bawdry."[69] He calls all the various pairs of lovers—including himself and Audrey—"country copulatives."[70] This is the love cynical.

Jaques, companion to none but often found in the company of Ferdinand and his men, is disappointed in, and has become only a spectator of, life and love. He has traveled widely, experienced much, and, like Faust—though Goethe's more than Marlowe's—has found nothing worthy of bidding stay. "I can suck melancholy out of a song as a weasel sucks eggs," he explains,[71] underscoring a bitterness that is life destroying. In his famous "all the world's a stage" speech, in which he ruminates on the seven ages of man, there is only misery, pointless longing, posturing, pomposity, and inevitable oblivion. This is the love negated.

Rosalind makes short work alike of Touchstone's cynicism and Jaques's melancholy. Turning his own words around on him, she tells Touchstone, "You'll be rotten ere you be half ripe."[72] But she does not reject the strongly sexual element of love, as her many double entendres make clear. As for Jaques, when he claims, " 'Tis good to be sad and say nothing," she retorts, "Why then, 'tis good to be a post."[73] And when Jaques insists that his experience was enriching, she responds, "And your experience makes you sad. I had rather have a fool to make me merry than experience to make me sad—and to travel for it too."[74] Rosalind is not immune to melancholy; yet her male dress and the freedom of the forest allow her to exercise an abundance of high spirits. Both Touchstone and Jaques seem dull and limited beside Rosalind. Not only does she have a wit to silence theirs, but her wit is deployed in the service of life and love, not cynicism and sadness. "Give me life," she could easily say with Falstaff.

Rosalind bears a more complicated relationship with Silvius. She calls him a "foolish shepherd,"[75] yet acknowledges that his passion "is much upon my fashion!"[76] After all, Orlando's own love for Rosalind veers strongly toward the sentimental and conventionally pastoral, and finds its expression in some very bad verses deftly parodied by Touchstone. Yet she would have love be clear-eyed and without too much illusion. In the guise of Ganymede, s/he tells Phoebe she has no more beauty "than without candle may go dark to bed."[77] Phoebe is beautiful only in the eyes and imagination of Silvius, Ganymede explains, and then advises her not to squander such an opportunity through self-delusion:

'Tis not her glass but you that flatters her,
And out of you she sees herself more proper
Than any of her lineaments can show her.
But, mistress, know yourself; down on your knees,
And thank heaven fasting for a good man's love.
For I must tell you friendly in your ear:
Sell when you can, you are not for all markets.[78]

Desentimentalizing love, without sacrificing its intensity and enchantment, or giving way to cynicism, is the lesson that Ganymede undertakes to teach Orlando. S/he begins by mocking Orlando for his rude and ruddy health, and for not showing the marks of a man in love:

A lean cheek, which you have not; a blue eye and sunken, which you have not; an unquestionable spirit, which you have not; a beard neglected, which you have not. . . . Then your hose should be ungartered, your bonnet unbanded, your sleeve unbuttoned, your shoe untied, and everything about you demonstrating a careless desolation. But you are no such man. You are rather point-device in your accoutrements, as loving yourself than seeming the lover of any other.[79]

Ganymede's portrait is of the stock lover, and s/he resolves to playact the misogynist's vision of the elusive beloved: proud, fantastical, everchanging, alternately encouraging and rejecting, smiling and scolding. This is Silvius and Phoebe squared. Such love is madness, Ganymede tells Orlando, and the only way to be cured of it is to mimic its most extreme manifestations. But, as the lessons progress, Ganymede exposes Orlando to a more and more sober view of love to test the strength of his vows. Womankind is inclined to be wayward, s/he insists, and yet will "make her fault her husband's occasion."[80] Conversely, of the tales of men dying for love, s/he tells him: "These are all lies. Men have died from time to time and worms have eaten them, but not for love."[81]

By this point in the play, Orlando—who is far from thick-headed— has apparently seen through the Ganymede disguise.[82] In a mock marriage ceremony performed by Celia with some reluctance—since it would in fact be civilly binding if both partners consent with knowledge of the other—Orlando earnestly responds, "I take thee, Rosalind, for wife."[83] But, when Orlando promises to love his Rosalind "for ever and a day," she responds:

Say "a day" without the "ever." No, no, Orlando, men are April when they woo, December when they wed. Maids are May when they are maids, but the sky changes when they are wives.[84]

Between the cynical and the sentimental, something deeper emerges. Love may all too often find its expression in bad verses and false promises. But, even stripped to its essentials by winter and rough weather, love can transform life. Love can make life seem transcendent, which is, of course, a form of madness. But "I would not be cured, youth," says Orlando.[85] Neither would Rosalind. She can be ironic about love while still embracing it. She can recognize its folly without forgoing its joy. Indeed, the folly itself is a large part of the joy. If we are not foolish in love, we are not in love, as even Touchstone recognizes:

TOUCHSTONE: We that are true lovers run into strange capers. But
    as all is mortal in nature, so is all nature in love mortal folly.
ROSALIND: Thou speak'st wiser than thou art ware of.[86]

The Forest of Arden persuades us what we are. It reduces life to its most basic form. When Touchstone chides the shepherd Corin for his lack of sophistication, Corin accepts the charge:

Sir, I am a true labourer. I earn that I eat, get that I wear; owe no man hate, envy no man's happiness; glad of other men's good, content with my harm; and the greatest of my pride is to see my ewes graze and my lambs suck.[87]

Touchstone jokes that Corin is a bawd living on the copulation of cattle, but the joke falls flat, even though it sets up his later, truly funny remark about country copulatives. Corin has the simple wisdom of a natural philosopher. He knows "that the property of rain is to wet and fire to burn; that good pasture makes fat sheep; and that a great cause of the night is lack of the sun."[88] Corin is what he is, and thereby stands immune to the distorting refinements of court life.

Yet in Rosalind alone, refinement is no distortion. She is "poetical" without being false, and poetry, despite its artifice, is the truest expression of life and love. Rosalind is more joyfully alive, physically, spiritually, and intellectually, than any other character in Shakespeare. She is endowed with such heavenly grace that she can o'er leap irony and happily accept the absurdity of love. As Harold Bloom notes, "if Rosalind cannot please us, then no one in Shakespeare or elsewhere in literature ever will."[89] Her appeal is universal.

Stephen Greenblatt has rightly identified self-fashioning (i.e., refinement) as a critical theme of the Renaissance. But self-fashioning can become rather a grim and calculating business in Petrarch, Machiavelli, and even Castiglione. The embrace of folly is a necessary counterpart in Erasmus, Rabelais, Montaigne, Cervantes, and Shakespeare. Without it, there is neither joy nor true wisdom.

Life stands before us in its infinite variety and absolute simplicity. We can take it cynically (Touchstone), gloomily (Jaques), sentimentally (Silvius), or triumphantly (Rosalind). Life, like love, is *As You Like It*.

THE WORLD AS WILL AND REPRESENTATION

Suppose Hamlet's love interest were Rosalind rather than the passive, easily led Ophelia. An idle thought, to be sure, but an interesting one nonetheless and in keeping with the various thought experiments essayed by Hamlet himself. Rosalind, of course, would not be deterred by a brother's warning to safeguard her "chaste treasure" or a father's injunction not "to give words or talk with the Lord Hamlet."[90] We could never imagine Rosalind agreeing to "keep … in the rear of [her] affection / Out of the shot and danger of desire."[91] Yet Ophelia does. She promises to hold her brother's lesson "as watchman to my heart" and meekly acquiesces to her father: "I shall obey, my lord."[92] Rosalind, we can be sure, would respond to brother and father alike with greater spirit, and she would assay the professed love of the prince with her own devices, rather than returning his letters and denying him access to her person.

But would it make a difference? Would the active love of a Rosalind rescue Hamlet from his despair? Of the three blows that descend upon the apparently once happy student—the sudden death of his father, the immediate remarriage of his mother, and Ophelia's withheld affection—would transforming the third be enough to change Hamlet's course? Could Rosalind tease him out of his funk and teach him to show more mirth than he is master of? With Rosalind by his side, would Hamlet take arms against a sea of troubles and play his assigned part as his father's avenger? Or would the two of them trip off to Wittenberg together, leaving the out-of-joint time to right itself, and thereby transform *Hamlet* into a comedy? More likely than either, Hamlet would shrink from a woman who is his rival in wit and spirit, a woman he is unable to reduce to the proportions of his bitter irony.

Rosalind in *Hamlet* would of course be in the wrong play. She is crafted for sunlit happiness. As Harold Goddard aptly put it, Rosalind is a "feminine Hamlet over whom the cloud never fell."[93] She does not feel Hamlet's compulsion to root about in the darkest shadows of the soul. Her emotions lie close to the surface. Hamlet, like the melancholy Jaques, would be equally out of place in the Forest of Arden. Yet there is something tender and lost in Hamlet to which Rosalind could respond. His early love poems to Ophelia are every bit as sincerely bad as those of Orlando to Rosalind. One feels he could, perhaps, in other circumstances, have been educated in love and thereby steeled against the slings and arrows of outrageous fortune. But it is, as I said, an idle thought. Hamlet's melancholic despair is less circumstantial than existential.

Even before he meets his father's ghost, and well before Ophelia's counseled rebuff, Hamlet is already disgusted with life:

How weary, stale, flat, and unprofitable
Seem to me all the uses of this world!
Fie on't, ah fie, 'tis an unweeded garden
That grows to seed; things rank and gross in nature
Possess it merely. . . .[94]

With the death of his father, and the prompt remarriage of his mother, Hamlet the student is forced to confront his own adult identity. "Who's there?" Barnardo cries from the battlements to open the play.[95] Hamlet looks within and doesn't like the answer. He looks without and likes what he sees even less. He has idealized his father as a warrior, a king, and a husband: "Take him for all in all, / I shall not look upon his like again."[96] He is correspondingly disgusted that his mother has so quickly and easily transferred her affections from "so excellent a king, that was to this / Hyperion to a satyr."[97] Literally, he sees his father as a divinity and Claudius as less than human. Yet his mother readily exchanged one brother for the other. "O God," Hamlet moans, "a beast that wants discourse of reason / Would have mourn'd longer."[98]

Such a double blow would send moral shock waves through any sensitive young man and lead him to question where once he loved and revered. Yet Hamlet is experiencing more than nausea at his mother "post[ing] / With such dexterity to incestuous sheets!"[99] The poet and critic T. S. Eliot dubbed *Hamlet* an "artistic failure."[100] He thought the play was too long, with "superfluous and inconsistent scenes" and "variable" versification.[101] It is a deliberately—and ludicrously—provocative judgment, akin to Henry James's dismissal of *War and Peace* and *Anna Karenina* as "loose, baggy monsters,"[102] and made for much the same aesthetic reasons. But Eliot is right on one point. Gertrude is not an adequate basis for the cosmic disgust felt by Hamlet: "His disgust envelops and exceeds her."[103] There is more going on here than a son's dismay at his father's death and his mother's hasty remarriage.

That something more is found necessarily in the character of Hamlet and the times in which he lived and whose ideals he had internalized before sounding their hollowness. Hamlet had long shown the promise of Castiglione's perfect courtier. As Ophelia describes him with retrospective despair: "O, what a noble mind . . . / The courtier's, soldier's, scholar's, eye, tongue, sword, / Th'expectancy and rose of the fair state, / The glass of fashion and the mould of form, / Th'observ'd of all observers. . . ."[104] By all indications, Hamlet as a student was open and candid; he endeared himself to friends and was beloved of the people. Even Claudius calls him "most generous, and free from all contriving."[105]

Hamlet articulates the Renaissance ideal in stirring terms: "What a piece of work is a man, how noble in reason, how infinite in faculties, in form and moving how express and admirable, in action how like an angel, in apprehension how like a god."[106] And yet, he adds, this "quintessence of dust" delights him not.[107]

By the time he wrote *Hamlet*, Shakespeare had certainly read Montaigne, perhaps in a prepublication draft of his friend John Florio's English translation. Montaigne's skepticism corrodes the lofty sunlit edifice of the Renaissance. Man is an imperfect creature, Montaigne taught. He is full of contradictions and vices that parade as virtues. Those who attempt to rise above human nature invariably fall below. "They want to get out of themselves and escape from the man. That is madness: instead of changing into angels, they change into beasts; instead of raising themselves, they lower themselves."[108]

Hamlet repeatedly echoes these sentiments. "I am myself indifferent honest," he explains to Ophelia, "but yet I could accuse me of such things that it were better my mother had not borne me. I am very proud, revengeful, ambitious, with more offenses at my beck than I have thoughts to put them in, imagination to give them shape, or time to act them in. What should such fellows as I do crawling between earth and heaven? We are arrant knaves all. . . ."[109] For Montaigne, it was a basic premise of his enterprise that each man bears within himself the seeds of man's estate. Hamlet recognizes that he bears within himself the seeds of the violence, treachery, and lust he sees around him. Hamlet the student, having forged a godlike vision of man, falls all the harder when forced to confront the bankruptcy of that vision. It is precisely because he was so high that he falls so low. He hardens his heart against those who disappoint him, such as his mother, Ophelia, and his erstwhile friends Rosencrantz and Guildenstern, but particularly against himself. He has become the polar opposite of Rosalind. He is dark where she is light; he is dissembling where she is candid (for Rosalind is candid even in her disguise as Ganymede); he is bitter where she is loving. And yet we are still drawn to the gloomy but charismatic prince.

It is a commonplace that Hamlet is in the wrong play. An earlier, lost play on the same subject, the so-called *Ur-Hamlet*, was probably written by Thomas Kyd, an important figure in the development of Elizabethan drama. Kyd's version was a straightforward revenge play, so full of melodrama as to have become an object of mirth. "Hamlet, revenge," the ghost would creak periodically. Shakespeare's Hamlet is not crafted for such a stock role, teetering between comedy and tragedy. It is not that he is incapable of acting the avenger. As he cautions Laertes: "Though I am not splenative and rash, / Yet have I in me something dangerous, / Which let thy wiseness fear."[110] When the occasion calls for it, Hamlet will act decisively and even impulsively: following the ghost on the darkened ramparts; boarding the pirate ship; and leaping into Ophelia's grave to grapple with Laertes. Nor, in the end, does he shrink from violence: stabbing Polonius through the arras; casually sending Rosencrantz and Guildenstern to their deaths; and running Claudius through with his sword and then prying his lips apart to force poison down his throat.

So why does Hamlet hesitate? Why does he recoil from his role as avenger even after the play within the play reveals the conscience of the king and Hamlet knows to a moral certainty that Claudius did indeed murder his father? He asks himself this question repeatedly and, despite his many soliloquies, never hits upon a satisfactory answer. "I do not know / Why yet I live to say this thing's to do, / Sith I have cause, and will, and strength, and means / To do't."[111]

There are as many answers to that question as there are readers and spectators of the play. Two of Shakespeare's greatest interpreters give diametrically opposing answers. According to A. C. Bradley, Hamlet has a moral obligation to avenge his father and shrinks from it only because mental illness, in the form of melancholia, has rendered him too depressed to act.[112] When he finally snaps out of his lethargy in act 5, it is too late. The tragedy of Hamlet is that, due to his indefensible delay, eight people die—Polonius, Ophelia, Rosencrantz and Guildenstern, Laertes, Gertrude, Claudius, and Hamlet himself—rather than just the one who deserved it.[113]

According to Goddard, Hamlet has a moral obligation *not* to avenge his father. The cycle of such violence traces back at least to Pyrrhus avenging the death of his father, Achilles, by brutally dismembering the elderly Priam at his household altar. It was set in motion again when Hamlet senior killed the father of Fortinbras and usurped his lands. It seizes young Fortinbras, who, in the name of honor, will sacrifice twenty thousand men to win a tract of land too small to bury them in. And it possesses Laertes, who will avenge his father even by underhanded and despicable means, thereby becoming a cat's-paw of Claudius. The tragedy of Hamlet is that, in the end, he abandons his moral scruples and engages in indiscriminate slaughter in a sinful cause.

The interesting thing is that each of these diametrically opposed views—which are presented here in only slightly exaggerated form—enjoys ample textual support. Indeed, Hamlet himself acknowledges that he is "prompted to [his] revenge by heaven *and* hell."[114] And those who pronounce Hamlet's epitaph take similarly contrary views. Fortinbras claims Hamlet as one of the warrior class, noting that, as king, he would have "prov'd most royal" and deserves to be borne by four captains accompanied by "the soldier's music and the rite of war."[115] Horatio bids him adieu in softer tones: "Good night, sweet prince, / And flights of angels sing thee to thy rest."[116]

Hamlet is caught between two contradictory cultural paradigms. Renaissance ideals of the noble use of reason, aesthetic refinement, and the peaceful arrangement of the social order clash with a warrior culture older than Homer. They clash within Hamlet himself. How is he to reconcile his artistic, moral, and spiritual longings with the rage, lust, and ambition he finds in himself and others? How is he to integrate the god and the beast into a coherent human being, with the grace and *sprezzatura* of Castiglione's courtier? He cannot do so, and he is disgusted and paralyzed by the disjunction between what man is and what he ought to be.

As Emily Dickinson beautifully put it, "Hamlet wavered for all of us,"[117] echoing William Hazlitt, who wrote, "It is *we* who are Hamlet."[118] Every thoughtful, self-reflective person, after Montaigne, recognizes the gap between the values we profess and the reality in our hearts, between "actions that a man might play" and "that within which passes show."[119] Hamlet has no faith in heroic action, either to perfect the inner man or to right the external world.[120] He has no faith that what we call greatness is anything more than rank ambition, which will reveal itself in time as empty and futile.

Rightly to be great
Is not to stir without great argument,
But greatly to find quarrel in a straw
When honour's at the stake.[121]

What we call greatness will find quarrel in a straw simply to manifest itself as greatness. Thus, Fortinbras "fight[s] for a plot / Whereon the numbers cannot try the cause."[122] Alexander conquered the entire world but to no greater effect. His "noble dust" may now be "stopping a bunghole."[123] Greatness of being—to which Hamlet has always aspired—finds no validation either in heaven or on earth. It is simply a word disguising a sordid reality, a sentiment with which Falstaff would surely concur.

In an earlier book on the eternal questions of philosophy, I wrote, "We live in a post-Wittgenstein age with Platonic longings."[124] By that I meant that Plato established our aspirations and expectations for human thought and language. He held out the promise of a comprehensive understanding in which every piece of the puzzle falls into place, and terms like "beauty," "courage," and "goodness" have an absolute, fixed meaning discernible to human reason. We can then gauge our conduct by those fixed standards. Wittgenstein, by contrast, showed us nothing but fragmentation and dismissed the false comfort of ideas that oversimplify and distort our messy everyday lives. There are no fixed standards. As Hamlet explains, "there is nothing either good or bad but thinking makes it so."[125] Hamlet is already post-Wittgenstein. He dismisses the products of human reason as "words, words, words"[126] that offer no coherent account of what it should mean to be a human being crawling between earth and heaven. Fine words hint at ideals that life constantly undermines. We cannot live up to our own speech. Everything we say is a lie. "The rest is silence."[127]

Friedrich Nietzsche may be the most incisive interpreter of Hamlet. He wrote that "action requires the veils of illusion," whereas Hamlet has "looked truly into the essence of things," and the resultant nausea inhibits action.[128] When the ghost first beckons Hamlet to follow, Horatio is horrified:

What if it tempt you . . .
to the dreadful summit of the cliff
That beetles o'er his base into the sea,
And there assume some other horrible form
Which might deprive your sovereignty of reason
And draw you into madness? Think of it.
The very place puts toys of desperation,
Without more motive, into every brain
That looks so many fathoms to the sea
And hears it roar beneath.[129]

The ghost has indeed tempted Hamlet to the dreadful summit, and throughout the rest of the play he teeters on the edge of that abyss. The constantly churning sea is nothing but blind, striving will, which can manifest itself equally in the most refined and polished works of art and thought and also in the basest and most despicable acts.

Hamlet loves the theater precisely because it maintains the veils of illusion so essential to life. It focuses on forms, tones, and words, and thereby purports "to hold as 'twere the mirror up to nature; to show virtue her feature, scorn her own image, and the very age and body of the time his form and pressure."[130] The theater is essentially Platonic. It distills characters and concepts to their essence. It reveals us to ourselves and to one another. And yet it is an illusion, however beautiful, a step removed even from the play of shadows on the wall of Plato's cave. Beneath this surface representation, what we hear, if we listen with the morbid sensibility of a Hamlet, is the undifferentiated roar of the constantly churning human will. Indeed, the sharper our perception, the greater the roar, as George Eliot so wonderfully noted:

That element of tragedy which lies in the very fact of frequency, has not yet wrought itself into the coarse emotion of mankind; and perhaps our frames could hardly bear much of it. If we had a keen vision and feeling of all ordinary human life, it would be like hearing the grass grow and the squirrel's heart beat, and we should die of that roar which lies on the other side of silence.[131]

Much is made of Hamlet's suggestion in act 5 that "there's a divinity that shapes our ends." But it is hardly a Christian vision; for the ways of providence are utterly unfathomable. Indeed, the only certainty is that our "deep plots . . . / Rough-hew them how we will," will end in our annihilation.[132] In the face of nothingness, in the face of the abyss shown to him by his father's ghost, Hamlet in act 5 effects an almost Buddhistic calm. Returning from his aborted trip to England, he knows that Claudius will make another attempt on his life. But he seems not to care.

> If it be now, 'tis not to come; if it be not to come, it will be now; if it be not now, yet it will come. The readiness is all. Since no man, of aught he leaves, knows aught, what is't to leave betimes? Let be.[133]

The readiness is all. There is a mode of being—aware, alert, resigned—that may not be intrinsically better than not being but is the best we can attain on this earth. It is the stance of the artist on whom nothing is lost.

Hamlet's actual death is messy due to the clumsy contrivances of Claudius. And Hamlet finally wreaks his long contemplated revenge in an impulsive act of rage. His will asserts itself even in death as he commands Horatio to "report me and my cause aright."[134] Why does he care about his "wounded name" if readiness is all and only nothingness awaits? It is the ultimate paradox of this most paradoxical character, who can never integrate the array of conflicting thoughts and impulses that constitute man. Hamlet, as Harold Bloom notes, "has no center."[135] He finds himself, like the cosmos, hollow at the core:

> Had I but time—as this fell sergeant, Death,
> Is strict in his arrest—O, I could tell you—
> But let it be.[136]

It is Hamlet's final tantalizing hint as he gazes into the abyss and hears the roar of the untamed human will. The rest is silence.

OUR REVELS NOW ARE ENDED

In Christopher Marlowe's last play, the eponymous Dr. Faustus undertakes to master all of human knowledge. Logic, medicine, law, and divinity are sounded in turn and found wanting. Of each he asks: "Affords this art no greater miracle? / Then read no more; thou hast attained that end. / A greater subject fitteth Faustus' wit!"[137] Having exhausted the liberal arts, he turns to necromancy in hopes of becoming "on earth as Jove is in the sky":

> All things that move between the quiet poles
> Shall be at my command. Emperors and kings
> Are but obeyed in their several provinces,
> Nor can they raise the wind or rend the clouds,
> But his dominion that exceeds in this
> Stretcheth as far as doth the mind of man.
> A sound magician is a demi-god.[138]

Faustus pledges his soul to the devil in order to gain such power for twenty-four years on earth, confident that there is no afterworld in which his debt will become due. His familiar, Mephistophilis, accordingly lets him "try the utmost magic can perform."[139] But Faustus gains no true knowledge and wastes his powers on vain pleasures and empty displays. When the twenty-four years have passed, it is too late to repent. Even his final plea—"I'll burn my books!"[140]—cannot prevent him from being dragged to eternal damnation.

Prospero, too, has attained the powers of a demigod, both through his own study and with the help of his familiar, Ariel. Together they raise the wind and rend the clouds to set in motion the tempest that delivers the king of Naples, the Duke of Milan, and others to Prospero's remote island in Shakespeare's *The Tempest*. "These mine enemies," Prospero exults, "now are in my power."[141] But what he will do with that power, and whether he has sold his soul to the devil to attain it, remains to be seen.

Twelve years earlier, Prospero explains to his daughter, Miranda, he was himself Duke of Milan. There, Prospero made "the liberal Arts . . . all my study."[142] He was so "transported / And rapt in secret studies" that he neglected worldly ends and turned the daily business of government over to his brother, Antonio.[143] For Prospero, his library was "dukedom large enough."[144] But Antonio wanted to be "Absolute Milan,"[145] duke in name and ceremony as well as substance. He therefore opened the gates of the city to Alonso, the king of Naples and longtime enemy of Milan, who, in exchange for annual tribute, contrived to exile Prospero along with the three-year-old Miranda, setting them adrift miles from shore in a leaky boat with no sails. Only the love of the people for the exiled pair stayed Antonio and Alonso from killing them outright. A faithful retainer, Gonzalo, secretly furnished father and daughter with food, water, and other necessities, and "from mine own library with volumes that / I prize above my dukedom."[146] "By Providence divine," Prospero concludes, they were brought safely to the island they now inhabit.[147]

For twelve years, then, Prospero has nurtured his daughter along with his grievance. Their only companions are the half-beast, half-man Caliban, and the airy spirits Prospero commands. Caliban's mother, the witch Sycorax, was banished to the island for her black magic, her life preserved only because of her pregnancy. She died before Prospero and Miranda arrived, leaving the misshapen Caliban without language or learning. She also left behind Ariel, her ethereal servant, "too delicate / To act her earthy and abhorr'd commands,"[148] and thus painfully imprisoned by Sycorax in a cloven pine from which Prospero finally freed him.

Caliban was at first extravagantly grateful for the attention of Prospero and Miranda, and he showed them "all the qualities o' th' isle, / The fresh springs, brine-pits, barren place and fertile,"[149] so that they could distinguish between the two, just as they in turn "endow'd [his] purposes

/ With words that made them known."[150] But education did not temper Caliban's natural urges, and when Miranda grew older he tried to rape her. Confined to a rock by Prospero and forced to do menial chores, Caliban nurses his own grievance. He was once king of this island. He had inherited it by right from his mother, Sycorax, just as Prospero had his dukedom by succession. He would people it with Calibans. But now he is a servant, and the gift of speech avails him nothing.

> You taught me language; and my profit on 't
> Is, I know how to curse.[151]

Ariel is wholly different from Caliban. He—or one might as easily say she, for Ariel is often played by a woman in performance—is a pure, sexless spirit, who can move with the speed of thought and weave spells and enchantments over foolish mortals. Yet Ariel, too, is servant to Prospero and longs for the freedom to "fly / After summer" and to live "merrily, merrily ... / Under the blossom that hangs on the bough."[152] Ariel is also the demiurge of the music that fills the island and moves even Caliban to eloquence—or, rather, especially Caliban, who, in his state close to nature, seems more attuned to it than anyone else:

> Be not afeard; the isle is full of noises,
> Sounds and sweet airs, that give delight, and hurt not.
> Sometimes a thousand twangling instruments
> Will hum about mine ears; and sometimes voices,
> That, if I then had wak'd after long sleep,
> Will make me sleep again: and then, in dreaming,
> The clouds methought would open, and show riches
> Ready to drop upon me; that, when I wak'd,
> I cried to dream again.[153]

The Tempest lends itself to allegorical interpretations. And it invites commentary on New World colonialism, servitude, political violence, and the varied promptings of nature and nurture. There is endless fodder here for committed scholars and directors. But if ever there was a play that called attention to forms, tones, and words—all of which lie dazzlingly upon the surface—it is *The Tempest*. As Hazlitt noted, "it is full of grace and grandeur,"[154] and it must be appreciated first and foremost on that level. The play is also, as critics have long recognized, "Shakespeare's farewell piece."[155] He cowrote a few other plays after this one, but *The Tempest* marks his valedictory. A simplistic equation of Prospero and Shakespeare may be indefensible, but it is nonetheless enriching to recognize that, in key passages, Shakespeare *cum* Prospero is speaking directly to his public in a way he has not done previously.

Prospero is the maestro who sets the stage and puts the characters in motion. His will constructs and controls three separate plot lines. First, Ferdinand, the son of Alonso, and Miranda fall in love. Ferdinand is alone and bereft, believing that his father and all their companions perished in the storm that stranded him on the island. When Ariel guides his heavy steps to Miranda, he is struck with wonder and is prepared to make her queen of Naples before they have exchanged a dozen words. Miranda, in turn—since the only men she has ever seen are her father and Caliban—would "call him / A thing divine; for nothing natural / I ever saw so noble."[156] "They are both in either's pow'rs," Prospero rejoices, "but this swift business / I must uneasy make, lest too light winning / Make the prize light."[157] He is accordingly severe with Ferdinand and sets him to work on onerous, menial tasks. But the course of true love does not deviate from its appointed path. For a prize so precious—"she will outstrip all praise, / And make it halt behind her"[158]—Ferdinand will happily endure any hardship.

The second subplot concerns Sebastian, the brother of Alonso. Antonio, believing Ferdinand to be dead, urges Sebastian to kill the grieving Alonso and himself become king of Naples, just as Antonio became Duke of Milan. Indeed, Antonio offers to kill the king himself in satisfaction of the tribute Milan owes to Naples. Sebastian all too readily agrees. The biblical violence of brother against brother is prepared to repeat itself yet again. But, although Prospero will give Sebastian and Antonio the freedom in which to develop their plot, he directs Ariel to prevent its completion.

In the third subplot, Caliban encounters two drunken sailors. After tasting their "celestial liquor," Caliban immediately pledges his allegiance and—eager to trade one tyrant for another, as if that were "freedom, high-day, freedom!"[159]—he proposes that they join together to kill Prospero and take over the island. "Burn but his books," he urges (echoing Faustus's own offer), "for without them / He's but a sot, as I am."[160]

Prospero fosters the first subplot and thwarts the second with equal ease. The third subplot is also readily countered; indeed, the drunken sailors themselves have no real appetite for violence and are readily distracted from Caliban's aims. Yet Caliban's aborted revolt disturbs Prospero deeply, as if he feels guilt for his failure to educate and civilize Caliban and for effectively displacing him as lord of his own island, while robbing him of what W. H. Auden calls his "savage freedom" and his "savage innocence."[161] There are at least tonal hints here, already found in Montaigne's essay "Of Cannibals," of a new myth of the natural man that Rousseau would seize upon more than a century later to usher in Romanticism. But Prospero, unlike Rousseau, is not sentimental.

With Ariel's help, Prospero's enemies are "all knit up" and in his power.[162] He can destroy them or torment them as he pleases. He can wreak his long-contemplated revenge. But Ariel reminds him of their common humanity in a deeply moving exchange. He describes the prisoners: distracted, mourning, and "brimful of sorrow and dismay"; and particularly the good lord Gonzalo, dear to Prospero, whose tears run down his old beard "like winter's drops / From eaves of reeds."[163]

> ARI . . . Your charm so strongly works 'em,
> That if you now beheld them, your affections
> Would become tender.

PROS. Dost thou think so, spirit?
ARI. Mine would, sir, were I human.
PROS. And mine shall.
    Hast thou, which art but air, a touch, a feeling
    Of their afflictions, and shall not myself,
    One of their kind, that relish all as sharply
    Passion as they, be kindlier mov'd than thou art?
    Though with their high wrongs I am struck to th' quick,
    Yet with my nobler reason 'gainst my fury
    Do I take part: the rarer action is
    In virtue than in vengeance: they being penitent,
    The sole drift of my purpose doth extend
    Not a frown further. Go release them, Ariel:
    My charms I'll break, their senses I'll restore,
    And they shall be themselves.[164]

Prospero renounces revenge as unworthy of nobler reason and tender affection. He embraces Gonzalo. He reunites Alonso with the son he thought was dead, and Alonso immediately blesses Ferdinand's proposed marriage to Miranda. Antonio must surrender his ill-gotten dukedom to Prospero. And Prospero himself abjures the magic that separated him from his fellow men:

    I'll break my staff,
    Bury it certain fadoms in the earth,
    And deeper than did ever plummet sound
    I'll drown my book.[165]

"My book" refers to his accumulated esoteric wisdom. Man is not meant to be a demigod. Such aspirations will overthrow the tender affections necessary for human connections. So Prospero gives up godlike control and will become again, for better or for worse, a man. He is redeemed by his love for Miranda: "O, a cherubin / Thou wast that did preserve me. Thou didst smile, / Infused with a fortitude from heaven."[166] Prospero includes even Caliban within his affections and promises to assume responsibility for him—"this thing of darkness I / Acknowledge mine."[167] Caliban, in turn, makes his own promise: "I'll be wise hereafter, / And seek for grace."[168]

The play ends in a remarkable moment of reconciliation, forgiveness, and mercy. But the moment is not untinged by ambiguity and sadness. Antonio and Sebastian are not redeemed; nor do they seek forgiveness. They simply escape punishment. Miranda may be filled with wonder and optimism:

> How beauteous mankind is! O brave new world,
> That has such people in 't![169]

But Prospero's response is more sober: "'Tis new to thee."[170] Prospero is not naive about the failings of mankind. He knows that Miranda will suffer disappointments and perhaps even betrayal. At best, and with grace, she will know the future Ferdinand predicts for them both: "quiet days, fair issue and long life."[171] That is as close to paradise as one might hope in an imperfect world.

Prospero's caution—"Let us not burthen our remembrance with / A heaviness that's gone"[172]—itself serves to recall that heaviness. He will "retire . . . to my Milan, where / Every third thought shall be my grave."[173] It is impossible not to substitute, in our minds, "Stratford" for Milan. For twelve years—from 1599 to 1611—Shakespeare has worked his own magic on the stage at the Globe, like a demigod whose dominion "stretcheth as far as doth the mind of man." He is ready to bid farewell.

> Our revels now are ended. These our actors,
> As I foretold you, were all spirits, and
> Are melted into air, into thin air
> And, like the baseless fabric of this vision,
> The cloud-capp'd towers, the gorgeous palaces,

The solemn temples, the great globe itself,
Yea, all which it inherit, shall dissolve,
And, like this insubstantial pageant faded,
Leave not a rack beyond. We are such stuff
As dreams are made on; and our little life
Is rounded with a sleep.[174]

Surely "the great globe itself" is a reference to his theater, as is the charmed "circle which Prospero had made," and into which the assembled cast is drawn and then dispersed.[175] Fortunately, Shakespeare did not drown his book or "bury it certain fadoms in the earth." But he did nothing to preserve it. That task was left to others, and we thankfully possess the inexhaustible riches of the First Folio. Yet Shakespeare himself still lies deeply hidden within those pages. His characters shine forth. They strut and fret their hour upon the stage, revealing to us the full range and depth of human thought, human passion, and human ambition. But Shakespeare himself is not to be found among them; or rather, he is so fully dispersed among them all as to melt into thin air, leaving only tantalizing hints. Shakespearean wisdom does indeed lie "deeper than did ever plummet sound."

ACKNOWLEDGMENTS

I have not attempted to document every source for the ideas in this book. But my extensive debt to generations of Renaissance scholars and translators will be obvious to those in the field. I have tried to list the books and articles on which I most relied, as well as those from which general readers would most benefit, in the section on Suggestions for Further Reading. I also cite there, and in the notes, the many excellent translations from which the quotations in the text are derived.

Oxford historian Emily Winkler read the chapters as they were written and made numerous helpful suggestions and corrections. My brother Peter—a distinguished playwright—read the chapter on Shakespeare and provided several key insights and comments, as did my daughter, Camille, to whom this book is dedicated.

Several of my colleagues played critical roles in putting this book in final form. Darrin Leverette scrupulously worked through the entire manuscript, checking the cites, the facts, and the prose, and saving me from numerous errors. His intelligence, attention to detail, willingness to track down obscure sources, and sensitivity to the nuances of language were all indispensable. So, too, was the work of Susan Cohen, who carefully and thoughtfully read each chapter. My longtime assistant, Marilyn Williams, without whom I would never accomplish anything, kept the entire project on schedule and put the manuscript in its final form.

Denise Roeper was my freelance editor from Prometheus Books. She has a wonderful ear for language and a sharp eye for imprecision. The book is much improved thanks to her efforts. She was also a delight to work with.

I would also like to express my gratitude and pay tribute to Steven L. Mitchell, the longtime editor in chief of Prometheus Books, who just retired after almost forty years. During that time, he helped make Prometheus Books into a model for independent publishers, offering serious books for thoughtful readers on a range of subjects. I am especially grateful that he was willing to take a chance on an unknown, previously unpublished author and that he stayed with me through five books.

My greatest joys are my wife, Lucy, and my three children—Baird, Cole, and Camille—who have sustained, encouraged, and inspired me throughout the writing of the books in this series.

CHRONOLOGY

Petrarch	1304–1374
Avignon Papacy ("Babylonian Captivity")	1309–1377
Boccaccio	1313–1375
Hundred Years' War	1337–1453
Western Schism	1378–1417
Henry the Navigator (Portugal)	1394–1460
Henry IV (England)	r. 1399–1413
Henry V (England)	r. 1413–1422
Council of Constance	1414–1418
Battle of Agincourt	1415
Marsilio Ficino	1433–1499
Gutenberg Printing Press	ca. 1440
Christopher Columbus	1451–1506
Leonardo da Vinci	1452–1519
Wars of the Roses	1455–1487
Vasco da Gama	ca. 1460–1524
Giovanni Pico della Mirandola	1463–1494
Erasmus	ca. 1466–1536
Machiavelli	1469–1527
Nicolaus Copernicus	1473–1543
Isabella I (Castile)	r. 1474–1504
Cesare Borgia	1475–1507
Vasco Núñez de Balboa	ca. 1475–1519
Michelangelo	1475–1564

Spanish Inquisition Established	1478
Castiglione	1478–1529
Thomas More	1478–1535
Ferdinand II (Aragon)	r. 1479–1516
Ferdinand Magellan	ca. 1480–1521
Raphael	1483–1520
Martin Luther	1483–1546
Rabelais	1483–1553
Huldrych Zwingli	1484–1531
Battle of Bosworth Field	1485
Thomas Cromwell	ca. 1485–1540
Hernán Cortés	1485–1547
Completion of Reconquista in Spain	1492
Girolamo Savonarola (Florence)	r. 1494–1498
Louis XII (France)	r. 1498–1515
Henry VIII (England)	r. 1509–1547
John Calvin	1509–1564
Protestant Reformation	1517–1648
Charles V (Holy Roman Emperor)	r. 1519–1556
Diet of Worms	1521
German Peasants' War	1524–1525
Luís Vaz de Camões	1524/5–1580
Troops of Charles V Sack Rome	1527
Montaigne	1533–1592
First Act of Supremacy	1534
Thomas More Executed for Treason	1535
Henry VIII Excommunicated from Catholic Church	1538
Society of Jesus (Jesuits)	1540

CHRONOLOGY

Sir Francis Drake	ca. 1540–1596
Council of Trent	1545–1563
Counter-Reformation	1545–1648
Cervantes	1547–1616
Peace of Augsburg	1555
Philip II (Spain)	r. 1556–1598
Elizabeth I (England)	r. 1558–1603
Index Librorum Prohibitorum Published	1559
Christopher Marlowe	1564–1593
Shakespeare	1564–1616
Galileo Galilei	1564–1642
Battle of Lepanto	1571
Johannes Kepler	1571–1630
St. Bartholomew's Day Massacre	1572
Ben Jonson	1572–1637
Spanish Armada Defeated	1588
Edict of Nantes	1598
Gunpowder Plot	1605
Jamestown Colony Founded	1607
Globe Theatre Destroyed by Fire	1613
Thirty Years' War	1618–1648
Ferdinand II (Holy Roman Emperor)	r. 1619–1637
Plymouth Colony Founded	1620
English Civil War	1642–1651
Peace of Westphalia	1648

SUGGESTIONS FOR FURTHER READING

INTRODUCTION

Fernand Braudel, *The Mediterranean and the Mediterranean World in the Age of Philip II* (New York: HarperCollins, 1992), translated by Siân Reynolds.

Jerry Brotton, *The Renaissance: A Very Short Introduction* (New York: Oxford University Press, 2005).

Jacob Burckhardt, *The Civilisation of the Renaissance in Italy* (London: Folio Society, 2004), translated by S. G. C. Middlemore with an introduction by Anthony Grafton.

Luís Vaz de Camões, *The Lusíads* (New York: Oxford University Press, 1997), translated with an introduction and notes by Landeg White.

J. H. Elliott, *Imperial Spain, 1469–1716* (1963; repr., London: Penguin Books, 2002).

Stephen Greenblatt, *Renaissance Self-Fashioning: From More to Shakespeare* (Chicago: University of Chicago Press, 2005).

John Hale, *The Civilization of Europe in the Renaissance* (New York: Atheneum, 1994).

Mark Hansen, *The Royal Facts of Life: Biology and Politics in Sixteenth-Century Europe* (Metuchen, NJ: Scarecrow, 1980).

Diarmaid MacCulloch, *The Reformation: A History* (New York: Penguin Books, 2005).

Garrett Mattingly, *The Armada* (Boston: Houghton Mifflin, 2005).

Peter Pesic, *Polyphonic Minds: Music of the Hemispheres* (Cambridge, MA: MIT Press, 2017), chaps. 1–9.

Giovanni Pico della Mirandola, *On the Dignity of Man* (1965; repr., Indianapolis, IN: Hackett, 1998), translated by Charles Glenn Wallis with an introduction by Paul J. W. Miller.

J. H. Plumb, *The Italian Renaissance* (New York: American Heritage, 1985).

Giorgio Vasari, *Lives of the Painters, Sculptors and Architects* (New York: Dell, 1968), edited by Edmund Fuller, translated by A. B. Hinds.

Robin W. Winks and Lee Palmer Wandel, *Europe in a Wider World, 1350–1650* (New York: Oxford University Press, 2003).

PETRARCH

Primary Sources:

The Essential Petrarch (Indianapolis, IN: Hackett, 2010), edited and translated by Peter Hainsworth.

Petrarch, *Canzoniere* (Bloomington: Indiana University Press, 1996), translated by Mark Musa.

Petrarch, *Letters of Old Age*, 2 vols. (New York: Italica, 2005), translated by Aldo S. Bernardo, Saul Levin, and Reta A. Bernardo.

Petrarch, *Letters on Familiar Matters* (New York: Italica, 2005), translated by Aldo S. Bernardo.

Petrarch, *Petrarch's Secret: The Soul's Conflict with Passion* (1911; repr., New York: Hyperion, 1978), translated by William H. Draper.

Secondary Sources:

Aldo S. Bernardo, *Petrarch, Scipio and the "Africa": The Birth of Humanism's Dream* (Baltimore: Johns Hopkins Press, 1962).

Morris Bishop, *Petrarch and His World* (Bloomington: Indiana University Press, 1963).

Maud F. Jerrold, *Francesco Petrarca: Poet and Humanist* (1909; repr., Port Washington, NY: Kennikat, 1970).

Petrarch: A Critical Guide to the Complete Works (Chicago: University of Chicago Press, 2009), edited by Victoria Kirkham and Armando Maggi.

Gur Zak, *Petrarch's Humanism and the Care of the Self* (New York: Cambridge University Press, 2013).

ERASMUS

Primary Sources:

The Colloquies of Erasmus (Chicago: University of Chicago Press, 1965), translated by Craig R. Thompson.

Erasmus, *Enchiridion* (Bloomington: Indiana University Press, 1963), translated with an introduction by Raymond Himelick.

Erasmus: The "Praise of Folly" and Other Writings (New York: W. W. Norton, 1989), edited and translated by Robert M. Adams.

Desiderius Erasmus and Martin Luther: Discourse on Free Will (London: Bloomsbury, 1989), edited and translated by Ernst F. Winter.

Martin Luther: Selections from His Writings (Garden City, NY: Anchor Books, 1961), edited with an introduction by John Dillenberger.

Secondary Sources:

Cornelis Augustijn, *Erasmus: His Life, Works, and Influence* (1991; repr., Toronto: University of Toronto Press, 1995), translated by J. C. Grayson.

Johan Huizinga, *Erasmus and the Age of Reformation* (Mineola, NY: Dover, 2001), translated by F. Hopman.

Lisa Jardine, *Erasmus, Man of Letters: The Construction of Charisma in Print* (Princeton, NJ: Princeton University Press, 1993).

James McConica, *Erasmus* (Oxford: Oxford University Press, 1991).

MACHIAVELLI

Primary Sources:

Niccolò Machiavelli, *Discourses on Livy* (New York: Oxford University Press, 2003), translated with an introduction and notes by Julia Conaway Bondanella and Peter Bondanella.

Niccolò Machiavelli, *The Prince*, 2nd ed. (New York: W. W. Norton, 1992), edited and translated by Robert M. Adams.

Niccolò Machiavelli, *The Prince* (New York: Alfred A. Knopf, 1992), translated by W. K. Marriott.

The Portable Machiavelli (New York: Penguin Books, 1979), edited and translated with an introduction by Peter Bondanella and Mark Musa.

Secondary Sources:

Peter E. Bondanella, *Machiavelli and the Art of Renaissance History* (Detroit: Wayne State University Press, 1973).

Quentin Skinner, *Machiavelli: A Very Short Introduction* (New York: Oxford University Press, 2000).

Maurizio Viroli, *Niccolò's Smile: A Biography of Machiavelli* (New York: Hill and Wang, 2002), translated by Antony Shugaar.

THOMAS MORE

Primary Sources:

Thomas More, *Utopia*, 3rd ed. (New York: W. W. Norton, 2011), edited and translated by George M. Logan.

Saint Thomas More: Selected Writings (New York: Vintage Books, 2003), edited by John F. Thornton and Susan B. Varenne.

A Thomas More Source Book (2004; repr., Washington, DC: Catholic University of America Press, 2008), edited by Gerard B. Wegemer and Stephen W. Smith.

Secondary Sources:

Peter Ackroyd, *The Life of Thomas More* (New York: Anchor Books, 1999).

Richard Marius, *Thomas More* (London: Fount, 1986).

James Monti, *The King's Good Servant but God's First: The Life and Writings of St. Thomas More* (San Francisco: Ignatius, 1997).

Thomas More (New York: Cambridge University Press, 2011), edited by George M. Logan.

CASTIGLIONE

Primary Sources:

Baldassare Castiglione, *The Book of the Courtier* (New York: W. W. Norton, 2002), edited by Daniel Javitch, translated by Charles S. Singleton.

Secondary Sources:

Castiglione: The Ideal and the Real in Renaissance Culture (New Haven, CT: Yale University Press, 1983), edited by Robert W. Hanning and David Rosand.

Wayne A. Rebhorn, *Courtly Performances: Masking and Festivity in Castiglione's "Book of the Courtier"* (Detroit: Wayne State University Press, 1978).

RABELAIS

Primary Sources:

The Complete Works of Rabelais: The Five Books of "Gargantua and Pantagruel" (New York: Modern Library, 1944), translated by Jacques Le Clercq.

François Rabelais, *Gargantua and Pantagruel* (London: Penguin Books, 2006), edited and translated with an introduction and notes by M. A. Screech.

Secondary Sources:

Erich Auerbach, *Mimesis: The Representation of Reality in Western Literature* (Princeton, NJ: Princeton University Press, 1968), chap. 11, translated by Willard R. Trask.

Mikhail Bakhtin, *Rabelais and His World* (Bloomington: Indiana University Press, 1984), translated by Hélène Iswolsky.

Barbara C. Bowen, *The Age of Bluff: Paradox and Ambiguity in Rabelais and Montaigne* (Urbana: University of Illinois Press, 1972).

The Cambridge Companion to Rabelais (New York: Cambridge University Press, 2011), edited by John O'Brien.

Donald M. Frame, *François Rabelais: A Study* (New York: Harcourt Brace Jovanovich, 1977).

M. A. Screech, *Rabelais* (London: Duckworth, 1979).

MONTAIGNE

Primary Sources:

The Complete Essays of Montaigne (Stanford, CA: Stanford University Press, 1965), translated by Donald M. Frame.

Montaigne's Travel Journal (San Francisco: North Point, 1983), translated with an introduction by Donald M. Frame.

Secondary Sources:

Erich Auerbach, *Mimesis: The Representation of Reality in Western Literature* (Princeton, NJ: Princeton University Press, 1968), chap. 12, translated by Willard R. Trask.

Sarah Bakewell, *How to Live, or, A Life of Montaigne* (New York: Other Press, 2010).

Donald M. Frame, *Montaigne: A Biography* (San Francisco: North Point, 1984).

Hugo Friedrich, *Montaigne* (Berkeley: University of California Press, 2010), edited with an introduction by Philippe Desan, translated by Dawn Eng.

Jean Starobinski, *Montaigne in Motion* (Chicago: University of Chicago Press, 1985), translated by Arthur Goldhammer.

CERVANTES

Primary Sources:

Miguel de Cervantes, *Don Quixote* (New York: HarperCollins, 2005), translated by Edith Grossman with an introduction by Harold Bloom.

Miguel de Cervantes, *Exemplary Stories* (New York: Oxford University Press, 1998), translated with an introduction and notes by Lesley Lipson.

Secondary Sources:

Harold Bloom, *The Western Canon: The Books and School of the Ages* (New York: Harcourt Brace, 1994), chap. 5.

Jean Canavaggio, *Cervantes* (New York: W. W. Norton, 1990), translated by J. R. Jones.

Cervantes: A Collection of Critical Essays (Englewood Cliffs, NJ: Prentice-Hall, 1969), edited by Lowry Nelson Jr.

Cervantes' "Don Quixote": A Casebook (New York: Oxford University Press, 2005), edited by Roberto González Echevarría.

Roberto González Echevarría, *Cervantes' "Don Quixote"* (New Haven, CT: Yale University Press, 2015).

William Egginton, *The Man Who Invented Fiction: How Cervantes Ushered in the Modern World* (New York: Bloomsbury, 2016).

Donald P. McCrory, *No Ordinary Man: The Life and Times of Miguel de Cervantes* (Mineola, NY: Dover, 2006).

José Ortega y Gasset, *Meditations on Quixote* (New York: W. W. Norton, 1963), translated by Evelyn Rugg and Diego Marín with an introduction and notes by Julián Marías.

SHAKESPEARE

Primary Sources:

The Complete Plays of Christopher Marlowe (New York: Odyssey, 1963), edited with and introduction and notes by Irving Ribner.

William Shakespeare, *As You Like It* (2006; repr., London: Bloomsbury, 2016), edited by Juliet Dusinberre.

William Shakespeare, *Hamlet* (1982; repr., London: Routledge, 1993), edited by Harold Jenkins.

William Shakespeare, *King Henry IV, Part I* (2002; repr., London: Bloomsbury, 2016), edited by David Scott Kastan.

William Shakespeare, *King Henry IV, Part 2* (London: Bloomsbury, 2016), edited by James C. Bulman.

William Shakespeare, *King Henry V* (New York: Cambridge University Press, 2005), edited by Andrew Gurr.

William Shakespeare, *King Richard II* (2002; repr., London: Bloomsbury, 2016), edited by Charles R. Forker.

William Shakespeare, *The Tempest* (1954; repr., London: Routledge, 1988), edited by Frank Kermode.

William Shakespeare, *The Tempest* (New York: W. W. Norton, 2004), edited by Peter Hulme and William H. Sherman.

Secondary Sources:

W. H. Auden, *Lectures on Shakespeare* (Princeton, NJ: Princeton University Press, 2001), edited by Arthur Kirsch.

Jonathan Bate, *Soul of the Age: The Life, Mind and World of William Shakespeare* (London: Penguin Books, 2008).

Harold Bloom, *Falstaff: Give Me Life* (New York: Scribner, 2017).

Harold Bloom, *Hamlet: Poem Unlimited* (New York: Riverhead Books, 2003).

Harold Bloom, *Shakespeare: The Invention of the Human* (New York: Riverhead Books, 1998).

A. C. Bradley, *Shakespearean Tragedy: Lectures on "Hamlet," "Othello," "King Lear" and "Macbeth"* (London: Penguin Books, 1991).

Bill Bryson, *Shakespeare: The World as Stage* (New York: Harper Perennial, 2008).

Harold C. Goddard, *The Meaning of Shakespeare*, 2 vols. (Chicago: University of Chicago Press, 1960).

Stephen Greenblatt, *Will in the World: How Shakespeare Became Shakespeare* (New York: W. W. Norton, 2004).

William Hazlitt, *Characters of Shakespear's Plays*, in *The Collected Works of William Hazlitt*, vol. 1 (New York: McClure, Phillips, 1902), edited by A. R. Waller and Arnold Glover with an introduction by W. E. Henley.

Park Honan, *Shakespeare: A Life* (New York: Oxford University Press, 1998).

Johnson on Shakespeare: The Yale Edition of the Works of Samuel Johnson, vol. 7 (New Haven, CT: Yale University Press, 1968), edited by Arthur Sherbo with an introduction by Betrand H. Bronson.

G. Wilson Knight, *The Wheel of Fire: Interpretations of Shakespearian Tragedy* (1961; repr., New York: Routledge, 1998).

Northrop Frye on Shakespeare (New Haven, CT: Yale University Press, 1986), edited by Robert Sandler.

A. D. Nuttall, *Shakespeare the Thinker* (New Haven, CT: Yale University Press, 2007).

Peter Saccio, *Shakespeare's English Kings: History, Chronicle, and Drama* (New York: Oxford University Press, 1977).

James Shapiro, *A Year in the Life of William Shakespeare: 1599* (New York: Harper Perennial, 2006).

Twentieth Century Interpretations of "As You Like It" (Englewood Cliffs, NJ: Prentice-Hall, 1968), edited by Jay L. Halio.

Twentieth Century Interpretations of "Henry IV, Part One" (Englewood Cliffs, NJ: Prentice-Hall, 1970), edited by R. J. Dorius.

NOTES

INTRODUCTION

1. See, for example, Frederick Hartt, *History of Italian Renaissance Art* (7th ed.). My own favorite book on the art of the Renaissance—albeit generally produced without illustrations—is Giorgio Vasari's *Lives of the Painters, Sculptors and Architects*. For a brilliant, synoptic account of the development of music through the Renaissance and beyond, see chapters 1–9 of Peter Pesic's *Polyphonic Minds: Music of the Hemispheres*.

2. See Michael K. Kellogg, *The Wisdom of the Middle Ages* (Amherst, NY: Prometheus Books, 2016), chap. 5.

3. See Fernand Braudel, *The Mediterranean and the Mediterranean World in the Age of Philip II*, trans. Siân Reynolds (New York: HarperCollins, 1992).

4. Ben Jonson, "To the Memory of My Beloved the Author, Mr. William Shakespeare," preface to the First Folio, reprinted at https://www.poetryfoundation .org/poems/44466/to-the-memory-of-my-beloved-the-author-mr-william-shakespeare.

5. Jacob Burckhardt, *The Civilisation of the Renaissance in Italy*, trans. S. G. C. Middlemore (London: Folio Society, 2004), p. 108.

6. Jerry Brotton, *The Renaissance: A Very Short Introduction* (New York: Oxford University Press, 2005), pp. 48–49.

7. Eratosthenes of Cyrene had provided a far more accurate estimate in the third century BCE. But, although he was aware of Eratosthenes's calculations, Columbus chose instead to follow an inaccurate map created in 1474 by Paolo dal Pozzo Toscanelli.

8. In searching for an analogy for his own feelings on first encountering the "wide expanse" of Homer, John Keats mistakenly gives this honor to Cortés:

Then felt I like some watcher of the skies
When a new planet swims into his ken;
Or like stout Cortez when with eagle eyes
He star'd at the Pacific—and all his men
Look'd at each other with a wild surmise—
Silent, upon a peak in Darien.

John Keats, "On First Looking into Chapman's Homer," reprinted at https://www.poetryfoundation.org/poems/44481/on-first-looking-into-chapmans-homer. Regardless, Keats beautifully captures the moment of exhilaration as explorers encountered new lands and new seas.

9. We require extensive notes when we read Shakespeare to explain archaic words and phrases. The King James Bible, written roughly in the same time frame, is transparent to all readers of modern English.

10. Thomas Carlyle, *On Heroes, Hero-Worship and the Heroic in History* (New York: A. L. Burt, [1840?]), p. 160.

11. Giovanni Pico della Mirandola, *On the Dignity of Man*, trans. Charles Glenn Wallis (1965; repr., Indianapolis, IN: Hackett, 1998), p. 3.

12. Ibid., pp. 5, 13.

13. Ibid., p. 23.

14. Ibid., p. 5.

15. Burckhardt, *Civilisation of the Renaissance*, p. 103.

16. It is a delicious irony, therefore, that opera arose from the mistaken belief that the individual speeches in Greek tragedy were sung, just like the chorale odes. Donald Jay Grout, *A Short History of Opera*, 3rd ed. (New York: Columbia University Press, 1988), pp. 11–15.

CHAPTER 1: THE THREE FACES OF FRANCESCO PETRARCA

1. Petrarch, *Rerum memorandarum libri*, 1.2, quoted in Morris Bishop, *Petrarch and His World* (Bloomington: Indiana University Press, 1963), p. 374.

2. See, for example, Maud F. Jerrold, *Francesco Petrarca: Poet and Humanist* (1909; repr., Port Washington, NY: Kennikat, 1970), p. 324.

3. For a full account of medieval thought, see Michael K. Kellogg, *The Wisdom of the Middle Ages* (Amherst, NY: Prometheus Books, 2016).

4. See Andrew M. Miller, trans., *Greek Lyric: An Anthology in Translation* (Indianapolis, IN: Hackett, 1996), p. 9 ("The fox knows many things, the hedgehog only one.") (quoting Archilochus of Paros).

5. Gur Zak, *Petrarch's Humanism and the Care of the Self* (New York: Cambridge University Press, 2013), p. 9.

6. Petrarch, *Familiares*, 6.2, in *Letters on Familiar Matters*, trans. Aldo S. Bernardo, vol. 1 (New York: Italica, 2005), p. 295.

7. For an account of the events leading up to Dante's exile, see Kellogg, *Wisdom of the Middle Ages*, pp. 228–29.

8. Petrarch, *Seniles*, 16.1, in *Letters of Old Age*, trans. Aldo S. Bernardo, Saul Levin, and Reta A. Bernardo, 2 vols. (New York: Italica, 2005), 2:600–601.

9. Ibid., 2:601.

10. Bishop, *Petrarch and His World*, p. 88.

11. See Kellogg, *Wisdom of the Middle Ages*, pp. 225–28.

12. Petrarch, *Familiares*, 21.15, in *Letters on Familiar Matters*, vol. 3, p. 203.

13. Petrarch, *Seniles*, 5.2, in *Letters of Old Age*, 1:160.

14. Bishop, *Petrarch and His World*, p. 144; see Michael K. Kellogg, *The Roman Search for Wisdom* (Amherst, NY: Prometheus Books, 2014), p. 138.

15. Kellogg, *Roman Search for Wisdom*, pp. 143–44.

16. Petrarch, *Familiares*, 13.4, in *Letters on Familiar Matters*, vol. 2, p. 181.

17. Peter Hainsworth, ed. and trans., *The Essential Petrarch* (Indianapolis, IN: Hackett, 2010), p. 213.

18. Virgil, *Aeneid*, trans. Robert Fagles (New York: Penguin Books, 2010), 4.774–84.

19. Aldo S. Bernardo, *Petrarch, Scipio and the "Africa": The Birth of Humanism's Dream* (Baltimore: Johns Hopkins Press, 1962), pp. vii-viii.

20. Petrarch, *Seniles*, 17.2, in *Letters of Old Age*, 2:648–52.

21. Ibid., 2:654.

22. The Italian text is from Petrarch, *Canzoniere*, trans. Mark Musa (Bloomington: Indiana University Press, 1996), 1.

23. Ibid., p. xiii.

24. Bishop, *Petrarch and His World*, p. 71.

25. Petrarch, *Canzoniere*, p. xiii.

26. Dante, *Vita Nuova*, trans. Mark Musa (Oxford: Oxford University Press, 2008), chap. 7. Musa comments on the reference to Dante in his introduction to the *Canzoniere*. Petrarch, *Canzoniere*, p. xiv.

27. Petrarch, *Canzoniere*, 334.4.

28. Ibid., 132.10–11.

29. Ibid., 118.14.

30. Ibid., 30.16–18.

31. Ibid., 127.18–22.

32. See Zak, *Petrarch's Humanism*, pp. 26–27.

33. Petrarch, *Canzoniere*, 119.14–15.

34. Ibid., 336.7.

35. William Shakespeare, "Sonnet 65," in *Shakespeare's Sonnets and Poems*, ed. Barbara A. Mowat and Paul Werstine (New York: Simon & Schuster, 2011).

36. Petrarch, *Canzoniere*, 6.1–4.

37. Ibid., 73.78.

38. Ibid., 272.1.

39. Zak, *Petrarch's Humanism*, pp. 24, 62.

40. Jerrold, *Francesco Petrarca*, pp. 149–50.

41. Petrarch, *Petrarch's Secret: The Soul's Conflict with Passion*, trans. William H. Draper (1911; repr., New York: Hyperion, 1978), p. 12.

42. Ibid., p. 16.

43. Ibid., p. 32.

44. Ibid., p. 18.

45. Ibid., p. 24.

46. Ibid., p. 50.

47. Ibid., pp. 51–52.

48. Ibid., p. 11.

49. Ibid., p. 55.

50. Ibid., p. 69.

51. Ibid., p. 71.

52. Ibid., p. 73.

53. Ibid., p. 79.

54. Ibid., p. 84.

55. Ibid., p. 107.

56. Ibid., p. 109.

57. Ibid., p. 125.

58. Ibid., p. 132.

59. Ibid., p. 133.

60. Ibid., p. 148.

61. Ibid., p. 172.

62. Ibid., p. 177.

63. Ibid., p. 192.

64. Ibid.

65. Ibid., p. 172.

66. Petrarch, *Seniles*, 6.2, in *Letters of Old Age*, 1:192.

67. Petrarch, *Familiares*, 1.6, in *Letters on Familiar Matters*, vol. 1, p. 34.

68. Ibid., 1.1, p. 9.

69. Bishop, *Petrarch and His World*, p. 280.

70. Petrarch, *Seniles*, 2.3, in *Letters of Old Age*, 1:61.

71. Petrarch, *Familiares*, 6.4, in *Letters on Familiar Matters*, vol. 1, p. 314.

72. Ibid., 1.9, p. 47.

73. Zak, *Petrarch's Humanism*, p. 78.

74. Petrarch, *Seniles*, 16.3, in *Letters of Old Age*, 2:612.

75. Ibid., 13.8, 2:493.

76. Quoted in Bishop, *Petrarch and His World*, p. 231.

77. Petrarch, *Familiares*, 4.1, in *Letters on Familiar Matters*, vol. 1, p. 172.

78. Ibid., p. 173.

79. Ibid., p. 174.

80. Ibid., p. 175.

81. Ibid.

82. Ibid., pp. 175–76.

83. Ibid., p. 176.

84. Ibid., p. 178.

85. Ibid., 24.12, vol. 3, p. 344.

86. Ibid., 8.1, vol. 1, p. 390.

87. Petrarch, *Seniles*, 1.3, in *Letters of Old Age*, 1:6.

88. Ibid., 10.4, 2:377.

89. Ibid., 13.1, 2:476.

90. Petrarch, *Familiares*, 6.2, in *Letters on Familiar Matters*, vol. 1, p. 290.

91. Ibid., 8.9, p. 422.

92. Petrarch, *Seniles*, 4.5, in *Letters of Old Age*, 1:148.

93. Petrarch, *Familiares*, 3.18, in *Letters on Familiar Matters*, vol. 1, p. 157.

94. Petrarch, *Seniles*, 1.5, in *Letters of Old Age*, 1:16.

95. Ibid., 1:23.

96. Ibid., 1:25.

97. Petrarch, *Familiares*, 10.4, in *Letters on Familiar Matters*, vol. 2, p. 69.

98. Ibid., 7.16, vol. 1, p. 378.

99. Ibid., 1.1, p. 13.

100. Petrarch, *Seniles*, 17.2, in *Letters of Old Age*, 2:651.

101. Petrarch, *Familiares*, 1.1, in *Letters on Familiar Matters*, vol. 1, p. 8.

102. See Kellogg, *Wisdom of the Middle Ages*, pp. 242–44.

103. Petrarch, *Familiares*, 1.9, in *Letters on Familiar Matters*, vol. 1, p. 49.

104. Petrarch, *Triumphus Eternitatis*, 20–21, quoted in Armando Maggi, "*You Will Be My Solitude*: Solitude as Prophecy," in *Petrarch: A Critical Guide to the Complete Works*, ed. Victoria Kirkham and Armando Maggi (Chicago: University of Chicago Press, 2009), p. 183.

CHAPTER 2: ERASMUS: THE MAN IN THE MIDDLE

1. "Erasmus laid the eggs, Luther hatched them." See H. R. Trevor-Roper, "Desiderius Erasmus," in *Erasmus: The "Praise of Folly" and Other Writings*, ed. and trans. Robert M. Adams (New York: W. W. Norton, 1989), p. 276.

2. Erasmus, "The Godly Feast," in *The Colloquies of Erasmus*, trans. Craig R. Thompson (Chicago: University of Chicago Press, 1965), p. 68.

3. William Butler Yeats, "The Second Coming," in *The Collected Poems of W. B. Yeats* (Ware, UK: Wordsworth, 2008), p. 158.

4. Cornelis Augustijn, *Erasmus: His Life, Works, and Influence*, trans. J. C. Grayson (1991; repr., Toronto: University of Toronto Press, 1995), p. 38.

5. Erasmus, *Praise of Folly*, p. 3.

6. Ibid., p. 4 and n. 3.

7. Clarence H. Miller, "Thomas More, a Man for All Seasons: Robert Bolt's Play and the Elizabethan Play of *Sir Thomas More*," *Moreana* 27, no. 104 (Dec. 1990): 101–10.

8. Erasmus, *Praise of Folly*, p. 4, n. 3.

9. Ibid., p. 11.

10. Ibid., pp. 12–13.

11. Ibid., p. 12.

12. Ibid., p. 20.

13. Ibid., p. 21.

14. Ibid., p. 22.

15. Ibid., p. 23.

16. Ibid., p. 25.

17. Ibid., p. 27.

18. Ibid.

19. Ibid., p. 32.

20. Ibid., p. 29.

21. Ibid.

22. Ibid., p. 30.

23. Ibid., p. 29.

24. Ibid., p. 30; see Michael K. Kellogg, *The Roman Search for Wisdom* (Amherst, NY: Prometheus Books, 2014), p. 34.

25. Erasmus, *Praise of Folly*, p. 39.

26. Ibid., p. 47.

27. Ibid., p. 54.

28. Ibid., p. 58.

29. Ibid., p. 57.

30. Ibid., p. 63.

31. Ibid., p. 70.

32. Ibid., p. 39–40.

33. Ibid., p. 43.

34. Ibid., p. 82.

35. Ibid., p. 39.

36. Ibid., p. 9.

37. See James McConica, *Erasmus* (Oxford: Oxford University Press, 1991), p. 63.

38. Erasmus, *Praise of Folly*, p. 5.

39. Ibid.

40. Mikhail Bakhtin, "Medieval and Renaissance Folk Humor," trans. Hélène Iswolsky, in Adams, *"Praise of Folly" and Other Writings*, p. 315.

41. Ibid., p. 317.

42. Johan Huizinga, *Erasmus and the Age of Reformation*, trans. F. Hopman (Mineola, NY: Dover, 2001), p. 71. Huizinga's most renowned work, *The Waning of the Middle Ages*, entered popular culture in the movie *Love Story*, when the character played by Ryan O'Neal goes to the Radcliffe College library and asks the student working there, played by Ali MacGraw, if they have a copy of *The Waning of the Middle Ages*, which he needs for a paper due the next day. Again, Folly would appreciate the irony.

43. Erasmus, *Praise of Folly*, p. 80 (quoting 1 Cor. 4:10).

44. McConica, *Erasmus*, p. 49.

45. Erasmus, *Enchiridion*, trans. Raymond Himelick (Bloomington: Indiana University Press, 1963), p. 38.

46. Ibid., p. 51.

47. Ibid.

48. Ibid., p. 133.

49. Ibid., p. 105.

50. Ibid., p. 106.

51. Ibid.

52. Ibid., p. 94.

53. Ibid., p. 85.

54. Ibid., p. 86.

55. Ibid., p. 125.

56. Ibid., p. 114.

57. Ibid., p. 101.

58. Ibid., p. 99.

59. Ibid., p. 116.

60. Augustijn, *Erasmus*, p. 92.

61. Erasmus, "Paraclesis: or, An Exhortation," in Adams, *"Praise of Folly" and Other Writings*, p. 121.

62. Ibid.

63. Erasmus, "Foreword to the Third Edition," in Adams, *"Praise of Folly" and Other Writings*, p. 134.

64. Erasmus, "Paraclesis," in Adams, *"Praise of Folly" and Other Writings*, p. 121.

65. Ibid., p. 123.

66. Augustijn, *Erasmus*, p. 68.

67. Erasmus, "Foreword," in Adams, *"Praise of Folly" and Other Writings*, p. 132.

68. Ibid., p. 133.

69. Scholars still debate whether Luther actually nailed the theses to the church door; regardless, the incident is now firmly fixed in our collective consciousness. See, for example, Diarmaid MacCulloch, *The Reformation: A History* (New York: Viking, 2004), p. 123.

70. Martin Luther, "Ninety-five Theses," in *Martin Luther: Selections from His Writings*, ed. John Dillenberger (Garden City, NY: Anchor Books, 1961), p. 493 (thesis 27).

71. MacCulloch, *Reformation*, pp. 14–15.

72. Luther, "Ninety-five Theses," in Dillenberger, *Martin Luther*, p. 499 (thesis 86).

73. Martin Luther, *The Freedom of a Christian*, in Dillenberger, *Martin Luther*, pp. 56–57.

74. Again, there is substantial doubt whether Luther in fact spoke those words. But they have passed into history, and no better answer could be imagined.

75. MacCulloch, *Reformation*, p. 160.

76. Giovanni Pico della Mirandola, *On the Dignity of Man*, trans. Charles Glenn Wallis (1965; repr., Indianapolis, IN: Hackett, 1998), p. 5.

77. Martin Luther, *The Bondage of the Will*, in Dillenberger, *Martin Luther*, p. 203.

78. Ibid.

79. Erasmus, "The Shipwreck," in Thompson, *Colloquies*, p. 142.

80. Erasmus, "The Abbot and the Learned Lady," in Thompson, *Colloquies*, p. 219.

81. Erasmus, "A Pilgrimage for Religion's Sake," in Thompson, *Colloquies*, p. 296.

82. Erasmus, "Charon," in Thompson, *Colloquies*, p. 392.

83. Ibid.

84. Letter from Desiderius Erasmus Roterodamus to the Reader, in Thompson, *Colloquies*, p. 630.

85. Ibid., p. 626.

86. Erasmus, "The Young Man and the Harlot," in Thompson, *Colloquies*, p. 156.

87. Erasmus, "An Examination Concerning Faith," in Thompson, *Colloquies*, p. 188.

88. Ibid.

89. Augustijn, *Erasmus*, p. 104.

90. Huizinga, *Erasmus*, pp. 188, 190.

CHAPTER 3: MACHIAVELLI AND POLITICAL REALISM

1. "No epitaph can equal so great a name"—inscription on the tomb of Machiavelli. See Felix Gilbert, "Fortune, Necessity, *Virtù*," in Niccolò Machiavelli, *The Prince*, ed. and trans. Robert M. Adams, 2nd ed. (New York: W. W. Norton, 1992), p. 155, n. 3.

2. Michael Hattaway, "The Shakespearean History Play," in *The Cambridge Companion to Shakespeare's History Plays*, ed. Michael Hattaway (2002; repr., Cambridge: Cambridge University Press, 2004), p. 8 (quoting *Henry VI, Part 3*, 3.2.193).

3. For a concise summary of more than a dozen different interpretations of Machiavelli's work, see Isaiah Berlin, "The Question of Machiavelli," in Machiavelli, *The Prince*, pp. 207–209.

4. Dominic Baker-Smith, introduction to *The Prince*, by Niccolò Machiavelli, translated by W. K. Marriott (New York: Alfred A. Knopf, 1992), p. ix.

5. Machiavelli, *The Prince*, chap. 15, p. 70 (Marriott translation).

6. Aristotle, *Politics*, 1.1253a, trans. Benjamin Jowett, in *The Complete Works of Aristotle: The Revised Oxford Translation*, ed. Jonathan Barnes, 2 vols. (Princeton, NJ: Princeton University Press, 1984).

7. Machiavelli to Vettori, 10 December 1513, in *The Prince*, p. 127.

8. Ibid.

9. Ibid., p. 128.

10. Ibid.

11. Maurizio Viroli, *Niccolò's Smile: A Biography of Machiavelli*, trans. Antony Shugaar (New York: Hill and Wang, 2002), p. 152.

12. Machiavelli, *The Prince*, chap. 26, p. 72.

13. Ibid. (quoting Petrarch, canzone 128).

14. Ibid., p. 70.

NOTES

15. William Shakespeare, *Julius Caesar*, ed. Barbara A. Mowat and Paul Werstine (New York: Washington Square, 2005), 4.3.249–55.

16. Machiavelli, *The Prince*, chap. 25, p. 68.

17. Ibid., chap. 18, p. 48.

18. Ibid., chap. 6, p. 17.

19. Quentin Skinner, *Machiavelli: A Very Short Introduction* (New York: Oxford University Press, 2000), p. 27.

20. Machiavelli, *The Prince*, chap. 3, p. 5.

21. Ibid., chap. 6, pp. 17–18.

22. Ibid., chap. 17, p. 46.

23. Ibid., chap. 8, p. 27.

24. Ibid., chap. 17, p. 45.

25. Ibid., chap. 8, p. 27.

26. Ibid., p. 25.

27. Ibid., chap. 21, p. 61.

28. Quoted (with a slightly different translation) in Ernst Cassirer, "Implications of the New Theory of the State," in Machiavelli, *The Prince*, p. 160.

29. Machiavelli, *The Prince*, chap. 8, p. 27.

30. Ibid., chap. 18, p. 48.

31. Ibid.

32. Ibid.

33. Ibid., chap. 17, p. 46.

34. Ibid.

35. Ibid., chap. 18, p. 48.

36. Ibid., p. 49.

37. Ibid., chap. 15, p. 43.

38. Ibid., chap. 14, p. 40.

39. Ibid., chap. 12, p. 37.

40. Ibid., chap. 25, pp. 68–69.

41. Ibid., chap. 19, p. 50.

42. Ibid., chap. 9, p. 27.

43. Machiavelli to Vettori, 10 December 1513, in *The Prince*, p. 129.

44. Skinner, *Machiavelli*, p. 43.

45. Cassirer, "New Theory of the State," in Machiavelli, *The Prince*, p. 159.

46. See generally Michael K. Kellogg, *The Greek Search for Wisdom* (Amherst, NY: Prometheus Books, 2012), chap. 10; Michael K. Kellogg, *The Roman Search for Wisdom* (Amherst, NY: Prometheus Books, 2014), chap. 3.

NOTES

47. See Michael K. Kellogg, *The Wisdom of the Middle Ages* (Amherst, NY: Prometheus Books, 2016), pp. 86–87.

48. Machiavelli, *The Prince*, chap. 15, p. 42 (emphasis added).

49. Federico Chabod, "Machiavelli's Method and Style," in Machiavelli, *The Prince*, p. 187.

50. David Morrice, *Philosophy, Science, and Ideology in Political Thought* (New York: St. Martin's, 1996), p. 135.

51. Chabod, "Machiavelli's Method and Style," in Machiavelli, *The Prince*, p. 186; see also Berlin, "Question of Machiavelli," in Machiavelli, *The Prince*, p. 213.

52. Chabod, "Machiavelli's Method and Style," in Machiavelli, *The Prince*, p. 189.

53. Cassirer, "New Theory of the State," in Machiavelli, *The Prince*, pp. 158, 168–69.

54. Berlin, "Question of Machiavelli," in Machiavelli, *The Prince*, p. 219.

55. Kellogg, *Greek Search for Wisdom*, pp. 278–81.

56. Niccolò Machiavelli, *Discourses on Livy*, trans. Julia Conaway Bondanella and Peter Bondanella (New York: Oxford University Press, 2003), 1.3, 1.7.

57. Kellogg, *Roman Search for Wisdom*, pp. 247–50.

58. Machiavelli, *Discourses*, 1.6.

59. Ibid., p. 152 (preface to book 2).

60. Ibid., 1.58.

61. Ibid.

62. Ibid., 1.3.

63. Ibid., 3.21.

64. Ibid., 1.58.

65. Ibid., 1.7.

66. Ibid., 1.4.

67. Ibid.

68. Ibid., 1.11.

69. Ibid.

70. Ibid., 1.12.

71. Ibid., 2.2.

72. Plato, *Republic*, trans. Allan Bloom, 2nd ed. (New York: Basic Books, 1991), 414c.

73. Machiavelli, *Discourses*, 2.2.

74. Kellogg, *Roman Search for Wisdom*, pp. 13–14.

75. Kellogg, *Greek Search for Wisdom*, pp. 19–20.

76. Machiavelli, *Discourses*, 1.11.

77. Ibid., 1.10.

78. Kellogg, *Roman Search for Wisdom*, pp. 235–41.

79. Machiavelli, *Discourses*, 1.42.

80. Ibid., 3.21.

81. Ibid., 1.25.

82. Ibid., 3.1.

83. Ibid.

84. Ibid., 1.38.

85. Ibid., 3.3.

86. Ibid., 3.9.

87. Ibid.

88. Ibid., 1.18.

89. Ibid., 1.27.

90. Ibid., 3.9.

91. Ibid., 1.27.

92. Ibid., 1.9.

93. Ibid., 3.20.

94. Ibid., 3.6.

95. Ibid., 2.23.

96. Ibid., 2.29.

97. Viroli, *Niccolò's Smile*, p. 258.

CHAPTER 4: THOMAS MORE: THE KING'S GOOD SERVANT BUT GOD'S FIRST

1. There is some dispute as to whether More used the word *and* rather than *but* in the sentence, stemming from an account of his words in the *Paris Newsletter*. The Paris publication was in French, however, and More spoke in English. Mistranslation or not, most biographers and historians follow the version in text, which is more in keeping with More's overall stance toward public life and, frankly, more dramatic. See, for example, Peter Ackroyd, *The Life of Thomas More* (New York: Anchor Books, 1999), p. 405; James Monti, *The King's Good Servant but God's First: The Life and Writings of St. Thomas More* (San Francisco: Ignatius, 1997), p. 449; Richard Marius, *Thomas More* (London: Fount, 1986), p. 514. Compare Gerard B. Wegemer and Stephen W. Smith, eds., *A Thomas More Source Book* (2004; repr., Washington, DC: Catholic University of America Press, 2008), pp. xv, 355.

NOTES

2. Federico Chabod, "Machiavelli's Method and Style," in Niccolò Machiavelli, *The Prince*, ed. and trans. Robert M. Adams, 2nd ed. (New York: W. W. Norton, 1992), p. 187.

3. Saint Augustine, *City of God*, trans. Henry Bettenson (London: Penguin Books, 2003), p. 213.

4. Thomas More, *Utopia*, ed. and trans. George M. Logan, 3rd ed. (New York: W. W. Norton, 2011), p. 34.

5. Details of More's life are taken largely from original sources contained in the *Thomas More Source Book* and *Selected Writings*, including *The Life of Sir Thomas More*, by More's son-in-law William Roper. I also found helpful the biographies by Ackroyd and Monti.

6. Wegemer and Smith, *Source Book*, p. 307.

7. Ibid., p. 308.

8. William Roper, *The Life of Sir Thomas More, Knight*, in Wegemer and Smith, *Source Book*, p. 37.

9. Erasmus to Ulrich von Hutten, 23 July 1519, in Wegemer and Smith, *Source Book*, pp. 3–13.

10. Erasmus to Richard Whitford, 1 May 1506, in Monti, *King's Good Servant*, p. 27.

11. More's original title used the Latin word *nusquam*, meaning "nowhere." See More, *Utopia*, p. 5, nn. 1, 3.

12. Erasmus to von Hutten, in Wegemer and Smith, *Source Book*, pp. 4, 6.

13. Ackroyd, *Life of Thomas More*, pp. 57, 63.

14. *Southern Pac. Co. v. Jensen*, 244 U.S. 205, 222 (1917) (Holmes, J., dissenting).

15. Ackroyd, *Life of Thomas More*, p. 66.

16. Ibid., p. 147.

17. Erasmus to von Hutten, in Wegemer and Smith, *Source Book*, p. 9.

18. Ibid., p. 10.

19. Roper, *Life of Sir Thomas More*, in Wegemer and Smith, *Source Book*, p. 40.

20. See Michael K. Kellogg, *The Roman Search for Wisdom* (Amherst, NY: Prometheus Books, 2014), pp. 64–69.

21. See Michael K. Kellogg, *The Greek Search for Wisdom* (Amherst, NY: Prometheus Books, 2012), pp. 281–85.

22. More, *Utopia*, p. 10.

23. Excerpt from *English Literature in the Sixteenth Century, Excluding Drama*, by C. S. Lewis, in More, *Utopia*, p. 201; see Samuel Taylor Coleridge, "The Rime of the Ancient Mariner," ll. 13–20, in *Selected Poetry*, ed. William Empson and David Pirie (New York: Routledge, 2002), p. 120.

24. More, *Utopia*, p. 14.

25. Ibid., p. 22.

26. Ibid., p. 17.

27. Ibid., p. 21.

28. Ibid., p. 27.

29. Ibid., p. 28.

30. Ibid., p. 33.

31. Ibid.

32. Ibid., p. 34.

33. Ibid., p. 35.

34. Ibid., p. 36.

35. Ibid., p. 37.

36. Excerpt from *The Dialogue of Comfort Against Tribulation*, by Thomas More, in Wegemer and Smith, *Source Book*, p. 250.

37. *Lucian's True History*, trans. Francis Hickes (London: A. H. Bullen, 1902), p. 4.

38. More, *Utopia*, p. 58.

39. Ibid., p. 74.

40. Ibid., p. 77.

41. Ibid., p. 86.

42. Ibid., p. 88.

43. Ibid., p. 60.

44. Ibid., p. 42.

45. Ibid., p. 53.

46. Ibid., p. 95.

47. Ibid.

48. Ibid., p. 96.

49. Ibid., p. 97.

50. Ibid., pp. 96–97.

51. Excerpt from *More's "Utopia,"* by Dominic Baker-Smith, in More, *Utopia*, p. 258.

52. Ackroyd, *Life of Thomas More*, p. 303.

53. See, for example, George M. Logan, ed., *Thomas More* (New York: Cambridge University Press, 2011), p. 93.

54. Excerpt from *A Dialogue Concerning Heresies*, by Thomas More, in Wegemer and Smith, *Source Book*, p. 286.

55. More to Erasmus, June 1533, in Wegemer and Smith, *Source Book*, p. 307.

56. Excerpt from *Dialogue Concerning Heresies*, in Wegemer and Smith, *Source Book*, p. 288.

57. Ibid., p. 289.

58. Ackroyd, *Life of Thomas More*, pp. 322–23 (my translation).

59. Lev. 20:21 (KJV).

60. More to Thomas Cromwell, 5 March 1534, in Wegemer and Smith, *Source Book*, p. 358.

61. More to Erasmus, 14 June 1532, in Monti, *King's Good Servant*, pp. 308–309.

62. Roper, *Life of Sir Thomas More*, in Wegemer and Smith, *Source Book*, p. 42.

63. Ibid.

64. Ibid., p. 44.

65. Ibid.

66. The original of Cromwell's portrait is lost, but three good copies remain, the best of which is at the Frick Collection.

67. Roper, *Life of Sir Thomas More*, in Wegemer and Smith, *Source Book*, p. 50.

68. Ibid., p. 48.

69. More to Margaret Roper, 2/3 May 1535, in Wegemer and Smith, *Source Book*, pp. 345–46.

70. Roper, *Life of Sir Thomas More*, in Wegemer and Smith, *Source Book*, pp. 59–60.

71. Wegemer and Smith, *Source Book*, p. 354.

72. Ackroyd, *Life of Thomas More*, p. 405.

CHAPTER 5: CASTIGLIONE: A GENTLEMAN IN URBINO

1. Count Alexander Rostov, the hero of Amor Towles's *A Gentleman in Moscow*, is the modern embodiment of Castiglione's ideal courtier.

2. Baldassare Castiglione, *The Book of the Courtier*, ed. Daniel Javitch, trans. Charles S. Singleton (New York: W. W. Norton, 2002), 1.1.

3. See Stephen Greenblatt, *Renaissance Self-Fashioning: From More to Shakespeare* (Chicago: University of Chicago Press, 2005).

4. Jacob Burckhardt, *The Civilisation of the Renaissance in Italy*, trans. S. G. C. Middlemore (London: Folio Society, 2004), p. 297.

5. Muriel C. Bradbrook, *Collected Papers Volume 4—Shakespeare in His Context: The Constellated Globe* (Totowa, NJ: Barnes & Noble Books, 1989), p. 50.

6. June Osborne, *Urbino: The Story of a Renaissance City* (London: Frances Lincoln, 2003), p. 168.

7. For a detailed discussion of the *Symposium*, see Michael K. Kellogg, *The Greek Search for Wisdom* (Amherst, NY: Prometheus Books, 2012), chap. 9.

8. Castiglione, *Courtier*, 3.1.

9. See Kellogg, *Greek Search for Wisdom*, chap. 9.

10. Castiglione, *Courtier*, p. 4.

11. Ibid., 1.1.

12. See Michael K. Kellogg, *The Wisdom of the Middle Ages* (Amherst, NY: Prometheus Books, 2016), chap. 9.

13. Castiglione, *Courtier*, 1.4.

14. Ibid.

15. Ibid., 1.12.

16. Ibid., 1.13.

17. Ibid., 1.14.

18. Ibid., 1.17.

19. Ibid.

20. Ibid., 1.18.

21. Ibid., 1.47.

22. Ibid., 1.22.

23. Ibid., 1.21.

24. Ibid., 1.25.

25. Ibid., 1.26.

26. See Kellogg, *Greek Search for Wisdom*, chap. 10.

27. Castiglione, *Courtier*, 1.26.

28. Ibid.

29. Ibid.

30. Ibid., 1.34.

31. Michael K. Kellogg, *The Roman Search for Wisdom* (Amherst, NY: Prometheus Books, 2014), p. 162.

32. Castiglione, *Courtier*, 1.27.

33. Ibid., 1.35; see generally Wayne A. Rebhorn, "The Enduring Word: Language, Time, and History in *Il Libro del Cortegiano*," in *Castiglione: The Ideal and the Real in Renaissance Culture*, ed. Robert W. Hanning and David Rosand (New Haven, CT: Yale University Press, 1983), chap. 5.

34. Robert W. Hanning, "Castiglione's Verbal Portrait: Structures and Strategies," in Hanning and Rosand, *Castiglione*, p. 134.

35. Castiglione, *Courtier*, 1.14.

36. Ibid., 2.2.

37. Daniel Javitch, "*Il Cortegiano* and the Constraints of Despotism," in Hanning and Rosand, *Castiglione*, p. 18.

38. Castiglione, *Courtier*, 2.18.

39. Javitch, "*Il Cortegiano*," in Hanning and Rosand, *Castiglione*, p. 18.

40. Castiglione, *Courtier*, 2.7.

41. Ibid.

42. Ibid., 2.18.

43. Ibid.

44. Ibid.

45. Ibid., 2.7.

46. Ibid., 2.10.

47. Ibid., 2.12.

48. Ibid., 2.40.

49. Ibid., 2.22.

50. Thomas M. Greene, "*Il Cortegiano* and the Choice of a Game," in Hanning and Rosand, *Castiglione*, p. 10.

51. Castiglione, *Courtier*, 2.22 (emphasis added).

52. Ibid., 2.23.

53. Ibid.

54. Ibid., 2.30.

55. Ibid., 2.14.

56. Ibid., 3.49.

57. Ibid., 3.5.

58. Ibid., 3.12.

59. Ibid., 3.9.

60. Ibid., 3.5.

61. Ibid., 3.10.

62. Ibid., 3.13.

63. Ibid., 3.32.

64. Dain A. Trafton, "Politics and the Praise of Women: Political Doctrine in the *Courtier*'s Third Book," in Hanning and Rosand, *Castiglione*, pp. 39–42.

65. Ibid., p. 38.

66. Castiglione, *Courtier*, 3.70.

67. Ibid., 3.51.

68. Ibid., 3.59.

69. Wayne A. Rebhorn, *Courtly Performances: Masking and Festivity in Castiglione's "Book of the Courtier"* (Detroit: Wayne State University Press, 1978), p. 183.

70. Castiglione, *Courtier*, 4.4.

71. Greene, "Choice of a Game," in Hanning and Rosand, *Castiglione*, p. 14.

72. Castiglione, *Courtier*, 4.1.

73. Rebhorn, *Courtly Performances*, p. 181.

74. Castiglione, *Courtier*, 4.5.

75. Ibid., 4.26.

76. Ibid., 4.42.

77. See Kellogg, *Greek Search for Wisdom*, pp. 255–58.

78. Castiglione, *Courtier*, 4.66.

79. Ibid., 4.59.

80. Ibid., 4.57.

81. Ibid., 4.67.

82. Ibid., 4.68.

83. Ibid., 4.70.

84. Ibid., 4.68.

85. Greene, "Choice of a Game," in Hanning and Rosand, *Castiglione*, p. 9.

86. Rebhorn, *Courtly Performances*, pp. 132–33.

87. Ibid., pp. 133, 148.

88. Virginia Woolf, *The Waves* (Ware, Hertfordshire, UK: Wordsworth, 2000), p. 91.

CHAPTER 6: RABELAIS AND THE WISDOM OF LAUGHTER

1. Jacques Le Clercq, trans., *The Complete Works of Rabelais: The Five Books of "Gargantua and Pantagruel"* (New York: Modern Library, 1944), p. xxxiii ("Better to write of laughter than of tears, / For laughter is the essence of mankind.").

2. François Rabelais, prologue to *Gargantua*, in *Gargantua and Pantagruel*, ed. and trans. M. A. Screech (London: Penguin Books, 2006), p. 206.

3. Ibid., p. 207.

4. Ibid.

5. Ibid., p. 208.

6. Ibid.

7. Donald M. Frame, *François Rabelais: A Study* (New York: Harcourt Brace Jovanovich, 1977), p. 199 ("I know of no writer, with the possible exception of Aristophanes, who has so successfully combined the serious and lofty with the comical and grotesque.").

8. Mikhail Bakhtin, *Rabelais and His World*, trans. Hélène Iswolsky

(Bloomington: Indiana University Press, 1984), p. 68 ("'Of all living creatures only man is endowed with laughter.'") (quoting Aristotle, *De Anima*, 3.10).

9. Floyd Gray, "Reading the Works of Rabelais," in *The Cambridge Companion to Rabelais*, ed. John O'Brien (New York: Cambridge University Press, 2011), p. 17.

10. John Cowper Powys, *Visions and Revisions: A Book of Literary Devotions* (London: Macdonald, 1955), p. 30, quoted in Le Clercq, *Complete Works*, p. xxvii.

11. See Michael K. Kellogg, *The Wisdom of the Middle Ages* (Amherst, NY: Prometheus Books, 2016), pp. 204, 207.

12. See Michael K. Kellogg, *The Roman Search for Wisdom* (Amherst, NY: Prometheus Books, 2014), p. 9.

13. Quoted in Frame, *Rabelais*, p. 12.

14. The remaining two sacraments were confirmation and anointment of the sick and dying (formerly called extreme unction).

15. M. A. Screech, *Rabelais* (London: Duckworth, 1979), p. 29.

16. Rabelais, prologue to *Pantagruel*, in *Gargantua and Pantagruel*, p. 13.

17. Bakhtin, *Rabelais and His World*, p. 4.

18. Ibid., pp. 66–67.

19. Rabelais, *Pantagruel*, chap. 3.

20. Ibid., chap. 5.

21. Ibid.

22. Ibid., chap. 7.

23. Ibid., chap. 8.

24. Ibid.

25. Ibid.

26. Ibid.

27. Ibid.

28. Ibid.

29. Ibid.

30. Ibid.

31. Ibid.

32. Ibid.

33. Ibid., chap. 19.

34. Ibid., chap. 9.

35. Ibid., chap. 13.

36. Ibid.

37. Ibid.

38. Ibid., chap. 22.

39. Ibid.

40. Ibid.

41. Erich Auerbach, *Mimesis: The Representation of Reality in Western Literature*, trans. Willard R. Trask (Princeton, NJ: Princeton University Press, 1968), p. 278.

42. Rabelais, *Pantagruel*, chap. 23.

43. Rabelais, *Pantagruel*, chap. 25.

44. Ibid.

45. Ibid., chap. 27.

46. Ibid., chap. 30. The words are spoken by Captain Braggart but endorsed by Picrochole.

47. Ibid.

48. See Kellogg, *Wisdom of the Middle Ages*, chap. 6.

49. Rabelais, *Gargantua*, chap. 48.

50. Ibid., chap. 44.

51. Ibid.

52. Ibid., chap. 50.

53. Ibid., chap. 38.

54. Ibid.

55. Ibid., chap. 55.

56. Ibid., chap. 56.

57. Rabelais, *Third Book of Pantagruel*, in *Gargantua and Pantagruel*, p. 401.

58. Ibid., prologue, p. 410.

59. Rabelais, prologue to *Fourth Book of Pantagruel*, in *Gargantua and Pantagruel*, p. 650.

60. Screech, *Rabelais*, p. 224.

61. Rabelais, *Third Book of Pantagruel*, chap. 3.

62. Ibid., chap. 5 (quoting Rom. 13:8).

63. Ibid., chap. 10.

64. Ibid., chap. 36.

65. Ibid., chap. 26.

66. Ibid., chap. 27.

67. Ibid., chap. 28.

68. Ibid.

69. Ibid.

70. Ibid.

71. Ibid., chap. 29.

72. See Kellogg, *Wisdom of the Middle Ages*, p. 244.

73. See Screech, *Rabelais*, pp. 293–461; Frame, *Rabelais*, pp. 66–84.

74. Rabelais, *Fourth Book of Pantagruel*, chap. 28.

75. Ibid., chap. 23.

76. Frame, *Rabelais*, p. 89.

77. Ibid., p. 100 ("The conclusion seems to me so superb and appropriate that I believe Rabelais must be at least the principal author.").

78. Rabelais, *Fifth Book of Pantagruel*, chap. 45.

79. Ibid.

80. Frame, *Rabelais*, p. 102.

81. Rabelais, *Fifth Book of Pantagruel*, chap. 45.

82. Auerbach, *Mimesis*, p. 276.

83. Rabelais, *Fifth Book of Pantagruel*, chap. 47.

84. Auerbach, *Mimesis*, p. 276.

85. Bakhtin, *Rabelais and His World*, p. 2.

CHAPTER 7: MONTAIGNE AND THE WISDOM OF EXPERIENCE

1. Ralph Waldo Emerson, "Montaigne; or, the Skeptic," in *Essays & Lectures*, ed. Joel Porte (New York: Library of America, 1983), p. 697.

2. Gustave Flaubert, quoted in Sarah Bakewell, *How to Live, or, A Life of Montaigne* (New York: Other Press, 2010), p. 221.

3. Friedrich Nietzsche, quoted in Hugo Friedrich, *Montaigne*, ed. Philippe Desan, trans. Dawn Eng (Berkeley: University of California Press, 2010), p. 2.

4. Virginia Woolf, "Montaigne," in *The Common Reader*, ed. Andrew McNeillie (1925; repr., San Diego: Harcourt Brace, 1984), p. 58.

5. That scandal has been only partly ameliorated by the welcome success of Sarah Bakewell's 2010 book, *How to Live, or, A Life of Montaigne*.

6. Friedrich, *Montaigne*, p. 3.

7. Woolf, "Montaigne," in *Common Reader*, p. 63.

8. Donald M. Frame, trans., *The Complete Essays of Montaigne* (Stanford, CA: Stanford University Press, 1965), 3.13, p. 844.

9. Ibid., 1.26, p. 129.

10. Ibid., p. 130.

11. Donald M. Frame, *Montaigne: A Biography* (San Francisco: North Point, 1984), p. 115.

12. Frame, *Complete Essays*, 1.8, p. 21.

13. Ibid., 2.8, p. 278.

14. Donald M. Frame, trans., *Montaigne's Travel Journal* (San Francisco: North Point, 1983), p. xxvii.

15. Frame, *Complete Essays*, 3.12, p. 798.

16. The essays are not presented in the precise order in which Montaigne wrote them. He himself chose their placement in the first edition. For example, the first essay of book 1 may have been written as many as eight years after the second essay. See Frame, *Montaigne*, pp. 324–26. A chronological reading of Montaigne is further complicated by the many interpolations he later added to the first edition of 1580, passages from which are marked by an *a* in Frame's translation. The letter *b* indicates additions made in 1588, and *c*, those of 1589 to 1592. Since the earliest essays were composed in 1572, a single sentence thus may contain material written more than two decades apart. Despite these difficulties, a general pattern of evolution in Montaigne's thought and method can be discerned. But see Barbara C. Bowen, *The Age of Bluff: Paradox and Ambiguity in Rabelais and Montaigne* (Urbana: University of Illinois Press, 1972), p. 138 ("The *a* text contains by implication everything that is in the final version.").

17. Frame, *Complete Essays*, 1.26, p. 121.

18. Although this is the standard view of Montaigne's early essays, it is not without controversy. Compare Friedrich, *Montaigne*, p. 66 (denying there was any "Stoic phase" in Montaigne), with Jean Starobinski, *Montaigne in Motion*, trans. Arthur Goldhammer (Chicago: University of Chicago Press, 1985), p. 27 (claiming Montaigne's "first hope" was to live up to the "moral imperative" of Stoicism).

19. Frame, *Complete Essays*, 1.14, p. 46.

20. Ibid., 1.50, p. 220.

21. Ibid., 1.31, p. 157.

22. Ibid., 2.6, p. 267.

23. Ibid., 1.20, pp. 56–68.

24. Ibid., 2.13, p. 461.

25. Frame, *Montaigne*, p. 170 (quoting Louis Cons).

26. Frame, *Complete Essays*, 2.12, p. 393.

27. Ibid., p. 443.

28. Ibid., p. 444.

29. Ibid., p. 450.

30. Ibid., p. 444.

31. Ibid.

32. Ibid., p. 438.

33. Ibid., 2.15, p. 463.

34. Ibid., 2.17, p. 499.

35. Ibid., 2.12, p. 457.

36. Ibid., p. 387.

37. Ibid., p. 401.

38. Ibid., p. 386.

39. Ibid., p. 393.

40. Ibid., 1.27, p. 134.

41. Ibid., 1.56, p. 233.

42. Ibid., 1.23, p. 79.

43. Ibid., 1.56, pp. 230–31.

44. Starobinski, *Montaigne in Motion*, p. 95.

45. François Rabelais, *Third Book of Pantagruel*, chap. 29, in *Gargantua and Pantagruel*, ed. and trans. M. A. Screech (London: Penguin Books, 2006).

46. Frame, *Complete Essays*, 3.13, p. 822.

47. Erich Auerbach, *Mimesis: The Representation of Reality in Western Literature*, trans. Willard R. Trask (Princeton, NJ: Princeton University Press, 1968), p. 308.

48. Ibid., p. 311.

49. Frame, *Complete Essays*, 3.13, p. 821.

50. Emerson, "Montaigne," in *Essays & Lectures*, p. 694 ("Why pretend that life is so simple a game, when we know how subtle and elusive the Proteus is?").

51. Frame, *Complete Essays*, 2.17, p. 499.

52. Ibid., 3.2, pp. 610–11.

53. Ibid., 2.6, p. 273.

54. Ibid., 3.2, p. 611.

55. Walt Whitman, "Song of Myself," sec. 51 (quoted in Bakewell, *How to Live*, p. 7).

56. Frame, *Complete Essays*, 2.6, p. 273.

57. Ibid., 3.2, p. 610.

58. Ibid., p. 611.

59. Ibid., 1.50, p. 219.

60. Auerbach, *Mimesis*, p. 290.

61. Emerson, "Montaigne," in *Essays & Lectures*, p. 700.

62. Frame, *Complete Essays*, 2.18, p. 504.

63. Ibid., 3.2, p. 611.

64. Michel de Montaigne, *Essais III* (Paris: Gallimard, 1973), 3.2, p. 45.

65. Frame, *Complete Essays*, 2.12, p. 331.

66. Bowen, *Age of Bluff*, p. 127.

67. Ibid., pp. 118–19, 127.

68. T. S. Eliot, "The Love Song of J. Alfred Prufrock," in *Collected Poems, 1909–1962* (New York: Harcourt Brace, 1991), p. 3.

69. Frame, *Complete Essays*, 1.26, p. 119.

70. Ibid., 3.13, p. 849.

71. See Friedrich, *Montaigne*, pp. 239–57.

72. Frame, *Complete Essays*, 3.10, p. 769.

73. Ibid., 1.28, p. 136.

74. Ibid., 3.8, p. 704.

75. Ibid., 3.9, p. 754.

76. Ibid., 1.9, p. 23.

77. Ibid., 2.18, p. 505.

78. Ibid., 1.39, p. 177.

79. Ibid., 3.10, p. 767.

80. Ibid., 1.14, p. 42.

81. Ibid., 3.5, p. 648.

82. Ibid., p. 647.

83. Ibid.

84. Ibid., 1.38, p. 173.

85. Ibid., 3.5, p. 644.

86. Ibid., p. 646.

87. Ibid., 1.28, p. 139.

88. Ibid., p. 136.

89. Ibid., p. 139.

90. Ibid., p. 143.

91. Ibid., 3.9, p. 728.

92. Ibid., 3.12, p. 805.

93. Ibid., 3.13, p. 830.

94. Ibid., 3.5, pp. 677–78.

95. Ibid., 2.1, p. 242.

96. Ibid., 3.9, p. 766.

97. Ibid., 3.13, p. 852.

98. Ibid., 3.2, p. 614.

99. Ibid., 3.13, p. 856.

100. Ibid., 1.3, p. 8.

101. Ibid., 1.39, p. 177.

102. Ibid., 3.13, p. 850.

103. Ibid., 3.12, p. 805.

104. See Michael K. Kellogg, *The Roman Search for Wisdom* (Amherst, NY: Prometheus Books, 2014), pp. 79–82.

105. Frame, *Complete Essays*, 3.2, p. 620.

106. Ibid.

107. Ibid., 2.37, p. 580.

108. Ibid., 3.9, p. 750.

109. Ibid., 3.5, p. 641.

110. Ibid., p. 640.

111. Ibid., 2.17, p. 494.

112. Ibid., 3.3, p. 628.

113. Ibid.

114. Ibid., 3.9, p. 744.

115. Ibid., p. 747.

116. Ibid., 3.12, p. 804.

117. Ibid., 3.4, p. 632.

118. Ibid., 1.50, p. 220.

119. Ibid., 3.9, p. 743.

120. Ibid., 1.20, p. 62.

121. Ibid., 3.13, p. 857.

CHAPTER 8: CERVANTES: LIFE AS LITERATURE

1. Harold Bloom, introduction to *Don Quixote*, by Miguel de Cervantes, trans. Edith Grossman (New York: HarperCollins, 2005), p. xxiii.

2. William Shakespeare, *King Lear*, ed. Barbara A. Mowat and Paul Werstine (New York: Simon & Schuster, 2016), 5.3.351.

3. Ibid., 4.2.60–61.

4. Ibid., 5.3.390–91.

5. Manuel Durán, "Cervantes' Harassed and Vagabond Life," in *Cervantes' "Don Quixote": A Casebook*, ed. Roberto González Echevarría (New York: Oxford University Press, 2005), p. 23.

6. Compare Echevarría, *"Don Quixote" Casebook*, p. 13, with ibid., p. 32, and Jean Canavaggio, *Cervantes*, trans. J. R. Jones (New York: W. W. Norton, 1990), p. 20.

7. William Shakespeare, *King Henry V*, ed. T. W. Craik (New York: Routledge, 1995), 4.3.44–59.

8. Roberto González Echevarría, *Cervantes' "Don Quixote"* (New Haven, CT: Yale University Press, 2015), p. 174.

9. Donald P. McCrory, *No Ordinary Man: The Life and Times of Miguel de Cervantes* (Mineola, NY: Dover, 2006), p. 126.

10. Miguel de Cervantes, *Exemplary Stories*, trans. Lesley Lipson (New York: Oxford University Press, 1998), p. 3.

11. See generally Stephen Greenblatt, *Renaissance Self-Fashioning: From More to Shakespeare* (Chicago: University of Chicago Press, 2005).

12. Cervantes, *Don Quixote*, 1.2, p. 25.

13. Ibid.

14. E. C. Riley, "Literature and Life in *Don Quixote*," in Echevarría, *"Don Quixote" Casebook*, p. 125.

15. Cervantes, *Don Quixote*, 1.4. p. 39.

16. Ibid., p. 41.

17. Ibid., 1.5, p. 43.

18. Ibid.

19. Ibid., 1.6, p. 50.

20. Ibid., p. 52.

21. Ibid.

22. Echevarría, *Cervantes' "Don Quixote,"* p. 40.

23. Cervantes, *Don Quixote*, 1.7, p. 55.

24. Ibid., 1.8, p. 61.

25. Ibid., 1.7, p. 55.

26. Ibid., 1.19, p. 137.

27. Ibid., 2.32, p. 674.

28. Ibid., 1.8, p. 58.

29. Donald M. Frame, trans., *The Complete Essays of Montaigne* (Stanford, CA: Stanford University Press, 1965), 1.28, p. 139.

30. Cervantes, *Don Quixote*, 2.33, pp. 678–79.

31. Ibid., 1.25, p. 195; see Echevarría, *Cervantes' "Don Quixote,"* p. 127.

32. Cervantes, *Don Quixote*, 1.8, p. 64.

33. Ibid., 1.9, p. 66.

34. Ibid., p. 68.

35. Ibid.

36. Ibid., 1.22, p. 164.

37. Ibid., p. 168.

38. Ibid., p. 169.

39. Ibid., p. 172.

40. Ibid., 1.25, p. 194.

41. Ibid., 1.28, p. 234.

42. Ibid., p. 227.

43. Ibid., 1.30, p. 257.

44. Ibid., 1.50, p. 430.

45. Ibid., 2.2, p. 271.

46. Ibid., prologue, p. 455.

47. Ibid.

48. Ibid.

49. See, for example, Ramón Menéndez Pidal, "The Genesis of *Don Quixote*," in Echevarría, *"Don Quixote" Casebook*, p. 86; Harold Bloom, *The Western Canon: The Books and School of the Ages* (New York: Harcourt Brace, 1994), p. 144; Echevarría, *Cervantes' "Don Quixote,"* p. 179.

50. Thomas Mann, "Voyage with Don Quixote," in *Cervantes: A Collection of Critical Essays*, ed. Lowry Nelson Jr. (Englewood Cliffs, NJ: Prentice-Hall, 1969), p. 53.

51. Echevarría, *Cervantes' "Don Quixote,"* p. 185.

52. Cervantes, *Don Quixote*, 2.1, p. 466.

53. Ibid., 2.7, p. 500.

54. Ibid., 2.3, p. 478.

55. Ibid., 2.13, p. 536.

56. Ibid., 2.30, p. 655.

57. Mann, "Voyage with Don Quixote," in Nelson, *Cervantes*, p. 62.

58. Cervantes, *Don Quixote*, 2.17, p. 563.

59. Ibid., p. 564.

60. Ibid., 1.15, p. 107.

61. Ibid., 1.16, p. 111.

62. See Michael K. Kellogg, *The Wisdom of the Middle Ages* (Amherst, NY: Prometheus Books, 2016), pp. 237–38.

63. Cervantes, *Don Quixote*, 2.23, p. 611.

64. Pidal, "Genesis of *Don Quixote*," in Echevarría, *"Don Quixote" Casebook*, p. 92.

65. Cervantes, *Don Quixote*, 2.41, p. 727.

66. José Ortega y Gasset, *Meditations on Quixote*, trans. Evelyn Rugg and Diego Marín (New York: W. W. Norton, 1963), p. 163.

67. Cervantes, *Don Quixote*, 2.65, p. 889.

68. Ibid., 2.72, p. 928.

69. Shakespeare, *King Lear*, 1.4.197–99.

70. Cervantes, *Don Quixote*, 2.59, p. 843.

71. T. S. Eliot, "The Love Song of J. Alfred Prufrock," in *Collected Poems, 1909–1962* (New York: Harcourt Brace, 1991), p. 7.

72. Cervantes, *Don Quixote*, 2.74, p. 939.

CHAPTER 9: SHAKESPEARE

1. Ben Jonson, "To the Memory of My Beloved the Author, Mr. William Shakespeare," preface to the First Folio, reprinted at https://www.poetryfoundation.org/poems/44466/to-the-memory-of-my-beloved-the-author-mr-william-shakespeare.

2. William Hazlitt, *Characters of Shakespear's Plays*, in *The Collected Works of William Hazlitt*, ed. A. R. Waller and Arnold Glover, vol. 1 (New York: McClure, Phillips, 1902), p. 238.

3. Stephen Greenblatt, *Will in the World: How Shakespeare Became Shakespeare* (New York: W. W. Norton, 2004), p. 12.

4. William Shakespeare, *The Tempest*, ed. Frank Kermode (1954; repr., London: Routledge, 1988), 5.1.56.

5. William Shakespeare, *Much Ado About Nothing*, 2.1.60, quoted in Greenblatt, *Will in the World*, p. 134.

6. Greenblatt, *Will in the World*, p. 210.

7. The oddness of the motto might indicate that the original application was denied with the notation *Non, sanz droict* (i.e., that the applicant, who was not a gentleman, had no right to a coat of arms). When the application was later granted, the new clerk simply copied the phrase without the comma, thus turning it into a "motto" for the coat of arms.

8. Bill Bryson, *Shakespeare: The World as Stage* (New York: Harper Perennial, 2008), pp. 126–27.

9. The reconstructed Globe Theatre, which opened in 1997, is not in the same location as the Globe of Shakespeare's day, but it is close and provides a wonderful sense of what it must have been like to see a performance there, especially as a groundling.

10. The significance of Shakespeare's odd bequest to his wife is unclear. In general, in 1616, a wife had a default dower right to one-third of her husband's estate, but it is possible that the specific bequest of the bed was meant to displace that right. Shakespeare presumably knew that his daughter and her husband would take care of

NOTES

Anne regardless, but he seems to have wanted, for whatever reason, to keep control of the estate out of her hands. See Park Honan, *Shakespeare: A Life* (New York: Oxford University Press, 1998), pp. 396–97. It is also possible that the "second best bed" was their marital bed and that he bequeathed it to Anne as a sentimental gesture.

11. Peter Saccio, *Shakespeare's English Kings: History, Chronicle, and Drama* (New York: Oxford University Press, 1977). Dr. Saccio's wonderful lectures on Shakespeare are available from The Teaching Company.

12. Keats to George and Tom Keats, December 1817, in *Letters of John Keats*, ed. Robert Gittings (1970; repr., Oxford: Oxford University Press, 1988), p. 43.

13. William Shakespeare, *King Henry IV, Part I*, ed. David Scott Kastan (2002; repr., London: Bloomsbury, 2016), 5.2.63–64.

14. Excerpt from *Shakespeare's Doctrine of Nature: A Study of "King Lear,"* by John F. Danby, in *Twentieth Century Interpretations of "Henry IV, Part One,"* ed. R. J. Dorius (Englewood Cliffs, NJ: Prentice-Hall, 1970), p. 93.

15. William Shakespeare, *King Richard II*, ed. Charles R. Forker (2002; repr., London: Bloomsbury, 2016), 5.5.43.

16. Ibid., 5.5.38.

17. Ibid., 5.1.55–65.

18. William Shakespeare, *King Henry IV, Part 2*, ed. James C. Bulman (London: Bloomsbury, 2016), 3.1.31.

19. Ibid., 4.3.173, 4.3.177.

20. Shakespeare, *King Henry IV, Part 1*, 1.1.80.

21. Ibid., 1.1.84–85.

22. Hazlitt, *Characters of Shakespear's Plays*, in Waller and Glover, *Collected Works*, pp. 283–84.

23. Shakespeare, *King Henry IV, Part 1*, 4.1.95–96.

24. Ibid., 1.2.5–11.

25. Ibid., 5.4.118.

26. Ibid., 3.3.19–20.

27. *Johnson on Shakespeare: The Yale Edition of the Works of Samuel Johnson*, ed. Arthur Sherbo, vol. 7 (New Haven, CT: Yale University Press, 1968), p. 523.

28. Ibid.

29. Ibid.

30. Harold Bloom, *Shakespeare: The Invention of the Human* (New York: Riverhead Books, 1998), p. 275.

31. Hazlitt, *Characters of Shakespear's Plays*, in Waller and Glover, *Collected Works*, p. 283.

32. Shakespeare, *King Henry IV, Part 1*, 1.2.185–93.

33. Shakespeare, *King Richard II*, 5.5.49.

34. William Shakespeare, *King Henry V*, ed. Andrew Gurr (New York: Cambridge University Press, 2005), 2.4.138–39.

35. Shakespeare, *King Henry IV, Part 1*, 1.2.176–80.

36. Ibid., 2.4.259–64.

37. Ibid., 5.1.89–92.

38. Ibid., 3.1.52–54.

39. Shakespeare, *King Henry IV, Part 2*, induction, l. 37.

40. Shakespeare, *King Henry IV, Part 1*, 5.2.85–86.

41. Ibid., 4.2.65–66.

42. Ibid., 5.125–40.

43. Shakespeare, *King Henry IV, Part 2*, 4.3.349–52.

44. Shakespeare, *King Henry V*, 4.1.220.

45. Shakespeare, *King Henry IV, Part 1*, 2.4.366–67.

46. Ibid., 2.4.435–36.

47. Ibid., 2.4.461–68.

48. Shakespeare, *King Henry IV, Part 2*, 5.5.55–58.

49. Ibid., 4.3.342–44.

50. Shakespeare, *King Henry V*, 2.1.99.

51. Ibid., 2.3.18–22.

52. Ibid., 2.3.6–7.

53. Friedrich Nietzsche, *The Gay Science*, trans. Walter Kaufmann (New York: Vintage Books, 1974), p. 38.

54. William Shakespeare, *As You Like It*, ed. Juliet Dusinberre (2006; repr., London: Bloomsbury, 2016), 1.2.2–3.

55. Ibid., 1.1.112–13.

56. Ibid., 2.1.5.

57. Ibid., 2.1.6–7.

58. Ibid., 2.1.62–63.

59. Ibid., 2.1.16–17.

60. Ibid., 2.1.11–12.

61. Ibid., 1.1.157.

62. Ibid., 3.5.111.

63. Ibid., 1.3.70–73.

64. Ibid., Epilogue, ll. 10–11.

65. Ibid., 2.4.31–40.

66. Ibid., 5.4.44–47.

67. Ibid., 2.4.15.

68. Ibid., 2.7.26–28.

69. Ibid., 3.3.88–89.

70. Ibid., 5.4.55–56.

71. Ibid., 2.5.10–11.

72. Ibid., 3.2.116.

73. Ibid., 4.1.8–9.

74. Ibid., 4.1.24–26.

75. Ibid., 3.5.50.

76. Ibid., 2.4.57.

77. Ibid., 3.5.40.

78. Ibid., 3.5.55–61.

79. Ibid., 3.2.359–69.

80. Ibid., 4.1.163.

81. Ibid., 4.1.97–99.

82. See James Shapiro, *A Year in the Life of William Shakespeare: 1599* (New York: Harper Perennial, 2006), pp. 212–13.

83. Shakespeare, *As You Like It*, 4.1.127.

84. Ibid., 4.1.135–39.

85. Ibid., 3.2.407.

86. Ibid., 2.4.50–53.

87. Ibid., 3.2.70–74.

88. Ibid., 3.2.24–27.

89. Bloom, *Shakespeare*, p. 204.

90. William Shakespeare, *Hamlet*, ed. Harold Jenkins (1982; repr., London: Routledge, 1993), 1.3.31, 1.3.134.

91. Ibid., 1.3.34–35.

92. Ibid., 1.3.46, 1.3.136.

93. Harold C. Goddard, *The Meaning of Shakespeare*, vol. 1 (Chicago: University of Chicago Press, 1960), p. 385.

94. Shakespeare, *Hamlet*, 1.2.133–37.

95. Ibid., 1.1.1.

96. Ibid., 1.2.187–88.

97. Ibid., 1.2.139–40.

98. Ibid., 1.2.150–51.

99. Ibid., 1.2.156–57.

NOTES

100. T. S. Eliot, "Hamlet and His Problems," in *Selected Essays* (New York: Harcourt, Brace, 1950), p. 123.

101. Ibid.

102. Henry James, *The Tragic Muse* (London: Penguin Books, 1995), p. 4.

103. Eliot, "Hamlet and His Problems," in *Selected Essays*, p. 125.

104. Shakespeare, *Hamlet*, 3.1.152–56.

105. Ibid., 4.7.134.

106. Ibid., 2.2.303–306.

107. Ibid., 2.2.308.

108. Donald M. Frame, trans., *The Complete Essays of Montaigne* (Stanford, CA: Stanford University Press, 1965), 3.13, p. 856.

109. Shakespeare, *Hamlet*, 3.1.122–29. Compare Frame, *Complete Essays*, 2.1, p. 242.

110. Shakespeare, *Hamlet*, 5.1.254–56.

111. Ibid., 4.4.44–46.

112. A. C. Bradley, *Shakespearean Tragedy: Lectures on "Hamlet," "Othello," "King Lear" and "Macbeth"* (London: Penguin Books, 1991), p. 109.

113. Ibid., p. 133.

114. Shakespeare, *Hamlet*, 2.2.580 (emphasis added).

115. Ibid., 5.2.403–404.

116. Ibid., 5.2.364–65.

117. Quoted in Goddard, *Meaning of Shakespeare*, p. 331.

118. Hazlitt, *Characters of Shakespear's Plays*, in Waller and Glover, *Collected Works*, p. 232.

119. Shakespeare, *Hamlet*, 1.2.84–85.

120. Shapiro, *Year in the Life of William Shakespeare*, p. 291.

121. Shakespeare, *Hamlet*, 4.4.53–56.

122. Ibid., 4.4.62–63.

123. Ibid., 5.1.197–98.

124. Michael K. Kellogg, *Three Questions We Never Stop Asking* (Amherst, NY: Prometheus Books, 2010), p. 21.

125. Shakespeare, *Hamlet*, 2.2.249–50.

126. Ibid., 2.2.192.

127. Ibid., 5.2.363.

128. Friedrich Nietzsche, *The Birth of Tragedy*, in *Basic Writings of Nietzsche*, ed. and trans. Walter Kaufmann (New York: Modern Library, 1968), p. 60.

129. Shakespeare, *Hamlet*, 1.4.69–78.

NOTES

130. Ibid., 3.2.21–24.

131. George Eliot, *Middlemarch: A Study of Provincial Life*, vol. 1, in *The Complete Works of George Eliot* (Boston: Colonial, 1890), p. 268.

132. Shakespeare, *Hamlet*, 5.2.9–11.

133. Ibid., 5.2.216–20.

134. Ibid., 5.2.344.

135. Bloom, *Shakespeare*, p. 406.

136. Shakespeare, *Hamlet*, 5.2.341–43.

137. Christopher Marlowe, *Doctor Faustus*, 1.1.9–11, in *The Complete Plays of Christopher Marlowe*, ed. Irving Ribner (New York: Odyssey, 1963).

138. Ibid., 1.1.57–63, 1.1.77.

139. Ibid., 1.3.15.

140. Ibid., 5.2.187.

141. Ibid., 3.3.89–90.

142. Ibid., 1.2.73–74.

143. Ibid., 1.2.75–77.

144. Ibid., 1.2.109–10.

145. Ibid., 1.2.109.

146. Ibid., 1.2.167–68.

147. Ibid., 1.2.159.

148. Ibid., 1.2.272–73.

149. Ibid., 1.2.339–40.

150. Ibid., 1.2.359–60.

151. Ibid., 1.2.365–66.

152. Ibid., 5.1.91–94.

153. Ibid., 3.2.133–41.

154. Hazlitt, *Characters of Shakespear's Plays*, in Waller and Glover, *Collected Works*, p. 238.

155. W. H. Auden, *Lectures on Shakespeare*, ed. Arthur Kirsch (Princeton, NJ: Princeton University Press, 2001), p. 296; see also, for example, excerpt from *The Pleasures of Exile*, by George Lamming, in William Shakespeare, *The Tempest*, ed. Peter Hulme and William H. Sherman (New York: W. W. Norton, 2004), p. 149 ("the poet's last will and testament").

156. Shakespeare, *Tempest*, 1.2.420–21.

157. Ibid., 1.2.453–55.

158. Ibid., 4.1.10–11.

159. Ibid., 2.2.186–87.

160. Ibid., 3.2.90–93.
161. Auden, *Lectures on Shakespeare*, p. 300.
162. Shakespeare, *Tempest*, 3.3.89–90.
163. Ibid., 5.1.14–17.
164. Ibid., 5.1.17–32.
165. Ibid., 5.1.54–57.
166. Ibid., 1.2.153–54.
167. Ibid., 5.1.275–76.
168. Ibid., 5.1.294–95.
169. Ibid., 5.1.182–83.
170. Ibid., 5.1.184.
171. Ibid., 4.1.24.
172. Ibid., 5.1.198–99.
173. Ibid., 5.1.310–11.
174. Ibid., 4.1.148–58.
175. Ibid., p. 116 (stage direction). See John Drydren, altered prologue to *The Tempest* ("Shakespeare's magic could not copied be, / Within that circle none dared walk but he."), quoted in Shakespeare, *The Tempest*, p. 121 (Norton edition).

INDEX

INDEX

INDEX

INDEX

INDEX

INDEX

St. German, Christopher, 153–54
Stoics and Stoicism, 51, 73–74, 76
    Erasmus echoing Epictetus, 82
    in Erasmus's work, 73, 75, 76
    and Montaigne, 232–34, 235,
      237–38, 239, 241, 243, 246,
      250, 251, 254
    and More, 142
    in Rabelais's work, 198, 213, 215
Suetonius, 73
Sulla, 124
Sycorax (in Shakespeare's *The
    Tempest*), 333–34
Symposium (Plato), 164–65, 182, 184,
    189, 295. *See also* Socrates

Tacitus
    and Machiavelli, 99, 115
    and Montaigne, 232
    and More, 153
Talleyrand, Charles-Maurice de, 111
Tallis, Thomas, 28
Tamburlaine the Great (Marlowe), 300
Taming of the Shrew, The (Shake-
    speare), 300
Tempest, The (Shakespeare), 258,
    332–39
Terence, 75, 226
Thaumaste (in the series of books by
    Rabelais), 204–205
Theatre, The (Shoreditch), 301–302,
    303
Thélème, Abbey of, founding of (in
    the series of books by Rabelais), 208,
    211–13

Third Book of Pantagruel (Rabelais),
    195, 196, 207, 213–17, 239
Thirty Years' War, 15, 26, 345
Titian, 66
Titus Andronicus (Shakespeare), 300
Torelli, Ippolita (Castiglione's wife),
    162
Tosetti, Lello di Pietro Stefano dei
    "Laelius," 36, 40, 61
*To the Christian Nobility of the
    German Nation* (Luther), 87–88
Touchstone (in Shakespeare's *As You
    Like It*), 318–19, 320, 321–22
trade and the Renaissance, 18–19
Treasons Act (England), 156
Trent, Council of, 196–97, 345
True History (Lucian), 140, 217
"Tudor myth," 300, 305
Twelfth Night (Shakespeare), 303
Two Gentlemen of Verona (Shake-
    speare), 300
Tyndale, William, 85, 146

Übermensch ["overman"], 117
Ulysses (Dante's), 63, 217, 218
Ulysses (Joyce), 199
Unamuno, Miguel de, 257
Urban V (pope), 56
Urbino
    Castiglione as a gentleman in
      Urbino, 159–87, 212
    as center of arts and literature,
      161
    portrayed in *Book of the Courtier*,
      212

INDEX

8/19